Understanding China

The series will provide you with in-depth information on China's social, cultural and economic aspects. It covers a broad variety of topics, from economics and history to law, philosophy, cultural geography and regional politics, and offers a wealth of materials for researchers, doctoral students, and experienced practitioners.

Yugui Zhang

Addressing Uncertainty

Logic of China's Economic Development in a Global Context

Springer

Yugui Zhang
School of Economics and Finance
Shanghai International Studies University
Shanghai, China

Jointly published with Peking University Press

ISSN 2196-3134 ISSN 2196-3142 (electronic)
Understanding China
ISBN 978-981-92-2691-7 ISBN 978-981-92-2692-4 (eBook)
https://doi.org/10.1007/978-981-92-2692-4

Translation from the Chinese Simplified language edition: "求解不确定:中国与世界经济发展的逻辑" by Yugui Zhang, © Peking University Press 2023. Published by Peking University Press. All Rights Reserved.

This Springer imprint is published by the registered company Springer Nature Singapore Pte Ltd.
The registered company address is: 152 Beach Road, #21-01/04 Gateway East, Singapore 189721, Singapore

Preface

China: An Anchor of Stability in an Uncertain World

The year 2023 marked a pivotal year with significant milestone importance for both China and the world.

Domestically, 2023 was the inaugural year of fully implementing the spirit of the 20th National Congress of the Communist Party of China (CPC) and promoting the great rejuvenation of the Chinese nation through Chinese-style modernization. It was also a transformative year for accelerating the construction of a new development pattern and vigorously promoting high-quality development after the comprehensive resumption of normalcy in economic and social life.

From a broader temporal perspective, and considering the strategic competition among major global economies, 2023 represented a rare window of opportunity for China. Despite rising rhetoric surrounding "decoupling" and "de-risking", China managed to stabilize its fundamental position in foreign trade and economic relations, as well as in the complex bilateral relationship with the United States—thereby safeguarding its core interests within the global value chains.

Internationally, 2023 coincided with several milestone events. It was both the 300th anniversary of the birth of Adam Smith, the British economist regarded as the "father of modern economics," and the midpoint for assessing progress on the United Nations' 2030 Agenda for Sustainable Development. Furthermore, it marked a crucial juncture for humanity to seek economic recovery and peaceful development following the COVID-19 pandemic (hereinafter referred to as "COVID-19") and regional turbulence. It was also a pivotal year for the international community to join hands in addressing poverty—the primary global challenge set forth in the 2030 Agenda—thereby bridging efforts from the past to the future.

A decade ago, China and the United States held the fifth round of the Strategic and Economic Dialogue in Washington, D.C., achieving broad consensus across 91 outcomes. These agreements spanned nearly all major areas, including politics, the economy, trade, finance, military affairs, security, climate change, energy, science and technology, judicial cooperation, maritime affairs, customs, nuclear safety, forestry, counter-terrorism, and law enforcement. Both countries reaffirmed their support for the multilateral trading system and their opposition to trade protectionism. The U.S. side pledged to provide fair treatment to China within its export control system reform process and to take China's concerns seriously. The two countries agreed to engage in timely dialogue on significant economic policy matters. This dialogue underscored the frankness, rationality, and constructiveness with which the world's two largest economies addressed global, long-term, and strategic issues concerning peace, development, and security for the two countries and the whole world. It has been demonstrated that maintaining strategic dialogue and communication coordination on major issues is an important guarantee to prevent systemic risks in China–U.S. relations.

For the leaders of both nations, it is imperative that the achievements of the past China–U.S. Strategic and Economic Dialogues not fade into mere historical memory.

Over the past decade, China has relentlessly pursued high-level opening-up and high-quality economic development, which has attracted worldwide attention, achieving an impressive average annual growth rate of 6.2% in its economy, lifting its economy to over CNY 120 trillion. This firmly secured its position as the world's second-largest economy, with its average contribution rate to world economic growth exceeding 30%, surpassing the combined contribution of all the Group of Seven (G7) countries, which made China the primary driving force of world economic growth.

This past decade also marked the crucial period for China to seize the precious strategic opportunities amidst increasing domestic and international uncertainties, to coordinate its own development and security, and to effectively resolve various risks. However, China has almost bid farewell to the low-risk development stage and entered a medium-to-high-risk stage with increasingly obvious internal and external constraints and multidimensional, complex, comprehensive challenges, especially after its total output first topped the $10 trillion threshold in 2014.

On the one hand, as the world's second-largest economy, largest trading nation, and one of the most important global sources of investment and financing, China faces problems such as economic structure inefficiencies, high macro leverage, the urgent need to improve total factor productivity and investment efficiency, unstable economic growth driving forces, and rising marginal costs of growth. These issues have led to what the Bank for International Settlements (BIS) identifies as the "risk trilemma" in China's economic performance: slowing growth or declining productivity, rising leverage, and narrowing macro policy space.

On the other hand, as China's demographic dividend fades and the cost of key production factors such as land and labor continues to rise, manufacturing costs are escalating. The new round of international industrial transfer, technological shifts, and changes in trade conditions, especially the resurgence of trade protectionism and technological hegemonism, have compelled China to vigorously promote the digital technology revolution, master self-reliance in core technologies, and enhance its human capital to promote comprehensive upgrades in its manufacturing sector, in order to respond to intensifying international competition and strategic containment.

Manufacturing and foreign trade are China's two trump cards for participating in international competition and maintaining its central position in global value chains. The financial competitiveness built upon industrial upgrading and enhanced global value chain positioning serves as a critical indicator of China's status in the international division of labor.

In recent years, China's pivotal role across the upstream, midstream, and downstream segments of global value chains, together with its central position in global supply chains, has faced mounting challenges. Furthermore, in today's world, where strategic competition among major economies is intensively focusing on the struggle for control over key industries and technologies, any shifts in national industrial competitiveness—whether gains or losses due to internal or external shocks—attract high attention from policymakers worldwide.

For G7 and even G20 decision-makers focusing on national economic security, it is hardly surprising to "rethink" the vulnerabilities of the global supply chains heavily dependent on China and to seek optimal responses and development strategies amid global economic restructuring. From the historical perspective of national competition, no established power willingly welcomes an emerging power to dominate the global economy, and China is unlikely to serve indefinitely as the primary maintainer of stability and resilience of global industrial and supply chains. Competitive cooperative games have thus become the new norm in great power relations throughout the twenty-first century.

Additionally, with the continuous increase in domestic business costs and the rise of some emerging economies, China's challenge to maintain its position as a global manufacturing hub is intensifying year by year. Emerging economies and developing countries such as India, Indonesia, and Vietnam are realistic or potential competitors that China must keep an eye on. These countries are characterized by a young and abundant workforce, improved infrastructure, and rapidly rising industrial support capacity. They are fully capable of becoming important competitors for China in the global export market and fields like attracting foreign investment in the future.

Optimistically speaking, driven by the dividends of maintaining high-level openness to the outside world, China is expected to retain a relatively stable central position in the global industrial and supply chains through around 2030. However, in the real world, economic development and industrial transformation often deviate from such static assumptions. China must ensure that no systemic economic or financial crises occur in the coming period and strive to avoid the recurrence of major public health "black swan" events. This would affirm the notion that enterprises are the most intelligent systemic entities. A clear testament to this is the fact that some of the most influential American business figures—Elon Musk, Bill Gates, Tim Cook, Jamie Dimon, among others—have all visited China ahead of their own political leaders.

Furthermore, U.S. Treasury Secretary Janet Yellen has repeatedly called for deeper economic ties between the world's two largest economies, warning that attempts to decouple from China would be a mistake. Even CIA Director William Burns has described decoupling from China as "foolish." These remarks suggest that some senior U.S. policymakers are increasingly concerned about the systemic risks associated with calls for "economic decoupling" and supply-chain disengagement" from China. A more pragmatic approach to competition and cooperation is also one of the key factors in avoiding systemic confrontation between the world's two largest economies.

Maintaining strategic composure is a key indicator of an emerging power's maturing international disposition and national mentality. As long as China sustains an average annual effective economic growth rate of 4%–5%, its economic scale is projected to catch up with or even surpass that of the U.S. by around 2035. By then, China will firmly establish itself as the world's largest capital exporter and the largest consumer market.

There is no doubt that China is among the foremost beneficiaries of economic globalization and has played a leading role in propelling it into a new higher phase in the twenty-first century. Despite facing multiple challenges today, globalization will never be reversed. In the foreseeable future, no country or vested interest group can bear the explicit and implicit costs of fragmenting the world into separate technological, industrial, trade, and even financial systems.

In general, from a rational business and transaction-cost perspective, neither developed Western countries like the United States nor international industrial and financial capital groups such as Apple, Tesla, ASML, Goldman Sachs, JPMorgan Chase, etc., can afford to completely decouple irrationally from the world's emerging largest economy; the burden would simply be too great. The policy logic of the so-called "de-risking" and "diversification" may be one of the options in the name of "political correctness" under most of the situations.

The evolution of the China–U.S. trade friction since its outbreak in 2018 shows that despite the strong desires within the U.S. and Western powers to decouple, markets and enterprises seldom support it. Artificially splitting the global industrial and technological division system only yields a zero-sum game with no real winners.

However, since 1945, the history of global economic development and the contest for order have proven and will continue to prove that great power competition is far from romantic. For emerging powers, the way of bottom-line thinking is indispensable, and the essence of having a plan is to prepare for the worst.

Nowadays, due to the ongoing fission of the global economic guarantor system, anti-globalization, trade protectionism, and various forms of "small yard, high fence" approaches are prevailing, the probability of "black swan" events is higher than before, while more ominous "gray rhino" threats add further ambiguity to the already uncertain world economy.

It is an undeniable fact that capitalism is deeply mired in a systemic crisis. How much superiority does the capitalist system still retain? Do Americans still possess the self-belief they once had in the twenty-first century? This is an issue of particular concern to American elites, including top strategists like Kissinger, Summers, and Paulson.

There is no doubt that the United States remains the world's only superpower. Nevertheless, from President Obama's confident assertion that "America can lead the world for another 100 years," to the "America First" doctrine aggressively promoted under President Trump, and now to the carefully constructed "Bidenism" of the current Biden administration, each reflects the intense effort and exhaustion of an overstretched superpower striving to preserve its existing hegemonic dominance.

Can the U.S. lead the world for another 100 years? Even the most insightful trend analysts cannot offer a definitive answer. Similarly, behind the resounding slogans such as "Make America Great Again" and "America is Back, Ready to Lead the World Again," it is worth thinking about the underlying mentality of the highest leaders of the United States. What people are interested in is why American leaders are particularly concerned with the durability of their leadership and what their deepest concern might be. Following this logic, perhaps one can understand the mindsets of Obama, Trump, and Biden during their tenures—after all, a country accustomed to being the global "leader" resists relinquishing its imperial stature, regardless of who sits in the Oval Office.

In this era where statesmen are becoming rarer and scarcer, while politicians are rampant, the credibility, particularly the marginal influence, of political leaders is far less meaningful than before. Few would take seriously this kind of propaganda-style publicity.

Precisely speaking, since the establishment of the Bretton Woods system in 1944, the United States has dominated global affairs for nearly 80 years. From the perspective of the imperial evolution life cycle over the past 300 years in modern history, sustaining dominance for 100 years is no small feat. The British Empire, once unrivalled in its global influence, has since declined into a second-tier power largely confined to the British Isles. Ultimately, imperial ambitions cannot withstand the tides of historical change. In contrast, the United States is still a superpower with cutting-edge technological innovation capabilities in the world, but after all, it is not an extraterrestrial visitor. Whether the U.S. can keep dominating the world in the twenty-second century is probably a far more daunting proposition than predicting long-term dominance in world football for the next century.

The biggest concern for the United States is China's comprehensive rise. As a realist power, the United States believes in absolute power supremacy, and that power growth determines the space for national action. From the end of World War II in 1945 to Brexit in 2020, despite challenges to its economic dominance from Europe and Japan, the U.S. maintained firm control over its self-designed international economic order through unmatched national competitiveness for over 70 years. However, compared to its economic status that was far ahead of other countries nearly 80 years ago, the relative economic strength of the United States is now declining. Its share of the world economy has dropped from 45% at the end of World War II to around 25%.

Although in the capitalist world, the absolute strength of the United States is far stronger than that of other countries such as Japan, Germany, the United Kingdom, and France, when it comes to global competition, the U.S. government and public have almost unanimously recognized in recent years that "China is the only country that intends to reshape the international order while continuously enhancing its economic, diplomatic, military, and technological strength."

The United States believes that the international financial crisis that broke out in 2008 was the watershed in the strategic competition and power shift between China and the U.S. The crisis inflicted severe internal damage, taking the U.S. five years to repair the financial system. It was not until December 16, 2015, when interest rates were raised, that the U.S. economy was declared to be back on a normal growth track. Fifteen years have passed now, and many American financial elites who experienced the once-in-a-century financial crisis were still haunted by the lingering fears, with a few keywords popping up in their minds from time to time: panic, uncertainty. Globally, the various measures the U.S. government has pursued, such as quantitative easing, deleveraging, manufacturing return, and trade protectionism were dedicated to repairing the financial system and boosting the real economy. However, the damage to its absolute strength and international reputation that it has paid for this is difficult to estimate, which has to some extent led Trump into the White House under the cover of "American First."

What most Americans did not foresee, however was that Trump not only prioritized personal preferences above sound policymaking, but also pursued a bewildering series of withdrawals from international institutions and maximum-pressure tactics during his four years in office, almost leaving the United States increasingly isolated on the global stage. Its international reputation was further tarnished, which then led the Biden administration to restore bilateral and multilateral relationships with considerable effort after taking office. The reality is that the overall performance of the United States in the past 15 years has been lackluster in terms of the four major goals that macroeconomic policies are most concerned about, namely economic growth, full employment, price level stability, and international balance of payments. On the micro level, American high-tech companies have shone, represented by Apple, Microsoft, Google, Amazon, NVIDIA, Tesla, etc., firmly occupying the top of the global high-tech industry, and somehow supporting the United States' status as an economic superpower.

It should be mentioned that in recent years, decision-makers and market participants in Western countries have also been reflecting on the lessons of financial crises. They recognize that permitting financial innovation to flourish—when economic growth is primarily driven by credit expansion and debt accumulation without concurrent performance gains in the real economy—is akin to "drinking poison to quench thirst" (a metaphor for short-term gain at great risk).

The history of economic development has proven that debt arrangement or debt expansion within certain limits is not only a powerful driving force of economic growth for a country's economy, but also an important reason for the continuous increase in systemic economic and financial risks in the country. How to find an equilibrium point between debt expansion and effective growth is the key to measuring a country's macroeconomic regulation level. The COVID-19 has become the past, but the Federal Reserve has issued massive bailout and rescue checks, resulting in an uncontrolled liquidity release. The multiple impacts of its spillover effects have damaged the international currency reputation of the U.S. dollar.

Since March of this year, the regional bank bankruptcy wave triggered by the collapse of Silicon Valley Bank in the United States has signaled clearly to the financial market that even if it is as powerful as the Federal Reserve, one cannot fully control the adverse effects of monetary policy adjustments on the domestic banking system. Small and medium-sized banks with weaker resistance to attacks are particularly vulnerable to becoming casualties of the Federal Reserve's interest rate hikes, if their internal controls are not strong and lacking forward-looking response capabilities.

Brzezinski once warned that the differences in abilities between countries are often reflected in their ability to distinguish between the following two states: what is persistent ambition, and what is self-righteous frivolity. This Polish Jewish hawkish strategist was worried shortly before his death that the United States might one day lose its superpower status. Obviously, in his eyes, the persistent ambition of the United States, especially the strategic determination to act after planning, is being overshadowed by a self-righteous frivolity and an imperial mentality that cannot tolerate others' rising power. Former U.S. Treasury Secretary Summers, known for his financial acumen, warns now and then that repeated missteps could inevitably undermine the U.S.'s role as a guarantor of the global system. Similarly, former Treasury Secretary Paulson, who is regarded as a key figure of the "Goldman Sachs faction," spoke candidly in *Foreign Affairs*, warning that "Washington risks pushing against economic gravity."

In the first half of the twenty-first century, as statesmen with a sense of global responsibility are becoming scarcer day by day, "beggar thy neighbor" often dominates the tone of the foreign economic policies of various countries. The "quantitative easing" policies implemented by the United States, Europe, and Japan after the financial crisis have proven to yield more of a false recovery. The proposition of modern monetary theory that sovereign states can never go bankrupt is essentially a theoretical extension of the logic of American hegemony into the field of finance. Nowadays, the global financial market is highly interconnected; the existing stability mechanisms have functional deficiencies; the guarantors of the financial system occasionally perform unethical behavior at the national level; various power systems are prone to the phenomenon of the "synthesis fallacy." No single actor or international economic organization can independently maintain global financial stability. Rising unemployment rates, mounting debt in many countries, declining sovereign debt ratings, the rise of populist forces in some countries, and the prevalence of anti-globalization, trade protectionism, and various forms of isolationism have added new uncertainties to the already uncertain world economy.

It is widely recognized that the trade frictions and even the competition for technology and talent initiated by the United States essentially stem from the fact that China's growing economic strength and rising global standing since its accession to the WTO have exceeded both U.S. expectations and what it regarded as the limits of its influence. In response, the United States has sought to constrain China's development to the greatest extent possible by adopting extraordinary measures that appear irrational but in fact form part of a broader strategy of interstate competition, including "massive trade frictions" (tariffs) and maximum-pressure tactics, while seeking to rewrite global trade, investment, and technology rules to secure its strategic interests.

China has become a super high-value target in the eyes of the United States and Europe, even defined by the West as the only systemic strategic competitor with both the ability and willingness to reshape the international order. The primary goal of the U.S. and Western strategic competition against China since the 2020s has been to strategically encircle China's increasingly powerful high-end manufacturing system. They employ tactics such as "decoupling and breaking chains," "small yard, high fence," "risk reduction," and "diversification" to constrain China's development trend within the existing order framework dominated by the U.S. and the West, until they turn China into a super economic vassal. Even if they themselves find it unreasonable, they still need to use the power of their alliance to slow down China's development pace.

The history of China's foreign relations since 1949 has proven, and will continue to prove, that no single power or even multilateral coalition in the world can easily undermine China's core interests, not even a superpower such as the United States has the capacity to do so.

Since 2018, China and the United States have engaged in rounds of games around trade friction, and China has gradually mastered the logic of dealing with uncertain competitors in the extremely complex great power game: it attaches great importance to resolving bilateral differences through dialogue and negotiation mechanisms, and appropriately reserves a trump card of countermeasures when necessary as a game choice; while gradually improving the early warning capability for various extreme situations, more emphasis is placed on exploring and constructing an effective cooperation range and risk management mechanism between China and the United States with a sense of great power responsibility and bottom-line thinking, demonstrating the unique national wisdom of a major Eastern nation.

Innovation drives human progress, and development is always the top priority for humanity. Both China and the world face an extensive list of tasks. How to solve the complex problems that constrain the sustainable development of human society and work together to address a series of uncertainties in the economic and financial fields is an urgent task for China and all countries around the world.

The pressing task facing China is no longer a general issue of openness and development, but rather how to consolidate the hard-won achievements of China's economy in opening-up and development amidst this increasingly uncertain and complex world, and how to coordinate development and security at a high level to make sure that there won't be systemic economic and financial risks.

There is also no doubt that the current Chinese economy has long passed the era where it could be launched with just a piece of approval. Nowadays, no one may dare to say that the vast Chinese economic system is flawless. In fact, all economies operate with imperfections, but the severity of the condition varies. When such conditions cannot be controlled, a systemic economic and financial crisis is on the way.

For China, with its complex economic system, it is almost impossible to initiate a new economic cycle on the basis of completed market clearing. Even achieving a basic level of market adjustment—including bringing capacity and inventories broadly into balance, resolving balance-sheet problems, and settling creditor–debtor relationships—is an extraordinarily difficult task. But this does not mean that we have to wait for the end of the previous stage of development to start the next, because the changes in global technological development are not entirely based on the static indicators used in government planning. A group of new enterprises focusing on technology research and industrial application as well as some innovative enterprises that seem small now but are closely attuned to technology and market change trends, have emerged in the market with the active support of the government, while China actively promotes economic strategic transformation and builds a new development pattern. The ability of these enterprises to extend in cross-industry integration and their forward-looking research and testing into future consumer experiences are reshaping the economic and technological landscape of China.

As long as the whole nation works together to boost the economy, the country will have hope.

Only by building a solid foundation through the development of the real economy and endogenous technological progress, always sticking to an awareness of ubiquitous risks, continuously strengthening the stability of the economic and financial system, and improving early warning capabilities for financial crises, can we be proactive, reserve sufficient policy tools, and ensure the steady and healthy development of China's economy.

China's development cannot be separated from the support of the world, and a developed China must, in turn, support the development of the world even more.

From a practical logic perspective, the 8 key areas of cooperation platforms established by China to implement global development initiatives, constructed with 32 practical measures, including poverty reduction, food security, epidemic prevention and vaccination, development financing, climate change and green development, industrialization, digital economy, and digital era connectivity, demonstrate concrete support for emerging economies and developing countries in advancing our respective modernization processes through practical actions. This marks that since the 2020s, emerging forces except for the United States and Western countries have spontaneously taken on the responsibility of promoting global development, which actively led responsible economies around the world to work together and overcome the so-called "Kindleberger Trap" set by the U.S. and the West.

In the *Report on the Implementation Progress of the Global Development Initiative*, China explicitly called on the international community to keep focusing on development, strengthen solidarity and cooperation, and promote synergy and efficiency in the development process of various countries, regions, and mechanisms. It also proposed to create more opportunities for the development and prosperity of all countries in practical cooperation, achieve all 17 sustainable development goals, and leave no country or individual behind. This is China's solemn commitment to the international community, reflecting its strong determination and national will to promote joint global development through practical actions. China will also perform the twenty-first-century development economics to promote global common development.

As the world's two largest economies, it is a natural policy logic for China and the United States to pursue strategic goals and take measures to safeguard their core interests in the global value chain, respectively. It is inevitable for the two countries to have conflicting interests and even fierce trade frictions. From the history of bilateral relations, the military and civilians of China and the United States fought side by side in the World Anti-Fascist War and achieved great victories. It is both the historical logic and the call of our times for the two countries to work together once again to solve world problems in the twenty-first century, which this epic strategic cooperation asks for!

The endogeneity of achieving global economic governance goals requires China and the United States to demonstrate a sense of international responsibility and great power responsibility in the process of a cooperative game. Global economic, trade, and financial stability call for decision-makers with a strong sense of international responsibility from both countries and powerful market entities to gradually eliminate disagreements through dialogue and communication, to promote the free flow of goods and capital through competition and cooperation, and to establish effective benefit-sharing mechanisms as soon as possible.

Moving beyond zero-sum competition toward mutual prosperity isn't merely China's goal—it's a shared mission for the world.

Shanghai, China
July 7, 2023

Yugui Zhang

Competing Interests The author has no competing interests to declare that are relevant to the content of this manuscript.

Contents

About the Author

Yugui Zhang Ph.D. in Economics; Professor of Economics; Doctoral Supervisor; Academic Committee Member, International Finance Forum (IFF); Board Member, China American Economic Association; Renowned Financial & Economic Columnist.

Dr. Zhang has long specialized in Chinese and global economic research, with a focus on international financial competition, industrial development, and evolving trade patterns. He has published over 40 scholarly articles in SSCI/CSSCI listed journals and authored several influential books, including *The Logic of the U.S. Dollar*, *China's Economic Breakthrough*, *Studies on Manufacturing Upgrading Paths*, and *Comparative Economics and China's Economic Reform*. He served as the primary translator of *The Global Economic System*. His nearly 1,000 columns have appeared in leading Chinese publications—*People's Daily*, *Guangming Daily*, *China Daily*, *Financial Times*, *Liberation Daily*, *Wenhui Daily*, *Global Times*, *China Securities Journal*, *Shanghai Securities News*, *Securities Times*, *China Business News*, *Ta Kung Pao*, and *Lianhe Zaobao*. Over 70 of these articles have been reprinted in notable outlets such as *Xinhua Digest*, *China Renmin University Press Reprints*, *China Economic Information*, *People's Daily Online*, *Qiushi Network*, *DRCnet*, *and China Economic Net*.

He is credited domestically with pioneering China's concept of an "Economic High Frontier" and forging China's "Financial Capital Power." Dr. Zhang has routinely provided economic, financial, and industrial policy advice to central ministries and the Shanghai municipal authorities. He received the "Outstanding Contribution to the First Flight of the C919" award and is a long-standing guest expert on CCTV, Phoenix TV, and Shanghai Media Group. His insights on "Rationally Addressing Sino–U.S. Trade Friction" were featured on *CCTV News Broadcast*, and his views on "Pudong's New Era as a Pioneering Zone" appeared on *CCTV Focus Interview*.

As Dean of the School of Economics and Finance at Shanghai International Studies University, he led the university's Master of Finance program to first place in the 2018 national assessment, and guided three undergraduate programs in International Economics and Trade, Accounting, and Finance to admission under the national "Double Ten-Thousand Plan."

Part I
When "Depression Economics" Knocks

Chapter 1
The Emerging Perils of Economic Darwinism

Responding to the Knock of "Depression Economics" with Robustness and Resilience

In the post-industrial era, where global economic confidence is highly dependent on the price transmission of financial markets, international financial markets have experienced significant turbulence in recent years. The obvious reason is the liquidity squeeze in global capital markets. The further reason is that the oil price wars pierced the irrational prosperity of the U.S. capital markets, whereas the inadequate response to the COVID-19 by the U.S. and Europe, coupled with the relative inability of monetary authorities to manage complex financial situations, exacerbated market fears over uncertain expectations. The underlying reason is that the actual economic growth and industrial technological progress since the 2008 financial crisis have failed to effectively offset the continuous accumulation of financial bubbles and financial risks. In addition, the absence of a global guarantor for the economic and financial systems has left the world ill-prepared to respond when "depression finance" comes knocking.

Today, the financial industry, especially the stock market, has deeply penetrated into human economies and social life. The violent fluctuations in the US and European stock markets, especially the U.S. stock market, which accounts for nearly half of the total market value of the global stock market, from February 20 to March 20, 2020, have become the most destructive risk impact in the global economy and financial operation ecology in 2020. The three major U.S. stock indexes, which are generally regarded as a symbol of the prosperity of the US economy, fell from the peak of prosperity to the area of the bear market in just 1 month. The stock prices of more than 2000 stocks had been cut by almost half, losing more than 10 trillion US dollars in market value, and the three major stock indexes circuit breaker kicked in four times within 10 days. (The trend of the Dow-Jones Average is shown in Fig. 1.1) In the post-industrial era where global economic confidence is highly dependent on the transmission of financial market prices, even the United States,

Y. Zhang, *Addressing Uncertainty*, Understanding China,
https://doi.org/10.1007/978-981-92-2692-4_1

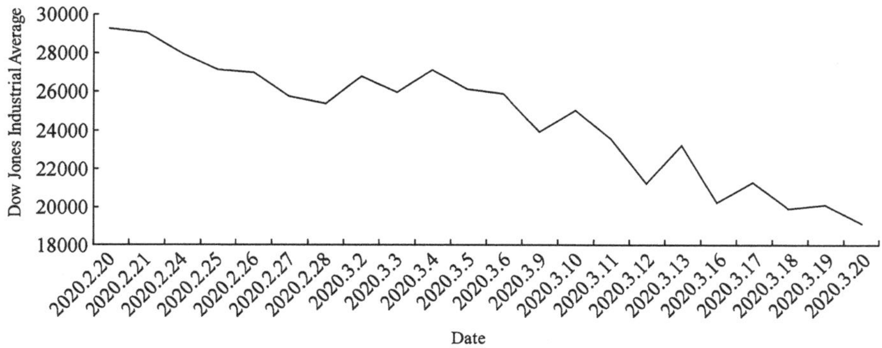

Fig. 1.1 The Trend of the Dow Jones Industrial Average. Data source: Sina Finance

which has the most powerful financial system in the world, will appear panicked to some extent when facing a super-large-scale market squall.

In a certain sense, the super shock that occurred in the international financial market in this month has already had the three characteristics of a financial crisis which are the uncertainty of the outbreak time, the high sensitivity of the transmission mechanism and the destructiveness to the economic system. However, in the case of these characteristics, we need to observe calmly before judging whether the world will enter the moment of the financial crisis. Although during the 2008 international financial crisis, some people were not positive about the "zero interest rate + QE" policy combination that the Federal Reserve made in response to on March 15, 2020 local time in the United States, and they believed that the 107-year-old super central bank may be facing a dilemma of not having enough abilities.

The author believes that although the U.S. financial market is indeed facing the most dangerous situation in the past 10 years, objectively speaking, the U.S. economic fundamentals are still the best among the major developed countries in the West and the health of its banking industry is also better than that during the 2008 international financial crisis, indicating that the capital and liquidity of banks or the ability to bail out are also stronger than 10 years ago. As the world's actual lender of last resort, the Fed also has privileges such as the Commercial Paper Facility (CPFF) and the Primary Dealer Credit Facility (PDCF), known as emergency loans, as granted by Sect. 13(3) of the *Federal Reserve Act*, as well as the ability to purchase corporate bonds directly with congressional authorization. At a critical time when the market continues to be volatile and systemic risk may occur at any time, cash is king and is the best strategy for companies in various countries. The US dollar, as the main international reserve currency and liquid asset, has shown signs of payment skipping in the international market, indicating that the evaporation of US financial assets. However, the international status of the US dollar is still difficult to shake in the short term, and the US still has the exclusive resource allocation ability to protect its financial system from eventual collapse. (The proportion of global foreign exchange reserves in the first quarter of 2020 is shown in Table 1.1).

Table 1.1 Global Foreign Exchange Reserves Proportion in the First Quarter of 2020

Currency	U.S. Dollar	Euro	Japanese Yen	RMB	Other currencies
Proportion	61.9%	20%	5.6%	1.9%	10.6%

Data source: IMF

Just as the return of "depression economics" has its own internal logic, since the 2008 financial crisis, the private sector in Europe and the United States as a whole has accelerated deleveraging, but governments have been increasing leverage to avoid excessive contraction in demand. To varying degrees, the world's major economies have seen a large amount of credit and money creation being used to buy stock assets rather than productive investment, resulting in lackluster global real economic growth.

Although the emerging technologies represented by big data and artificial intelligence and their industrial applications are promising, they have not been able to produce global economies of scale due to the technological fragmentation of some countries. A long period of excessive easing in major industrialized countries has led to bad investments all over the world, and some irrational monetary policy, while producing some good-looking economic data, is misleading enough to obscure the fragile side of the US economy, including the US economy. Moreover, after 2017, due to the fission of the global economic and financial guarantor system, coupled with the prevalence of anti-globalization, trade protectionism and various forms of isolationism, the probability of "black swan" events is greater than before, adding new uncertainty to the already uncertain global financial market.

Crisis has always been a combination of asset catastrophe and confidence blows with no winners. Judging from the risk transmission mechanism of the previous financial crises since the 90 s of the last century, in the open world where the global economy and financial system are increasingly interlinked, every large-scale systemic economic and financial risk is accompanied by a "Darwinist" impact. Because of the weak ability to prevent risks and absorb the damage of crises, the most injured were often emerging economies and developing countries, regardless of whether sources of the crises were developed or developing countries. Since late January 2020, the size of emerging market outflows has surpassed the level of the 2008 international financial crisis. On the other hand, banks and non-bank institutions around the world are increasing their demand for US dollar financing, but the assets they acquire through US dollar financing are essentially US assets, including US Treasury bonds. As a result, the Fed, as the world's actual lender of last resort, still has the advantage of a base currency and vested interests in times of crises.

As the world's second largest economy, China must maintain a prudent and rational policy in a more uncertain external environment. In the future, China's financial system may face major tests in the following aspects. Firstly, the long-term accumulation of systemic risks in the existing financial system will continue to test the financial breakwater. Secondly, the next global financial crisis that may break out in the future will have a major impact on China's economic system; Thirdly, after the high internationalization of the RMB, there may be a contradiction between China's global responsibilities as an important guarantor of the global financial system and the continuous supply of risk prevention capabilities.

Although China has rich experience and strong financial tools in preventing systemic economic and financial risks, and the use of monetary policy tools has also reached a high level, the explicit and implicit risks of China's debt cannot be ignored.

The global spread of the COVID-19 in 2020 put new pressure on China's efforts to stabilize financial markets, especially the RMB exchange rate. It is recommended to closely follow the relevant actions of domestic and foreign trading entities, effectively manage risks, and maintain sufficient external reserve liquidity positions, especially off-balance sheet assets and off-balance sheet transactions, as well as the scale of external reserve assets and financial leverage involved in these transactions. At the same time, it is recommended that China, on the basis of effective coordination with the United States, Europe, Japan and other BRICS countries, take the lead in convening an online special summit of G20 members at an appropriate time and take special actions to inject confidence in the global economic and financial system, preventing the eventual outbreak of systemic financial risks in the world.

Protectionism Is By No Means a "New Type of Globalization"

There have been articles in the Western media saying that Brexit[1] and *The United States-Mexico-Canada Agreement* (USMCA) all reflect the development direction of a "new type of globalization", in which the old trade rules are rewritten and the new rules pay more attention to national interests, so globalization has not stagnated or reversed, but exists and develops in a new form. This kind of assessment and discretion based on the position of a single country or a specific interest group is obviously biased.

Since 1985 when the American scholar Theodore Levitt first proposed "globalization", the concept has become a reality and has been the dominant force in promoting the globalization of the world in past 30 years.

International organizations such as the World Trade Organization (WTO), the World Bank and the International Monetary Fund (IMF), as well as relevant participants, influential scholars and market participants, have attached great importance to the role of globalization in promoting global economic growth and sustainable human development over the years. At the national level, the major developed countries tended to support globalization until at least 2016, despite the occasional prevalence of protectionism, unilateralism or action. Emerging economies and many developing countries have been playing the role of promoters or defenders of globalization.

[1]According to statistics, the most supportive group in the U.K. to stay in the EU are young people. Among Britons over the age of 65, only 39% choose to stay in the EU. These people have lived through Europe's darkest years and have deep suspicions about the European Union.

Today, although facilitating the free flow of goods, services, capital, and technology around the globe is more often seen as the scene of "blackboard economics", most of the world still believes that this should be the ultimate goal of globalization. The reason why globalization has been interfered with by protectionism in recent years is to a large extent because the motivation and preference of the major Western developed countries, which are the biggest promoters and beneficiaries of globalization, have declined significantly. In their view, the trend towards globalization and its resulting explicit and implicit benefits are increasingly beyond the limits of national capacities. At a time when their willingness and ability to pay for globalization are also declining marginally, the gradual abandonment of multilateralism has become the logic of some countries' foreign policies.

When the USMCA was about to replace the 26-year-old *North American Free Trade Agreement* (NAFTA), the U.S. International Trade Commission (ITC) released a report saying that, compared to NAFTA, the USMCA would increase U.S. real GDP by.35% per year and increase U.S. exports while increasing 1760,00 jobs. The U.S. Trade Representative even stressed that the agreement "will be a model for future U.S. trade agreements." As for the concern of many groups in Mexico that the main beneficiary of this agreement is the United States, it is not at all not a concern of mainstream American public opinion.

And Brexit, which was unthinkable in the 80 s of the last century, is now a reality that more than 60 million Britons have to face. In the days of Margaret Thatcher, although there was no lack of "glorious isolation" in Britain, both elites and ordinary people had a strong sense of national superiority and global responsibility. For a long time after joining the European Community in 1973, Britain's GDP per capita was among the fastest growing in Europe's largest economies, and for the previous 20 years it had been among the slowest growing large economies. In the view of economists who prefer to speak with data, for a long time after joining the European Community in 1973, Britain's GDP per capita was among the fastest growing in Europe's largest economies, and for the previous 20 years it had been among the slowest growing large economies. (Changes in UK's per capita GDP before and after joining the European Community is shown in Fig. 1.2) A range of evidence suggests that the UK's relatively close trade links with the EU promote competition and productivity growth, because the EU's red tape does not burden the UK too much, and there is not enough evidence that tens of thousands of migrants every year take jobs away from native British residents, and that migration does little damage to the original welfare. Therefore, time will be the best judge whether Brexit is a phenomenal expression of "alternative globalization" or an extension of the logic of refined national egoism.

The current ebb of globalization is obviously related to the inadaptability of developed countries in the face of the growing strength and the increased ability to participate in the reform of global economic governance of emerging economies. Since the Industrial Revolution, European and American capital, which has long been at the top of the global industrial and financial division, also showed a certain degree of discomfort when they found that transnational capital from emerging economies has increasingly become an important participant in the allocation of

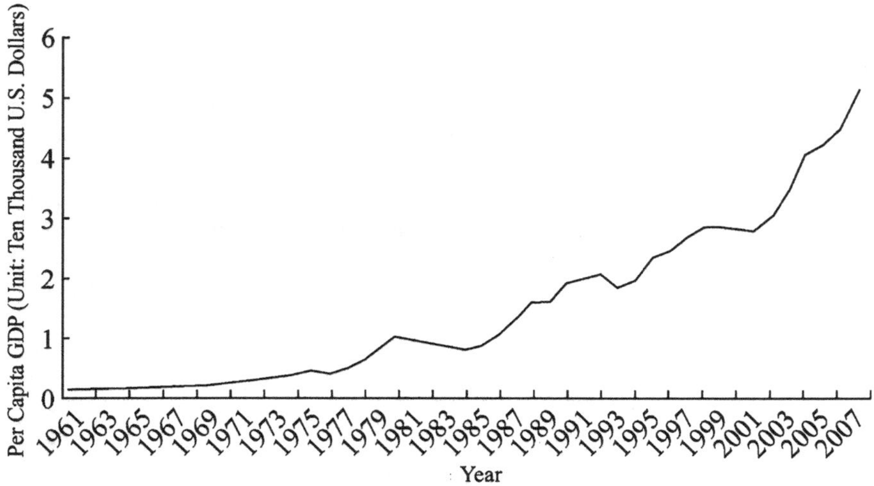

Fig. 1.2 Changes in UK's per Capita GDP before and after Joining the European Communities (in 1973). Data source: World Bank

global resources. However, in any case, in the context of irreversible scientific and technological progress and the impossibility of technological exchanges and cooperation being artificially blocked, it is difficult to contain the endogenous driving force of globalization which is based on factors such as scientific and technological progress, free flow of factors, and transaction cost savings.

At a time when the global economy and trading system are facing a structural lack of guarantors, the obvious rise of egoism at the national level, and the development of free trade and multilateralism are "lacking oxygen" from time to time, countries need to work together to promote the free flow of capital, technology and related factors, building an effective benefit-sharing mechanism. History has proven, and will continue to prove, that globalization, while not perfect, is an effective way to avoid "beggar-thy-neighbor" and promote global economic and trade growth to share the dividends of development.

Accusations of China's "Economic Coercion" Are a Case of Strategic Reversal

In recent years, western politicians and public opinion have frequently accused and hyped China of engaging in so-called "economic coercion". The early hype mainly focused on China's "coercive diplomacy" with anti-pandemic materials, and also interpreted the cooling of China-Australia relations as caused by China's "economic coercion" against Australia. Recently, they have attributed the partial rupture of the global supply chain to China's "economic coercion", claiming that in order to ensure global economic stability and normalization, it is necessary to work together to deal with China's "economic coercion". For example, at the Liverpool Foreign Ministers' Meeting that ended on December 12, 2021, the G7 made a big noise about the so-called "economic coercion" of China.

Even the European Union, which has the highest concentration of classical capitalist countries and a strong sense of institutional superiority, has tried to portray itself as a "vulnerable group" who are bullied by China. The world has noticed that in the joint statement issued by Europe and the United States after the second "Dialogue on China", China was portrayed as a destroyer of the international economic order, claiming to enrich and strengthen supply chains and solve the problem of "economic coercion". The European Commission, which has always been known for its "rationality" and "prudence", has also been instigated by some politicians to introduce a policy tool against China, the core issue of which is the so-called "response to economic coercion".[2]

Sufficient information, accurate data and scientific analysis framework are the prerequisites for rational judgment and decision-making. A careful analysis of the reasons behind the recent intensive hype of the West on the topic of China's "economic coercion" is nothing more than the following:

Firstly, China's economic development achievements since the reform and opening up, especially since its accession to the World Trade Organization (WTO) in 2001, have greatly exceeded Western expectations, and some Western countries, led by the United States, have increasingly shown great discomfort with China's rise. As we all know, since the seventeenth century, the international economic order has been controlled by Western capitalist countries for a long time. Since the beginning of the twenty-first century, the United States, as the only superpower, still controls the international economic, trade and financial order relatively firmly through institutional hegemony. However, the long-term calculating Western countries did not expect that after China's accession to the WTO, it has continuously adapted to international trade rules, expanded the scale of trade, improved product competitiveness, and steadily built a bilateral and multilateral trading system, becoming the world's most important exporter and the core hub of the global industrial chain and supply chain in less than 20 years.

According to the logic of classical economists such as Adam Smith and David Ricardo, global economic development, investment and trade facilitation, and financial stability especially require countries like China to exert their comparative advantages to promote the free flow of goods and capital, so that countries can reap the benefits of sharing. However, in the views of many Western politicians, in the 20 years since China's accession to the WTO, China's economic strength and position on the global trade map have risen far beyond their expectations and the boundaries of their actual control. A few years ago, Western countries often used their

[2]The Anti-China Economic Coercion Act was made public in the U.S. House of Representatives on October 15, 2021, and its sponsors include Ami Bera, Ann Wagner, and other bipartisan lawmakers. In fact, the term "economic coercion" has become a tool for some US and foreign politicians to frequently manipulate anti-China issues.

"market economy status" to clamp down on China's economic development, but after China has taken the initiative to connect with international high-standard economic and trade rules with high-level opening-up in recent years, it is obvious that this way didn't work.

Secondly, after the "economic coercion" diplomacy represented by the United States' trade bullying against China suffered a lot, Western countries tried to form a united front of economic encirclement against China by claiming China's "economic coercion", attributing the cause of their own governance failure to China. The first phase of the economic and trade agreement between the United States and China was reached almost two years after unilaterally provoking economic and trade conflicts with China in 2018, which is not only due to pressure from enterprises and markets, but also the result of changes in the political and economic situation at home and abroad. As the economic and trade conflicts between China and the United States have reached a stalemate in the past few years, the illusion of a "quick fix" that the United States originally predicted has been shattered. There is also no possibility that the United States will attempt to force China to make significant concessions on its core key interests or even its fundamental system through tariff barriers. However, if Sino-US economic and trade relations continue to deteriorate or even a systematic all-round confrontation occurs, it is very likely to cause a tsunami-like impact on the global political, economic, and financial systems. The U.S. is clearly not prepared for this, so it chose a partial break or a phased compromise, and escalated tensions between China and the United States from time to time at the tactical level, intending to force China to make concessions on major core interests through "decoupling" and other means, but this trick is also ineffective for China.

Thirdly, Western countries tried to subvert international perceptions and divert international contradictions, achieving the strategic intention of maximizing collective interests at the lowest cost by demonizing China's economic image. The world should not forget that at the beginning of the pandemic, some Western media smeared and said that Western anti-China politicians had failed to decouple China from the West, but that nature and the virus were helping to achieve this goal. They predicted that this would accelerate the process of "decoupling" the industrial chain between China and developed countries such as the United States, which would prompt more multinational companies to rethink the vulnerability of supply chains dependent on China and then make developed countries forecast that the COVID-19 may trigger a major reshuffle of industrial chains in Asia and even the world. Regrettably, all the predictions made so far by Western public opinion have failed. On the contrary, it is precisely because China plays the role of the pivot and stabilizer of the global industrial and supply chain that it has ensured that the global economy can remain relatively stable and resilient in the face of the continuous impact of the pandemic.

In the era of globalization encountering headwinds, economic competition between countries is increasingly concentrated on the control of core technologies and the layout of important industries. In such a severe situation, if some Western countries ignore their own misgovernance and instead try to hype up China's "economic coercion" as a panacea to divert domestic conflicts, they will only swallow the bitter fruits they have sown.

Developed Economies Must Not Pursue Recovery at the Expense of Others

The two-day G20 Finance Ministers and Central Bank Governors' Meeting was held in Jakarta, the capital of Indonesia, starting from February 17, 2022. A previously disclosed document showed that the European members of the G20 were particularly concerned about the issue of inflation and believed that the monetary policy communication among major central banks was crucial to the global economy, prices and financial stability. To some extent, this set the tone for this meeting, which was that Europe and the United States were tightening their monetary policies and emerging market countries should be well-prepared for this to avoid uncontrollable spillover effects caused by sudden market fluctuations. In a word, developed countries might once again try to get the best deal from emerging market countries for their own economic recovery.

As the communication and coordination mechanism with the strongest action ability in global economic governance, the G20, together with the International Monetary Fund (IMF), the World Bank and others, jointly constituted the main guarantors of the global economic and financial system after the 2008 international financial crisis. In recent years, in coordinating responses to major international issues such as the impact of the COVID-19 on the global financial markets, industrial chains and supply chains, climate change and the global minimum tax, the G20 has often been able to play a crucial and central role through concerted actions, and thus has become the main force in today's global economic governance.

However, an obvious fact is that the developed countries represented by the G7 and the European Union among the G20 members have long occupied a dominant position in agenda setting and the discourse system, making it difficult to fundamentally change the disadvantaged position of emerging market countries in the short term. In particular, the issue of the inequality between rights and obligations urgently needs to be addressed. It is easier said than done to make global economic governance return to true multilateralism.

Taking the spillover effects of the tightening of monetary policies in Europe and the United States, which has drawn special attention from the international community recently as an example, the first thing that needs to be clarified is: What was the starting point for the developed countries represented by Europe and the United States to adopt extremely loose monetary policies in the past 2 years? Who were the ultimate beneficiaries? And under the logical framework of global economic and financial integration, how can the world avoid the fallacy of composition and beggar-thy-neighbor policies? In particular, when the controversial Modern Monetary Theory (MMT) prevailed under the backdrop of the COVID-19,

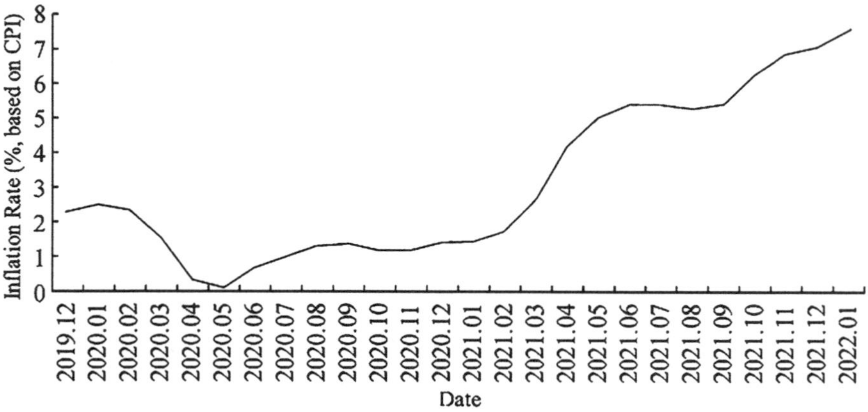

Fig. 1.3 The Inflation Rate of the United States Since the Outbreak of the COVID-19. Data source: OECD

becoming the main tool in the monetary policy toolbox of the ruling authorities in Europe and the United States and even getting out of control, should emerging markets bear the mess it left behind globally?

After the outbreak of the COVID-19, developed countries successively introduced quantitative easing (QE) monetary policies in an attempt to alleviate the impacts on their domestic financial markets and real economies. The International Monetary Fund (IMF) tracked the fiscal, monetary and macro-financial policies, as well as exchange rate and import-export policies adopted by more than 190 countries in response to the pandemic shocks. Among them, the monetary and fiscal policies of the United States had the greatest impact. According to the Fiscal Monitor released by the IMF in October 2021, from January 2020 to the release of the report, the global fiscal expenditures to counter the COVID-19 amounted to as high as 10.79 trillion US dollars, with the United States alone accounting for 5.5 trillion US dollars.

One of the biggest dilemmas faced by the quantitative easing monetary policy is that it is easy to implement but difficult to withdraw. Although the United States managed to achieve a superficial prosperity in the financial market by releasing a huge amount of liquidity and, to some extent, stabilized the economic fundamentals of the US, the Federal Reserve, no matter how strong its coordination ability is, cannot avoid the consequence of inflation as warned by Milton Friedman, the founder of the Modern Monetary Theory. Currently, inflation in the United States has approached an out-of-control level, which is surely a matter of great concern for the Biden administration and has significantly raised the expectation that the Federal Reserve will raise interest rates soon. (The inflation rate of the United States since the outbreak of the COVID-19 is shown in Fig. 1.3.) In 2020, many mainstream economists even claimed that the main risk for the US economy was not inflation.

This can't help but remind people of 2008, when President George Walker Bush consulted his economic advisors about the security of the US financial system after the collapse of Bear Stearns and those financial officials and renowned economists who had access to core information surprisingly generally believed that the US financial system was solid and sufficiently resilient. Even the internal monitoring report of the US Securities and Exchange Commission (SEC) had accurately identified many risk factors that led to the outbreak of the financial crisis as early as 2006. However, the overly confident SEC did not use its regulatory power to guide financial institutions to reduce risks, ultimately resulting in the complete outbreak of that once-in-a-century financial crisis.

Nevertheless, in the context where the global economic and financial system is still largely controlled by the US dollar, the United States and its major allies in the capitalist world can basically freely adjust their monetary policies. Of course, they will make a big fuss in the international public opinions before loosening or tightening their monetary policies, that is, giving risk warnings in the economic sense. They intended to convey information to emerging markets and developing countries that they will issue risk warnings or so-called "friendly reminders" before making major decisions, and these countries need to prepare early, otherwise they will bear the consequences. Just as Europeans warned before the 2022 G20 Finance Ministers and Central Bank Governors' Meeting, the central banks of developed countries will try to reduce the spillover effects that their actions may cause to emerging markets and developing countries, but policymakers in emerging markets must strive to enhance the resilience of their domestic financial markets.

As the saying goes, it's easy for those who are not in the situation to give advice. Asking emerging markets, which have relatively fragile economic and monetary policy space and whose domestic economic performance relies more on the stability of the international market, to bear the costs or consequences of the monetary policy shifts in Europe and the United States is the hegemonic logic under the unequal economic order in today's world.

Is the Petro-Dollar System Facing a Cliff Moment?

In March 2022, according to foreign media reports, Saudi Arabia was considering using RMB for settlement in oil transactions with China and incorporating RMB-denominated futures contracts into the pricing system of Saudi oil companies. On the other hand, India, the world's third-largest oil importer, took advantage of the sharp drop in Urals crude oil prices to snap up Russian crude oil that was mainly targeted at the European market before. At the same time, the Reserve Bank of India was also exploring to establish a "Rupee-Ruble" trade payment mechanism with the Central Bank of Russia. Western public opinion generally believes that these may lead to the weakening of the dominant position of the US dollar in the global oil market.

From a technical perspective, there are no major obstacles for Saudi Arabia to export oil to China denominated in RMB. Important oil-producing countries such as Iran and Venezuela have already made relevant arrangements before. As for other currencies, such as the Euro, it has long been the settlement currency for some oil-exporting countries, but its share is incomparable to that of the US dollar.[3]However, if Saudi Aramco, a super giant with an income of over $350 billion and a net profit of approximately $1100 billion in 2021, were to use RMB instead of the US dollar in large-volume oil trade with China, the impact on the global commodity trading market would be explosive. Therefore, the speculative reports in Western media are more like a pre-set signal test.

Regardless of whether the above speculations will eventually come true, simply from the perspective of trend changes, as the world's largest oil importer and one of the most important participants in the global currency and financial markets, it is a very natural logic to use or expand the use of RMB in bilateral or multilateral trade systems. However, from the history of global currency and financial changes, once a currency penetrates into the transaction and settlement systems of the global real economy and virtual economy and occupies the dominant position in reserve currencies, it will have a strong gravitational pull of holding and using preferences for ordinary market entities, enterprises, and even central banks of various countries, thereby forming an international prestige mechanism for this currency.

As for the supporting system, it generally includes strong real economy competitiveness (manufacturing industry), the extension of the global trade value chain, flexible commercial rules and financial pricing power, as well as a global maritime power projection and strike system to ensure the stability of the country's position as the guarantor of the global economic, trade and financial system. Since the nineteenth century, the pound and the US dollar have successively played the above roles. As superpowers in different periods, Britain and the United States have spared no effort in maintaining the hegemonic position of their domestic currencies.

Some studies believe that the cycle of a country's currency serving as the international dominant currency is generally about 100 years. If the foresight of this view holds true, then since the establishment of the Bretton Woods system in 1944, the hegemonic dividend cycle of the US dollar is running out. This may be the reason why American strategists and economic authorities, including Zbigniew Brzezinski and Paul Samuelson, are deeply worried about the impending collapse of the US dollar's status.

Certainly, it seems that the petrodollar still has a long time to enjoy the dividends. Strictly speaking, the concept of petrodollars originated in 1973. It was jointly proposed by Peter Peterson, the then US Secretary of Commerce, and Ibrahim Oweiss, an American economist, against the backdrop of the fourth Middle East War triggering another global oil crisis. Through the lobbying of Henry

[3]In 2016, the Chinese yuan was included in the basket of Special Drawing Rights (SDR), which marked that the Chinese yuan had become one of the major global currencies. On May 11, 2022, the composition of the basket currencies after the valuation review by the International Monetary Fund (IMF) is shown in Fig. 1.4.

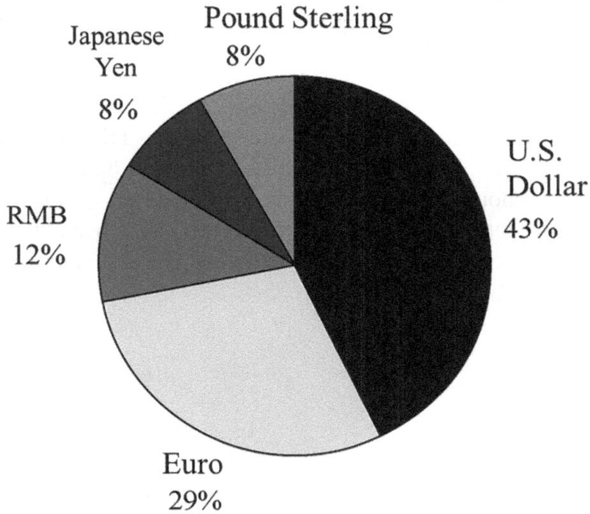

Fig. 1.4 Composition of Basket Currencies. Data Source: The State Council of the People's Republic of China Website: www.gov.cn

Kissinger, the then US Secretary of State, Saudi Arabia, as the leading oil-producing country, decided to use the US dollar as the sole pricing currency for oil exports. This led to the Organization of the Petroleum Exporting Countries (OPEC) unanimously agreeing in 1975 to price oil products in US dollars and invest oil revenues in US government bonds in exchange for US military security protection. Since then, the "petrodollar" system has been established.

On the surface, the United States and the oil-exporting countries seem to have achieved mutual benefit and win-win results by meeting each other's needs. However, from the perspective of international political economy, the United States has successfully embedded the US dollar in the central nervous system of oil, the world's most important commodity, by providing military security protection, thus grasping the "dominant strategy" in the economic sense, and thus being able to form a certain degree of control over the strategy of the major oil-producing countries in the Middle East in terms of politics, economy, finance, and security, and then form an institutionalized financial hegemony system with petrodollars and capital asset pricing power as strategic support on a global scale. Exactly how much the United States has gained from this, both explicit and implicit, is probably clear only to the core bureaucracy of the United States.

However, any hegemonic currency system will eventually collapse. The so-called "a currency will only die in its own bed" means that the excessive use of the power of a currency will ultimately lead to an irresistible cycle of metabolism and rebalancing in the global currency system.

For petrodollars, the main short-term challenge is the increasing cost for the United States to maintain the existing system, and due to the relative decline of its national strength, it is difficult for the United States to bind the preference choices of the major oil-producing countries in the Middle East at once. The main medium-term challenge is that oil itself, as a fossil energy, will gradually lose its dominant position in the context of "dual carbon" (carbon peaking and carbon neutrality), resulting in the petrodollar system either continuing to exist under a new guise or accepting the fate of being partially replaced. Of course, this cycle may be relatively long. In the long run, as the United States is likely to no longer be the most important economy in the world by the middle of the twenty-first century, and with the economic scale of multiple G20 members accounting for more than 10% of the global total, new currency power centers will inevitably appear. At that time, the most likely scenario in the world will be a trilateral or even multilateral currency balance of landscape.

Chapter 2
Who Is Seeking Quick Fixes During the Pandemic?

There Is No "Magic Pill" for the Rescue of the Global Economy[1]

The outbreak of the COVID-19 pandemic in 2020 has damaged the mature production, living and trading systems that countries around the world rely on so much, not only far exceeding the consequences of most previous "black swan" events, but also a costly and long-term test of human collective intelligence, scientific and technological progress, and the resilience or ability of the economic system to absorb losses. The gap in global trade and growth, created by the pandemic, though enormous, was not necessarily a leading factor to the Great Depression. Further, whether the global economy can avoid a new recession depends on the ability of the USA and European countries to act.

The rapid spread of the pandemic around the world has caused significant and implicit losses to the capital market and the real economy, and the statistical departments of various countries and relevant international economic organizations have failed to provide accurate analysis data. People in the world may be more concerned about whether the USA, which has the world's most advanced medical means, technologies and the most developed economic and financial system, will fall into a new round of deep recession after its recovery results and fairly good economic trend since the 2008 international financial crisis due to the severe impact of the pandemic?

The Federal Reserve's Beige Book released on April 15, 2020 showed that economic activities in all regions of the United States has contracted sharply in recent weeks due to the impact of the COVID-19. The U.S. Department of Labor's weekly unemployment benefits application report released on April 9 showed that about 6.6 million people filed for unemployment benefits for the first time in the week of March 29 to April 4, 2020, and about 16.6 million people filed for unemployment benefits for the first time in the past three weeks. The Associated Press commented

[1] This section was originally published in *Shanghai Securities News* on April 18, 2020.

Y. Zhang, *Addressing Uncertainty*, Understanding China,
https://doi.org/10.1007/978-981-92-2692-4_2

that this figure means that about 1 in 10 workers in the United States have lost their jobs in the past three weeks. On the other hand, the International Monetary Fund (IMF) warned in its *World Economic Outlook* report released in April 2020 that the global economy is likely to experience the worst recession since the Great Depression, and that the recession will be far greater than the economic downturn caused by the 2008 international financial crisis. A worried IMF Chief Economist Geeta Gopinath predicted at the time that the pandemic would cost the cumulative global GDP loss of about $9 trillion in 2020 and 2021, more than the economies of Japan and Germany combined, while the USA, the world's number one economic power, would have its worst report card that its economy would shrink by 5.9%; In addition, the Eurozone economy would have negative growth for the whole of 2020 7.5%, the Japanese economy would also shrink by 5.2%.

However, although the actual economic data, financial market indicators, and economic confidence indices of the United States and globe all experienced a more-than-expected decline in March 2020, and the subsequent wave of corporate bankruptcies and unemployment will also cause heavy damage to the world economy. The author believes that this is to a large extent due to the significant external variable of the pandemic, and the pandemic cannot rage globally endlessly. On the other hand, the sharp contraction of the US economy and the surge in the number of people applying for unemployment benefits are the short-term reactions of the economic operation system and ordinary people to the pandemic. Since the breakthroughs achieved by humanity so far in the fields of technology and cognition are not enough to deal with the risks brought by the pandemic, it is a very normal market logic for the economic operation system to directly enter the instantaneous recession track. But to judge whether the global economy will suffer the most severe depression and collapse since the "Great Depression" of the last century, three key indicators still need to be observed: Firstly, the short-term damage absorption and self-repair capabilities of the economic and financial systems of major economies, especially the USA; Secondly, whether the major global economies can put aside their "beggar-thy-neighbor" foreign policies after communication and coordination, and then inject confidence into the market; Thirdly, whether the global financial markets can stop the bleeding as soon as possible and stabilize the basic situation.

Regarding the first indicator, from the major response mistakes and a certain degree of incompetence shown by the United States in the face of the initial impact of the pandemic to the rapid adoption of unconventional monetary and fiscal policies after the pandemic spread, it indicates that the United States still possesses a relatively mature self-correction mechanism, corresponding monetary policy tools, and a strong financial foundation, demonstrating the damage absorption and self-repair capabilities that cannot be ignored. The most significant challenge faced by the USA is whether it can control the pandemic as soon as possible and eliminate the source of market panic.

Regarding the second indicator, with the successful convening of the G20 Extraordinary Leaders' Summit on COVID-19 and the positive progress made in the relevant ministerial meetings in implementing the *G20 Action Plan in Response to the COVID-19*, it shows that various countries have sent a major signal to the world that they unanimously agree to jointly adopt various policy tools to deal with the impact of the pandemic on the economy, maintain financial stability, and at the same time create positive conditions for a strong recovery of the global economy.

As for the third indicator, it is the most difficult to predict. This is mainly because it depends on the capabilities and collaborative effectiveness of individual countries and the global community in responding to the pandemic. The recurrence of the pandemic, as well as the global willingness to cooperate in maintaining the integrity of the supply chain and industrial chain, are all important uncertainties. If major countries can uphold a bottom-line mentality, earnestly adopt the strictest prevention and control measures, and carry out substantial cooperation in global joint prevention and control, it is still possible for the global financial markets to truly stabilize before the end of 2020.

What worries people a lot is that, with the partial shutdown of major economies such as those in Europe and the United States, output has declined significantly, and an unexpected drop in fiscal revenue will be inevitable. To put it bluntly, where will the money come from? The IMF reminded countries in its *Fiscal Monitor* released in April 2020 that the pandemic and its impact on the financial and economic sectors will lead to a significant increase in the fiscal deficit and the public debt ratio compared to previous forecasts. In the baseline scenario for 2020, the proportion of fiscal revenue in global GDP will be 2.5% lower than the forecast in October 2019. The deterioration of the fiscal situation will greatly restrict the government's bailout capabilities. However, the prescription proposed by the IMF, which aims to promote economic recovery through extensive fiscal stimulus while ensuring debt sustainability, is an extremely difficult proposition to achieve in the real world.

Since the last financial crisis, the private sectors in European and American countries, on the whole, have been accelerating deleveraging. However, in order to avoid excessive demand shrinkage, governments have been continuously increasing leverage. In major global economies, a large amount of credit and money creation has been used to purchase existing assets rather than for productive investment to varying degrees. The history of economic development has proven that debt arrangements are not only an important driver of a country's economic growth but also the root cause of a new round of crises. The pandemic, as a major public health event, will eventually pass, but the money overissued by the Federal Reserve due to large-scale market rescue and bailout plans will be difficult to withdraw quickly. The unrestrained release of liquidity by the Federal Reserve will ultimately backfire on the US financial system and damage the global reserve currency status of the US dollar.

Emerging economies should learn from the monetary policy of the Federal Reserve. They must base economic growth and financial stability on deeply cultivating the development of the real economy and building a flexible and robust financial system. Without consistent attention to the real economy and the adoption of truly protective measures, it is impossible to build a flexible and robust financial system. Only economic growth based on knowledge and driven by technological innovation is sustainable and effective. Emerging economies must by no means introduce the debt-driven growth model of the United States and must avoid falling into the strange cycle of using credit expansion to support economic confidence.

What Is Holding Back America's "Infrastructure Dream"?

Strengthening domestic infrastructure construction in the United States and increasing infrastructure spending to boost the US economy have become one of the key governance items that Joseph Robinette Biden has been striving to promote since taking office. As early as during the congressional nomination hearing, Pete Buttigieg, the US Secretary of Transportation, called on both the ruling and opposition parties to jointly support the improvement of US infrastructure, describing it as an "opportunity of the generation." He even elevated the promotion of infrastructure to a strategic level, stating that if such an opportunity is missed, the domestic racial and economic inequality in the US may intensify, leading to social division and weakening the rights of the American people to prosperity and development.

As early as August 2020, when he was elected as the Democratic Party's presidential candidate, Biden's policy preference for infrastructure had already become evident. At that time, he promised that if elected, infrastructure would be one of the major important items to be prioritized. Subsequently, Biden once again stated that he would ask Congress to "make historic investments in infrastructure, manufacturing, innovation and research, and clean energy."

As the 46th President of the United States, Biden's policy vision for expanding infrastructure construction seems to have a certain logical connection with the New Deal implemented by Franklin Roosevelt, the 32nd President of the United States, also from the Democratic Party, in 1933. The US economy today has similarities to that of 90 years ago. Although US still holds the top position in the world, it has been severely damaged under the impact of large-scale crises. The former prosperity is no longer there, and the morale of the people and the market is low. There is an urgent need for the "visible hand" of the government to play the role of a positive government.

Looking at the current situation of US infrastructure construction, although the US is the world's only superpower, the old-age and dilapidation of its infrastructure have long been an indisputable fact, and it is even inferior to some emerging economies. The report *The State of US Infrastructure* published by the Council on Foreign Relations in 2018 detailed the backward situation of US dams, bridges, airports, urban drinking water pipelines, and power facilities. For example, it pointed out that the drinking water pipelines in many US cities were built in the 1920s before the implementation of the New Deal and have long been in disrepair. The author visited some cities and rural areas in the Midwest of the US a few years ago and has a certain understanding of the local backwardness in the field of infrastructure. (Shown in Figs. 2.1 and 2.2).

Therefore, whether from the perspective of the demand side or considering the significant value that the "Roosevelt's New Deal" played in reviving the US

Fig. 2.1 An old train parking lot in New York, USA

Fig. 2.2 An apartment building collapsed in Miami, USA

economy, it has certain practical significance and even historical legitimacy for the Biden administration to revisit the "infrastructure dream" of its predecessors. Moreover, the infrastructure mentioned today also includes "new infrastructure" such as clean energy and 5G networks. The US urgently needs to increase investment in these areas to avoid being left behind by other major economies.

However, the economic reality in the real world has always been difficult to fulfill static policy assumptions. Since the beginning of the twenty-first century, both the Bush administration and the Obama administration have attempted to make a difference in changing the status of US infrastructure. Former President Donald Trump claimed in 2019 that he would invest $2 trillion in infrastructure construction over the next 10 years. But none of the three former presidents were able to make substantial achievements in the field of infrastructure.

Nowadays, China is dubbed the "infrastructure maniac" by netizens. However, many people may not know that the US was also a veritable global "infrastructure maniac" in the first half of the twentieth century. At that time, the US set many world records in the construction of highways, airports, and bridges. A number of super projects still support the prosperity of the US economy today. But for the US to relive its past "infrastructure dream" and lead the US economy to take on a new look, it faces at least the following three constraints:

The first is the lack of funds. Infrastructure construction is an industry with a large investment volume, a long cycle, a low rate of return, and even the need to accept losses in medium to long term. Generally, it requires government leadership or initiative to establish an effective profit-sharing mechanism through project cooperation to attract private investment. But the government must first be "willing and able" to invest money, which is a necessary prerequisite for infrastructure projects to be implemented.

Even according to the assessment of the American Society of Civil Engineers in 2014, the US, with an infrastructure rating of D +, needs to invest at least $3.6 trillion to significantly change its backward appearance. Moreover, an additional investment of $200 billion per year is required to keep up with the global infrastructure development trend. The problem is that the US government, already heavily in debt, simply can't afford this amount of money. Biden took over a mess with a total government debt of $27.55 trillion (as of December 31, 2020). His predecessor added an average of $1.89 trillion in debt each year over the past 4 years, leaving the new government with limited room for expansionary fiscal spending to meet the infrastructure investment needs. (The total debt of the US federal government from 2001 to 2020 is shown in Fig. 2.3). Facing the embarrassing situation of an empty US treasury, even former President Clinton, who is considered to have the "strongest fiscal management ability" in the US after World War II, would probably be at a loss.

Secondly, there is a shortage of labor. Current infrastructure construction is also an industry that encompasses both traditional and cutting-edge technologies. It requires a workforce proficient in design and construction techniques to support. The reason why Europe and the United States took the lead in achieving modernization and even full-scale modernization is, to a large extent, due to the

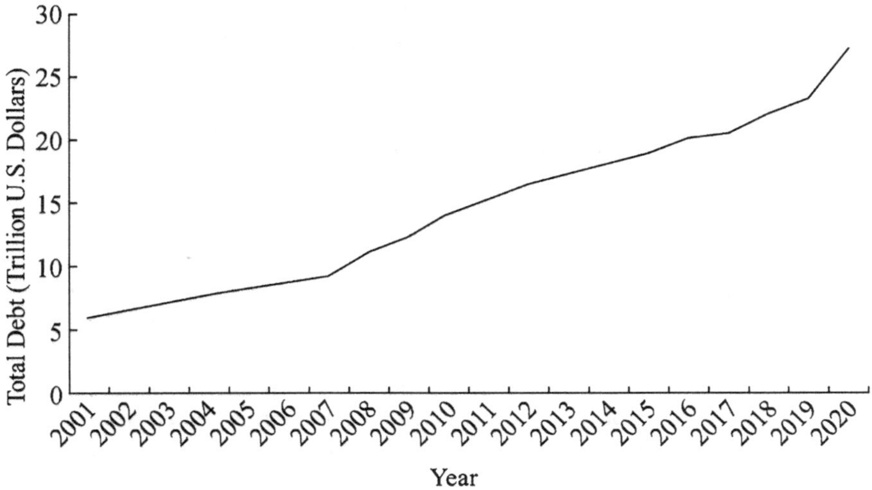

Fig. 2.3 Total U.S. Federal Government Debt, 2001–2020. Data Source: US Department of the Treasury

demand-driven effects of a series of factors including infrastructure construction during the process of industrialization, as well as the strong support of a large army of infrastructure industry workers based on the demographic dividend.

In other words, although traditional infrastructure and today's "new infrastructure" have significantly reduced the base demand for labor with the development of technology and the increasing proportion of alternative construction, they still rely on a large number of infrastructure industrial workers who learn while working and are willing to endure hardships. Unfortunately, in the United States, due to the disruption and discontinuity of infrastructure construction, a large number of industrial workers have either left the industry or changed jobs. When young people make career choices, they often favor industries that can bring quick profits, resulting in a growing scarcity of "craftsmen" in the United States.

Thirdly, there is a "lack of policy". The Biden administration's policy vision of boosting the US economy through infrastructure modernization is positive and a strategic design with a long-term perspective. However, on the current emergency list of the US government, infrastructure certainly does not rank first or even among the top three priorities. The $1.9 trillion rescue package signed by Biden on March 11, 2021, includes direct rescue for US residents, extension of unemployment insurance, and subsidies to state and local governments. These are all measures that the Biden administration deems necessary for emergency rescue. But it was extremely difficult for this plan to pass through both the Senate and the House of Representatives, let alone an infrastructure plan that cannot provide immediate relief.

Therefore, for the US to realize its "infrastructure dream", it not only needs an appropriate time window, but also the support of relevant matching conditions, and more importantly, the timely demonstration of national wisdom. But currently, it is precisely stuck on these factors and links, making it difficult to move forward.

Short-Term Stimuli Cannot End America's "Middle-Class Stagnation"

At Biden's first press conference after taking office, he said that the US government would increase investment in areas such as technology and physical infrastructure. This was widely regarded as an echo of the "trillion-dollar stimulus plan" previously reported by the US media. Part of the funds would be invested in infrastructures such as 5G, green power grids, universal broadband Internet access, semiconductor production, and carbon-free transportation. Another part would be used for universal pre-school education, free community colleges, child tax credits, and subsidies for low- and middle-income families to participate in health insurance. On March 11, 2021, Biden signed a $1.9-trillion rescue package. By rolling out or formulating such large-scale economic stimulus plans in succession, apart from hoping to promote the rapid recovery of the US economy and increase labor productivity, Biden is also fulfilling his campaign promise, that is, to ensure that the US middle class can receive higher wages and benefits, so as to help achieve his so -called goal of "building back better".

These economic stimulus plans are actually part of the Biden administration's "100-day plan". Its high-level attention to the interests of the middle class and practical measures are reminiscent of Roosevelt's actions in 1933. Roosevelt is regarded as one of the greatest presidents of the US in the twentieth century. The New Deal he implemented at that time achieved great success and even became a classic case in economic history of an effective government kick-starting economic recovery after market failure. That is, during a critical period when the external economic environment deteriorated sharply and market entities such as manufacturers and consumers lacked confidence seriously, expanding government public spending played a key role in boosting economic confidence and reviving the economy.

Western public opinion that is optimistic about Biden's New Deal believes that the Biden administration's rescue package may give it the opportunity to "reset US capitalism" and enable it to lead the US to end the "middle-class stagnation" dilemma. Many Chinese economists, including the author, are also willing to see the US usher in a new round of economic growth and hope that the US middle class can get out of the state of hesitation under uncertain expectations as soon as possible. From a rational perspective, after all, the US is currently the country with the largest economic scale in the world. If the US economy remains sluggish for a long time, it will take more time and effort for the global economy to recover and then move towards strong growth. And the middle class, which occupies an important position in the US economy and social life, their income and living conditions are directly related to the stability of the US economic and social order.

Many economic indicators in the US are calculated on a household basis, including the middle class, tax and welfare policies. According to the definition of the Pew Research Center, the US middle class refers to households with an income ranging from two-thirds to twice the median income in the US. Pew's survey data in 2019 showed that the median household income of US residents was $68,700, with an average of 2.52 people per household. At that time, the household income of the US middle class ranged from $45,800 to $137,400. However, after the outbreak of the COVID-19, more than ten million middle-class people in the US fell back into poverty. It is estimated that there are currently around 35 million people with incomes below the middle-class level.

Recently, the author asked middle-class people who have been working and living in the US for a long time. The relevant information is that once one of the family members loses their job, life quickly falls into a difficult situation, and daily expenses become tight. Regarding the Biden administration's economic recovery plan and the Democratic Party's measures of raising taxes on the rich, or in a sense, "robbing the rich to help the poor", they think the effects may not be optimistic. These US middle-class people have long been tired of various narrative scripts of politicians. Moreover, they have a good level of economic literacy and intuitive ability, and they have their own independent judgments about all kinds of "deceptions", even at a high level.

As for the current situation of the US economy, for any economic revitalization or recovery plan to achieve the expected results, it not only requires real-money investment but also needs to be based on the effective growth of the real economy. The problem is that the funds required for the previous rounds of US economic stimulus plans were not real money but rather the "helicopter drop" approach of living beyond its means. The US is already heavily in debt, and its fiscal deficit has repeatedly exceeded the internationally recognized 3% benchmark. By the end of the 2022 fiscal year, the scale of US national debt reached $31 trillion, equivalent to 122% of the total GDP; the US fiscal deficit was as high as $1.375 trillion, accounting for 5.5% of GDP.

Therefore, if the US fails to face up to the economic risks caused by the serious inversion of its virtual economy and real economy, does not reflect on its "quenching thirst with poison" economic development model, and does not withdraw its fiscal and monetary policies that harm others and actually do not benefit itself as soon as possible, then any economic prosperity realized by relying on short-term stimulus plans will ultimately be an illusion. Before the economy truly enters a virtuous development track, it is doomed to be a dream for the Biden administration to end the long-standing "middle-class stagnation" state.

The Resurgence of "Resource Nationalism"

The COVID-19 and the Russia–Ukraine conflict have profoundly influenced the international landscape. Against this backdrop, some emerging economies that possess critical and advantageous resources are increasingly emphasizing the control of resources of strategic significance to themselves, and gradually mastering the "art of transaction" at the national level. Developed countries represented by the United States, Australia, and Canada have successively released lists of critical minerals, and they are already highly proficient in maximizing national interests by leveraging resource-based means.

In general, even with the overall trend of global economic integration remaining unchanged, as long as national interests exist and will continue to exist rigidly in the long-term future, countries with resource-endowment advantages will occasionally exhibit a preference for "resource nationalism".

In the history of global economic changes after World War II, the two oil crises that broke out in the 1970s were typical manifestations of "resource nationalism". From a perspective of the origin of the crises, they had profound ethnic conflict and geopolitical backgrounds. Arab countries' use of oil as a weapon against Israel and Western countries was a last resort. The resulting global "great inflation" was comparable to the global "great depression" in the 1930s, and these two events can be regarded as the two "darkest moments" of the global economy in the twentieth century. Therefore, the nearly decade-long confrontation was a lose-lose situation for global economic development with no ultimate winner.

Decades later, "resource nationalism" has shown a clear resurgence, adding new uncertainties to the world economy, which is already facing multiple shocks. On the one hand, due to the rise of nationalism and protectionism, the global supply of key resources faces short-term shortages. This not only drives up resource prices but may also cause partial disruptions or adjustments in the supply chain. On the other hand, facing the most severe inflation in 40 years, the United States may introduce unexpected and highly intense monetary policies. Although this may stabilize inflation expectations, it will hardly avoid causing economic impacts on other countries, especially emerging economies and developing countries. From the perspective of past policy practice, in an era when Darwinism prevails, developing countries with low damage-absorption capabilities or a lack of economic immunity often end up as victims of adjustments in US economic policies.

Worryingly, neither the G7, whose marginal influence is gradually waning, nor the G20, which is playing an increasingly important role in global economic governance, can quickly find an "optimal solution", or even a "sub-optimal solution", when facing protectionist tendencies including "resource nationalism". The G20 Finance Ministers and Central Bank Governors' Meeting held in Washington on April 20, 2022, should have focused on key and urgent issues such as the global economy and risks, global health, the international financial architecture, and sustainable finance. However, against the backdrop of the Russia-Ukraine conflict at that time, the fragmentation of global economic governance and non-cooperative games intensified, seriously affecting the concerted actions of powerful entities on key issues. The World Trade Organization, which shoulders the heavy responsibility of regulating global trade relations and order and promoting global trade liberalization and facilitation, also faces the practical bottleneck of having a long list of problems and insufficient action capabilities.

Protectionism has always been a cancer to the stability and sustainable development of the global economy. Although the "fallacy of composition" is a normal phenomenon in countries' foreign economic and trade policies, history has proven and will continue to prove that in today's globally integrated economy, "resource nationalism" and "zero-sum games" are harmful and unbeneficial. Two hundred years ago, the British classical economist David Ricardo proposed that under a system of full free trade, countries will naturally invest capital and labor in industries that are most profitable for them. Through common interests and mutual exchanges, it is possible to connect individuals with society, and individual countries with the entire civilized world.

At this crucial moment, as the two major economies in the world, China and the United States, despite having many complex issues to be resolved, also bear the important responsibility of maintaining global economic growth and financial stability. No matter how intricate their contradictions are, they should not prevent the two countries from jointly addressing increasingly difficult regional and global economic problems.

Part II
Why Is Global Development Uncertain?

Chapter 3
Global Economic Imbalance from a Macro Perspective

The World Bank's Hopes for Endogenous Growth in All Economies

On July 18, 2016, the World Bank Appointed Paul M. Romer, a Professor of Economics at the Stern School of Business, new York University and a Representative Figure of the New Growth Theory (shown in Fig. 3.1), as its New Chief Economist. This Is Regarded as One of the most Sensational and Constructive Measures in the World Bank's Selection of Research Directors in the Past 20 Years, Provided that Romer Can Live up to the Mission.

As a world-renowned economist, although Romer's famous endogenous growth model is inevitably influenced by Joseph Schumpeter's innovation ideas, his integration of knowledge into the economic and technological systems as an endogenous variable of economic growth not only makes up for some limitations of the neoclassical economic growth model but also systematically expounds on the important role of human capital in economic growth. In general, Romer's research shows that the most important factors driving economic growth are knowledge innovation, technological progress, and the increase of human capital. And the economic practices in the real world have proven that Romer's new growth theory can not only explain many economic growth phenomena but also promote the economic growth transformation of many countries and regions.

If in 2008, Robert B. Zoellick, then President of the World Bank, appointed Lin Yifu, an economist from China, as the senior vice-president and chief economist, hoping that Lin Yifu's research and China's poverty alleviation experience would help developing countries out of poverty, then Jim Yong Kim, then President of the World Bank with a Ph.D. in anthropology from Harvard University, in his attempt to transform the World Bank into a "knowledge bank", apparently wanted to draw on Romer's research experience to help backward economies get rid of poverty and stimulate economic growth and reform.

Y. Zhang, *Addressing Uncertainty*, Understanding China,
https://doi.org/10.1007/978-981-92-2692-4_3

Fig. 3.1 Economist Paul Romer

Although it is an era of globalization today, economic development is seriously imbalanced, and the gap in economic and financial division of labor continues to widen. In the author's view, in terms of economic and social development levels, the world today can be roughly divided into six levels: at the top of the pyramid is the United States, which holds the most economic and financial resources and dominates the top-level division of labor; the second level consists of classic European capitalist countries and developed countries such as Japan, Canada, and Australia; the third level includes countries in the Organization for Economic Co-operation and Development (OECD) with relatively weak economic and social development levels; the fourth level is represented by emerging economies such as China, Russia, India, and Brazil; the fifth level is general developing countries; and the last level is the 46 least-developed countries.

According to *the Least Developed Countries Report* 2021 released by the United Nations Conference on Trade and Development (UNCTAD), the 46 least-developed countries on the periphery of the global economy, under the impact of the health, economic, and social crises brought about by the COVID-19, have significantly declined in the resilience of their economic systems and the ability to absorb losses. Their economic growth in 2020 hit a 30-year low, and their vaccination rates are far lower than those of developed countries. In 2020 alone, about 32 million people were pushed into extreme poverty (i.e., with a daily income of less than \$1.90), about 244 million people suffered from malnutrition, 466 million people had no access to electricity, 665 million people had no access to safely managed drinking water, and 874 million people had no access to clean fuels and cooking technologies.

The suggestion given by UNCTAD is to develop and improve productive capacity, and the prerequisite for improving productive capacity is the effective supply of development funds. For example, just to eliminate extreme poverty in the least-developed countries, an average annual investment of \$485 billion is required. And to achieve economic structural transformation, the average annual fixed investment required will exceed \$1 trillion, which is more than three times the fixed investment of the least-developed countries in 2019. Obviously, without the participation of powerful investment, financing, and aid entities in the international community, it is difficult to fill the huge funding gap. On the other hand, the recent food and energy security crises have further tormented the least-developed countries.

According to *the Least Developed Countries Report 2015* released by UNCTAD, in some rural areas of African countries among the 48 least-developed countries, the lowest income is as low as \$0.10–\$0.20 per day. To eradicate poverty in these countries, their income needs to be increased by 5–13 times in the next 15 years, water supply needs to be provided to about 600 million people, electricity and sanitation facilities need to be provided to about 900 million people, and the primary and secondary school enrollment rates of rural children need to be significantly increased. To achieve these goals, it depends on major donor countries allocating 0.35% of their national income to targeted official aid. It is estimated that by 2030, this aid amount should reach at least \$250 billion.

However, although developed countries' aid to less-developed countries, including the least-developed countries, has achieved certain results in the fields of education, health, and even climate change, overall, the enthusiasm for aid is on the decline. On the other hand, due to the structural defects and obvious political factors in the Western-dominated aid system, the global achievements in poverty alleviation and promoting economic growth are not significant. In 2005, Western countries proposed the aid effectiveness agenda in Paris, but these concepts and related measures did not deeply reflect on the root causes of aid failures and were limited to improving aid management. Moreover, the relevant reform measures have instead strengthened the "institutional change" factor, making the aid conditionalities more stringent and thus weakening the self-development ability of developing countries. Although the High-Level Forum on Aid Effectiveness in Busan, South Korea in 2011 proposed to improve "development effectiveness", the relevant constructive measures were lackluster.

Now, with the slowdown of economic growth, weak demand, low commodity prices, rising debt levels, and increased economic growth uncertainty in developed countries, the external constraints faced by developing countries in economic growth are becoming increasingly harsh. Even emerging economies that have maintained relatively high growth rates in the past have significantly slowed down. And according to the World Bank's report, the sluggish economic growth means that it will take at least 30–70 years for these countries to catch up with the per capita GDP of the United States. As for the least-developed countries, what lies ahead of them is not catching up but how to get out of extreme poverty.

The World Bank's appointment of Paul Romer as chief economist not only reflects the concern of this most important global development institution dedicated to poverty alleviation about the continued widening of the North-South gap and its attempt to take new measures but also, to a large extent, expresses its expectation of endogenous growth to developed countries and emerging economies such as China: in the long run, economic growth must rely on endogenous technological progress and significant improvement of human capital. And economic financialization has always been a double-edged sword and is not the driving force for economic growth.

The author has said that the so-called phased recovery of the global economy since the 2008 financial crisis is essentially a false recovery with huge uncertainties. This is because major developed countries have not placed the logical starting point of a new round of economic growth on reviewing the shortcomings of the existing growth model and increasing investment in technology research and development and the improvement of human capital. Instead, they have occasionally launched irresponsible monetary policies, trying to radiate the costs of their own economic development externally and stimulate their domestic economic growth through the re-allocation of global wealth. Especially after the Brexit referendum, although negative interest rates have become prevalent and the debt market has fallen into a vicious cycle of negative returns, if central banks of various countries rely on "helicopter dropping" again, I'm afraid it will not be able to "hot-start" the economy. Without the real recovery of the real economy, how can we expect the global economy to embark on a track of effective growth?

At this delicate moment, one of the strategic considerations of the World Bank in appointing Romer, who has always advocated "endogenous growth", as its chief economist is to send a strong signal to major economies including the United States, Europe, and China: The growth exploration and recovery efforts of the global economy over the past decade have been largely unsuccessful. All countries must bring economic growth back to its endogenous track in order to form a joint force.

G7's Policy Missteps Must Not Become a Negative Force in Global Governance

The 2019 Biarritz Summit of the Group of Seven (G7) in France concluded on August 26, and the participating parties failed to issue a joint communique. As the host, President Macron, who is eager to be the leader of Europe, of course hoped to avoid such a situation. However, in today's world where the preferences of individual leaders deeply influence and even hijack the trend of the global economy, the effectiveness of the existing communication and coordination mechanisms is difficult to guarantee, and even the G7 Summit, which still has great ambitions, is no exception.

The world should remember that at the 2018 G7 Summit in Canada, due to serious differences between the USA and other members on the issue of tariffs, the atmosphere of the meeting was once highly tense. Although a joint communique was issued at the end of the summit, the arrogant former US President Trump not only left the meeting early but also directly refused to recognize it after the communique was released. This fully shows how intense the non-cooperative games among the seven major industrialized countries are when it comes to issues related to their respective national core interests.

The current situation of the G7 Summit reflects that against the backdrop of a turbulent international pattern, the major Western countries, as the leaders of the existing political and economic system, are struggling in the face of long-accumulated global problems such as trade, finance, energy, climate, environmental protection, education, inequality, and security, whose complexity coefficients are constantly increasing. It also reflects the "fallacy of composition" of member states as single entities in relevant issues and policy proposals.

The G7 Summit, which was born in 1975, was regarded as a consultation and coordination mechanism established by major developed countries to respond to globalization and safeguard their own interests before the 2008 international financial crisis. At the same time, during the 33 years from 1975 to 2008, the G7 actually played a leading role in global economic governance. At each annual summit, the leaders and relevant officials of member states, who held the discourse power of the global economy, not only "guided" the development of the world economy and "cared" about the world situation but also demonstrated an unprecedented sense of economic and institutional superiority and extraordinary cultural confidence. During that period, the economic policy trends of Europe, the United States, and Japan were the vane of other countries' economic policies. And the G7 indeed played a major driving force in the development of the global economy to a large extent and, through the IMF, also assumed the important responsibility of stabilizing the global financial system to a certain extent.

However, the severe 2008 international financial crisis completely exposed the huge loopholes in the US economic and financial models: Endless financial innovation and the reliance on credit expansion to support economic growth, without a synchronous improvement in the performance of the real economy, are tantamount to quenching thirst with poison. Financial deepening can lift the US economy to the clouds, but it can also be an important driving force for the US economy to go astray. If the virtual economy and the real economy are seriously inverted, even a financial derivative that looks normal can create a financial plague.

When the G7 was at a loss, the G20 Summit, initially established as a bailout mechanism to deal with this crisis, quickly came to the forefront. In just one year after the outbreak of the financial crisis, the G20 held successive summits in Washington, Pittsburgh, and London, achieving a series of positive results. As the leader of the G7, the United States, deeply mired in the crisis at that time, attached particular importance to the role of the G20. Because it could not only cover the functions of the G7 but also added elements of emerging economies represented by China. And China, which held one-third of the world's foreign exchange reserves at that time, was the most important external force that could assist the US economy at a critical moment. So much so that in March 2009, Robert B. Zoellick, then President of the World Bank and former US Deputy Secretary of State, wrote that China and the USA must become the engines of the G20. "Without the strong development of the G2, the G20 will be disappointing." Subsequently, David Wright Miliband, then British Foreign Secretary, also expressed support for Zoellick's proposition.

However, in the 21st century, when statesmen with a sense of global responsibility are becoming increasingly scarce, "beggar-thy-neighbor" has become the keynote of the foreign economic policies of some countries, and the instrumental use of policies has increasingly become the norm for developed countries towards emerging economies. Although the G20 has gradually become a key player in promoting international economic cooperation and global economic governance over the past decade or more, in the eyes of the United States, with the increasingly prominent role of emerging economies in the G20, the dominant position of the United States is bound to decline, and emerging economies represented by China are bound to seek more say, which the "rich club" will never readily agree to. In such a situation, only by building the G20 into a constructive mechanism, making its marginal promoting effect on the stability and prosperity of the world economy show an increasing trend, can the G20 be given strong vitality in the future.

Regrettably, the evolution of trends in the real world often fails to meet general static assumptions. Once the financial systems of some developed countries have been repaired to a certain extent, the selfish nature at the national level immediately comes to light, and the reform of the global governance system quickly stalls after making some progress. Nowadays, anti—globalization, trade protectionism, and various forms of isolationism are on the rise. The probability of "black swan" events is higher than before, and the more alarming "grey rhinos" add new uncertainties to the already uncertain world economy.

The global economic guarantor system is undergoing fission. In fact, the United States has abandoned its role as the guarantor of the global economic system since World War II. Although France and Germany aspire to restore the former glory of the G7, they both face the awkward situation where their national strength cannot support their policy ambitions. For example, in 2018, France, with a GDP of only $2.78 trillion, has little chance of influencing the United States, whose economic scale is 7.3 times that of France, and leading the US government to cooperate with its "little brothers" at the G7 level. In addition, France passed a digital tax bill in July 2019, and US technology companies such as Google, Apple, Meta, and Amazon will all face taxation. In such a situation, it is even more unrealistic to expect the US government to be calm in EU-US cooperation, not to mention the powder keg of automobile tariffs that could be ignited at any time. The United Kingdom, which has been exhausted by "Brexit" and whose economic strength is even less than that of France, also has a shrinking scope for action in global affairs. As for Germany and Japan, what they may care more about at present is how to stabilize the domestic economic fundamentals.

Overall, most G7 members are not as influential as they used to be. Their global task lists are too long, and it seems difficult to complete them one by one. The G7 Summit, which is becoming increasingly "apathetic", may gradually degenerate into a high-level talk-shop with little real significance. The G7 can no longer share the concerns of the international economic order, and some developed countries, through multilateral or bilateral mechanisms, are obstructing emerging economies within the G20 from fully playing their roles. If this continues, global economic governance will truly be a cause for concern.

Global Tax Reform May Trigger a New Round of Digital Industry Realignment

The finance ministers and central bank governors of the G20 held a meeting in Venice, Italy, on July 10, 2021, and issued a statement supporting the "two-pillar" plan for global tax reform, backing the re-distribution of multinational enterprises' profits, agreeing to set a global minimum corporate tax rate of 15%, and calling on more countries to join the consultations. This meeting has reached a historic agreement on a more stable and fair international tax framework.

The so-called "two-pillar" plan for global tax reform is an inclusive framework determined in the *Blueprint for Pillar One and Pillar Two* report released by the OECD in October 2020, aiming to promote global tax reform. The first pillar of this framework is to re-allocate some tax rights of multinational enterprises to the markets where they conduct business activities and earn profits. The second pillar is the global minimum corporate tax rate, which is of great concern to the market. For example, under the benchmark of a 15% global minimum tax rate, if a multinational company earns profits in a country or region outside its home country, and the corporate tax rate of the host country or region is lower than 15%, the company not only has to pay corporate tax in the host country or region but also has to pay tax to its home country according to the tax rate difference between the two countries or regions. Of course, there are strict scope definitions for multinational companies included in the relevant tax scope, that is, large-scale and high-profit multinational companies with a profit margin of not less than 10%. The market country, that is, the country where the multinational company operates, has the right to tax 20% or more of the company's remaining profits (i.e., the part exceeding 10% of the profits). Allowing countries to increase tax revenues from large multinational companies without using digital service taxes is expected to, on the one hand, end the situation where some countries or regions compete to lower corporate tax rates to attract multinational companies. On the other hand, it also cracks down on profit-shifting and base-erosion behaviors of multinational enterprises. A previous calculation by the OECD shows that if a 15% minimum tax rate is implemented globally, it is expected to bring an additional $150 billion in tax revenue to the world every year.

It has been noted that the global minimum corporate tax has not entered the OECD's reform process as an independent issue but has been incorporated into the "inclusive framework" as part of the "reform plan to address the tax challenges of the digital economy." In fact, in the agreement reached at the 2021 G20 Finance Ministers and Central Bank Governors' Meeting, large multinational enterprises in almost all fields have been included in the tax scope, not just those in the digital economy field.

It is worth noting that after this G20 Finance Ministers and Central Bank Governors' Meeting, the EU has suspended the digital tax collection plan originally scheduled to be introduced at the end of July 2021, so as not to impede the achievement of a more equitable global tax agreement. This shows that the US and the EU have adopted a cooperative-game strategy on the major issue of global tax reform.

However, the competition between the two sides for the dominance of digital technology and the digital industry will not stop.

In recent years, in response to the accelerated transformation of economic digitalization, the EU took the lead in proposing the "Digital Services Tax Proposal" in March 2018 to promote tax reform. In December 2020, the EU proposed the drafts of the *Digital Services Act* and the *Digital Markets Act*. Regarding the violations of tech giants, the acts propose severe punitive measures, with the maximum fine reaching 10% of the annual turnover. At the same time, for platforms with "systematic non-compliance behaviors," the acts suggest taking "structural-level" rectification measures for the companies. The European operations of tech giants that do not comply with the new EU regulations may be split up.

In addition, Europe also regulates the order of the digital market by adjusting taxes, etc. The effective tax rate that traditional European enterprises need to pay is 23.3%, but the average tax rate paid by large tech companies in the EU is only 9.5%. In July 2019, the French Senate passed a bill to levy a digital tax. According to this bill, France will levy a digital tax on Internet companies with a global annual revenue of over 750 million euros and a revenue in France of over 25 million euros, at a rate of 3% of the revenue from the French market. On April 1, 2020, the UK began to levy a new 2% digital services tax on companies such as Meta, Google, and Amazon. After that, other EU members such as Spain also followed suit.

Large US tech companies such as Meta, Google, and Amazon are the products of revolutionary changes in technological development and business models. They have become the most globally influential Internet technology companies, far ahead of their European counterparts, and have long penetrated into all aspects of the European economy and social life. The winner-takes-all pattern is becoming more and more obvious. If no effective measures are taken, it is likely to trigger regional systematic economic and technological risks. The tax actions of European countries against large US tech companies aim to establish the boundaries of digital economy and digital industry services, prevent super-large US tech platforms from controlling the market and mastering consumer information by relying on technology and data, and thus build a monopolistic ecosystem aimed at obtaining excess profits, and ultimately form a non-open business empire or even an "independent kingdom".

Therefore, under the trend of global industrial and technological changes, this long-brewing global tax reform reflects Europe's anxiety and sense of urgency in cultivating and fostering super-digital enterprises in the region since the twenty-first century. This may increase the relevant costs for global multinational enterprises to adjust their regional operations and create uncertainties in their operations. For example, they may reduce investments in original tax havens. It is expected that some low-tax investment centers will comprehensively take measures including fiscal subsidies and income tax exemptions to stabilize the investment expectations of existing digital enterprises.

Of course, the key factors determining the investment and layout adjustments of the world's 100 largest multinational companies still lie in their assessment of the business environment, business costs, and comprehensive supporting capabilities of the investment destination countries or regions. However, the tax rate is an important variable that cannot be avoided. It can be predicted that the implementation of the global minimum tax rate system may prompt the world's 100 largest multinational companies, especially digital technology enterprises, to make adaptive adjustments and optimizations to the profit distribution pattern in the global market based on the existing transfer pricing rules, thus triggering a new round of global industrial layout adjustments.

The G7's "Global Minimum Corporate Tax Rate" Is About More Than Just Revenue

On June 4, 2021, the finance ministers of the G7 held negotiations on tax reform in London, UK, and issued a statement supporting the setting of a global minimum corporate tax rate at 15% to end decades of low-tax competition. On the other hand, countries are allowed to tax the profits of super-enterprises that have no physical businesses but digital businesses. However, relevant countries will abolish unilateral digital service taxes.

Looking closely at the core issues of this G7 finance ministers' meeting, the key point is that major economies aim to form a united front to levy a 15% tax rate on the overseas profits of the 100 largest and highest-revenue multinational companies globally. This is to prevent super-enterprises such as Apple, Google, Meta, and Amazon from evading taxes by registering most of their profits in low-tax jurisdictions and to avoid "tax havens" attracting business activities or profits through low tax rates.[1]

At first glance, it might seem that the EU, the UK, etc. are about to "target" the ace enterprises of the USA, and the US seems to be in favor of it. However, this is not the case. In the author's opinion, this long-brewing regional and even global tax reform is a major international move by the US to "replenish its blood" by seizing the opportunity of this round of global tax reform under the situation of an increasingly long list of fiscal expenditures. It is an attempt to regain the dominance of international economic rules. In fact, this is a multi-round, long-cycle cooperative game among global "players" in terms of rule-making and wealth redistribution. Of course, this also reflects, from another perspective, the strong rule-arbitrage and government-capture capabilities of some global companies that exceed the capacity boundaries of countries and international organizations in today's world.

The G7 members within the EU and the UK have a shrewd calculation. According to relevant estimates, if the minimum tax rate is set at 15%, the medium-and long-term tax dividends will be far more than 50 billion euros. EU members such as Ireland, Luxembourg, and the Netherlands are currently low-tax countries, which

[1]On March 9, 2021, the UK non-governmental organization "Tax Justice Network" released the latest global tax haven rankings. Three overseas territories of the UK (the British Virgin Islands, the Cayman Islands, and Bermuda) topped the list. The Netherlands ranked fourth, Switzerland ranked fifth, Hong Kong, China ranked seventh, and the UAE was among the top ten.

have attracted the establishment of regional or national headquarters by companies like Meta and Alphabet, the parent company of Google, but these companies only need to pay a small amount of tax. On the other hand, OECD members have long been arguing about the tax location of multinational companies, that is, whether all revenues should be taxed in the home country or the investment destination, because this involves the issue of where the real money goes to. Under the impact of the COVID-19, Western countries are generally short of money. And tax revenue, which cannot be obtained by printing money, must rely on production and business activities. Especially, the Biden administration, which has taken over a lot of problems, within less than half a year of taking office, requires an enormous amount of funds for its infrastructure and economic revitalization plans. Except for replicating the previous administration's unlimited monetary policy, it also attempts to accelerate the repatriation of super-enterprise earnings to enrich the national treasury by launching global tax reform and tax-increase plans. Relevant research shows that in the past more than 10 years, the difference between the taxable amount and the actual tax paid by US tech giants such as Amazon, Google, and Apple has exceeded $150 billion, and this is a relatively conservative estimate. Looking at Apple's extremely wealthy financial situation, finance ministers of various countries need to consider: why are countries getting poorer while super-enterprises are getting richer?

As is well known, tax is one of the most important levers for the redistribution of national wealth. From the perspective of saving transaction costs and activating the innovative endowment of market entities, the reduction of the global average corporate tax rate is an inevitable trend. However, the common "race to the bottom" in corporate tax rates often leads to the fallacy of composition. Therefore, since 2013, the OECD has been promoting global tax reform actions through the G20 platform, calling on countries to jointly combat unreasonable cross-border tax avoidance. In 2019, the OECD put forward the second-stage initiative for tax reform, including setting a global minimum corporate tax rate, etc. But at that time, it did not attract sufficient attention from all countries. It was not until today, when countries are generally "anemic" due to the impact of the COVID-19, that it has received high attention. (The corporate tax rates of some developed countries in 2021 are shown in Fig. 3.2). To put it bluntly, money comes first.

Of course, there is also the competition for the international dominance of tax rules. In recent years, the EU has been attempting to establish new international tax rules based on the OECD framework and has announced multiple development strategies to regain "digital sovereignty". In December 2020, the European Commission proposed the drafts of the *Digital Services Act* and the *Digital Markets Act*, aiming to regulate the order of the digital market and restrict the unfair competition behaviors of tech giants. In addition, Europe regulates the order of the digital market by adjusting taxes and other means. The effective tax rate that traditional European enterprises need to pay is 23.3%, while large tech companies, which often operate across borders, pay an average tax rate of only 9.5% in the EU. The dispute between the US and the EU over the digital tax collection of large tech enterprises actually concerns the competition for industrial dominance.

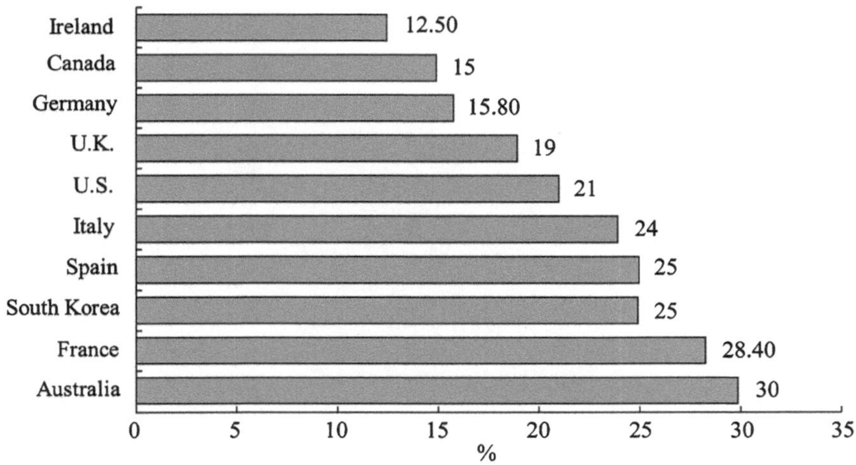

Fig. 3.2 Corporate Tax Rates of Some Developed Countries in 2021. Data Source: OECD

In the short term, this round of global tax reform will not have a significant impact on China, because China's current corporate income tax rate is higher than the proposed global bottom line of 15%. Moreover, in terms of the objects of taxation, the global minimum corporate tax rate advocated by the OECD only applies to large multinational companies with revenues exceeding 750 million euros, and the vast majority of small and medium-sized enterprises in China are not included. However, in the medium and long term, as a country with a highly developed digital industry, a number of Chinese Internet technology enterprises have had a worldwide impact. With the improvement of enterprises' ability to allocate global resources, they will encounter various constraints, including digital taxes. Therefore, in the context of global cooperation in the supervision of large-scale technology platforms, it is recommended to build a high-standard financial system in light of China's actual situation, actively promote the sharing of anti-monopoly information of platform technology enterprises under the G20 framework, strengthen forward-looking supervision of expectations, strengthen coordination with the United States, the European Union, the United Kingdom, Japan and other members, and introduce digital rule standards with a more balanced rights and obligations of platform-based enterprises, so as to establish a new benchmark for global digital rules.

Chapter 4
The Absence of a Global Economic System Guarantor

The Underlying Logic Behind Divergences on Deep Reform of the Global Trade System

In 2019, at a time when the global trade order was fraught with uncertainties, the leaders of various countries participating in the G20 Osaka Summit temporarily injected a stabilizer into it.

The Declaration Avoids Direct Criticism of "Trade Protectionism"

The declaration issued by the G20 leaders at the summit stated: "The G20 is committed to achieving a free, fair, non-discriminatory, transparent, predictable and stable Trade and investment Environment and keeping markets open." The G20 leaders warned that against the backdrop of increasingly tense trade and geopolitical Situations, global economic growth remains weak, and at the same Time, it is facing downward risks. They also confirmed the basic principles of freedom, fairness and non-discrimination regarding the trade System.

However, just like at the G20 Buenos Aires Summit in 2018, the USA still did not accept the wording of resisting trade protectionism in the declaration, while the leaders of other member countries sought to issue a clearer warning against trade tensions. Eventually, the declaration avoided direct criticism of trade protectionism.

As is well known, the declaration is just a form of rhetoric and does not have much binding force in itself. At most, it records the content on which countries can reach a consensus and the positions that everyone is willing to accept.

Y. Zhang, *Addressing Uncertainty*, Understanding China,
https://doi.org/10.1007/978-981-92-2692-4_4

The alarm of a new global trade conflict has not been lifted either. Lee Hsien Loong, the Prime Minister of Singapore, who is deeply worried, even issued a warning that "it is worrying that the G20 has failed to make progress on core issues."

As for the much-concerned WTO reform, G20 leaders have promised to take more forceful actions to improve the WTO's dispute settlement system and strongly advocate reforming the WTO to promote the organization's development in the right direction. However, a few countries still hold reservations about the multilateral trading system, and such resistance is often fatal to the survival and development of the WTO.

WTO Reform Is at an Extremely Delicate Time Window

In essence, free trade is often a false proposition because absolute free trade does not exist. Promoting trade facilitation is the realistic goal pursued by all countries. However, the history of global economy and trade has proven and will continue to prove that promoting trade and investment facilitation and consolidating and developing the multilateral trading system are not only the most effective institutional arrangements for market players at all levels to save transaction costs, but also the "soul" of the WTO, one of the three pillars of the global economy. Moreover, due to its role as a core variable in national and regional relations, it has become the cornerstone of global economic stability.

However, with the increasing integration of the global economic and trade system, the United States, which originally held a firm grip on the dominance of changes in the global trade order, has increasingly found that since the 21st century, China, India and other emerging economies that were basically on the periphery of global trade in the last century have continuously adapted to international trade rules, expanded trade scale, enhanced product competitiveness and steadily built bilateral and multilateral trade systems. As a result, their trade scale has been growing larger and larger, the added value of their exported goods has been continuously increasing, and the position of their export manufacturing industries in the industrial chain has been gradually rising. Obviously, the USA has difficulty adapting to the above achievements of the emerging economies.

Today, the WTO reform, which has entered the deep water area, is at an extremely delicate time window. Apparently, whether to maintain or cut the "Special and Differential Treatment" (SDT) enjoyed by developing members under the WTO framework is the main disagreement between developed members represented by the United States and developing members represented by China. However, the deep-seated disagreement is that since China joined the WTO in 2001, its economic strength, influence and the improvement of its position in the global trade value chain have significantly exceeded the United States' expectations and actual control boundaries. Moreover, the globalization firmly defended by China and its pursuit of free trade and multilateralism are in sharp contrast to the "America First"[1] trade protectionism pursued by the U.S. government. China is expected to lead a new round of globalization and the evolution of the free trade order, which may cause the United States to lose its dominance over the global trade system and the evolution of rules. The United States attempts to restrict China's development with the "market economy status" and "developed country status" and incorporate China's development path into the order framework controlled by the USA.

Judging from the *2018 Report on China's WTO Compliance* (hereinafter referred to as the *2018 Annual Report*) submitted by the Office of the United States Trade Representative to Congress in February 2019, compared with the relatively positive *2016 Annual Report* and the *2017 Annual Report* with gradually increasing negative comments, the *2018 Annual Report* is filled with negative evaluations of China throughout. Regarding the proposal supported by developing members such as China to endow the WTO Appellate Body with more powers, the USA believes that the purpose of doing so is to protect their domestic "non-market economy" systems.

The United States believes that the vast majority of developing members need the WTO more than developed members. In recent years, through means such as retreating to advance and high-level intimidation, the United States has partially achieved the strategic goal of amending bilateral or multilateral trade agreements in accordance with its will. In the reform of key issues of the WTO, the United States is fully likely to follow the same approach. By paralyzing or even shutting down the WTO dispute settlement mechanism, it can divide the forces supporting the multilateral trading system, and use Brazil and other countries as a breakthrough to induce some emerging economies to follow in its footsteps, so as to achieve the goal of reforming the WTO.

The USA advocates that the direction of WTO reform is to build a so-called undifferentiated WTO. On January 15, 2019, it submitted a document titled *An Undifferentiated WTO: The Threat of Self-Designated Developing Status to the Relevance of the System* to the WTO. Later, it also proposed a draft decision of the General Council, demanding the cancellation of the rights of a large number of developing members to enjoy special and differential treatment.

According to the proposed standards of the United States, if a WTO member meets any of the following conditions: being listed as a high-income economy by the World Bank, being a member of the OECD, being a member of the G20, accounting for more than 0.5% of the global trade share, etc., it cannot be regarded as a developing member. This proposal aims to deprive developing members of the most-favored-nation treatment principle, the principle of non-discrimination, the multilateral framework for rule-making, special and differential treatment, etc. enjoyed in the WTO, and it is no wonder that it has been firmly opposed by members such as China, India, and South Africa.

[1] "America First" was the foreign policy of Donald Trump, the 45th President of the United States, emphasizing American nationalism and non-interventionism.

However, Brazil, a member of the BRICS countries, has been successfully persuaded by the United States. This is because, in order to join the OECD, Brazil promised to give up the "special and differential treatment" as a developing member enjoyed in the WTO as an exchange condition. Based on this, the United States believes that emerging economies and developing members are not a monolithic bloc in the WTO reform, and the USA is fully capable of defeating them one by one.

The USA Tries to Reshuffle the Order of Global Trade Governance

The United States is very wary of China's development achievements in terms of trade scale, adaptation to rules, improvement in the global value chain, industrial competitiveness, and comprehensive national strength since China joined the WTO. Since joining the WTO, China has rapidly grown into one of the only two super economies in the world with a GDP exceeding $10 trillion in less than 20 years. In contrast, Japan, the USA' long-term economic rival, has seen its GDP size hovering around $5 trillion over the past 20 years.

According to the logic of the United States, China's development has far exceeded its expectations, and it claims that it was the United States that "single-handedly" led China to the center of the global economic and trade stage. Nowadays, the global wealth center is shifting from the United States to China, and it is possible that the global wealth allocation and asset pricing center will also shift to China in the future. Moreover, China is actively taking the lead in restructuring regional and even global trade rules, which the USA cannot tolerate.

As for the market economy standard, there has never been a unified benchmark globally. In fact, judging from the market economy measurement standards established by the USA and Europe in anti-dumping practices, the understandings of the market economy standard are not completely the same. For example, the U.S. Department of Commerce has six criteria for judging a market economy: the degree of currency convertibility, the degree of freedom in wage negotiations between labor and management, the degree of freedom in establishing joint ventures or foreign-funded enterprises, the degree of government control over resource allocation, enterprise output, and price determination, the degree of government ownership and control over the mode of production, and other judgment factors.

The criteria for judging a market economy stipulated by the European Union mainly include five aspects: whether prices are determined by the market, whether enterprises have basic accounting books in line with international accounting standards, whether the production costs and financial status of enterprises are distorted by non-market factors, whether enterprises have the freedom to transfer profits and capital abroad, the freedom to independently decide on exports and other business activities, whether enterprises are bound by bankruptcy laws and asset laws, and whether exchange rates are determined by the market, etc.

However, judging from the actual economic operation situations in the United States and Europe, even they selectively implement these so-called market economy standards. In fact, the United States' protection intensity for its domestic market and industries even far exceeds that of emerging economies such as China in some aspects. The United States has never given up subsidies to agriculture and has long been closely monitoring the technological progress and industrial development of its main (potential) competitors in the industrial field. Once it finds that they pose a competitive squeeze on the USA, it will immediately take suppressing measures. The Section 201 and Section 301 of the U.S. *Trade Act of 1974* are clear evidence of this.

In fact, since the trade friction between China and the United States broke out, the USA has frequently wielded the tariff stick and undisguisedly used the suppression of individual Chinese enterprises as a bargaining chip in trade negotiations, which in itself shows the hypocrisy of the label of a market economy.

If China were to reform its domestic economic system and operation mechanism according to the United States' standards for a market economy, give up the efforts to make state-owned enterprises bigger and stronger, abandon the support for state-owned enterprises to enhance their global resource allocation capabilities, and even let state-owned enterprises gradually withdraw from the market and fully open up the domestic market, then even if China could obtain an expansion of the export market to the United States and an incremental introduction of sub-new technologies, in essence, China would gradually become a super economic vassal of the USA.

In terms of the much-concerned reform of the WTO dispute mechanism, the United States has made great efforts to obstruct the initiation of the selection process for new judge candidates of the Appellate Body under the WTO dispute settlement mechanism and has rejected all proposals. This can only show that the United States is trying to use the paralysis of the WTO dispute settlement mechanism as a threat to reshuffle the order of global trade governance, and coerce members such as China to de facto recognize that U.S. domestic laws can override WTO laws, thereby negating multilateral rules and multilateral mechanisms.

In fact, the United States is bypassing the WTO multilateral system and, taking the *United States-Mexico*-Canada *Agreement* as a model, forcefully promoting new international economic and trade rules and standards based on U.S. preferences, including trade policies, industrial policies, environmental standards, labor standards, etc., to replace international multilateral trade rules, reshape the U.S. paradigm of trade agreements in the 21st century, and achieve the goal of continuing to control the dominance of global trade and industrial development.

Will the WTO Face "Brain Death" Due to the Paralysis of Its Appellate Body

The WTO, known as the "Economic United Nations," is facing the most serious survival crisis since its establishment a quarter of a century ago.

The cause lies not only in the endless trade disputes among countries that are weakening and even destroying the core values of the existing free trade and multilateralism system, but also in the fact that the Appellate Body, the settlement mechanism responsible for adjudicating trade disputes in the WTO, may fall into a state of no one being in charge due to the interference of the United States, leading to functional paralysis. The USA once threatened to cut off the funding for the WTO, which directly put the organization at risk of closing down.

The Appellate Body is the "Supreme Court" responsible for adjudicating trade disputes in the complex operation system of the WTO, and it is also an innovative mechanism compared with its predecessor, the General Agreement on Tariffs and Trade (GATT). Its most important feature is its independence.

According to Article 17 of the *Understanding on Rules and Procedures Governing the Settlement of Disputes*, a basic document of the WTO dispute settlement mechanism, the Appellate Body shall have seven standing judges, and each ruling shall be made by at least three judges. The term of office of a judge is 4 years and can be renewed once. When there is a vacancy in the Appellate Body, the Dispute Settlement Body composed of all WTO members shall promptly appoint a new member through a consensus approach.

However, this dispute settlement mechanism, which is crucial to the future and destiny of the WTO, has been paralyzed due to the continuous obstruction of the United States in the selection of Appellate Body justices. Since January 2018, there were only three justices left, namely the U.S. justice Graham, the Indian justice Bhatia, and the Chinese justice Zhao Hong. Among them, the terms of office of the U.S. and Indian justices expired in December 2019. As a result, since December 11, 2019, the WTO Appellate Body, which should be composed of 7 members, had only 1 member left and was unable to hear cases. On November 30, 2020, with the formal expiration of the term of the last member of the Appellate Body, that is, the Chinese justice Zhao Hong, all members of the Appellate Body left their positions. Subsequently, the USA repeatedly vetoed relevant proposals to restart the selection process of the Appellate Body, making it impossible for the "brain" of the WTO to operate normally, and the global multilateral trading system faced a serious crisis.

Is the WTO Preventing the USA from Becoming Great Again?

According to the relevant rules of the WTO dispute settlement mechanism, the appointment of Appellate Body justices requires the consensus of all WTO members, and the United States has shown no signs of loosening its position so far. Why is the United States determined to obstruct the effective operation of the WTO dispute settlement mechanism? Because according to the assessment of the United States, the existing mechanism of the WTO has led international trade into a state of market failure. The USA believes that Appellate Body justices often "overstep the boundaries" in the process of interpreting WTO laws and in fact abuse the powers that have not been granted to them by WTO laws.

For example, in 2018, the WTO ruled that a $7.3 billion countervailing duty system of the United States against China was illegal and required the United States to modify the system to comply with WTO regulations. However, the United States did not fully correct its illegal practices and believed that the WTO's judgment was unfair. China continued to appeal to the WTO. In early November 2019, the WTO ruled in China's favor and allowed China to impose taxes on U.S. products worth $3.6 billion. This move further deepened the dissatisfaction of then U.S. President Trump with the WTO, believing that the WTO was one of the stumbling blocks preventing the USA from making it great again.

If the Appellate Body of the WTO eventually collapses, it is really possible that the WTO will face the danger of "brain death". Because once the Appellate Body is unable to work effectively, most of the WTO appeal cases will be unable to be handled, and even fall into an endless loop.

Generally, the losing party will choose to appeal against the report of the panel. In the case of the paralysis of the Appellate Body, the extreme situation will occur where the appeal can never be finally adjudicated. The losing party can also arbitrarily veto the report of the panel according to its national interest preferences without being held accountable. If this is really the case, the fragmented WTO will become a direct victim of unilateralism in the history of global trade changes in the twenty-first century.

Diverging Agendas Between the U.S. and the EU

On the other hand, as the two most powerful economies in the WTO, trade frictions and mutual retaliations between the United States and the European Union have always been frequent. On October 14, 2019, the WTO officially authorized the United States to take trade retaliatory measures against the European Union based on the WTO's latest ruling on the "Airbus subsidy case". According to the relevant ruling of the WTO, since the European Union and some of its members have not fully implemented the previous relevant rulings of the WTO dispute settlement mechanism and still provide illegal subsidies to Airbus, the United States has the right to impose tariffs and other measures on EU goods and services exported to the USA worth about $7.5 billion annually.

Although $7.5 billion only accounts for 1/50 of the total EU exports to the United States in 2018, the symbolic significance is very obvious. Because this protracted trade dispute mainly reflects the open and covert struggles between Airbus, jointly established by France, Germany, the United Kingdom and Spain, and Boeing.

As early as 2004, after Airbus replaced Boeing as the world's largest civil aircraft manufacturer, the United States filed a lawsuit with the WTO on the grounds that the European Union and its four members, including France, Germany, the United Kingdom and Spain, provided illegal subsidies to Airbus. The European Union immediately retaliated in kind and sued the U.S. government in the WTO dispute settlement mechanism on the grounds that Boeing received illegal subsidies.

The WTO ruled in 2011 that both the USA and the European Union had violated WTO rules and both needed to compensate for each other's losses. However, this compromise ruling has instead sown the seeds of greater conflict. Since then, Boeing and Airbus have continued to receive huge subsidies from their respective governments, have gone further and further down the path of unfair competition, and the lawsuits have also become more and more intense until the WTO made a new ruling this time.

Judging from the reaction of the U.S. government to the WTO ruling, in addition to cheering for victory, the United States has taken great pains in drawing up the list of tariff increases. It has precisely targeted the ace industries of France, Germany, the United Kingdom and Spain, listed the highly competitive wine and agricultural products of the European Union as the targets of attack. At the same time, it has also limited the tariff increase on Airbus to the whole aircraft, excluding subcontractors and suppliers, in order to protect the relevant U.S. enterprises that provide important components for Airbus and ensure the stability of 275,000 jobs. However, for the European Union, which is also a master of trade, it certainly has no shortage of strength and means to counter the USA.

The European Union immediately threatened to take reciprocal or even excessive retaliatory measures. The European Union also filed a complaint with the WTO on November 4, 2019, demanding that the United States cancel the tariffs on imported metals. This is one of the most thorny cases facing the WTO. Because the focus of this case lies in the "national security exception" clause, that is, the WTO allows its members to violate WTO obligations on the grounds of "national security". The USA insists that national security should be judged by each country itself and is by no means something that can be evaluated by a three-person panel authorized by the WTO. It is expected that the dispute between the two sides will last for a long time.

All kinds of signs show that the U.S. government is becoming increasingly impatient with the WTO. It has not only repeatedly threatened to withdraw from the WTO but also prepared to take unilateral actions against its major trade competitors.

In terms of the WTO reform issue, the United States is fully likely to follow the same approach. By paralyzing or even shutting down the WTO dispute settlement mechanism, it can divide the forces supporting the multilateral trading system, and use countries such as Brazil as a breakthrough to induce some emerging economies to follow in its footsteps, so as to achieve the goal of reforming the WTO.

Another trump card for the United States to force the WTO to reform is to directly cut off its funding. For example, the U.S. representative to the WTO hinted on November 12, 2019, that it might obstruct the WTO's budget for the next 2 years. The reason is that part of the WTO's annual budget funds may be diverted for other

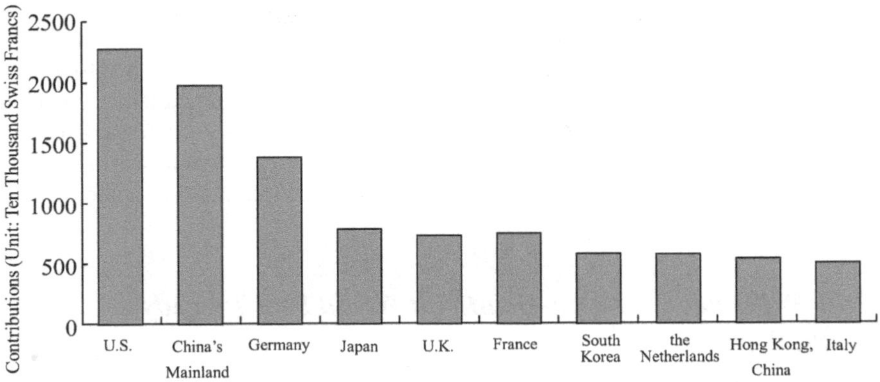

Fig. 4.1 The top ten members in terms of WTO budget contributions in 2019. Data Source: WTO Annual Report

purposes. The WTO's budget in 2019 was $197 million, and the United States was the largest contributor, contributing $22.8 million. According to the relevant rules, decisions related to the WTO must be reached by consensus among all 164 members. If all members cannot approve the organization's budgets for 2020 and 2021 before December 31, 2019, it will directly lead to the shutdown of the WTO. (The top ten members in terms of budget contributions to the WTO in 2019 are shown in Fig. 4.1.)

WTO Members Are Taking Actions to Save the Institution

To save the WTO that is beset with crises, various members are also accelerating their actions. For example, the European Union and Canada are discussing the establishment of a temporary appellate arbitration procedure based on WTO laws, which is applicable to disputes between the European Union and Canada. However, this temporary mechanism cannot replace the overall dispute settlement mechanism and is time-consuming and labor- intensive.

At a regular meeting of the WTO dispute settlement mechanism on October 28, 2019, 116 members called for the prompt initiation of the recruitment and selection process for Appellate Body justices, but the United States rejected this proposal again.

In addition, during the second China International Import Expo held in Shanghai in early November 2019, China took the lead in hosting a small-scale WTO ministerial meeting. Ministers or ministerial representatives from 33 WTO members, including the European Union, Russia, and India, as well as more than 200 representatives such as Roberto Azevedo, the former Director-General of the WTO, were invited to the meeting. However, the results seemed to be not significant. On

February 27, 2023, 127 WTO members jointly proposed a motion to launch the selection process for new Appellate Body justices at a regular meeting of the WTO Dispute Settlement Body, but the United States once again exercised its veto power. This move means that there is little hope for the WTO dispute settlement mechanism, which has been out of operation for more than 3 years, to "come back to life" in the short term. The United States also sent a signal to the whole world through this that it is the ultimate decisive force in reshaping the international trade order.

If the WTO Faces "Brain-Death", it Would be a Tragedy for the World

The U.S. government has repeatedly and publicly questioned the rationality of multilateral rules and multilateral mechanisms, criticized the WTO for being "unfair to the United States", demanded that the WTO initiate comprehensive reforms, and even verbally threatened to "withdraw from the WTO" many times, but has not put forward a constructive reform plan acceptable to most WTO members. This can only show that the United States is attempting to use the paralysis of the WTO dispute settlement mechanism as a threat to reshuffle the order of global trade governance.

The United States coerces members such as China to de facto recognize that U.S. domestic laws can override WTO laws, and then deny multilateral rules and multilateral mechanisms. This also, to some extent, confirms the harsh reality that free trade essentially must serve the fundamental interests of countries or groups, and makes the vision of free trade and free competition envisioned by Smith and Ricardo in those days nothing more than a dream for economists in the real world.

If the WTO, as the most important international organization promoting fair competition in the trade field and ensuring the effectiveness of multilateral mechanisms, were to face "brain death" 1 day, it would obviously be a sorrow for the world.

The WTO certainly needs reform. If the WTO reform stalls or fails to adapt to the new trends in global trade development, then the trend of fragmented and bloc-based games in trade rules will seriously impede the process of global economic integration, significantly increase trade frictions and transaction costs, and lead to a serious regression in global economic governance. The goal of reform is to enable each member to provide trade and service facilitation to each other in an environment of equal competition. With the rapid development of the digital economy, there is an urgent need to establish international standards for digital trade.

However, in today's world where statesmen are increasingly scarce and politics is pervasive, whether it is international organizations, countries, enterprises, or other market participants, they must be prepared for the worst-case scenarios that may occur.

Why Is WTO Reform Progressing So Slowly?

The final round of consultations on the candidate for the new Director-General of the WTO ended on October 27, 2020. The international public opinion generally expected that the finally determined new Director-General could bring the driving force for reform and progress to the WTO that was in a difficult situation. However, at least judging from the current situation, the reality is still harsh, especially the obstruction and destruction by the United States still show no signs of stopping. At the WTO General Council meeting in October 2020, the United States submitted two proposals. One was about canceling the "Special and Differential Treatment" enjoyed by developing members such as China, and the other was related to the "market-oriented conditions". The purpose was to promote the multilateralization of the discriminatory trade remedy rules in the United States, and the target was also directed at China.

In response to the United States' hackneyed provocation, China gave a stern retort on the spot. In addition to reaffirming that it is meaningless for members to have endless debates on the classification criteria for developing countries, China also conducted a thorough analysis of the "Special and Differential Treatment" clauses that the United States has always emphasized. Among the 155 "Special and Differential Treatment" clauses in the current 16 WTO agreements, at least 105 clauses are too broad and not operable. Among the remaining 50 clauses, at least 25 are transitional period or technical assistance clauses. In other words, there are only 25 "Special and Differential Treatment" clauses directly related to the rights and obligations of members in the existing agreements. As for the situation of China, the actual number of "Special and Differential Treatment" clauses that China can enjoy is only 8. Therefore, the United States' frequent references to the above clauses actually amount to an abuse of the hegemony of the power of rule interpretation.

In the difficult situation of the WTO reform, why has the United States been fixated on the issue of "Special and Differential Treatment"? The United States believes that since China joined the WTO, it has achieved outstanding development achievements in terms of trade scale, adaptation to rules, improvement in the global value chain, industrial competitiveness, and comprehensive national strength, which have far exceeded the United States' expectations. Nowadays, China has become the core of the global supply chain and industrial chain and the leading export powerhouse. In the future, it is possible that the global wealth allocation and asset pricing center will also shift to China. Moreover, China is actively promoting the reform of regional and even global trade rules. According to the logic of the United States, it was precisely the "Special and Differential Treatment" that the United States granted to China that enabled China to obtain asymmetric trade competitive advantages. Therefore, the United States now requires China to give up its status as a developing member, participate in the WTO as a developed member, cut the tariff level of the manufacturing industry to the level of developed members, and eliminate non-tariff barriers in the fields of services, goods, and agriculture. Only when

China does all these can it be considered a basic return for the United States' long-term "selfless assistance".

On the other hand, the United States believes that since China joined the WTO, while benefiting to the greatest extent from the "Special and Differential Treatment", it has not adopted a market economic system with the characteristics of the U.S. paradigm, even though the United States selectively implements the market economic standards it has set in its actual economic operation. In fact, the United States' protection intensity for its domestic market and industries even far exceeds that of China in some aspects. Taking agriculture as an example, in 2016, the per capita agricultural subsidy in the United States was 70 times, 176 times, and 267 times that of China, Brazil, and India respectively. In the fields of industry and technology, the United States has not only been closely monitoring the technological progress and industrial development of its main or potential competitors in the industrial field for a long time, but also, once it discovers market entities of competitors that pose a threat to the United States, it will immediately launch various forms of suppression. For example, on the grounds that high-tech Chinese enterprises investing and developing in the United States pose a threat to its national security, the United States has carried out unexpected suppression or issued ultimatums to many Chinese enterprises, paralyzing or even specifically eliminating those enterprises that have a certain influence in the U.S. market and pose a significant challenge to their U.S. counterparts. The purpose is to eliminate any threats from real or potential competitors to the United States by creating a super white terror in the era of globalization, and to ensure that the United States always maintains its generational advantage over its competitors.

If China were to reform its domestic economic system and operation mechanism according to the United States' standards for a market economy, and give up the efforts to make its domestic enterprises bigger and stronger, as well as the support for domestic enterprises to enhance their global resource allocation capabilities, then there is only one outcome for Chinese enterprises, that is, sooner or later they will become vassals of U.S. enterprises in the same industry.

The WTO certainly urgently needs reform, which is also the reason why the international community has high hopes for the new Director-General. However, the direction of its reform should be, on the premise of enhancing the organization's effectiveness, authority, and dispute settlement capabilities, to strive for the maximum international support to jointly safeguard the multilateral trading system based on rules and with the WTO as the core.

In the subsequent process of WTO reform, as the most powerful participants, China and the United States need to show a high level of wisdom to resolve their differences. Of course, China will adhere to its bottom line and principles. For example, it demands that the United States cancel the discrimination against enterprises from specific countries in investment security reviews and anti-monopoly reviews, and requires the United States to reduce or even eliminate the abuse of export control measures. At the same time, China is also showing appropriate flexibility, aiming to prevent the "shock" of the WTO operation mechanism, prevent the comprehensive "derailment" of China-U.S. economic and trade relations, and explore the possible cooperation areas between China and the United States in WTO reform.

On the other hand, regarding the issue of WTO reform, while there are differences between China and developed members such as the European Union, Japan, Canada, and Australia, there is also a certain consensus in opposing U.S. unilateralism. This is an important basis for China to carry out constructive cooperation with the above economies. In addition, China's cooperation with India, Brazil, Russia, and the vast number of emerging economies and developing members on the issue of WTO reform outweighs the differences. China should not only unite emerging economies and developing members to the greatest extent and firmly safeguard the legitimate rights and interests that developing members deserve, but also take the initiative to reduce tariff rates when conditions permit, especially by implementing structural tariff reductions in the consumer field to achieve mutual benefits between China and WTO members, and demonstrate the unique wisdom of a major Eastern country in handling complex issues.

WTO Reform: Seeking Equilibrium in a Non-Zero-Sum Game

The WTO, which has endured multiple hardships such as the paralysis of the Appellate Body, the vacancy of the Director-General, as well as unilateralism and trade protectionism, finally has a person at the helm for its normal operation after Ngozi Okonjo-Iweala, the new Director-General, officially took office on March 1, 2021.

However, for Okonjo-Iweala, who has 25 years of working experience at the World Bank, it is easier said than done to lead the 25-year-old WTO to effectively play the role of a referee in the multilateral trading system in an extremely complex international environment, and further promote multilateral trade governance onto a virtuous development track that is non-discriminatory, predictable, fair, inclusive and orderly.

The WTO, known as the "Economic United Nations", and its predecessor, the GATT, are the most important multilateral trade organizations established globally after World War II. They play an irreplaceable role in promoting investment and trade facilitation, reducing tariffs and non-tariff barriers, eliminating differential treatment in international trade to promote trade liberalization, optimizing the global allocation of resources, and expanding the production and flow of goods. Even in the 2020s of the twenty-first century when free trade areas are densely distributed around the world, the WTO still has a broad scope of operation. The fact that the Biden administration quickly took corrective actions against the previous administration's policies and supported Okonjo-Iweala's appointment as the WTO Director-General after taking office is clear evidence of this.

The WTO: The Most Important Public Good in Global Trade

In terms of its historical origin and essential attributes, the WTO is a global public good established in the trade field by developed capitalist countries led by the United States. The dominance in formulating its main rules and resolving disputes through the dispute settlement mechanism has long been in the hands of major developed countries. However, in the past decade, with emerging economies continuously integrating into the global trade system and actively participating in the governance and reform of the WTO based on their growing strength, and with trade disputes among developed countries becoming increasingly fierce, the major developed countries that originally supported free trade and the multilateral trading system have begun to change their attitudes towards the WTO. In particular, the United States, as the main designer of the WTO's mechanisms, during the Trump administration, not only repeatedly demanded that the WTO be reformed in accordance with the will of the United States, but also took drastic measures against the Appellate Body, the dispute settlement mechanism responsible for adjudicating trade disputes in the WTO, leading to the functional paralysis of the institution. It even threatened to withdraw from the WTO several times, putting the organization in an unprecedented survival and development dilemma.

There is no doubt that today, with significant changes in the global trade patterns, trade structures, as well as technologies and industries, the WTO must be reformed. Otherwise, if the reform stalls or fails to adapt to the new trends in global economic, technological, and trade development, the trend of fragmented and bloc-based games in trade rules will seriously impede the process of global economic integration, significantly increase frictions and transaction costs, and lead to a serious regression in global economic governance. Especially during the global response to the impact of the Covid-19, the digital economies and digital trades of various countries have made rapid progress. Many countries or regions have proposed to comprehensively promote digital transformation, giving rise to new business forms, models, and application scenarios in digital trade, which has greatly accelerated the digitalization process of global trade. It can even be said that to a certain extent, the dominant position of digital trade has been established. There is an urgent need to establish international standards for digital trade, which is the driving force and urgency for the WTO to transform itself to adapt to technological progress and trade development.

WTO Reform Struggles to Identify a Convergence Zone for Collective Action

Although Okonjo-Iweala stated during her campaign for the WTO Director-General that "the world needs a revitalized WTO more than ever" and called for strengthening the multilateral trading system to be in line with the interests of all countries, especially the least developed countries and African countries. However, like the reform of the IMF, the WTO reform is an extremely complex systematic project. All countries advocate reform, but it is very difficult to find a consensus on how to carry out the reform.

The European Union took the lead in proposing a WTO reform plan in 2018, advocating strengthening the supervision of "market-distorting" behaviors; reclassifying "developing countries"; implementing "flexible multilateralism" and promoting multilateral negotiations; improving the efficiency and transparency of the dispute settlement mechanism, etc. In September of that year, the European Union also reached an agreement with the United States and Japan on a joint proposal for WTO reform, which was highly targeted. However, as the two economies with the most say in the WTO, the European Union and the United States have always had continuous trade frictions and retaliations against each other, and they have long had different goals despite their apparent cooperation. There are also significant differences between them regarding the priority order of WTO reform. In February 2021, the European Union announced that it would list WTO reform as the core of its trade strategy for the next 10 years, including urging all WTO members to make greater commitments in the fields of trade and climate change, formulating new rules for digital trade, increasing efforts to deal with unfair competition, restoring the WTO dispute settlement mechanism, and so on. Although the EU's reform proposals have a certain degree of practical relevance and forward-looking nature, they are more considered from the perspective of its own interests, and there has always been a deviation between the EU's policy announcements and the implementation of actions.

During the Trump administration, the United States became the biggest opponent of the WTO, which it had played a leading role in establishing. This is not only related to the U.S. judgment that China has been the biggest beneficiary of global free trade since the twenty-first century, but also related to the fact that the United States does not have a key veto power in the WTO as it does in the World Bank and the IMF.

As is well known, the United States is one of the main founders of the WTO and its predecessor, the GATT, and is also one of the most important promoters of international trade and investment. The United States advocated and promoted trade liberalization and investment facilitation for a long time after World War II and played the role of a major guardian of free trade.

Although the United States laid the tradition of trade protectionism at both the theoretical and practical levels at the beginning of its founding. For example, by looking into the *Report on Manufactures* written by Alexander Hamilton, the first U.S. Secretary of the Treasury, in 1791, it can be found that the core ideas of a series of industrial subsidy policies with a strong protectionist color that the United States is implementing today are in the same vein as the policy designs of the so-called founding fathers of the United States more than 200 years ago. However, the fact that the United States has long been the world's largest importer shows that the United States is still one of the most important participants in international trade.

In the past decade, with emerging economies continuously integrating into the global trade system and actively participating in the governance and reform of the WTO based on their growing strength, and with trade disputes between the United States and the European Union becoming increasingly fierce, the United States, which originally supported free trade and the multilateral trading system, has begun to change its attitude towards the WTO. Especially, China became the world's second-largest economy and the largest exporter of goods within less than 10 years after joining the WTO, and its significant improvement in the position in the global trade value chain has far exceeded the expectations and actual control boundaries of the United States. In recent years, China has actively promoted a new round of globalization and the evolution of the free trade order, which has made the United States more and more anxious, fearing that it will 1 day lose its dominance over the global trade system and the evolution of rules.

The United States demanded that the WTO initiate comprehensive reforms. Even during the Trump administration, it threatened to withdraw from the WTO several times, and repeatedly "upset the table" on the "Economic United Nations" that it had personally helped to create. As a result, the "Supreme Court" responsible for adjudicating trade disputes within the organization remained in a state of no one being in charge for a long time, leading to functional paralysis. It even went so far as to destroy the core values of the existing free trade and multilateralism system at the cost of damaging its national prestige system. The ultimate goal is nothing more than to turn its "willful behavior" into an objective fact that other countries must accept.

Since China joined the WTO in 2001, while benefiting from global economic and trade integration, it has firmly safeguarded economic globalization, free trade, and multilateralism, and is committed to promoting a new round of globalization and the reform of the trade governance system. In November 2018, China put forward three principles and five proposals for WTO reform, emphasizing that the WTO reform should maintain and strengthen the core values of the multilateral trading system, namely non-discrimination and openness. It also emphasized that the WTO reform should protect the interests of developing members, and should follow the decision-making mechanism of consensus. In particular, it is necessary to ensure that the vast majority of members, especially developing members, jointly participate in the reform process, and there should be no "exclusive cliques".

After the Appellate Body of the WTO dispute settlement mechanism was paralyzed, China, together with other members such as the European Union, jointly established the "Multi-Party Interim Appeal Arbitration Arrangement". After the WTO selected a new Director-General, China advocated that the WTO reform should first restore the normal operation of the Appellate Body.

At this critical moment when the WTO has entered a time window for reform, as a responsible emerging economy, on the one hand, China, together with the members of the *Regional Comprehensive Economic Partnership* (RCEP) whose levels of economic and social development in the Asia-Pacific region vary greatly, by reaching a high-level free trade agreement, has not only effectively countered the trade fragmentation, block-like patterns, and national-level egoism that have been prevalent in recent years, but also hopes that through the subsequent implementation, it can provide a new development paradigm for the replication and promotion of new global multilateral investment and trade agreements. On the other hand, through structural reforms, especially by accelerating the implementation of the pre-establishment national treatment plus negative list management system, and a series of institutional arrangements such as effectively strengthening the protection of the legitimate rights and interests of foreign investors in China, especially the protection of intellectual property rights, China has made the operating environment of its market economy highly consistent with the common understanding of a market economy in the United States and Europe. China has also reached an important consensus with the European Union on WTO reform, which is also an important reason why the two major economies were able to reach a high-level investment agreement negotiation at the end of 2020.

WTO Reform Is Not a Zero-Sum Game

In conclusion, although the WTO reform is a multi-faceted strategic game involving both cooperative and non-cooperative games, it does not essentially constitute a zero-sum game. After the Biden administration took office, it has shown a certain willingness to cooperate in a multilateral context and demonstrated a certain degree of flexibility in addressing climate change and restoring the normal functions of the WTO.

On the premise of insisting that the WTO must undergo necessary reforms to enhance its effectiveness, authority, and dispute settlement capabilities, China should strive to the greatest extent possible to rally international forces to jointly safeguard the multilateral trading system based on rules and with the WTO as its core. It should constructively integrate China's three principles and five proposals for WTO reform with the reform proposals or demands of other members. Taking the implementation of the RCEP as an opportunity, China should firmly safeguard the global connectivity of the economic production chain and the trade value chain. By building a high-standard market system, China should make every effort to urge major developed countries to fulfill their promised commitment to recognize China's "market economy status". In the process of multiple rounds of games with the United States on WTO reform, China should not only adhere to its bottom line and principles but also show appropriate flexibility, and explore the possible cooperation areas between China and the United States in WTO reform. For example, further dialogues can be carried out on issues such as tariffs and non-tariff barriers, technology transfer, market access, anti-dumping, and countervailing measures. Because in today's era of global economic integration, zero-sum games are harmful and unbeneficial. For far-sighted politicians and business leaders in China and the United States, whether it is global economic growth, financial market stability, the reconstruction of new trade rules, the response to climate change, or the effective resolution of complex economic, financial, and trade issues in China and the United States respectively, all depend on the close cooperation between the two countries.

U.S. Strategic Intentions in Setting Constraints on WTO Reform

In October 2021, Katherine Tai, the U.S. Trade Representative, sent out a so-called "positive signal" that the United States intended to thaw its relations with the WTO during her visit to the WTO. As the first U.S. Trade Representative to visit the WTO headquarters since 2015, Tai's visit did have a certain symbolic significance. On the same day, she also held talks with Li Chenggang, China's Permanent Representative to the WTO, and exchanged views on the work of the WTO, especially on issues related to the 12th Ministerial Conference. This shows that although there are differences on major core issues of WTO reform and bilateral trade, it is still considered a rational choice for the world's largest and second-largest economies to face the reality and explore ways to resolve their differences.

Of course, Tai's words and deeds only indicate that the Biden administration intends to change the unilateral and arbitrary practices of the Trump era. Tai herself also does not want to leave the impression that she shares the aggressive attitude towards the WTO as her predecessor, Robert Lighthizer. Instead, she wants to restore the United States' leadership position in the WTO through cooperative games.

No matter how sophisticated or seemingly elegant Tai's speech is, it cannot hide the United States' hostile and even coercive attitude towards the WTO. For example, on the much-concerned issue of the WTO dispute settlement mechanism, not only did Tai not propose a clear path to get the mechanism out of the "brain death" trap, but she also echoed the wave of criticism of the mechanism during the Trump era, accusing it of having become "synonymous with litigation", which is both long and expensive, and has seemingly become a platform for countries to file trade lawsuits to obtain concessions rather than a place for negotiation.

As is well known, the Appellate Body of the WTO is the "Supreme Court" responsible for adjudicating trade disputes in the organization's complex operation system. It is also an innovative mechanism of the WTO compared with its predecessor, the GATT, and its most important feature is its independence. According to Article 17 of the *Understanding on Rules and Procedures Governing the Settlement of Disputes*, a basic document of the WTO dispute settlement mechanism, the Appellate Body shall have seven standing judges, and each ruling shall be made by at least three judges. The term of office of a judge is 4 years and can be renewed once. When there is a vacancy in the Appellate Body, the Dispute Settlement Body composed of all WTO members shall promptly appoint a new member through a consensus approach.

This dispute settlement mechanism is crucial to the future and destiny of the WTO. However, the Trump administration obstructed the recruitment of new judges and the timely completion of the reappointment process in various ways, resulting in the mechanism being paralyzed since December 2019 and unable to make rulings on trade disputes. Although the WTO appointed Angela Ellard, a U.S. trade expert, as Deputy Director-General in May 2021, which indicates that the Biden administration is fulfilling its international commitment of "America is back", from a technical perspective, this is just a routine operation of the WTO. Because according to the organization's tradition, the Deputy Director-General of the WTO generally comes from the United States, the European Union, Asia, and a developing member. Against the backdrop that Zhang Xiangchen, China's representative, was basically confirmed to be appointed as Deputy Director-General at that time, the United States obviously did not want its room for action in the WTO to be occupied by other members.

From the perspective of U.S. national interests and the logic of the Biden administration's foreign policy, the United States certainly understands that the long-term suspension of the WTO dispute settlement mechanism is not conducive to the development of U.S. and global trade, because the United States itself is one of the biggest beneficiaries of the WTO dispute settlement mechanism. However, the Biden administration has still maintained some of the practices of the Trump era 10 months after taking office, mainly due to three policy considerations:

First, the United States intends to actively take the lead in having the right to speak on major and thorny issues of the WTO. In recent years, the United States has often sent out self-contradictory and wrong messages on issues related to WTO reform and development. On the one hand, it has criticized the organization for being unfair to the United States, repeatedly and publicly questioned the rationality of the multilateral rules and multilateral mechanisms upheld by the WTO, and demanded that the WTO initiate comprehensive reforms. On the other hand, it has not put forward a constructive reform plan acceptable to most WTO members and has directly resorted to simple and crude sanctions and tariff measures in dealing with Sino-U.S. trade disputes. However, the cold economic data shows that the previous policy logic of the United States simply does not work. After weighing the pros and cons, the Biden administration decided to adopt an attitude of returning to tradition and cooperative games, and regain leadership of the WTO, which has fallen into difficulties, with its strength and international coordination ability.

Second, to incubate the United States' right to formulate and interpret the new round of international trade rules within the WTO framework. The United States is well aware that the WTO must be reformed; otherwise, it will not be able to adapt to the new trends in global trade development. Especially with the rapid development of the digital economy, there is an urgent need globally to establish international standards for digital trade. At this critical moment, the United States certainly cannot be absent, otherwise, it will mean voluntarily giving up the right to formulate and interpret the rules.

Third, to form a "new rules frontier" against China based on the institutional camp. In recent years, the United States has been trying to use domestic laws or presidential executive orders to resolve differences with its main trade partners, directly leading to the fragmentation, unilateralization, and even intensification of global trade or bilateral trade disputes between countries. Even so, the United States itself has not become a winner. Moreover, China has demonstrated strong national governance capabilities and institutional resilience in responding to the major external shock of the Covid-19, which has further reduced the institutional superiority complex that Western countries such as the United States have enjoyed for hundreds of years.

After repeated weighing, the United States decided to return to tradition and the institutionalized trade system. On the one hand, it seeks to actively repair its trade relations with the European Union and create a new regional and even global trade paradigm based on the USMCA. On the other hand, it sends out a strong expectation of reform to the WTO, attempting to use "all available tools" to enhance U.S. economic interests in leading the process of WTO reform and ultimately forming a new strategic advantage against its main trade partners.

Bretton Woods System 3.0: Is a Turning Point Approaching?

Major financial issues in today's world are often, to a certain extent, political issues in essence. Since the outbreak of the Russia-Ukraine conflict, the Western world represented by the United States and Europe has launched successive financial sanctions against Russia, aiming to cut off Russia's external financial channels and strangle the Russian economy. Measures such as prohibiting Russia from repaying debts with U.S. dollars actually amount to a declaration that once a country is defined as a political enemy of the United States, the U.S. dollar assets legally held by that country will, for a certain period, become assets under the control of the United States. If the country defaults on its debts as a result, it cannot be ruled out that it will be demanded to pay sky-high liquidated damages by its creditors.

Under the framework of the current international monetary order, assets denominated in either U.S. dollars or other currencies are, in essence, sovereign wealth with national credit, and their ownership and right of use have clear boundaries. In particular, the U.S. dollar, as a fully-fledged international currency, has five major functions simultaneously: a measure of value, a medium of exchange, a means of payment, a store of value, and a world currency. Even in the face of competitive pressure from the euro, the U.S. dollar remains the reserve currency, the pricing and settlement currency for commodities that holds an absolutely dominant position in the world today.

According to the composition of global official foreign exchange reserve currencies in the fourth quarter of 2021 released by the IMF, among the total global foreign exchange reserves of over $12 trillion, the proportion of U.S. dollar reserves is 58.86%, as high as $7.06 trillion. The euro, ranking second, accounts for 20.58%, which is only 35% of the proportion of the U.S. dollar, showing a significant gap. As for commodities represented by oil, natural gas, etc., although the euro, the Chinese yuan, and the Russian ruble have already penetrated into the trading system, the dominant position of the U.S. dollar is still difficult to shake in the short term. (The proportion of each currency in global foreign exchange reserves is shown in Table 4.1.)

Table 4.1 The proportion of various currencies in global foreign exchange reserves (unit: %)

Currency	Fourth quarter of 2021	First Quarter of 2022
U.S. Dollar (USD)	58.86	58.88
Renminbi (CNY)	2.79	2.88
Pound Sterling (GBP)	4.8	4.97
Japanese yen (JPY)	5.51	5.35
Euro (EUR)	20.58	20.05

Data Source: IMF.

Therefore, to a considerable extent, the current international monetary system is still the "post-Bretton Woods System" or the so-called "Bretton Woods System 2.0" dominated by the U.S. dollar. The supporting forces that enable this system to maintain relative stability mainly come from two aspects: First, the proportion of the U.S. economy in the total global economic volume has remained relatively stable over the years, and at the same time, the credit of the U.S. dollar as a reserve currency in the global financial market remains relatively sound. Second, the pattern of global industrial and financial division of labor has remained relatively stable in the past 20 years. In particular, the two most important economies, the United States and China, have formed a relatively stable and orderly division of labor and cooperation in the fields of manufacturing, trade, and finance. In fact, its stability and resilience have withstood the severe test of the Sino-U.S. economic and trade frictions in the past 2 years.

From a historical perspective, today's international monetary system has some similarities with that of a hundred years ago: According to John Keynes' explanation of the legitimacy of the pound standard system at that time, although the United Kingdom was no longer the world's leading industrial country, the pound standard system could still operate smoothly, mainly due to the United Kingdom's dominant position in the global financial system and the central role of London, as the largest capital market and trade center, in supplying gold to its partners. As the "conductor of the international symphony orchestra," the Bank of England successfully regulated the international flow of gold and maintained a relatively small gold reserve through floating discount rates. The dominant position of the United Kingdom in the international financial market enabled the Bank of England to achieve a net capital inflow by adjusting the discount rate. The centralized international settlement methods in the London market and other favorable conditions made the pound replace the previous precious metal currencies.

According to a similar logic, although the United States has now lost its status as the world's largest industrial country, the U.S. dollar support system composed of the U.S. dollar, the New York international financial center, the Federal Reserve, the U.S. Department of the Treasury, and still powerful industrial and financial capital has maximized the tension of the United States' national credit in the era of credit currency and floating exchange rates. Coupled with the fact that the United States has a relatively mature self-correcting mechanism and strong abilities to absorb losses and self-repair, even at the critical moment when the United States encounters a major crisis, few countries, enterprises, and residents choose to abandon the U.S. dollar voluntarily.

However, since the outbreak of the Russia-Ukraine conflict, the United States and its major allies have imposed extreme financial sanctions on Russia, including excluding some Russian banks from the international payment and settlement system SWIFT, freezing the assets of the Central Bank of Russia and prohibiting transactions with it, and even preventing Russia from using U.S. dollars to pay its due debts. This has forced Russia to link the ruble with export commodities such as oil and natural gas, forming the concept of "gas ruble" that runs parallel to or even conflicts with the "petrodollar." This has led to the peculiar phenomenon of "active decoupling" in the history of the evolution of the global monetary system, that is, the reserve currency issuing country has severed ties with specific users, causing large-scale disruptions in the originally relatively smooth international currency settlement system and giving rise to a certain amount of "gas rubles."

In terms of economic consequences, this is obviously an unwise move that harms oneself as much as the enemy. In other words, the United States, at the cost of damaging the reputation of the U.S. dollar as the cornerstone of the international credit currency, has achieved its political goals by launching extreme financial sanctions, which has undermined the credit foundation of the international monetary system since World War II, and a huge crack has thus been torn in the "Bretton Woods System 2.0."

As a result, there is a saying in the market about the "Bretton Woods System 3.0," in which the internal currency credit system represented by the U.S. dollar is on the verge of collapse, and the "commodity currency" supported by "external currencies" (gold and commodities) is rising again. This view has been spread by financial analysts in the United States and Europe and international public opinion, creating a discourse phenomenon that the international monetary system is about to undergo a major transformation.

The reform of the international monetary system, which has already been in progress, will definitely be affected by the Russia-Ukraine conflict. This geopolitical conflict with complex historical backgrounds and real motivations may play a considerable "assisting" role. However, from a rational perspective, the driving force for the fundamental reform of the international monetary system does not ultimately depend on the non-cooperative games between the reserve currency issuing country and the secondary important participating entities, but rather on the evolving trend of the ebb and flow between the main issuing countries of the existing reserve currencies and other reserve currency issuing countries in terms of absolute economic strength, the influence of the financial market, especially the asset pricing power of capital, and international coordination and mobilization capabilities.

By referring to the development logic of the pound and the U.S. dollar as the international dominant currencies successively, when the currencies representing emerging forces, as important participants in the existing international monetary system, gradually assume increasingly important roles, the international monetary system will reach a crucial inflection point at a certain time window. Of course, it will take a long time to wait for the arrival of this inflection point, but it will definitely not be too far away.

Chapter 5
The Consequences of the U.S. "Maximum Pressure" Strategy Against China

Why Is the U.S. Increasingly Violating Global Trade Norms?

On July 6, 2018, the Trump administration initiated a trade dispute with China, forcing China to fight back in kind and triggering a confrontation within the trade systems between the world's two largest economies today. A little earlier before that, facing the protectionist actions of the powerful neighbor, the United States, Canada, which could no longer tolerate it, launched the most aggressive trade actions since World War II. Prime Minister Justin Trudeau declared that Canada had no choice but to retaliate and called on all sectors in Canada to support the government in imposing retaliatory tariffs on the United States. Subsequently, the more shocking trade war between the United States and the European Union ultimately became inevitable. Almost any country other than the United States had to be prepared to fend off the Trump administration, in an attempt to minimize the impact and harm caused by the biggest variable in today's world political and economic order to their own countries.

According to the logic of the Trump administration, as the guarantor of the global trade system, the United States has provided an enormous amount of trade opportunities, market space, and welfare effects to other countries since World War II, especially since the twenty-first century. However, the United States has been suffering from the long-term "plundering" by its major trade partners, including China. Therefore, the United States was forced to launch the "301" investigation and use tariff measures to punish competitors who do not abide by trade rules. (The *2017 Special 301 Report* released by the Office of the United States Trade Representative (USTR) is shown in Table 5.1.) But this logic is obviously not tenable.

As is well known, the United States is the biggest beneficiary of free trade, and also the main designer and system maintainer of the GATT and later the WTO. Americans will not forget the advocacy of free trade by David Ricardo, the classical economist they respect, nor will they be unaware of how Sir John Maynard Keynes, who once played the role of saving the fate of the United States, opposed

Y. Zhang, *Addressing Uncertainty*, Understanding China,
https://doi.org/10.1007/978-981-92-2692-4_5

Table 5.1 *The 2017 Special 301 Report* Released by USTR

Priority watch list of countries	Watch list of countries
China, Indonesia, Thailand, India, Algeria, Kuwait, Russia, Ukraine, Argentina, Chile, Venezuela	Vietnam, Pakistan, Turkmenistan, Uzbekistan, Egypt, Lebanon, Bulgaria, Greece, Romania, Switzerland, Turkey, Canada, Mexico, Costa Rica, Dominican Republic, Guatemala, Barbados, Jamaica, Bolivia, Brazil, Colombia, Ecuador, Peru

Note: The United States has placed China, India, and nine additional countries—11 in total—on its Priority Watch List

trade protectionism. Although the Bretton Woods System, which was established under the leadership of the United States in 1944, has already disintegrated, the global economic, financial, and trade rules and practices formed based on this system are still playing a supporting role to this day. Its core concepts and practical expressions include: expanding the production and trade of goods and services based on the recognized and signed rules of various countries, adopting an integrated multilateral trading system, gradually eliminating tariff and non-tariff trade barriers, etc. Eventually, based on bilateral or multilateral free trade areas, it aims to eliminate trade discrimination, meet the effective demands of various countries, and promote global economic growth by significantly reducing transaction costs among trading partners. The United States has long played the role of system builder and change driver in this trading system and has thus obtained both explicit and implicit benefits.

Those familiar with economic history know that since the Industrial Revolution, it is difficult to count the wealth plundered by Western capitalist countries represented by the United States and Europe under the banner of free trade. How was the North-South divide created? Presumably, it would be very embarrassing for them to answer this question. Even now, the U.S. government still believes that the global trade system and rules must allow the United States to profit comfortably. Otherwise, it is considered unfair to the United States. Unfortunately, the changes in the real-world international economic and trade landscape do not entirely follow the will of the United States. Before 2001, China was basically on the periphery of the global trade value chain. By joining the WTO, China continuously learned and adapted to international trade rules, and continuously improved its export competitiveness through the enhancement of technology and service quality. It has thus become an important participant in the high-end part of the international trade value chain. Moreover, based on the rules, China has steadily built bilateral and multilateral free trade systems. These achievements are clearly difficult for the United States to accept.

In my exchanges with people from the U.S. business and political circles, I found that although the United States is not fully confident about the outcome of a systemic trade collision with China, most of them believe that China's development has far exceeded the United States' expectations. There is a trend of the global wealth center shifting from the United States to China, and it is also possible that the global wealth allocation and asset pricing center will shift to China in the future. Moreover,

China is promoting the reconstruction of regional and even global trade rules, which the United States absolutely cannot tolerate. The United States must take "extraordinary measures" to contain the improvement of China's export competitiveness, and even cut off China's core trade value chain, forcing China to "join the WTO" for the second time in accordance with the will of the United States, so as to achieve strategic encirclement of China and enable the United States to continue to maintain its dominance in the new round of global wealth allocation.

On the surface, the United States' wanton trampling on international trade rules is to achieve short-term national goals through "extraordinary means" such as trade frictions. At a deeper strategic level, it is to ensure that the United States maintains its generational advantage over its main competitors by mobilizing its comprehensive competitive strength in high-end industries, flexible business rules, and institutionalized hegemony.

Long-Term and Responding Calmly to the World's "New Trade Frontiers"

Today, with the global value chain relationships already deeply intertwined and the Chinese economy having entered a stage of deep-opening up, whether it is the United States and the European Union, or the United States, the European Union and Japan, their construction of a "new trade frontier" targeting China, to some extent, is not only an instrumental arrangement to cut off China's core value chain, but also an alternative exploration to eventually establish a moderate interest-sharing mechanism with China.

When the Sino-U.S. trade dispute was in a stalemate, the European Union, as an important pole in the global economy and trade, sent its highest-level delegations to visit China, Japan and the United States successively, achieving a series of visit outcomes. Among them, on July 17, 2018, the European Union and Japan officially signed an Economic Partnership Agreement (EPA) in Tokyo, aiming to create a "super free trade area" covering 600 million people and accounting for nearly one-third of the global GDP. According to this agreement, the European Union will abolish tariffs on 99% of Japanese imported goods; Japan will abolish tariffs on 94% of EU imported goods, including 82% of agricultural and aquatic products. In the following years, Japan will gradually abolish tariffs on 99% of EU imported goods. Subsequently, the European Union and the United States issued a joint statement on July 25 and reached an agreement to defuse trade tensions. The two sides agreed to work towards eliminating tariffs and trade barriers. The United States agreed not to impose tariffs on European cars, and the European Union agreed to import more U.S. soybeans and natural gas. After that, the Trump administration followed up promptly. Robert Lighthizer, sent by the administration, stated before the Senate Appropriations Committee that the United States would start consultations with Japan within the next 30 days and strive to sign a bilateral Free Trade Agreement (FTA) with Japan.

As the three most developed economies in the world today, the United States, the European Union and Japan not only possess the world's strongest R&D foundation and the most advanced technological level, but also have long ranked among the top three in the fields of manufacturing (including high-end manufacturing), trade value chain and top-level financial division of labor. More importantly, as the main designers and interest defenders of the world economic order, the United States and the European Union have long played the role of guarantors of the global economic, financial and trade systems. Japan, on the other hand, realizes its national goals by participating in a series of international organizations such as the G7, the World Bank, the IMF, the Asian Development Bank, and through its multinational corporations distributed globally. Objectively speaking, in recent years, the United States, the European Union and Japan have faced challenges from emerging economies in the economic, trade and some financial fields, but they still firmly hold the dominance of the existing order.

However, for U.S. strategists who highly value trend changes, today's world cannot be simply summarized by terms like the "Anglo-Saxon system" or the "New Victorian Era". It is a world where the old-fashioned economic, trade and financial clubs are depreciating rapidly and the influence of the existing order is gradually declining. It is also an era in which reform -related factors and new public-product tools keep emerging. Americans have found that since the 2008 global financial crisis, emerging economies representing global change forces not only have the will, but also are gradually capable of providing new public goods in the financial and trade fields globally. For example, Lawrence Summers, a former U.S. Treasury Secretary with extremely sensitive financial instincts and a strategic vision among U.S. financial leaders, pointed out in an article a few years ago that due to Washington's failure to respond to the Asian Infrastructure Investment Bank (AIIB) project led by China in a positive and open manner, especially its failure to persuade more than a dozen of its traditional allies to participate in the institution, the United States was at risk of losing its role as the guarantor of the global economic system. Some Western observers are worried and predict that the responsibility for protecting the global commons will spread from one country to multiple countries, and competition and instability will become the new normal.

In fact, what the United States is most worried about is the replacement of the functions of the U.S. dollar. Although the United States still has a unique special advantage, that is, a global-wide maritime power projection and strike system, a flexible commercial intervention system and an intangible financial control system. However, the trend of the changing economic strength between the United States and China makes U.S. strategists and Wall Street financial oligarchs constantly feel uneasy. Zbigniew Brzezinski, who has already passed away, was particularly worried during his lifetime: Will the United States lose its superpower status one day? And Hank Paulson, a former Treasury Secretary regarded as a core representative of the "Goldman Sachs Gang", has been working extremely hard over the years to maintain the United States' position as the leading financial power. Because modern finance is widely regarded as an effective integration of a strong manufacturing industry, the high frontier of global trade and financial pricing power, and a comprehensive extraction of a country's science and technology, output, transactions, creativity, as well as international coordination and leadership capabilities. Since the Bretton Woods System, whether it is Japan or Europe, due to certain weaknesses in the above-mentioned comprehensive competition areas, coupled with geopolitical constraints, they have ultimately been unable to replace the United States as the guarantor of the global economic system. Coincidentally, in the history of global economic development so far, only China, following the United States, has reached an economic scale of more than $10 trillion. The United States believes that once China completes its industrialization and builds a relatively complete financial service system, it will sooner or later challenge its hegemonic position. Therefore, the West must use all kinds of forces to suppress China's development before China becomes strong enough, or control China's influence within the framework of the order dominated by the United States.

Therefore, from the perspective of the changes in global economic and financial competition and trade patterns in the past decade, whether it is the "one-body, two-wings" strategy of the Obama administration (taking the North American Free Trade Area as the body, and the *Comprehensive and Progressive Agreement for Trans-Pacific Partnership* (CPTPP) and the *Transatlantic Trade and Investment Partnership* (TTIP) as the two wings), or the series of "America First" policies successively introduced by the U.S. government, as well as the relevant economic and trade agreements reached by the European Union with Japan and the United States, although they have different manifestations, they essentially all attempt to, through reaching multilateral or bilateral free trade agreements and relying on the unshakable dominant position of the United States in the financial field, while consolidating the global trade system based on the U.S.-EU paradigm, suppress to the greatest extent the room for emerging economies to upgrade their trade value chains. Coupled with the technology-locking against China in the high-tech field, the ultimate goal is to construct a "new frontier of technology, finance and trade" mainly targeting China, and continue to reap the dividends of institutionalized hegemony to the greatest extent.

However, it is very difficult to find an optimal solution to the structural contradictions between the United States and Japan, as well as between the European Union and Japan. Even if the three join forces against China, in today's globally-integrated economy, it is an extremely difficult task. Moreover, China already has considerable counter-measures. The United States, which is well-versed in the laws of global economic competition and industrial changes, actually knows very well that the trend of China's transformation from a manufacturing and trading power to a strong industrial, trading and capital-based country cannot be completely curbed. Sooner or later, the Chinese yuan will become one of the world's major pricing and reserve currencies, and Shanghai will one day become the global wealth allocation and asset pricing center. What the United States can do is to, when China's economic ambitions and specific elements are temporarily not in line, make the most of its dominant position in the existing economic, financial and trade rules to compress China's space for strength growth and international influence to the greatest extent.

Therefore, at this critical moment when the global trade pattern is facing a major reshuffle, China must have a long-term vision, summarize the experience and lessons of its previous foreign trade development. It should not only moderately abandon some policy-making mindsets that do not conform to the current global situation, but also release the dividends of economic development through deep-level domestic opening-up and reform progress in key areas, and focus on increasing the coverage of the welfare effects of economic growth for the public. In addition, since the most important factors driving economic growth are knowledge innovation, scientific and technological progress, and the improvement of human capital, in the coming period, while increasing investment in human capital, China should lead the overall upgrading of the industrial structure with forward-looking technological investment and high-quality technological transformation, promote economic strategic transformation, and purify the impetuous concept of wealth pervading the whole society. It should increase efforts in forward-looking technology research and development and independent innovation, strive to achieve key breakthroughs in strategic emerging industries, and make them a new engine leading China's sustainable economic growth. Finally, China must analyze the trends of global trade development and rule changes in a forward-looking manner. While effectively improving the level of dealing with trade friction games, it should intensively engage in the research and development of core technologies and the international promotion of independent brands, actively explore the establishment of an effective interest-sharing mechanism with major trading partners, and master the art of cooperative games with uncertain competitors.

The Reality of "Made in the USA" Is Bound to Disappoint Washington

Since taking office, Trump has been strongly pushing the federal government to increase its procurement of "Made in the USA" products, in order to fulfill his campaign promise of "Buy American, Hire American". In July 2019, he signed an "upgraded" executive order, requiring the U.S. Federal Procurement Regulatory Commission to draft a new rule within 180 days. The rule stipulates that for goods procured by the federal government, the cost of using domestic materials should account for more than 55% of the total product cost, which is higher than the 50% stipulated in the then-effective *Buy American Act*. The executive order also specifically proposed that the proportion of the cost of using domestic materials in steel and aluminum products procured by the federal government should be increased to more than 95%, in order to promote the return of manufacturing to the United States.

Today, with the global economy already highly integrated, the above-mentioned executive order is far from what one would expect from the world's largest and most mature market-economy country since World War II. For the U.S. government, its role seems more in line with the "active non-interference" advocated by Milton Friedman, a proponent of laissez-faire capitalism. Mainstream U.S. economists believe that only in this way is it possible to achieve the optimal allocation of resources.

However, real-world economic practices and policies never rigidly conform to general static assumptions. As early as 1894, the United States replaced the United Kingdom as the world's largest industrial country. Subsequently, under the influence of historical opportunities and multiple favorable factors, the United States continuously consolidated its position as the world's leading manufacturing power. The Bretton Woods Conference in 1944 officially marked the United States' ascent to the peak of global industrial and financial division of labor. At that time, the industrial output value of the United States accounted for more than 40% of the world's total. The "201" and "301" clauses in the *Trade Act of 1974* are clear evidence of this.

As is well known, the scale and level of the manufacturing industry are important indicators for measuring the comprehensive strength and modernization level of a country or region. Without a strong manufacturing industry as a foundation, there can be no mention of upgrading the trade value chain, let alone the financial pricing power that represents the highest level of division of labor. However, the United States over-emphasized the development of the financial industry, real estate, and other service industries for nearly 30 years after the 1980s, which weakened the international competitiveness of its manufacturing industry to a certain extent. It was not until the painful lessons of the 2008 international financial crisis that Americans began to attach importance to the real economy again. In times of economic prosperity, even if there are serious ecological distortions in the financial industry, which is at the top of the economic division of labor, its negative externalities are easily overlooked. But when the real economy that supports the development of the financial industry collapses due to the impact of the financial crisis, the self-serving nature of the financial industry and its inability to promote extensive employment are fully exposed. The development of the real-economy industries represented by the manufacturing industry, on the other hand, can achieve a reasonable distribution of wealth along a long industrial chain, and is especially beneficial for increasing the employment rate, which the government is highly concerned about.

It was precisely because of seeing these weaknesses of the financial industry that the United States decided to face up to the long-standing problems in its economic development. As early as 2008, Laura Tyson, an economic advisor to former President Barack Hussein Obama, stated that China could not remain the supply-chain center forever, and the "U.S. consumption-China production" model would become ineffective. Lawrence Summers, on the other hand, called on the Obama administration: "The United States must become an export-oriented economy rather than a consumption-based one, and must rely on real engineering and technology, not financial gimmicks." After taking office, the Obama administration began to adjust its economic policy focus to emphasize real-economy industries and an export-oriented approach, strongly promoting the "reshoring of manufacturing" and the " Export Doubling Plan". This was done to repair economic imbalances and reverse the United States' decline in international economic competition. After the Trump administration came to power, this policy was not only effectively carried forward but also further strengthened, becoming an important part of the "America First" policy.

However, the development of the global manufacturing industry, industrial changes, and the division-of-labor pattern have already undergone fundamental changes that do not conform to the will of the United States. Some countries represented by China have become the most important centers for manufactured goods and the core links in the global supply chain. This is not only the result of giving play to factor-endowment advantages and adapting to market competition but also constitutes the most important foundation for the global manufacturing division of labor and a well-ordered ecosystem. This relatively stable division-of-labor pattern cannot be broken by the U.S. government's measures that distort the laws of the market economy, such as offering preferential policies to enterprises that set up factories in the United States or using tariffs as a lever to guide the "reshoring of manufacturing".

Apple, a company with a thorough understanding of industrial division of labor, responded to the Trump administration's request in 2017 by promising to invest $1 billion in a new advanced manufacturing fund in the United States to create more job opportunities. Amazon and Intel have also made similar attempts. However, the fact is that in June 2019, Apple decided to transfer the production of its only main device assembled in the United States, the desktop computer, to China. Just as a forced melon is not sweet, the clumsy plans and economic thinking that "force" enterprises to return to the United States or wave the flag of "domestic products" while peddling "America First", going against the laws of market selection and industrial division of labor, are doomed to failure. The reality of "Made in the USA" simply cannot meet Washington's eagerness.

Why Do Figures Like Soros Fantasize About "Defeating China"?

On September 9, 2019, George Soros, a U.S. speculator notorious in the international financial community, declared in *The Wall Street Journal*: "I am more interested in defeating China at present than in caring about the national interests of the United States." At the same time, media in Hong Kong, China, exposed that he was frequently mobilizing his short-selling funds and tools such as the "Open Society Foundations" at that time, colluding to create a "color revolution" in Hong Kong, China, taking advantage of the chaos to profit, and trying to wash away the humiliation of his failed attempt to attack the Hong Kong dollar in the past. Why is Soros so persistent in his attempt to "defeat" China? This is a proposition worthy of in-depth exploration.

Soros was born into a Jewish family in Budapest. When he was young, his family fled Nazi -occupied Hungary and moved around through places like Bern and London, and he studied at the London School of Economics and Political Science. Unlike his compatriot Andy Grove, who was also born in Budapest and persecuted by the Nazis and took the path of technological innovation, becoming a Silicon Valley leader by participating in founding Intel, Soros moved from the UK to the United States to engage in stock trading. On Wall Street, where money never sleeps, Soros learned the tricks of deception and ruthless exploitation. After getting rich, he didn't forget to disguise himself as a "philanthropist" and gradually became a super speculator who was well-versed in the law of the jungle and the art of taking risks for personal gain.

Looking at Soros's life trajectory, especially the speculative and extremely destabilizing roles he played in financial markets and changing societies, it can be found that this financial tycoon, deeply influenced by liberal philosophical ideas and market Darwinism, not only has the greedy genes commonly shared by Wall Street financial capitalists, but also, due to his tortuous life experiences and gratitude for the opportunities that American-style capitalism gave him to realize his life dreams, plays the role of a persistent defender of ideology.

On the one hand, he is a big speculator in the capital market: he attacked the British pound, leaving the Bank of England in a difficult situation; he targeted the Thai baht, triggering the Asian financial crisis; and he made a fortune by short-selling the Japanese yen.

On the other hand, he is an alternative and extremely complex dreamer of capitalism. Based on his substantial capital, he attempts to export American ideology and values to the world through tools such as the "Open Society Foundations" he founded. The "regime changes" in countries like Georgia, Ukraine, and Kyrgyzstan were all involved with the participation and instigation of this foundation. Soros's foundation tries to incite "color revolutions" in many countries while also maximizing his personal influence in the global political landscape as much as possible.

Sometimes, Soros also disapproves of American-style capitalism that he believes in. For example, at the World Economic Forum in Davos in 2009, he exclaimed that the theory of the "efficient-market hypothesis" had died. However, at his core, as a representative of the interests of international financial capital, what Soros cannot tolerate the most are those countries and forces that do not abide by the game rules set by the Western world. Against this background, China, which is continuously developing and growing, is precisely the super-sample that Soros least wants to see.

As early as before Hong Kong's return to the motherland in 1997, Soros wanted to create large-scale financial panic in Hong Kong, but he didn't have the opportunity. From October 1997 to June 1998, international speculators attacked the Hong Kong dollar three times and made profits. On October 28, 1997, the Hang Seng Index fell below 9000 points, and Hong Kong was once reduced to a "super ATM" for Wall Street. So in August 1998, Soros frantically sold off stocks, causing the Hong Kong stock market and foreign exchange market to be in turmoil for a time. However, with the strong support of the Chinese government, the Hong Kong Special Administrative Region government decisively intervened in the market and

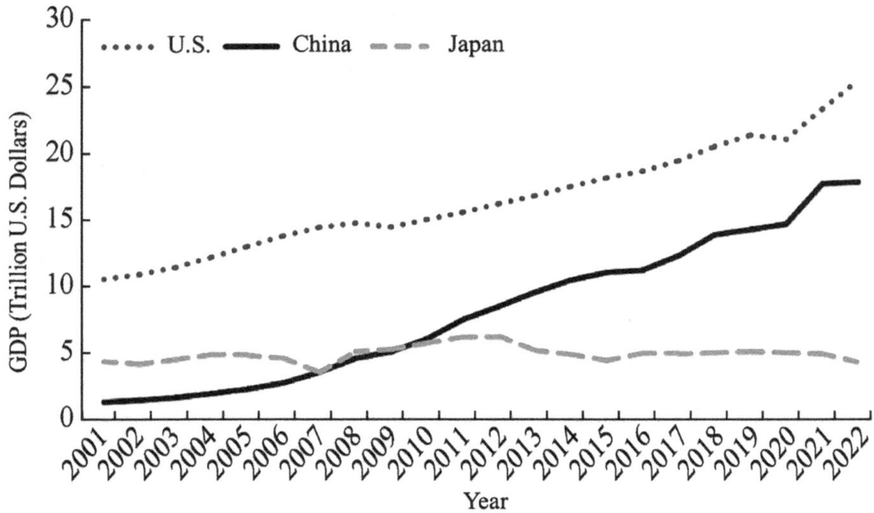

Fig. 5.1 Changes in the GDP of China, the United States, and Japan since 2001. Data Source: World Bank

had a major confrontation with international speculators led by Soros, ultimately winning that bloodless financial defense battle.

Now, 25 years have passed. China has not only gone through the uncertain stage of fully integrating into the world trade and financial systems, but also, in the more than 10 years since joining the WTO in 2001, it has rapidly grown into a super economy with a GDP exceeding $10 trillion, becoming one of the only two members of the "trillion-dollar club". In contrast, Japan, the United States' long-term main economic competitor, has seen its GDP size hovering around $5 trillion for more than 20 years. (The changes in the GDP of China, the United States, and Japan since 2001 are shown in Fig. 5.1.) The changing economic development and power growth between China and major capitalist powers have greatly exceeded the expectations of some Wall Street financial capitalists represented by Soros.

In their view, it was the United States that single-handedly led China onto the global economic and trade stage, and it was they who taught Chinese financial professionals about investment. However, over the years, the global economic and wealth center has gradually shifted from the United States to Asia, and the focus of economic vitality has also turned towards China. In the future, the global wealth allocation and asset pricing center may also shift from Wall Street in the United States to places like Shanghai and Shenzhen in China.

Moreover, China is actively advocating the construction or improvement of regional and even global investment and trade rules. International public goods such as the Belt and Road Initiative, the Asian Infrastructure Investment Bank, and the New Development Bank of the BRICS countries are continuously developing and growing. This is clearly not only a challenge to the institutionalized economic, financial, and trade system dominated by the United States, but also a so-called non-"Anglo-Saxon" model that people like Soros, who have a strong sense of institutional and psychological superiority, cannot tolerate. People like Soros are very surprised by China's achievements in terms of trade scale, adaptation to rules, improvement of the global value chain, industrial competitiveness, and comprehensive national strength since China joined the WTO. They believe that if China is not contained, divided, and comprehensively attacked, the "Chinese path" rooted in China's history, culture, and institutional paradigm will become an important variable driving the changes in global order at a faster pace. For the Western capitalist world, isn't this a thorn in the side?

Retarding the pace of China's rejuvenation by disrupting Hong Kong, China, or even instigating "color revolutions" has become the goal of people like Soros. However, the history of global economic and financial development and industrial changes since the twenty-first century has proven and will continue to prove that no force in the world can "short-sell" China, and no force can halt the great rejuvenation of the Chinese nation.

Will Financial Sanctions Lead to U.S.–China Financial Decoupling?

Trump once threatened that "the United States has only used a few tools against China so far." This is by no means a joke. The United States is fully capable of taking a series of extreme measures against China, including higher-level financial sanctions, without prior warning. The strategic and economic dialogue mechanism established between China and the United States back then may become history.

According to a Reuters report on September 26, 2019, former U.S. Secretary of State Michael Richard Pompeo said on the 25th (local time) that the United States was imposing new sanctions on certain Chinese companies and individuals because the latter "intentionally transferred oil from Iran, violating Washington's sanctions against Iran."

Previously, the U.S. Department of the Treasury announced the targets of this round of sanctions on its official website, including five Chinese citizens and six Chinese entities. The six sanctioned Chinese entities are COSCO Shipping (Dalian) Co., Ltd., Dalian COSCO Shipping Tanker Crewing & Ship Management Co., Ltd., Zhonghe Petroleum Co., Ltd., Kunlun Shipping Co., Ltd., Kunlun Holding Co., Ltd., and Pegasus 88 Ltd.

It was disclosed that these sanctions will prohibit U.S. citizens and companies from dealing with the above-mentioned Chinese companies, effectively excluding them from the U.S. banking industry, which is at the core of the global financial system. At the same time, any property or interests owned by these companies or individuals in the United States will be frozen, and any payment or transfer of U.S. assets to them will be prohibited.

Financial Sanctions: The Unique Trump Card of the United States

According to relevant statistics, since the Office of Foreign Assets Control (OFAC) of the U.S. Department of the Treasury began releasing sanction information in 2001, as of June 30, 2019, as many as 152 Chinese individuals or entities (including enterprises) had been successively included in the OFAC sanction list, making China one of the countries with the largest number of entities on the list. Among them, there were 68 Chinese individuals, 83 Chinese enterprises, and one military department. 150 of them were included in the "specially designated nationals" (SDN) list, one was included in the 561 list (a special list for OFAC's financial sanctions against Iran), and another one was included in the list related to Iran-sanctioning legislation. U.S. financial sanctions against China mainly focus on the individual and corporate levels.

In recent years, OFAC has continuously increased the intensity of sanctions against China. Since 2017, as many as 110 Chinese individuals and entities have been sanctioned, accounting for more than 70%.

As the Sino-U.S. trade frictions have become somewhat stalemated, the quick victory originally anticipated by the Trump administration has become increasingly unlikely. There is also no possibility for the United States to force China to make major concessions on core and key interests, or even in terms of fundamental systems through tariff barriers. However, the United States, with its deeply-ingrained "hegemon" mentality, has taken the initiative to provoke Sino-U.S. trade frictions and has constantly escalated the intensity of confrontation. Moreover, as the degree of goal-achievement so far is far from what was originally expected, the evolution and impact of this trade friction will not be subject to China's will.

On August 6, 2019, the U.S. Department of the Treasury labeled China as a "currency manipulator." The United States' decision to target the Chinese yuan at this time was not a whim, but a long-planned strategic choice by extreme hawks represented by former U.S. Trade Representative Robert Lighthizer and former Director of the White House National Trade Council Peter Navarro. Due to China's appropriate response, and the fact that the main allies of the United States and the IMF did not follow suit, the U.S. move failed to achieve the expected results, and its symbolic significance outweighed its practical significance.

However, the United States did not stop there. The U.S. government believes that although its advantages in the real-economy and high-tech fields are being gradually eroded by China, finance remains China's weak point. Taking financial sanctions of different levels and intensities against specific Chinese enterprises or individuals when necessary may yield unexpected results.

In fact, the United States has already started to show its fangs in imposing financial sanctions on China: As early as 2012, on the grounds that it was involved in business with Iran, the United States sanctioned Bank of Kunlun in China and threatened to sever the connection between Bank of Kunlun and the U.S. financial system, forcing Bank of Kunlun to strictly abide by U.S. sanction regulations. A similar situation also occurred with Dandong Bank in China. In 2017, the United States accused Dandong Bank of providing channels for North Korea's so-called illegal financial activities, and thus cut off Dandong Bank's connection with the U.S. financial system.

In March 2019, during the investigation of North Korea's sanctions-violation cases, a U.S. judge accused three Chinese banks, namely the Bank of Communications, China Merchants Bank, and Shanghai Pudong Development Bank, of non-compliance. There were rumors that the connection between these three banks and the U.S. financial system would be severed. However, due to the lack of direct evidence, the three banks were not investigated by the U.S. judicial department for suspected violations of any sanction laws. In July 2019, Pompeo revealed in a speech that Zhuhai Zhenrong, a state-owned energy enterprise in China, was sanctioned by the United States.

Previously, using the excuse of Iran's attack on Saudi oil fields, the United States intensified its financial sanctions against Iran, cutting off most of Iran's sources of funds, leaving Iranian banks almost isolated from the international financial community. Only the banks of a very few countries, such as Russia, still maintained contact with Iranian banks.

The financial sanctions imposed by the United States on Iran are an extreme measure, other than warfare, that the U.S. takes against hostile countries. Since the Iranian economy is highly dependent on oil exports, has a relatively single economic structure, and has always faced a harsh external environment, its domestic economy has been greatly affected by U.S. financial sanctions.

In contrast, China has a large-scale economy, with its GDP equivalent to two-thirds of that of the United States. It is the world's largest trading nation, has a huge financial market, is deeply involved in the global financial market, and has a very high degree of international connectivity. The number of global systemically important banks in China is second only to that in the United States. Moreover, extremely close economic, trade, and financial ties have long been established between China and the United States. As a result, for the United States to impose financial sanctions on China at the same level as those on Iran and Russia is not only technically difficult to implement but also will cause far more harm to the United States itself than the impacts of the financial sanctions on Iran and Russia.

However, based on an analysis of how the United States has suppressed its main competitors after World War II, during the multi-round strategic games between China and the United States, the United States is fully likely to use excuses such as threats to national security and resort to means like the *International Emergency Economic Powers Act, the National Emergencies Act, the National Defense Authorization Act*, and the issuance of presidential executive orders to impose medium-to-low-level sanctions on certain enterprises with symbolic significance in China or specific individuals. These sanctions include fines, asset freezes, and cutting off transactions with the U.S. financial system, in an attempt to achieve high-value strategic goals at a relatively low cost.

The factors supporting the United States' ability to impose financial sanctions globally are nothing more than the powerful institutionalized financial hegemony it has constructed since World War II, along with its supporting laws and enforcement systems. To some extent, this is also a form of containment after its status as the global economic and security guarantor has been challenged or faced with asymmetric threats.

As the United States controls the global currency settlement network and the most important payment currency system, that is, the dollar-centered pricing and settlement system, it has become the only hegemonic country in the world capable of launching real-world financial sanctions against other countries. Moreover, the superpower status of the United States allows it to override international law and directly launch unilateral financial sanctions bypassing major international organizations. The sanctioned countries or entities almost have no channels or mechanisms for appeal and international legal remedies, and they have nowhere to complain.

On the other hand, in today's world, there is no payment and clearing system that can replace the Clearing House Interbank Payments System (CHIPS) in New York and the Society for Worldwide Interbank Financial Telecommunication (SWIFT), which is de facto controlled by the United States. (The development history of SWIFT is shown in Table 5.2.) Most of the global cross—border dollar payment and clearing operations are carried out through CHIPS, while SWIFT is a message-sending system responsible for transmitting transaction information among the world's major banks and financial institutions. Together, they handle more than 95% of inter-bank dollar payment and clearing and more than 90% of foreign exchange transaction clearing. If an economic entity (market entity) is removed from the SWIFT system, all of its foreign exchange trading businesses will be interrupted.

Currently, although China has established the Cross-Border Interbank Payment System (CIPS) for the renminbi, almost all countries, including China, rely on the Society for Worldwide Interbank Financial Telecommunication (SWIFT) for message transmission services in cross-border payments. As the U.S. dollar remains the most important reserve currency, pricing currency, and investment currency, for any transactions in U.S. dollars, whether in trade or investment, the final clearing

Table 5.2 The development history of SWIFT

1970–1979	1980–1989	1990–1999	2000–2009	After 2010
In 1973, due to the needs of international trade and finance, SWIFT was established. By the end of 1979, a total of 239 members from 15 countries had joined SWIFT	The SWIFT community was established, and a central bank was introduced. By the end of 1989, a total of 2814 members from 79 countries had joined SWIFT	With the advancement of technological modernization, the SWIFT inter—bank message transmission system was introduced. By the end of 1999, a total of 6797 members had joined SWIFT	SWIFTNet was introduced, and innovation was enhanced. By the end of 2009, a total of 9281 members from 209 countries had joined SWIFT	It has been developing rapidly. By the end of 2021, a total of 11,000 members from over 200 countries had joined SWIFT

process takes place in the United States. The United States can also monitor other global transaction information systems.

Once the United States initiates financial sanctions and removes an economic entity (market entity) from the Clearing House Interbank Payments System (CHIPS), that entity will be unable to conduct cross-border U.S. dollar transactions. Once the United States severs the connection between a financial institution and the SWIFT system, the cost of message transmission for the institution's cross-border business will increase significantly, or it may even become impossible to conduct such business.

In addition, through its tangible and intangible control over the global financial system in recent years, the United States has established a "financial intimidation system" worldwide based on financial hegemony and extraterritorial jurisdiction. That is, under the pressure of U.S. financial sanctions, financial institutions in other countries dare not have substantial connections with U.S.—sanctioned entities for fear of being added to the sanction list. As a result, the sanctioned institutions are highly likely to become financial islands, creating a chilling effect.

Testing China's Response Ability after Financial Decoupling

The financial sanctions imposed by the United States on Chinese enterprises and individuals are not only one of the "trump cards" played by the U.S. to achieve its goals in the Sino-U.S. trade frictions but also a practical test of China's security defense capabilities and international mobilization capabilities in the economic, financial, and technological fields as the world's second-largest economy. In other words, the United States wants to see to what extent China can counter it, or whether China can operate and develop independently after being detached from the financial system dominated by the United States.

Essentially, financial sanctions are a strategic choice that serves the United States' medium-to-long-term strategic goals towards China. The medium-to-long-term strategic goal of the United States is to lock China's absolute strength and say within the institutionalized hegemony system it controls, and not allow China to have the ability to be on an equal footing with it in terms of economy, technology, trade, finance, and the supply of global public goods.

The United States believes that if it can strike China at the tactical level while China's leverage in the financial field is still being cultivated and is not yet fully developed, it can not only gain real economic benefits but also produce a deterrent effect, and divide China's economic and financial ties with its major trading partners. This, in turn, can delay to a certain extent the process of China's upgrading from a manufacturing and trading power to an industrial and financial powerhouse.

The United States does not want to see China transform its huge financial assets and financial market into financial pricing and settlement capabilities. In particular, the gradual replacement of U.S. dollar-denominated assets by renminbi-denominated assets will undermine the foundation of the U.S. dollar. For the United States, which

Table 5.3 China's banking sector foreign financial assets as of end-March 2019

Currency	U.S. Dollar (USD)	Renminbi (CNY)	Euro (EUR)	Japanese Yen (JPY)	Pound Sterling (GBP)	Swiss Franc (CHF)	Others
Amount (Hundred Million U.S. Dollars)	807.0	119.0	59.2	9.0	6.8	0.7	163.7
Proportion (%)	69.25	10.21	5.08	0.77	0.58	0.06	14.05

Data Source: State Administration of Foreign Exchange of China

attaches great importance to trend changes, it must find ways to disrupt this development trend, and financial sanctions can precisely play an "assisting" role.

As of the end of March 2019, China's external financial assets had exceeded $7381.7 billion, of which external liabilities were $5430.6 billion, and external net assets were $1951.1 billion. By the end of August of the same year, China's reserve assets were $3107.2 billion, accounting for more than 42% of external financial assets. Among them, U.S. dollar-denominated assets accounted for about 51% of reserve assets, and U.S. Treasury bonds accounted for about 38%. The value of U.S. dollar-denominated assets held by China was approximately $1.8 trillion.

In terms of banks' external financial assets, as of the end of March 2019, the external financial assets of China's banking industry were $1165.4 billion. Among them, renminbi-denominated assets were $119 billion, U.S. dollar-denominated assets were $807 billion, accounting for 69.25%, and assets denominated in other currencies were $239.4 billion (Shown in Table 5.3). Evidently, the U.S. dollar dominates China's external financial assets. This has also led to a high degree of dependence on U.S. dollar—denominated assets, with a relatively large risk exposure.

Sanctioned Chinese Enterprises May Become "Isolated Islands"

The financial sanctions imposed by the United States on relevant Chinese banks will not only significantly affect the international business operations of relevant Chinese institutions but also, by creating an "isolation" effect, demonize the international image of these institutions. For relevant listed Chinese enterprises under sanctions, their stock prices may experience panic-driven declines, thus affecting the stability of the stock market and the foreign exchange market.

Once the United States imposes financial sanctions on China, in an extreme scenario, if certain Chinese banks are removed from the Clearing House Interbank Payments System (CHIPS) and their connections with the Society for Worldwide Interbank Financial Telecommunication (SWIFT) system are severed, the U.S. dollar-denominated assets held by China's banking industry will, in a sense, become mere "currency values", unable to be used for settlement or cross-border

U.S. dollar transactions. At that time, the United States may use this as a tool for bargaining with China, putting China in a passive position.

On the other hand, due to the large scale of China's assets in the United States, and the serious asymmetry in the scale of assets that China and the United States hold in each other, with China holding far more U.S. assets than the United States holds Chinese assets, China's financial assets in the United States are vulnerable to being "held hostage".

Once the United States deems that the business operations of Chinese financial institutions pose a threat to U.S. national security, China may fall into the sanction trap set by the United States. According to the extraterritorial jurisdiction regulations of the United States, U.S. courts can exercise jurisdiction over any foreign bank that has branches and conducts business in the United States. Even according to the minimum-contacts principle, even if a Chinese-funded bank has nothing to do with the disputes between the plaintiff and the defendant, as long as the defendant has an account with the Chinese-funded bank, as a third-party assisting in enforcement, the Chinese-funded bank will be involved in the lawsuit, and thus must cooperate and may even be punished.

In recent years, according to the revised U.S. laws, any foreign company that signs contracts denominated in U.S. dollars, or simply sends, receives, stores (or even just transits) emails through servers located in the United States (such as Gmail or Outlook), will fall within the scope of U.S. "extraterritorial jurisdiction". This is something that the Bank of China and related enterprises must guard against.

Although there is a certain level of financial mutually assured destruction (MAD) equilibrium between China and the United States, a systemic financial confrontation between the two countries would seriously damage their respective economic systems and have an irreparable negative impact on the global financial ecosystem. However, for the U.S. government, which has no upper limit and no bottom-line in its actions, if conventional extreme-pressure measures such as imposing additional tariffs cannot quickly achieve short-term goals, financial sanctions and extraterritorial jurisdiction, as tools for the United States to conduct strategic blackmail at a low cost, are fully likely to become important means for the United States to bargain with China. In this regard, China must remain highly vigilant and formulate practical response plans.

Peter Navarro's Fabrications: A Laughingstock Destined for Global Ridicule

In Western countries like the United States, where rational politicians are increasingly scarce and politicians are becoming more and more prevalent, various lies and deceptions under the guise of national interests for individual selfish purposes can easily prevail. Even when lies are exposed, some fabricators can still act with a straight face. Peter Navarro, the chief China policy advisor to former President Trump, is a "remarkable" example of this.

According to reports from multiple U.S. media outlets, after being exposed by an Australian scholar, Navarro finally admitted that the "economist" Ron Vara, who was extremely hostile to China in his books such as *Death by China*, didn't actually exist at all. Instead, the name was derived from rearranging the letters of his own surname "Navarro". However, Navarro showed little remorse for his fabricating behavior. He even brazenly claimed that Ron Vara was his "whimsical pen-name used over the years to express opinions, which had entertainment value rather than being a source of facts", and he exclaimed that "someone has finally discovered this joke that has been hidden for years". Navarro's words and deeds not only vividly illustrate the saying "shameless people fear nothing", but also provide a vivid real-life script for Machiavellianism in the United States in the twenty-first century. His words and deeds coincide with what Mike Pompeo publicly admitted in his speech at Texas A&M University in April 2019: "We lie, we cheat, we steal. We have a whole course that teaches that. That's the glory of the United States' continuous exploration and progress."

In his seventies, Navarro was persistent yet conflicted before joining Trump's policy team. Born into a poor family, he was often mocked by mainstream U.S. economists for not understanding economics. However, Navarro, who holds a Ph.D. from Harvard University and has long taught at the University of California, Irvine, has always been unwilling to be mediocre. He knew that to stand out in the complex U.S. political arena, he had to be bold and outrageous in his words and deeds, which would increase his chances of seizing opportunities. Therefore, after careful consideration, Navarro targeted China, a country with a booming national strength.

Navarro has written 13 best- selling books, three of which are related to China. All three books share a common theme: using various sensational means to accuse China of being the main cause of job losses in the U.S. manufacturing industry and alleging that China manipulates its currency. In his most well-known anti-China book, *Death by China*, Navarro claimed that China poses a deadly threat to the United States. He slandered China as a hub for producing defective products, not only expanding its military power and conducting extensive espionage activities against the United States, but also being incompatible with the United States in terms of political systems. More seriously, in the second part of the book, he portrayed Sino-U.S. trade as a weapon that destroys U.S. job opportunities; in the fifth part, he directly labeled China as an evil "currency manipulator", claiming that China deprives U.S. national interests by manipulating the exchange rate of the renminbi and that this is the root cause of the unequal and unfair trade relationship between China and the United States.

Navarro's "deadly" views and propositions have found some resonance among far-right U.S. elites and the general public. Because his series of views on Sino--U.S. economic and trade relations coincided with those of Trump, Navarro got a "once-in-a-lifetime" opportunity and became the top White House advisor who was "best at turning Trump's intuitive ideas into policies". However, this "ultra-hawk" in Washington has been frequently mocked and refuted by mainstream media such as *The Wall Street Journal* due to his common-sense errors in understanding issues like the impact of additional tariffs on U.S. enterprises and households, and even confusing tariffs with value-added tax.

Even so, in the eyes of some Washington policymakers with extreme views on China policy, whether Navarro's policy recommendations are supported by sufficient facts is not important. What matters is that his "patriotic enthusiasm" and "loyalty" have never wavered. This has made Navarro's position relatively stable despite much criticism. In fact, during the past Sino-U.S. consultations on economic and trade issues, Navarro's extreme pressure-exerting and ultra-tough attitude, along with his unconventional negotiation ideas, have often become the dominant opinions in the White House, and sometimes his views on China were even tougher than those of Robert Lighthizer.

From his works and interviews, it can be seen that Navarro's goal for the rest of his life is to do everything in his power to crush China. Even if he fails to achieve this goal, he at least wants to disrupt China's pace of catching up with the United States and slow down China's rise, so as to prevent China, based on its manufacturing industry, from seizing the territory of the U.S. dollar by enhancing its trade value chain and financial competitiveness.

The short-term goal of his strong advocacy for launching a trade war against China and continuously exerting extreme pressure is to reduce the scale of the U.S. trade deficit with China and even achieve bilateral import-export balance, cutting off China's access to "real economic benefits" from the United States. The medium-term goal is to sever China's technological ties with developed countries, forcibly remove China from the global high-end value chain, and even "eliminate" China's prospects of integrating into the global high-end value chain. The long-term goal is to confine the international role of the renminbi within the scope of the U.S. dollar system and turn China, which has already become the world's second-largest economy, into a super economic vassal of the United States.

However, today, with the trend of global economic integration impossible to be artificially blocked or reversed, the zero-sum game mindset has been fully proven to be harmful. Only extremely radical people would believe that Sino-U.S. economic and trade relations can be completely decoupled and would be willing to go to great lengths to bring the annual bilateral trade volume of approximately $600 billion and the two-way investment volume of approximately $250 billion between China and the United States to a standstill. (The bilateral goods import and export volumes between China and the United States before and after the Sino-U.S. trade frictions in 2018 are shown in Fig. 5.2.) Far-sighted politicians and business leaders in both China and the United States should be aware that whether it is about global economic growth, financial market stability, the reconstruction of new trade rules, the development of forward-looking technologies, or the effective resolution of the complex economic problems in China and the United States, close cooperation between the two countries is indispensable.

Navarro, who has backed himself into a corner, might as well make a good comparison with Lawrence Summers, who became the youngest tenured professor in the history of Harvard University at the age of 28 and later served as the 8th Chairman of the U.S. National Economic Council, and carefully sort out the latter's thinking on economic policies towards China. The 71st U.S. Treasury Secretary, whose very being is steeped in economic genes, although he is also reluctant to see

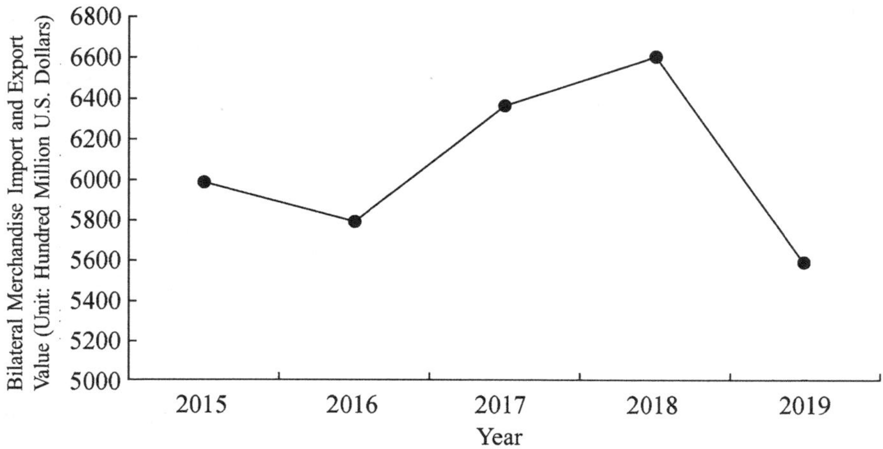

Fig. 5.2 China–U.S. bilateral merchandise import and export value before and after the 2018 trade frictions. Data Source: China Customs

the rapid growth of China's economic and financial strength in his heart, firmly opposes taking extreme and irrational measures against China. This is because China is neither the former Soviet Union nor today's Iran. Instead, it is a super emerging economy that has already been deeply integrated into the global division of labor in industry, technology, trade, and finance. When it comes to handling various connections between the United States and China, one must first rely on sufficient information, accurate data, and a suitable analytical framework to conduct cost-benefit accounting. This is the prerequisite for rational decision-making. Otherwise, relying on lies and fabrications to support the logic of economic policies towards China is doomed to make a huge fool of itself.

The United States, which has the largest number of Nobel laureates in Economics, should make a rational choice now.

Chapter 6
Modern Monetary Theory Cannot Save the U.S. Economy

The Federal Reserve's Market-Salvage Measures in Response to the COVID-19 Shock: Characteristics and Theoretical Analysis

Under the constraints of highly interconnected international financial markets, where the normal development of production, services and trade in various countries highly dependent on the stability of the industrial chain and supply chain, the COVID-19 epidemic, as a major public health and security event, has unleashed systematic risks and faced mankind with its gravest challenge since World War II.

The United States and European countries utterly failed to capitalize on the critical time window that China won from January to February 2020 to fight against the COVID-19 outbreak, resulting in the rampage of the epidemic in the world since March. Both the number of confirmed cases and fatalities skyrocketed beyond all projections. The rapid spread of the epidemic has caused production and service shutdowns in various countries in the short term, thereby transmitting panic to financial markets.

In March 2020, in order to staunch market sentiment, prevent liquidity depletion and the bankruptcy of large financial institutions, which could trigger a systemic financial crisis, the Federal Reserve quickly intervened after the sharp decline of the three major stock indexes and launched an aggressive "zero interest rates + unlimited QE" policy package. The speed and intensity of the Federal Reserve's rescue efforts are unprecedented, far exceeding the policy framework of traditional monetary theory and general market expectations, and also attracting widespread attention from the international community.

To study the policy logic and relevant characteristics of the Federal Reserve's rescue plan and its relationship with the recently controversial Modern Monetary Theory (MMT), and analyze the reasons for the sharp turbulence in the US financial market after the spread of the COVID-19 epidemic are very important. It is also particularly necessary to study the medium and long-term risks of the Federal

Y. Zhang, *Addressing Uncertainty*, Understanding China,
https://doi.org/10.1007/978-981-92-2692-4_6

Reserve's implementation of Modern Monetary Theory, taking into account its rise Modern Monetary Theory and the impact of its policy proposals.

The Impact of COVID-19 on U.S. Financial Markets

Like the 2008 financial crisis, the COVID-19 pandemic, as a "black swan" event, has its sudden or unexpected nature. It is really difficult for human beings to achieve accurate early warning and minimize losses through effective response mechanisms. Nouriel Roubini, known as the "Dr. Doom," has been warning in recent years that the chasm between financial markets and the real economy is becoming so perilously wide it could trigger another global financial crisis. Worse still once a financial crisis erupts, policy makers will find themselves shackled by dwindling tools. Because returning to unconventional monetary policies may be hindered by the inflated balance sheets of central banks around the world. In 2019, when the overall performance of the global stock market was relatively outstanding, although some research institutions occasionally issued risk warnings, few people truly paid attention to the warnings of market bears.

Fueled by a tidal wave of loose liquidity, trade patterns reshaping, and the successive hype of related technology concepts, the US stock market has been surging all the way up, and the Dow Jones Industrial Average reached a historical high of 29,568 on February 12, 2020. But as the epidemic rapidly spread in the United States after March, the stock market, which was originally not sensitive to it, continued to experience rising panic. The three major stock indices in the United States fell into bear market territory in a mere month, and experienced four circuit breakers within 10 days. On the other hand, the Chicago Board Options Exchange Volatility Index (VIX), the market's fear gauge, hit a record high of 82.69 on March 16, surpassing the peak value of 80.74 on November 21, 2008. The yield of treasury bond fluctuated significantly. The seismic panic effect of the spread of the COVID-19 on the financial market exploded into the most significant external risk impact in the global economic and financial operation in 2020.

Statistics show that by March 31st, the Dow Jones Industrial Average, one of the three major stock indexes in the United States, fell by 13.74%, marking the largest monthly decline since October 2008, and on a quarterly basis, a sharp drop of 23.2%. The S&P 500 index also recorded its largest monthly and quarterly decline since the 2008 international financial crisis. The Nasdaq Composite Index, shielded relatively strong by its focuses on technology stocks, still plunged quarterly decline to 14.18% high.

Under the impact of the epidemic, the inverted yield curve of US government bonds, which is one of the most accurate predictive indicators for measuring economic recession in the United States, has reappeared. On March 9, the yield of 3-month US treasury bonds was 0.481, while the yield of 10-year treasury bond was 0.477, which is an important signal of market panic. In the 50 years prior to this, the inverted curve indicated the approaching pace of economic recession. On March 25, the yields of 1 month and 3-month US treasury bonds fell to negative values. In the Asian trading session on March 26, the yields of 1-month and 3-month US treasury bonds, which are generally regarded as cash by investors, hit −0.046% and −0.056%. It can be seen that the liquidity released by the Federal Reserve has not achieved the expected effect.

The cataclysmic volatility that gripped US financial market in March 2020 bore eerie parallels to the panic selling and stock collapse of September 2008s global financial crisis, but with apocalyptic differences in scale and severity.

By comparing the performance of the three major U.S. stock indexes in September 2008 and March 2020 (see Figs. 6.1, 6.2, and 6.3), it can be found that the intensity of the U.S. stock market's response to the COVID-19 greatly exceeded the impact of the financial crisis triggered by the bankruptcy of Lehman Brothers in 2008 on the stock market. After the outbreak of the 2008 international financial crisis, although the three major stock indexes in the United States experienced a sharp decline, they did not trigger the circuit breaker mechanism. The US stock market has endured a total of five circuit breakers so far, occurring on October 27, 1997, as well as March 9, March 12, March 16, and March 18, 2020. Over just 10 days of March 2020, there were four consecutive circuit breakers, with the one on March 16th causing the most severe market panic: the circuit breaker was triggered again at the opening, and the Dow Jones Industrial Average fell 2997.10 points at the close, making a decrease of 12 93%, setting a record for single day point drops in history. The Nasdaq Composite Index and S&P 500 Index fell by 12.32% and 11.98%, indicating the degree of panic selling in the market. The successive circuit breakers of the three major stock indexes have dealt a heavy blow to the confidence of the US economy, leading to the most dangerous situation in the US financial market since the 2008 international financial crisis.

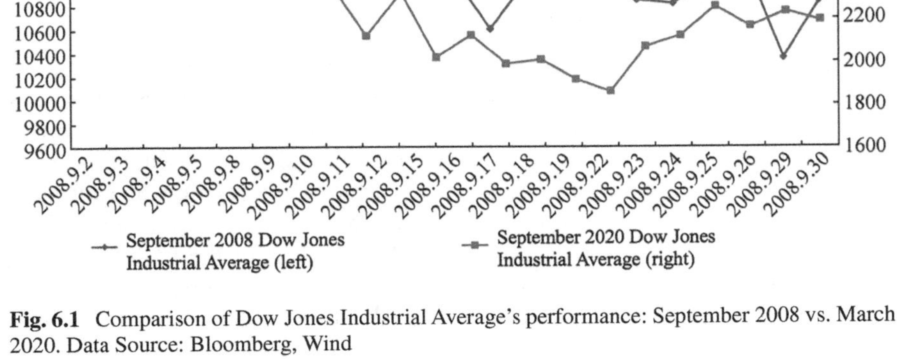

Fig. 6.1 Comparison of Dow Jones Industrial Average's performance: September 2008 vs. March 2020. Data Source: Bloomberg, Wind

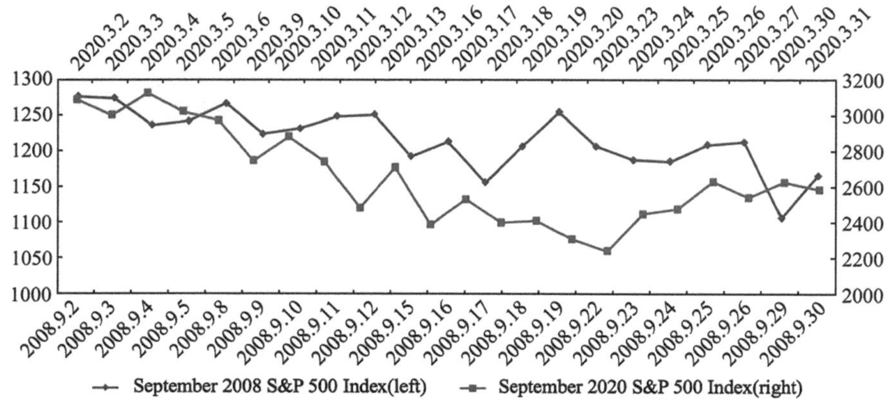

Fig. 6.2 Comparison of the S&P 500 index performance: September 2008 vs. March 2020. Data Source: Bloomberg, Wind

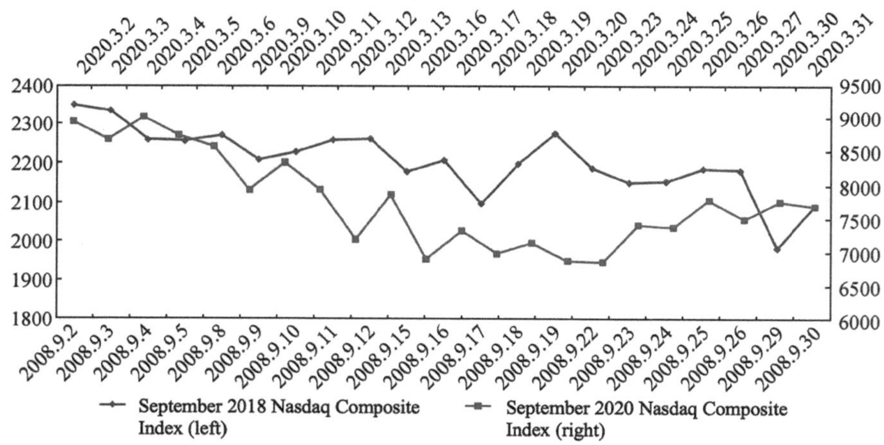

Fig. 6.3 Comparison of the NASDAQ composite index performance: September 2008 vs. March 2020. Data Source: Bloomberg, Wind

The sharp decline and repeated shocks of the US stock market in March 2020 are both the market's response to the massive uncertainty brought about by the spread of the COVID-19 in the US and even the world, and the government's ineffective response. It also reflects investors' concern that the bubble of economic prosperity in the United States, which has been mainly achieved through credit expansion since the 2008 international financial crisis, may burst at any time. From the cyclical perspective of the stock market, even without the impact of the COVID-19 epidemic, the bull market in the US stock market, which has lasted for 11 years, may face huge adjustment pressure. The tight liquidity in the capital market, the sharp drop in oil prices, and the government's inadequate response to the epidemic are also important factors contributing to the severe turbulence in the market. The sharp fall of the three major stock indexes is more likely related to the fact that the real economic growth and industrial technological progress of the United States since the 2008 international financial crisis cannot effectively hedge the financial bubble and the relentless accumulation of financial risks.

Characteristic Analysis of the Fed's Market-Salvage Measures

The sharp decline of the three major stock indexes in the United States not only caught global investors off guard, but also greatly shocked the Federal Reserve. This global super central bank, established in 1913 and long playing the role of lender of last resort in critical moments, introduced a series of very aggressive market rescue plans in response to the impact of the COVID-19 epidemic in the short 4 weeks from March 3 to March 31. These measures included drastic interest rate cuts and even the adoption of zero interest rate, zero reserve rate policies, unlimited quantitative easing monetary policy, unlimited repo operations and other audacious market rescue measures. Beyond this, the Federal Reserve has also restarted multiple policy tools adopted during the 2008 international financial crisis while creating new market rescue mechanisms. Overall, its efforts, frequency, and determination to rescue the market far exceed those of 2008. The Federal Reserve has also used this opportunity to shift itself from the lender of last resort for commercial banks during periods of economic normalcy, directly to the role of a super commercial bank and ultimate guarantor.

The Federal Reserve's rescue plan, in summary, has the characteristics of unconventional, high yield, and fast pace, closely focusing on the policy logic of stabilizing market sentiment and restoring economic confidence. It strives to inject unlimited liquidity into the market through multiple policy tools and directly purchase various risky assets to curb market panic selling and prevent the transmission of financial assets to the real economy due to irrational depreciation. The purpose is to mend the severely battered US economic and financial system due to the ravages of the COVID-19 as soon as possible, and prevent another Great Depression in the United States with the help of fiscal policy.

Firstly, break through the limitations of traditional monetary theory and use unconventional monetary policies to hedge against market uncertainty.

In response to the 2008 international financial crisis, the Federal Reserve broke through the policy proposition of traditional monetary theory and adopted unconventional monetary policies to address market risks. Generally speaking, the traditional regulatory mechanism of the Federal Reserve mainly includes two aspects: one is to regulate the target interest rate, mainly by buying and selling US short-term Treasury bonds (with commercial banks); The second is to lend directly to banks. However, during the 2008 crisis, the Federal Reserve found that traditional monetary control mechanisms had little effect and instead adopted bolder and more aggressive policies, including credit rescue mechanisms such as the Commercial Paper Financing Facility (CPFF), Primary Dealer Credit Facility (PDCF), Asset-Backed Commercial Paper Money Market Mutual Fund Liquidity Facility (AMLF), Money Market Investor Financing Facility (MMIFF). Among them, CPFF is regarded as a "miracle tool" by "spreading money on a flying helicopter" for rescuing the market by directly providing credit to non-financial enterprises and households. This mechanism utilizes Special Purpose Vehicles (SPVs), to purchase commercial paper directly from qualified issuers using funds. From October 2008 to early 2010, the Federal Reserve purchased a total of $738 billion in commercial paper, which to some extent helped stabilize market sentiment.

In its rescue plan to deal with the COVID-19, the Federal Reserve not only reactivated a number of policy tools during the 2008 international financial crisis, but also put forward more bold and unconventional policy tools. The most representative one was that the Federal Reserve held an emergency meeting on March 15, 2020 and announced a 100 basis point reduction in the federal funds rate to 0–0.25%, and announced that it will purchase $500 billion more of US treasury bond and $200 billion of mortgage-backed securities of financial institutions in the next few months, and implement the policy combination of "zero interest rate + QE". On March 23rd, it was announced that an unlimited quantitative easing monetary policy (QE) would be implemented, with unlimited on-demand purchases of US Treasury bonds and institutional mortgage-backed securities (MBS). In addition, when necessary, it could directly purchase investment grade corporate bonds (including newly issued and secondary market circulating bonds, with a holding ratio of no more than 10% for a single issuer), as well as mortgage-backed securities for student loans, car loans, credit card loans, and small business loans, with no upper limit on the total purchase quantity. This is the first time that the Federal Reserve has purchased assets that are not subject to stock or liquidity restrictions. In addition, the Federal Reserve established two new liquidity instruments on March 23rd: the Primary Market Corporate Credit Facility (PMCCF) and the Secondary Market Corporate Credit Facility (SMCCF). These two tools are aimed at corporate bonds, with the former used for issuing new bonds and loans, and the latter used to provide liquidity for outstanding corporate bonds. This indicates that the Federal Reserve can use all necessary policy tools to stabilize the market.

Despite the various unconventional rescue measures launched by the Federal Reserve in March 2020, which did not receive immediate positive reactions from the financial market, with the Dow Jones Industrial Average even fell by 12.93% the day after announcing the launch of the "zero interest rate + QE" policy combination on March, but from the perspective of the market reaction mechanism of monetary policy itself, the subsequent sharp decline in the market was not caused by the Federal Reserve's excessive monetary policy, that is, there is no "panic spiral" between financial markets and monetary policy itself. Rather, the huge uncertainty brought about by the spread and evolution of the epidemic was the true culprit behind the market turmoil.

Secondly, maximize the function of the US dollar and inject liquidity into the world through reckless credit expansion.

As the actual lender of last resort globally, the Federal Reserve holds privileges such as commercial paper financing tools granted under Section 13 item 3 of the Federal Reserve Act and primary dealer credit facility tools, namely emergency loans. Congress also authorized it to directly purchase corporate bonds to provide a backing function to the market, while in times of sustained turbulence in the international market, liquidity depletion, and potential systemic risks, fully leverages the function of the US dollar as the main international reserve currency. For example, injecting a large amount of liquidity funds into the market through the purchase of medium-and long-term like treasury bond, to deal with problems such as payment defaults in the international market and the shortage of US dollar liquidity.

During the 2008 international financial crisis, in order to address the shortage of US dollar liquidity in many foreign banks at that time, the Federal Reserve signed temporary US dollar liquidity swap agreements with the European Central Bank, the Bank of England, the Bank of Japan, the Swiss National Bank, the Bank of Canada, and other central banks. This allowed them to exchange US dollars in their own currency with the Federal Reserve in the event of a shortage of US dollars, and agreed to swap back at the same exchange rate in the future and pay a certain amount of interest. From the 2008 international financial crisis to the establishment of the long-term swap mechanism in 2013, the Federal Reserve provided nearly $600 billion in currency swaps to foreign central banks through the swap mechanism, forming a global foreign exchange swap network centered around the US dollar and the Federal Reserve. This continuous injection of US dollar liquidity into the global central bank system not only resolved the US dollar shortage, but also strengthened the position of the US dollar in the international monetary system, and to some extent replaced the IMF's rescue mechanism. At the institutional level, this "interbank QE" enables the Federal Reserve and its strategic partners (foreign central banks) to create any amount of currency. Through this process, the Federal Reserve has fortified its role as the global lender of last resort.

The Federal Reserve implements an unlimited QE policy with the aim of resolving the liquidity crisis in the credit and bond markets. Because the size of these two markets is much larger than that of the stock market, only when the crisis in the former is resolved can the latter be stabilized. The Federal Reserve's move not only replaces the original risk management functions and market mechanisms of the credit and bond markets, but also makes investors anticipate the possibility of more aggressive negative interest rate policies in the future. This move actually indicates that the Federal Reserve is implementing Modern Monetary Theory policies, namely long-term zero interest rates, monetization of fiscal deficits, and using tax policies to regulate inflation.

The Federal Reserve has initiated four rounds of quantitative easing, with the first three rounds lasting 6 years from November 2008 to November 2014. From the perspective of policy effects, the first round of signal effects is the most obvious, the second round begins to weaken, and there is already an expectation of interest rate hikes in the third round. The Federal Reserve has set the intensity of its fourth round of quantitative easing policy to be unlimited, indicating that its policy decision no longer considers the rapid expansion of its balance sheet as a major risk, but rather believes that the US economy is facing great difficulties and the risk of the financial system failing to function properly also a severe economic recession. It is necessary to hedge against market collapse at any time by releasing massive liquidity.

Finally, with the priority of American interests, it will ensure to safeguard the stability of US financial market with unprecedented efforts.

The Federal Reserve learned the lesson from its sluggish and overconfident response to the 2007 subprime crisis. On March 3, 2020, when the impact of the COVID-19 on the financial market was not particularly serious, it immediately took strong emergency action, and constantly improved the level, intensity and breadth of response according to the subsequent development and changes of the epidemic, showing its determination to rescue the market vigorously at all costs. Despite some market participants viewing the relevant measures as overreactions, the US financial market, especially the stock market, is at the heart of the global financial market and is also a barometer of global asset prices, given the special nature of the epidemic, and from a global perspective. If the Federal Reserve had not immediately taken drastic emergency measures to stabilize the US market, investors' panic about the spread of the epidemic would rapidly ferment in the US market and spread globally, which may trigger a systemic financial crisis.

The Federal Reserve's policies, including unlimited bond purchases, the creation of special financing instruments with approval from the Treasury Department under Section 13 item 3 of the Federal Reserve Act, and the establishment of temporary repurchase facilities and other special relief measures, are based on unprecedented efforts to ensure the stability of the US financial market and the international status of the US dollar, prioritizing the protection of US interests as the main focus of policy implementation.

For example, the Federal Reserve established the Foreign and International Monetary Authorities Repo Facility(FIM Repo facility) on March 31, 2020, which is applicable to overseas monetary authorities and international institutions. According to the statement of the Federal Reserve, foreign central banks and international financial institutions holding FIMA accounts in the New York Federal Reserve are allowed to use this tool to pledge their own U.S. treasury securities, so as to exchange U.S. dollar liquidity from the Federal Reserve and use it within its jurisdiction. The interest rate level is IOER+25 basis points, that is, 0.35%. This facility was launched on April 6th and will be maintained for at least 6 months.

From the perspective of the policy starting point of the Federal Reserve, the introduction of this tool is to provide an alternative temporary source of US dollar funds to prevent related entities from selling US treasury bonds in the market, thus helping to support the smooth operation of the US treasury bond market. On the other hand, this tool can also help alleviate pressure on the global dollar financing market, along with other dollar liquidity swap lines established by the Federal Reserve and central banks of various countries. However, as far as the target of this policy is concerned, it is actually aimed at China, Japan and other major creditor countries that hold large-scale U.S. treasury bond. Because collateral (US treasury bonds) is required to obtain dollars through repo, central banks without large-scale reserves won't be able to use it. The introduction of this policy by the Federal

Reserve has to some extent prevented major creditor countries from selling off US dollar assets on a large scale in the market and causing a shortage of US dollar liquidity. The Federal Reserve has also used this tool to strengthen its position as the lender of last resort for central banks holding US bonds, indicating that it remains the world's most liquid releasing super central bank, while other central banks play a role as commercial banks to some extent.

Theoretical Analysis of the Fed's Market-Salvage Measures

The aggressive rescue measures launched by the Federal Reserve since March 2020, from a monetary policy perspective, are highly consistent with many policy proposals of the controversial Modern Monetary Theory (MMT) in recent years, indicating that the Federal Reserve has, in effect, implemented MMT on a large scale. If this theory becomes a policy paradigm for central banks around the world to respond to systemic financial risks and economic recession shocks through the policy practice of the Federal Reserve, it will not only have a profound impact on the development of the US economy and finance, but also affect the medium and long- term trajectory of the global economy and finance.

Firstly, the rise, policy proposals, and evaluation of Modern Monetary Theory.

Among various schools of Western economics, Modern Monetary Theory, which emerged in the 1990s, initially garnered little attention. Its research was centered at the Department of Economics at the University of Missouri Kansas City and the Levi's Institute of Economics at Bard College in the United States. The main representatives were M. Forstater from the University of Missouri Kansas City, L. Randall Wray from Bard College, Warren Mosler from the University of Connecticut, and Stephanie Kelton from the State University of New York at Stony Brook. Although they branded their theory as "modern", its theoretical origins can be traced back to the state theory of money proposed by German historian Georg F. Knapp in the 1920s, and to some extent, integrating economic theories such as A. Mitchell Innes' endogenous monetary theory, Abba Lerner's functional fiscal theory, Hyman Minsky's financial instability hypothesis, and Wynne Godley's sectoral equilibrium approach.

The reason why MMT has continuously expanded its influence and received attention from central banks, economists, and market participants in recent years is mainly due to the problem of "insufficient capabilities" faced by central banks in various countries, including the Federal Reserve, after the outbreak of the 2008 international financial crisis. Furthermore, in response to financial crises and economic downturns, a policy model of debt expansion was adopted to drive economic recovery and stimulate economic growth, but this resulted in a rapid expansion of government debt.

After the 2008 international financial crisis, the United States, the European Union, and Japan implemented large-scale quantitative easing policies, which led to a significant increase in fiscal deficits and inflationary pressures, and debt risks continued to rise. The monetary authorities of the United States, the European Union, and Japan are facing increasing pressure from society, and are believed to be pushing their countries towards an irrational and prosperous path of debt-free prosperity. In this context, MMT provides a certain theoretical defense for the debt driven economic growth models implemented by the United States, the European Union, and Japan with its particularly eye-catching and bold viewpoints.

The core viewpoints and policy proposals of MMT are encapsulated in Randall Wray's three works: *Understanding Modern Currency: The Key to Full Employment and Price Stability* published (1998), *Modern Money Theory 101* published (2012), and *Modern Money Theory: A Primer on Macroeconomics for Sovereign Monetary Systems* published (2017). Its main viewpoint is that currency is not tied to any commodity but serves as a government debt instrument used for issuing bonds and collecting taxes. Finance can also play a role in creating currency. The government first creates currency through fiscal expenditure, and then recovers it through taxation. Therefore, the purpose of taxation is not to provide funds for government spending, but to promote the issuance and circulation of currency. As long as the government borrows in its own currency and the inflation rate is not out of control, there is no need to worry about the deficit problem. Because the government can repay debts by printing money, and borrowing local currency debt will not trigger government bankruptcy.

In general, in the view of modern monetary theorists, as long as a government's debt is entirely issued in its own currency and the government controls the monetary system, in the context of moderate inflation, the government can repay its debts by continuously printing money without causing any adverse consequences, and the sovereign state can achieve eternal bankruptcy.

In terms of policy choices and advocacy, MMT advocates monetizing fiscal deficits to defend government debt. It believes that government deficits not only increase the net financial assets of the private sector, but also increase the total financial wealth of the public, leading to income growth and increased investment expenditures. Taxation, government spending, and borrowing are all means of creating and reducing the sovereign money supply, with the aim of maintaining total expenditure at a predetermined level. As for the fiscal deficit, it should not become a hard constraint on government spending. There is no good or bad between surplus and deficit, it depends on the level of private sector expenditure. The government controls the level of inflation, and inflation will not be linked to price increases until full employment is achieved. After reaching a predetermined level of employment, excess purchasing power can be drained through tax increases. In terms of the relationship between monetary policy and fiscal policy, MMT advocates that the central bank directly purchases treasury bond from the Ministry of Finance to support the fiscal deficit, which negates the independence of the central bank. Finally, the government needs to establish a "final employer" program for those who are unemployed, providing jobs for anyone who wants to work.

These propositions and policy proposals of MMT are quite tempting, not only catering to the monetary policy preferences of the United States in recent years, but also providing a strong defense for the economic development model of the United

States living beyond its means. Therefore, the theory has received widespread attention from the political, financial, and economic circles in the United States, but also caused huge controversy. The left-wing of the Democratic Party in the United States is an important supporting force for MMT. In their view, Modern Monetary Theory provides a theoretical basis for large-scale fiscal expenditure proposals such as the "Green New Deal" and universal healthcare insurance. Ray Dalio, founder of Bridgewater Fund, is also a supporter of MMT. What's more, the Republican government also advocates supporting MMT, although it has not been publicly stated. Federal Reserve Chairman Jerome Powell explicitly opposes the policy proposition of MMT and does not agree with the idea of unconstrained government finances. While former US Treasury Secretary Lawrence Summers, Kenneth Rogoff (former Chief Economist of the IMF), Paul R. Krugman (Nobel laureate in economics), Warren E. Buffett (CEO of Berkshire Hathaway), Laurence D. Fink (Chairman and CEO of BlackRock), and others have explicitly opposed it. As for Chinese scholars, they have also increased their attention to MMT and judged and even criticized it recently.

It is not surprising that MMT, which essentially belongs to non-mainstream macroeconomics and advocates "rebellious" policies, has been questioned by mainstream Western economics. Because Western mainstream economics, based on neoclassical economics, has always advocated for a balance between fiscal and monetary neutrality, even though the balance itself is a policy goal that is difficult to achieve in the real world.

However, the widespread critique of MMT by the global economic community also stems from its huge logical flaws. The policy logic of the government continuously expanding debt without facing bankruptcy was proven to have great flaws in the European debt crisis that erupted in 2009. Especially in open economies, the government cannot simply issue unlimited money without bearing the consequences, as this is only possible under the condition that the government can only borrow local currency debt. In today's world, theoretically only the United States can repay foreign debts in its own currency. But even the United States needs to set a debt ceiling. From 1940 to 2019, the United States raised the debt ceiling a total of 85 times, averaging at least once a year. The debt ceiling was raised from 10.6 trillion US dollars at the end of December 2008 to 23.2 trillion in 2020 (See Fig. 6.4). This also illustrates from another perspective that even the United States, which has the strongest economic strength, has boundaries in its government debt and cannot expand credit indefinitely.

In terms of research paradigm, although Modern Monetary Theory draws on macroeconomic models such as consistency of deposit and flow to enhance academic legitimacy, overall, it is considered difficult to withstand economic policy tests due to the lack of rigorous logical deduction and mathematical model expression.

Secondly, the Federal Reserve's market-salvage measures are actually promoting Modern Monetary Theory.

Although MMT has been opposed by Powell and many mainstream economists in the United States have "laughed it off", the reality is that the Federal Reserve

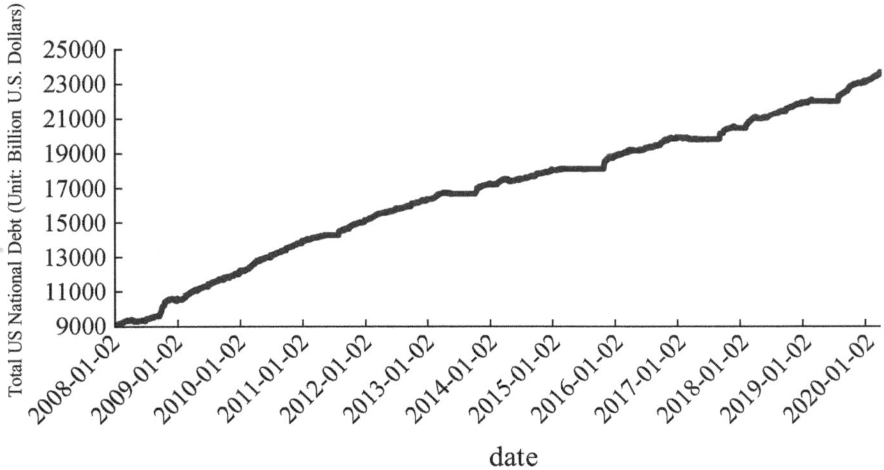

Fig. 6.4 Changes in total U.S. National debt since 2008 (as of January 2, 2020). Data Source: Wind

appears to oppose it and its international counterparts such as the Bank of Japan strongly deny using it as a basis for monetary policy implementation, but it is getting closer and closer to MMT in specific policy practice.

The COVID-19 has provided a good opportunity for the Federal Reserve to merge with MMT. On the one hand, supporters of MMT firmly believe that the United States, with its monopoly on the issuance of the US dollar, can to some extent rely on fiscal spending to achieve the dual mission of full employment and inflation goals; On the other hand, the Federal Reserve also seems to be encouraged by the fact that the size of US treasury bond is rising year by year without inflation. Therefore, when dealing with the major impact of the COVID-19, in order to stabilize the market, the Federal Reserve not only turned on the money tap again, but even directly purchased any risk assets that might trigger the crisis. According to Powell, the Federal Reserve will continue to use all tools to maintain extremely low interest rates until the US economy begins to recover. In short, as long as systemic collapse can be avoided, the Federal Reserve will not reject any feasible market-support or bailout mechanism.

The Federal Reserve's implementation of monetary policy marked by unlimited QE not only breaks through the constraints of traditional monetary theory, but also fully embraces MMT policy proposition. For example, in order to stimulate economic development and stabilize social employment, as long as the government borrows in its own currency and inflation rate remains under control, there is no need to worry about deficit problems. The government can totally repay its debts by printing money. The central bank can transcend the traditional restrictions of "lender of last resort" and "zero lower bound", and if necessary, implement a "negative interest rate" policy to directly purchase structured bonds issued by the government at zero interest rates, or directly issue loans to specific objects in need of support such as small enterprises. However, whether the above-mentioned radical rescue policies will deliver the anticipated outcomes still needs time to be tested.

The 2008 international financial crisis and a series of economic policy practices by various countries in response to the crisis have proven that, under the constraint of the inability of the real economy to achieve endogenous growth, relying mainly on the continuous expansion of credit supply cannot sustain economic confidence in the long run. The "no debt, no joy" policy in developed countries has led to a large-scale fourth wave of debt worldwide.

At the beginning of 2020, the World Bank issued the aforementioned warning in its Global Economic Outlook. The Global Debt Monitor report by the International Finance Association shows that in 2021, the global debt scale reached 303 trillion US dollars, accounting for 351% of global GDP, setting a new historical high. Among them, the scale of US debt exceeded 30 trillion US dollars for the first time, accounting for 130% of GDP. The scale of Japan's debt has reached 12.69 trillion US dollars, accounting for 25.96% of GDP, with a debt ratio nearly twice that of the United States, and the debt levels of various sectors, from the household sector to the government sector, from the financial enterprise sector to the non-financial enterprise sector, have reached worrying levels.

Economic recession and financial crisis are essentially closely related to a significant decrease in labor productivity and capital return rate. In the past decade, the private sector in European and American countries has been accelerating deleveraging overall, but governments have been continuously increasing leverage to avoid excessive demand contraction. Major economies around the world have seen varying degrees of credit and money creation being used to purchase existing assets rather than productive investment. Debt expansion is not only an important driver of a country's economic growth, but also might sow the seeds of a new crisis. The IMF has repeatedly warned that high debt ratios may not necessarily trigger an economic crisis, but countries should no longer prioritize using fiscal stimulus to boost demand.

Over 70 years since the establishment of the Bretton Woods system, it has proven that linking the security of the global economy and financial system to the United States is not only an opportunity given to the United States by history, but also a dangerous logic.

In a sense, it is the United States that has kidnapped the world economy and finance. The deep-seated problems facing the US economy cannot be completely solved with quick acting drugs. The Federal Reserve surged its balance sheet by $2 trillion in just 1 month in March 2020, and this unrestrained release of liquidity actually placed the global economy in greater uncertainty and risk.

Conclusion and Policy Recommendations

Just as the resurgence of "depression economics" follows its inherent logic, in 2020, when global economic confidence is highly dependent on the transmission of financial market prices, the US financial market quickly fell into a bear market and repeatedly fluctuated under the impact of the COVID-19. The reasons are not only related to the US's weak response to the COVID-19, or the Federal Reserve's relatively insufficient ability to control complex financial situations and the expected uncertainty brought by the rapid spread of the epidemic, but also because the actual economic growth and industrial technological progress of the United States since the 2008 international financial crisis cannot effectively hedge the accumulation of financial foam and financial risks.

In recent years, emerging technologies represented by big data, artificial intelligence, and their industrial applications in the United States, although promising, have not generated global economies of scale. The long-term excessively loose monetary policy of the United States has led to the spread of poor investments around the world. Although the corresponding economic data looks good, these are actually misleading data that precisely conceal the fragile side of the US economy.

The emergence of MMT and its policy impact have indeed brought conceptual breakthroughs and even a certain degree of subversion to the traditional monetary theory framework regarding the functional positioning of central banks, monetary policy objectives, and protection of central bank independence. On the surface, the Federal Reserve, which opposes Modern Monetary Theory, directly pursued it in the face of the impact of the COVID-19, which is far beyond the expectation of the economic community, and is also a topic that deserves special attention and research.

The COVID-19 is a major external shock event that is difficult to find a baseline scenario, and it is also an important test of the resilience of countries' economic and financial systems. In responding to the COVID-19, the logic of macro policies should not only focus on eliminating the source of panic, and fight against the invisible impact of the virus with stronger prevention and control efforts, but also need to stabilize market expectations through sustained policy implementation, especially structural reforms. Whether it is the Federal Reserve or central banks of various countries, they should not only be highly vigilant about the possibility of liquidity depletion in the market at any time, but also truly connect the pain points of the market and enterprises through policy transmission mechanisms, and release policy dividends including structural tax cuts. History has proven that the widespread activation of micro subject innovation and business endowments is an important reliance for hedging systemic risks. To truly stabilize market confidence, it is not only necessary to rescue those "too big to fail" enterprises, but also to deeply cultivate the development of the real economy from the strategic height of activating effective economic growth, and repair the already imbalanced global economic ecology.

Faced with an increasingly complex external environment, especially the constantly changing international economic and financial situation, China must be proactive and closely monitor potential major risks. The theoretical community should also maintain close attention to MMT and its policy impact. Generally speaking, the consequence of excessive use of monetary policy is the continuous expansion of debt scale. It is very important for central banks to maintain the instrumental rationality of currency issuance. After all, any bubble formation traces back to monetary policy. Without sustained and stable growth of the real economy, building a resilient and robust financial system is impossible. Only economic growth based on knowledge and driven by technological innovation or revolution is sustainable and effective. China must avoid embracing MMT as a theoretical guide for economic development, and must steering clear of irrational prosperity track driven by debt expansion. It must avoid falling into a vicious cycle of credit expansion supporting economic confidence.

America's Massive Stimulus Is Like "Pouring Oil on Fire"

In May 2021, while I was participating in a television debate program on US inflation, a former senior Federal Reserve economist made the judgment right on the spot that "there is no sign of inflation erupting in the United States at all". There is no doubt that this judgment is quite staggering, given the increasingly evident inflationary signs in the United States, and the abnormal state of the entire economic system. The economy was fragmented under the impact of the COVID-19, while the stock market was enthusiastic under the support of massive liquidity, yet offering minimal support to the real economy. This irrational prosperity only allows mainly a few powerful participants to benefit.US President Biden signed a COVID-19 rescue bill at a total of 1.9 trillion US dollars in March 2021, providing about half of Americans with checks of about $1400 per person. While some people who received the check used the money to improve their personal balance sheet, most spent it on consumption, which significantly contributed to a 9.8% surge in US retail sales in March. But the negative effect of this so-called "cheque illusion" and the generous unemployment insurance during the epidemic is that many Americans became reluctant to return to work at all, and nearly three million people petitioned to urge Congress to issue "monthly stimulus checks and regular payments". And once the wishes of the American people cannot be met, the Biden administration's approval rating will inevitably decline, forcing the government to continue releasing liquidity and relief to the market and consumers to maintain relative economic and social stability.

The partial interruption of the global supply chain coupled with the fact that many American residents have long been accustomed to begging from the government instead of seeking employment, creating a realistic scenario in the US where "too much money, chasing too few goods" at that time, and its direct consequence was rising inflation. According to the US Bureau of Labor Statistics, in October 2021, the US Consumer Price Index (CPI) rose by 6.2% year-on-year, breaking the highest records since 1990, which also shows a significant acceleration compared to the previous year's 5.4% increase. If economist Friedman were still alive, he would definitely curse at the absurdity of the Modern Monetary Theory and policies that the United States is currently pursuing, as well as the severe medium to long-term damage it has caused to the US economy. He would emphatically declare that the United States must control its currency issuance! Because inflation is primarily a monetary phenomenon at anytime and anywhere.

The US presidency has traditionally been measured against the so-called "333" barometer, which measures whether the president's governance performance is good based on three economic indicators: economic growth rate above 3%, inflation rate under 3%, and unemployment rate under 3%. Significant deviations in one or more indicators can lead to an unstoppable decline in approval ratings, even if the president is successful in foreign policy. And if running for re-election, it would often ends in failure. For example, despite Trump's claim during his administration that he was the President of the United States who had kept the unemployment rate to the lowest level in 50 years, his poor performance in dealing with the COVID-19 led to voters disillusionment. More than 30 years ago, when George H.W. Bush had just won the Gulf War, he was once in the limelight and had high international prestige. However, he still won diplomacy and lost domestically, ultimately losing the battle against Clinton. Looking back at the American economy under Clinton's administration, although there were some problems, the sense of harvest of Americans in that period was undoubtedly much greater than that of today when the Democratic Party was also in power. Perhaps because the super intellectual Clinton was always a lucky dog, he balanced Keynesianism, monetarism, supply side economics, and rational expectations economics, forming a "Clinton economics" that opposed both complete laissez faire and excessive intervention. As a result, the US economy experienced unprecedented prosperity at that time. In his last year in office, Clinton recorded a fiscal surplus of 237 billion US dollars, and when he left office, the size of the US treasury bond was 5.6 trillion US dollars. Successive presidents of the United States all failed to achieve such fiscal surplus, instead they left with only increased fiscal deficit and treasury bond.

According to data released by the US government, the federal fiscal deficit for the fiscal year 2021 (from October 1, 2020 to September 30, 2021) was 2.77 trillion US dollars, only slightly lower than the 3.13 trillion record for the fiscal year 2020, when the COVID-19 rampaged the most severely. As for federal debt, in November 2020, the size of the US federal debt was 27.44 trillion US dollars, an increase of $3.4 trillion from the end of 2019. By October 2021, the size of federal debt had approached $29 trillion. US Treasury Secretary Janet L. Yellen stated in a letter to Congress in mid-November 2021 that the US Treasury Department's cash would run out by December, and there will be another dilemma of raising the debt ceiling after October.

In addition, in order to revitalize the real economy, activate the competitiveness of emerging industries, and promote so-called sustainable development, the Biden administration has issued the largest infrastructure investment bill in nearly 50 years, with a total amount of 1.2 trillion US dollars. This infrastructure investment and employment bill has received rare bipartisan support and can be considered a milestone. On the other hand, the Biden administration has actively sought approval from Congress to support so-called "Building **Back Better**" social spending bill worth up to 1.75 trillion US dollars in total. The bill has been passed in the House of Representatives, but has been blocked in the Senate. From the content of the bill, this expenditure is mainly used for major issues such as childcare, family support, healthcare, solving housing subsidies and other livelihood issues, as well as addressing climate change.

The goals of the Biden administration's two major spending bills can be described as ambitious, aiming to address both the weaknesses related to the US's medium- and long-term strategic competitiveness and the wide-ranging social issues such as people's livelihoods and welfare. But for the US government, which is heavily in debt, financially strapped, and struggling with fiscal revenue and expenditure, how to allocate these two funds and whether it can maintain policy stability and continuity are not so easy to solve.

As the world's top economic and financial power, the United States is not short of money while extremely short of it. The former refers to the fact that the United States can still rely on the hegemony of the US dollar to release massive liquidity without being held accountable, while the latter refers to the fact that the United States, which has already overused its power, cannot rely solely on its own strength to cure its flawed economic system. Although the United States has a group of super enterprises with a market value exceeding 1 trillion US dollars or even approaching 3 trillion US dollars, history will eventually prove that if the country and its people do not put themselves into the right place for a long time, instead of thinking about how to strengthen and expand the real economy, but always want to play the game of "monetizing fiscal deficits" thoroughly, the outbreak of its systemic economic and financial crisis will never be late.

Part III
China Bridging the Fault Lines

Chapter 7
The New Development Paradigm and the Smooth Flow of Domestic and International Dual Circulation

Accurately Positioning the Guangdong-Hong Kong-Macao Greater Bay Area in the Competition Among Poles of the World Economy

The Hong Kong-Zhuhai-Macao Bridge (HZMB), acclaimed as the longest overseas bridge globally, has been officially inaugurated. This large-scale project, with an investment exceeding RMB 120 billion, holds not only symbolic significance in the annals of international bridge engineering but also serves a critical function in advancing the strategic framework aimed at fostering the development of the Guangdong-Hong Kong-Macao Greater Bay Area.

It is widely recognized that the terrestrial transportation networks interlinking Hong Kong, Zhuhai, and Macao have historically experienced disconnection. This lack of connectivity has hindered the efficient distribution of resources within the Guangdong-Hong Kong-Macao Greater Bay Area, while also constraining the development of trade and economic relations with adjacent regions such as Guangxi, Yunnan, Guizhou, and Hong Kong. With the recent completion and activation of the Hong Kong-Zhuhai-Macao Bridge, transaction costs are expected to decrease significantly, fostering the growth of the "9+2" mega-city cluster in the Guangdong-Hong Kong-Macao Greater Bay Area. This development will guide the region towards its aspiration of establishing itself as an international financial hub, a center for technological innovation, and a prominent cluster for advanced manufacturing and modern service industries.

Within the framework of China's economic landscape, the Guangdong-Hong Kong-Macao Greater Bay Area stands out as a pivotal region characterized by distinctive elements and resources that effectively complement one another, making it the leading zone for mainland China in terms of engaging in international industrial transfer, extending trade value chains, and importing financial capital. Upon examining the regional economic structures of China and the United States, one observes that both nations possess three principal economic circles: China features the

Y. Zhang, *Addressing Uncertainty*, Understanding China,
https://doi.org/10.1007/978-981-92-2692-4_7

Hangzhou Bay Economic Circle, the Guangdong, Hong Kong and Macao Economic Circle, and the Bohai Economic Circle, while the United States encompasses the New York Economic Circle, the Chicago Economic Circle, and the Los Angeles and San Francisco Economic Circle. The three principal economic circles in the United States notably exhibit a pattern of gradient development from east to west, historically facilitating Europe's industrial migration and serving as the cradle of the Second Industrial Revolution and its subsequent stages, thereby maintaining a persistent focus on emerging technological advancements. Over the past four decades of accelerated development, China's three significant economic zones have ascended to become prominent industrial clusters on the west coast of the Pacific Ocean, significantly altering and likely continuing to shape the trajectory of the global economic landscape.

Currently, although the Guangdong-Hong Kong-Macao Greater Bay Area continues to confront issues such as disparities in economic development, the medium- and long-term developmental outlook reveals that the region has already been established as one of the six world-class city clusters acknowledged by the international community. It holds significant potential to develop into an international super-economy comparable to that of New York's Greater Bay Area, notwithstanding challenges such as industrial isomorphism and market segregation.

From the perspective of fundamental indicators for global economic hubs, the GBA has begun to emerge as a significant region. Generally, there are three key benchmarks to determine whether a region (or city cluster) can become an international economic hub: first, the economic scale of the region must account for at least 5% of the international economy; second, its industrial competitiveness must be among the world's leading positions; and third, it should possess an innovation ecosystem capable of continuously activating the business potential of micro entities and fostering a robust R&D foundation. Evaluating the GBA against these criteria reveals its trajectory toward becoming an international super-economy. As the economic core of China, with a total GDP exceeding $1.8 trillion, the GBA currently accounts for approximately 2% of the international economy. Although this is still some distance from the 5% benchmark, its rapid development momentum suggests that it could reach this target by around 2030. (The 2021 GDP of the GBA cities and their respective shares are detailed in Table 7.1.) Another significant advantage of the GBA lies in its prominent position within the international manufacturing and trade value chains. The competitiveness of several real economies within the region has reached advanced global levels. Moreover, the GBA is one of the most dynamic regions on the China innovation map. In 2021, its R&D expenditure as a percentage of GDP reached 3.14%, comparable to that of the United States and Germany. In particular, Shenzhen and Hong Kong have emerged as the leading hubs within international innovation clusters.

However, the GBA still faces several constraints and bottlenecks in its quest to become an international economic hub. The most critical challenge is to establish an effective division of labor between Hong Kong and Guangdong, leveraging their respective factor endowments. Unlike Shanghai's dominant role in the Yangtze River Delta, the relationship between Hong Kong, Guangzhou, and Shenzhen

Table 7.1 GDP and proportion of cities in Guangdong-Hong Kong-Macao Greater Bay Area in 2021

City	GDP (Unit: billion yuan)	Proportion (%)
Shenzhen	30,664.85	24.03
Guangzhou	28,231.97	22.12
Hong Kong	24,771.67	19.41
Foshan	12,156.54	9.52
Dongguan	10,855.35	8.51
Huizhou	4977.36	3.9
Zhuhai	3881.75	3.04
Jiangmen	3773.41	2.96
Zhongshan	3566.17	2.79
Zhaoqing	2649.99	2.08
Macao	2100.01	1.65

Data source: WIND

within the GBA's "9+2" city cluster is more reciprocal. On the one hand, as the mainland economy becomes increasingly integrated with the international economy and the comprehensive competitiveness of Guangzhou and Shenzhen—particularly Shenzhen—continues to rise, Hong Kong's role as the regional "leader" and "intermediary" is gradually diminishing. Should Hong Kong lose this position, the economic repercussions would be unprecedented. On the other hand, Hong Kong's industrial structure has not been upgraded in a timely manner, and its leading industries, such as finance and trade, face increasing pressure from upstream competition with international supercities like New York and London. Simultaneously, the industrial competitiveness of the main cities of mainland China, represented by Shanghai and Shenzhen, continues to grow. This competitive dynamic between the two sides has naturally led to a decline in Hong Kong's economic confidence. However, Hong Kong remains one of Asia's most important business hubs. Its clean and fair business environment still serves as a critical benchmark for cities such as Shanghai, Guangzhou, and Shenzhen as they further optimize their own business climates. Hong Kong's international market network, extensive management experience, and advantages in areas such as the rule of law, taxation, marketing, and public relations will continue to be its key strengths, enabling it to maintain a competitive edge in the Asia-Pacific region for the foreseeable future.

Therefore, accelerating the integrated development of Guangdong, Hong Kong, and Macao is both an inevitable trend and an inherent requirement. For the Greater Bay Area (GBA) of Guangdong-Hong Kong-Macao to become a super bay area comparable to those of New York and Tokyo, as well as a pivotal hub on the international economic map, it is essential to fully leverage the unique strengths of its core cities. Hong Kong should take the lead in driving integration in finance, information, trade, business, and other professional services. Meanwhile, core cities like Guangzhou and Shenzhen must proactively grasp the evolving trends in international industry and finance, benchmark themselves against the development logic of international megacities such as New York and London, leaders in industrial division of labor, and effectively integrate regional resources. With a broader vision and the courage to embrace self-revolution, they must deepen the cultivation of core competencies in manufacturing, focus on upgrading the international trade value chain, and accelerate the construction of a financial center that supports the real economy, particularly innovative enterprises. This will enable the GBA, in collaboration with Hong Kong, to reach the pinnacle of the international economy.

Building Dual Centers of Supply and Demand in the Global Value Chain Through Domestic and International Dual Circulation

On August 12, 2020, the General Office of the State Council issued a document reintroducing 15 measures to stabilize foreign trade and foreign investment, each of which serves as a targeted solution to the practical challenges faced by foreign trade and foreign-invested enterprises.

As is widely recognized, the essence of foreign trade, which includes trade in goods and services, lies in the global-scale transfer of production factors and the alignment of trading conditions. Its survival and development depend on a series of supporting conditions. From the end of World War II to the end of the twentieth century, international trade experienced prolonged growth driven by developed nations. During this half century, the flow of commodities, technology, capital, and labor across borders, coupled with the enhanced international resource allocation capabilities of multinational corporations, spurred the development of foreign trade in emerging economies and developing countries. This process unleashed successive waves of industrial and technological transfer dividends. Germany and Japan emerged as pivotal forces in the external cycle of international trade. However, the shifting international trade landscape during this period led to frequent trade frictions, not only between developed countries but also between developed and developing nations, with particularly intense trade conflicts between the United States and Japan, as well as the United States and Europe.

Reflecting on the historical evolution of the global value chain's supply and demand dynamics, when a country transitions from a manufacturing and trade powerhouse to an industrial and capital powerhouse, it often prioritizes gains from the high end of the value chain while neglecting the consolidation of its traditional comparative advantages. As these advantages erode, the competition of emerging forces intensifies, creating growing pressures. This phenomenon reflects the internal and external economic imbalances caused by industrialization, globalization, and the deepening integration of trade and financialization.

Since the beginning of the twenty-first century, particularly after China's accession to the World Trade Organization (WTO) on December 11, 2001, the international market structure and global industrial and supply chains have undergone the most significant transformation since the Industrial Revolution, driven by China's active participation. China has rapidly evolved from a mid-tier trading partner with annual import and export volumes below $500 billion before the WTO accession to one of the world's most important trading partners, with annual trade volumes exceeding $6 trillion. In less than 22 years, the breadth and depth of China's foreign trade have expanded substantially. Data from the Ministry of Commerce reveal that by 2020, China had become the largest trading partner for more than 120 countries and regions, with imports accounting for approximately 11% of the global total. The trade surplus from net exports remains a critical source of China's substantial foreign exchange reserves.

Since its WTO accession, China's position as a core country in the global industrial and supply chains has become firmly entrenched. Major international market players, including S&P, widely acknowledge that U.S. manufacturers struggle to find alternatives to Chinese suppliers. Moreover, China's vast market opportunities are too significant for any forward-thinking entrepreneur to overlook or easily relinquish.

China is advancing high-standard opening-up through sound institutional design and high standards in the twenty-first century. By globally allocating high-quality production capacity, providing replicable business models, and employing other strategies, China continues to release the dividends of economic openness and foreign trade development. These efforts constitute a core component of globalization's benefits in the first half of the twenty-first century. Consequently, China's proposal and promotion of the "dual circulation" strategy not only contribute to global economic rebalancing but also serve as an indispensable condition for establishing a dual supply and demand center in the global value chain. This approach aligns with China's goals of achieving high-standard opening-up and sustainable, high-quality development.

In terms of the foundational conditions and supporting elements required for implementing the "dual circulation" strategy, China is in the mid-to-late stages of industrialization and urbanization. Significant tasks remain to build a competitive domestic market system, particularly a modernized economic system, and it is expected that the overall transfer of the gradient of industries will persist for years to come. This provides substantial room for maneuvering within the domestic macro-cycle. In fact, the growth potential of more than 500 million people in the central and western regions, driven by the domestic cycle, may rival the growth dividends previously generated by the coastal economic cycle. On the other hand, China, deeply integrated in the global industrial division of labor and closely linked to international markets, has the conditions to expand and strengthen the external cycle by adhering to the rules of the international market and broadening foreign economic trade and cooperation. Once China fully integrates its internal and external cycles and establishes a dual supply and demand center in the global value chain, it will become the true "anchor" of global economic and industrial development.

Understanding the CIIE: The Optimal Link Between Domestic and International Dual Circulation

Introduction: The third China International Import Expo (CIIE) opened on November 4, 2020 in Shanghai. After the success of the first two sessions, the Fair has become a popular trade event around the world. As President Xi Jinping said in his keynote speech at the opening ceremony of the fair, after 3 years of development, the fair has transformed exhibits into commodities and exhibitors into investors, exchanging ideas and concepts, and connecting China and the world. What is the special significance of organizing the Fair as scheduled? What is the role of the Fair in building a new development pattern? This program invites Zhang Yugui, Dean of the School of International Finance and Trade of Shanghai International Studies University, to give you an explanation.

China.org.cn: At the opening ceremony of this year's Fair, President Xi Jinping delivered a keynote speech. What aspects impressed you deeply? In your opinion, what kind of signal does it release to the world in the current situation?

Zhang Yugui: President Xi Jinping's keynote speech at the opening ceremony of the Fair impressed me in three ways: first, he made a very good judgment of the international political and economic situation under the current circumstances. Although we are currently encountering many difficulties, including unilateralism, hegemony and protectionism, the world cannot stop the pace of economic globalization, including global governance. As the world's second-largest economy, China's hosting of the Fair is a signal to the world that it will continue to open up, and to do so at a high level. President Xi's speech also specifically mentioned that China is going to expand opening up at a deeper level in several areas, including the introduction of a negative list for cross-border trade in services, which is very important.

Second, we may expand our total imports to 22 trillion dollars in the next 10 years, which will provide a huge dividend to the world economy.

Third, President Xi's speech revealed that no matter how the world changes, China, as a responsible global major economy, will work together with like-minded countries, or regions, or trade organizations, including the thousands of foreign manufacturers participating in the Fair, to promote the Fair as a public product on the world stage, which shows China's responsibility to the world. This shows China's responsibility to the world. I think these three points have profound significance.

In the current delicate international situation, China is probably the only major economy that has the conditions to organize such a large-scale national exhibition, that is to say, only China has the ability, willingness, and international coordination to organize such a safe, large-scale import exposition, which is the first signal.

The second signal is that in the face of the new epidemic, China is the first of the world's major economies to recover, and will achieve positive economic growth. The share of the total global economy has exceeded 16%, and our annual imports total about 2 trillion US dollars. This Import Expo is an extremely important platform for those manufacturers and consumers who have been hit by the new crown epidemic.

The third signal is that the organization of the fair proves that we have purchasing power and that we have access to the world's most advanced commodities, trade, services and technology at our doorstep. This is crucial to the launch of a new round of opening up after the Fifth Plenary Session of the 19th Central Committee of the Communist Party of China (CPC), and it is also an important practical platform for China to connect with economic globalization and promote the effective growth of global commodities and trade in the new era.

China.org.cn: What are the new highlights and new features of this year's Fair?

Zhang Yugui: First, the transaction volume is large. In less than 2 days after the start of the conference, a large-scale transaction volume came out, which shows that the offline and online communication in advance is very good, especially online communication. At the same time, it also shows that we have released dividends to the world through the Fair.

Second, there are a lot of technologies and equipment that China needs in this fair, such as German large-scale technologies and equipment, especially in the field of manufacturing. This year's fair may be a bit different from the previous one in terms of certain consumer goods, but there are some key technologies that we need urgently, which have been imported and introduced.

Third, we found that a consumer brand like Nike entered the Fair for the first time, which also sends a signal that Nike's annual sales in China are about 120 billion, and such a large-scale enterprise did not participate in the Fair in the past, so this time to make up for it. I believe that this Fair will help improve our business environment and promote our future high-quality development.

China.org.c: As the world's first import-themed national exhibition, the Fair has been successfully held for two times. What kind of effect did the first two editions of the Fair bring, and what impact did it have both internationally and domestically?

Zhang Yugui: At the first edition of the Fair in 2018, the General Secretary, on behalf of China, sent some important signals to the world, including the integration of the Yangtze River Delta, the expansion of the Shanghai Free Trade Zone, the launch of the Science and Technology Innovation Board and so on. In the next 10–5 years, China will open up on a large scale. By organizing the Fair in Shanghai, the radius and influence of the Fair is not regional, but international. We have attracted the world's top 500 companies, as well as a number of specialty companies, through the first two editions of the Fair. Our manufacturers can seamlessly connect with these enterprises, which have the most advanced technology and services in the world, right at their doorsteps. In terms of introduction, digestion, absorption and re-innovation, we are very successful.

Secondly, the General Secretary said that all the promises made at the Expo have been honored. This shows that a big country like ours not only has the purchasing power, but also the level of fulfillment of trade commitments.

Through the Fair, China has demonstrated to the world that it can continue to release economic and trade development dividends, reflecting the international responsibility of a responsible big country.

China.org.cn: In the extraordinary period when the new crown epidemic is spreading globally and the world economy continues to be in the doldrums, many large-scale international exhibitions have been canceled or postponed, but the 3rd Fair is coming as scheduled. What do you think is the special significance of organizing the Fair as scheduled under such a special background?

Zhang Yugui: As the biggest external uncertainty in the world, the new crown epidemic has disrupted our economic expectations and the normal order of production, trade and life of human beings, ushering in the return of global depression economics.

Under such circumstances, a single country alone cannot stabilize the global economic forces, especially the need for each country and its market players, including enterprises, consumers and international organizations, to coalesce on a platform, and this year's platform is China's third Fair. We have attracted more than 2600 foreign enterprises, 39 domestic trade missions and nearly 600 sub-trade missions, 112,000 buyers registered and 400,000 professional visitors through the Fair. Some manufacturers are "first-time visitors", "repeat visitors" more than 70%. Among them, there are nearly 50 of the world's top 500 enterprises and industry leading enterprises.

Under such a special circumstance, China's holding of the fair is to show the world that China is capable of participating in stabilizing the global economic and trade order.

China.org.cn: President Xi Jinping mentioned in his keynote speech at this year's fair that "the series of initiatives to expand opening-up announced by me at the Second China International Import Expo have been fully implemented", and judging from the implementation situation in the past 2 years, what positive effects have these initiatives had on China's opening-up to the outside world in the new round?

Zhang Yugui: From the President in the first two sessions of the Expo announced China's deep opening-up initiatives, very important points have been implemented: first, the business environment. The business environment is extremely important, our country in the past in the global business environment ranking has been in the median or low. In this regard, we have made great improvements through sustained efforts over the past few years.

Second, the negative list. We now have so many free trade zones, including the Shanghai Free Trade Zone, Hainan Free Trade Zone and so on. Through the Fair, we have found China's openness should be in which time slot, which areas are suitable for foreign investment at a high level of docking.

Third, in recent years, the level of trade and investment facilitation has been greatly improved, whether it is the central bank, the foreign exchange bureau, or the relevant Securities and Futures Bureau, Banking and Insurance Regulatory Commission and so on, these financial regulators of foreign financial institutions have significantly relaxed the threshold of access, including joint venture brokerage firms and so on.

The implementation of the above initiatives is through such an important platform as the Fair, which plays a significant role in promoting and facilitating. President Xi Jinping has declared that the major opening-up initiatives have been well committed one after another, and have been widely recognized by major global manufacturers, including some multinational companies. Therefore, the pace of foreign investment in the Chinese market has accelerated significantly in recent years.

China.org.cn: As you have just mentioned, there are a lot of "first-time visitors" and "returning visitors" at the Fair, indicating that our "circle of friends" at the Fair is getting bigger and bigger. Do you think that the growing attractiveness of the Fair is related to our pragmatic measures, efficient promotion and intensive implementation? Besides, what are the other important factors?

Zhang Yugui: The circle of friends of the Fair is getting bigger and bigger, first of all, because our country is the largest trading partner of more than 100 countries in the world. In addition, through the consecutive organization of several sessions of the Fair, foreign manufacturers generally believe that: first, China's level of national governance is very high, ranking in the global "first tier".

Secondly, there are many business opportunities in China. The General Secretary has made it very clear that China has a population of 1.4 billion, with nearly 400 million middle-income groups, and our purchasing power is sky-high. So under these circumstances, it is a natural extension of logic that there are "repeat customers" and "first-time customers" who flock to this market on a large scale. The President of the American Chamber of Commerce in Shanghai made it very clear: no one can ignore the business opportunities that China offers. This is the best proof.

China.org.cn: The recently concluded Fifth Plenary Session of the 19th CPC Central Committee made the major deployment of "accelerating the construction of a new development pattern with the domestic macro-cycle as the main body and the domestic and international double-cycle promoting each other", and the keynote speech at the opening ceremony of this year's Jinfei Fair also emphasized this important deployment again. In your opinion, what role does the Fair play in building a new development pattern?

Zhang Yugui: The strategic positioning of a country's development is extremely important, which is why the Fifth Plenary Session of the 19th Central Committee of the Communist Party of China (CPC) introduced the important development concept of focusing on the domestic macro-cycle and mutually promoting the domestic and international double cycle.

In order to effectively implement the domestic and international double cycle, we need to consider the following aspects: first, continuously expanding opening up. For example, China needs to find a win-win platform for cooperation with major or large international trading organizations. We need to go out and come in. The Expo is to let you come over to see what China is like, so as to eliminate the misunderstanding of the outside world. This is about the international cycle. Secondly, the domestic cycle, our per capital income has already exceeded 10,000 dollars, and our GDP will exceed 100 trillion yuan. This is a very important time, we can go up a little better, a little more solid; if we do not do a good job, we may face a lot of problems. At this time we organized the Fair, our domestic and international double cycle, played a role in the communication of valuable business information between China and foreign countries, through the Fair to see the global technology, trade and the development of the industry as a whole new trends.

Through the Fair, we can see the new trend of global technology, trade and the development of the whole industry. The Fair has played such a platform role for the domestic and international double cycle. We find that although our technology and commodities have developed rapidly in recent years, and we are a very important global investment body, but there is still a big gap compared with other developed countries. This gap is an important driving force for us to open up, reform and develop.

The Fair is a platform that connects domestic and foreign market players and consumers, and is in itself the best link between the domestic and international double cycle?

Zhang Yugui: Because the Fair is organized by the state and held in Shanghai. In the next 10–15 years or even longer, Shanghai will have to undertake a very difficult task. That is to say, Shanghai, as the leader of the Yangtze River Delta, should be built into a global economic and financial center, science and technology innovation center. The Fair can not be limited to just a few thousand manufacturers, tens of thousands of enterprises registered, hundreds of thousands of visitors to participate. How to find better Chinese and foreign exhibitors, traders, visitors and consumers through the online and offline mega-size of this never-ending Fair, docking facilitation platform window, which requires in-depth thinking.

In addition, we need to look forward to the future. The Fair is not a platform to undertake the task of reaching tens of billions of dollars in turnover, but how to make it China's version of a new twenty-first-century public product that will continue to promote the release of China's opening dividend to the world? This public good should play its role as an incremental dividend, that is to say, people come here once and want to come again, come here this time and want to bring things over or bring Chinese goods back through our vendors, that is, traders. They think that someday their countries may want to organize a fair like China's, which is a two-way promotion. What role does China play? As an emerging economy, China plays a role in economic development and trade models that can be replicated and scaled up. This is a promising prospect.

There are about three suggestions: First, because we now have some stable "repeat customers", how to win those "repeat customers" and "first-time customers" on a larger scale in the future? How to win those "repeat customers" and "returning customers" on a larger scale in the future, so that they are willing to bring the best technology, the best goods, the best service, need to think carefully.

Second, people are willing to come, how do we achieve a high level of docking. Although Shanghai is currently the best city in China to hold large-scale expositions, the hardware has reached a world-class level, but there is still a lot of software that can be further optimized.

Third, through the platform of the Fair, we can meet the aspirations of Chinese consumers to pursue a better life. How can we achieve a higher level of fulfillment? Some products are really good, but they are unaffordable or can only be purchased as one-time purchases. How can we further reduce tariffs? Our country's tariffs have dropped considerably in recent years, and the world, including the WTO, has taken a positive view of us. Therefore, we can do better in this regard.

The CIIE Puts China at the Center of Global Attention, Sharing the Dividends of Openness and Development with the World

Introduction: The fourth China International Import Expo (CIIE) was held in Shanghai as scheduled. A total of 58 countries and three international organizations to participate in the national exhibition, from 127 countries and regions, nearly 3000 exhibitors appeared in the enterprise exhibition, country, the number of enterprises are more than the previous session. (See Table 7.2 for the regional distribution of exhibitors.) As the world's first import-themed national exhibition, the Fair has become a globally shared international public goods and an important window for the world to observe China's open-door policy. What are the "report cards" of this year's Fair? Where will the role of import trade in the new development pattern be further reflected, and what signals have been released by the high-standard opening-up initiatives announced in 2021? On November 10, 2021, China Net's China Talks program invited Zhang Yugui, Dean of the School of International Finance and Trade at Shanghai International Studies University, to share his views with readers.

China.org.cn: Since it was first organized, the Fair has become an international public product shared by the whole world. According to statistics, more than 80% of the world's top 500 companies and industry leaders have returned to the fair. The "circle of friends" of the Fair is expanding and upgrading. From the current point of view, what are the highlights on the "report card" of the Fair?

Zhang Yugui: The fourth session of the Fair and the previous three sessions compared to the scale, content, quality and impact of a great change. First of all, this session of both the national exhibition and enterprise exhibition in the scale has been expanded, buyers using online and offline content and form, compared with the past, there is a major breakthrough. Some exhibits have been turned into commodities, which can be sold on the spot and docked through the offline interface. In terms of content, this exhibition of technology, goods and services has many characteristics, such as the emergence of many cutting-edge technologies; European and American exhibitors brought China's current high-quality development needs of medical care, people's livelihood-related products; there are also some products and people's livelihood docking products, such as barley bread, that is, the French technology and Chinese raw materials combined, which meets China's needs. In

Table 7.2 Regional distribution of exhibiting enterprises at the 4th China international import expo

Continents	Asia (including China, Hong Kong, Macao and Taiwan)	Europe	Africa	America	Oceania
Number of enterprises as a percentage (%)	45	33.3	3.0	13.9	4.8
Percentage of Exhibit Space (%)	38.4	36.8	0.7	20.3	3.9

Data source: China International Import Expo

Table 7.3 Exhibition highlights of the 4th China international import expo

Participating countries in the Online National Exhibition	58
Online National Exhibition Exhibitors International Organization	3
Total exhibition space for corporate exhibitions	36.6 million square meters
The world's top 500 and industry leading enterprises exhibition turnover rate	Over 80%
Corporate Exhibition Exhibitors	Over 2900
Procurement Missions	39
New products, new technology, new service display	422
Intent to sell on a 1-year basis	707.2 billion of dollars

Data source: China International Import Expo

addition, there are lipsticks, printers and so on, which are more in line with China's consumption trends and changes. (See Table 7.3 for details.)

From the quality point of view, the fair compared with previous years increased the content of science and technology, a greater degree of docking China's "2030", "2060", "double carbon" goals and technological development of cutting-edge trends, including artificial intelligence, robotics, smart medical and so on. The exhibition will also feature a wide range of technology trends, including artificial intelligence, robotics, and smart healthcare. Another highlight is the impact of China's accession to the WTO over the past 20 years, and its active participation in a number of important high-standard investment and trade agreements. With China's per capital GDP exceeding 10,000 US dollars and consumption constantly upgrading, Chinese people and Chinese and foreign exhibitors can actually feel that the Fair, as the world's only national import exhibition platform, its world height determines its influence.

China.org.cn: The fair has been held offline for 4 consecutive years as scheduled, and the opening-up initiatives announced every year are full of "dry goods". In his keynote speech this year, President Xi Jinping expressed three "unchanging determination" and put forward four "unswerving" initiatives. In your opinion, what signals have been released by this year's announcement of high-standard liberalization initiatives? What do you think about this?

Zhang Yugui: The Fair is a heavyweight, national-level import platform personally planned, designed and promoted by President Xi Jinping. This year's fair combines China's high level of openness and the highest international investment and trade standards, as well as China's high level of opening up to the outside world in the 20th anniversary of its accession to the World Trade Organization (WTO), including a series of actions such as joining the RCEP, applying for membership in the CPTPP, and the Digital Economy Partnership Agreement (DEPA). These measures are not just major oaths, but some are about to be implemented and others are being negotiated. This shows that the path of China's opening up is progressive and deep-rooted, and that no matter what happens to the country, the door to opening up will never be closed, because opening up is a distinctive national symbol of China's external development and interaction. This can be seen from President Xi Jinping's important speech at the Expo. Whether it is the extremely important promotion of high-quality development of the domestic economy and the external radiation of the welfare effect of high-standard opening-up, or the global sharing of the opportunities of China's development, including the expansion of imports and the promotion of the trend of globalization, the actual path of our development will not change.

President Xi Jinping's speech sent out four signals: the first one is that China has the ability to continue to provide the welfare arrangements and related market opportunities for China's economic development to the world through high-standard opening-up and high-quality development. The second signal is that China will release China's development dividends to the world through the platform, leverage and public products of the Fair. Over the past 20 years since its accession to the WTO, China has been one of the biggest beneficiaries of globalization, and at the same time one of the biggest adherents and centers of strength in promoting globalization. The third signal is that the world is facing a lot of uncertainties, including unilateralism, national-level egoism and even bullying, which have led to some major ruptures or divisions or even decoupling of the global value chain and industrial chain in a sense?

Zhang Yugui: The exhibitors and traders of this year's Fair have reached an unprecedented level in terms of scale, system, capacity and products, which shows that the world has cast a vote of confidence in China, and China has cast a warm vote for the world. Whether online or offline, China has practiced the concept of a community of human destiny through organic integration with the world, which has been well reflected through the platform of the Fair. We can note that President Xi Jinping has proposed that China should build a "Silk Road" platform. Through the expansion of the Silk Road, we can attract the products and services of many least developed countries to this platform, so that Chinese people and Chinese enterprises can effectively connect with them. This shows that while China has developed, it has not forgotten the countries that have helped us in the past. We have helped them get rich and strong, and we have helped them go global, and this platform of the Fair has played a very good role.

China.org.cn: China has not only organized the Fair, but also held large-scale exhibitions such as the Canton Fair and the China Apparel Fair. Through these trade fairs, what kind of momentum has China provided for the recovery of the world economy? And what development dividends have been shared by other countries and enterprises?

Zhang Yugui: The success of the Canton Fair, the Fair for Trade in Services and the Fair for Import and Export over the years reflects that our country's economy is in the take-off stage of development, a critical moment, and that we will introduce the "Chinese paradigm" to the international community. These import and export platforms of global significance, on the one hand, show that our country's development has always maintained good interaction with international trade, production and people, and that no one can lock themselves in a "dark room" in the context of global economic integration; on the other hand, it shows that today China has the ability, platforms, technologies and support systems, as well as such a system. On the other hand, it shows that today China has the ability, platform, technology, support system and purchasing power. China to buy, the world to sell, Shanghai is building a global consumer center, shopping center.

Whether it is the Canton Fair, Trade in Services or the Expo show the world two points: on the one hand, China and the world can not be detached, because China is the world's largest exporter of goods trade, is the world's largest trading partner of more than 100 countries or regions. On the other hand, after China has become rich and developed, it has found a very good and large-scale consumption docking platform for the services of other countries in the world through the import platform, which is actually a natural international extension of the dividend effect released to the world through our development.

China.org.cn: China has been the world's second largest import market for 12 consecutive years, and actively expanding imports has become an important part of our new round of high-standard opening-up to the outside world. In your opinion, the role of import trade in the new development pattern will be further reflected in where?

Zhang Yugui: From 1978 to the present more than 40 years, China's economic development has gone through the following stages: the first stage is the reform and opening up to the end of the twentieth century, when China's foreign exchange was in extreme shortage, we through some processing trade, including the "three to one complementary", to the world's exports of inexpensive, labor-intensive, finished products, including agricultural products, agricultural products, and labor-intensive, and the world's exports to the world.

Through this Fair, we found that China is a "super net-roots", this "net-roots" to the world released real money and real market opportunities. A Russian commentator said that in a few seconds their live broadcast with goods earned several million yuan, which is the welfare effect of the import platform provided by the Fair. We also found that China is doing high-quality development and opening up to the outside world at a high level. At present, many of our science and technology and the world's developed countries compared with a large gap, in the general feasible path, many foreign advanced manufacturers and enterprises are still willing to put these high-tech content of the products, technology, services through the Fair to China to release, the role of imports at this time is irreplaceable.

China.org.cn: There are views that the Fair not only has a direct effect, but also has an indirect effect, and its comprehensive effect is increasingly apparent. The future will be how to further release this comprehensive effect to more efficiently promote a new round of opening up?

Zhang Yugui: The success of each session of the Fair has obvious spillover effects. Whether through the initiative of some powerful exhibitors, or through the perception of the market, we will find that the Fair in Shanghai is a success. Because Shanghai is exactly the bridgehead of the domestic and international double cycle, is practicing a high level of opening up to the outside world, and plans to make Pudong a high-standard leading area. Qingpu, where the Fair will be held, is the demonstration zone for the integration of the Yangtze River Delta, which is the core of China's economy and one of the most important growth points of the global economy in the future.

In addition, the Fair will not only have a gradient impact on the domestic market, but also an integrated impact, because everyone is equal on this platform, which will have an external radiation effect. By showing the demonstration effect of China's Fair to the international market, its debut effect, and its cluster effect of connecting the most advanced technology, products, services and consumption concepts at home and abroad will continue in the future.

Finally, since 2021 to 2025 is the critical period for China's import capacity to undergo major upgrading changes, the international market and some international enterprises will not give up such an opportunity. It can be expected that on the basis of the success of the first four sessions of the Fair, it will do even better in the next 10 or 20 years. The Fair will become one of the best windows for the world to see the world, share China's dividends, and organically combine production capacity, industrial chain, supply chain and value chain with China.

Record-High Foreign Trade Volume Highlights the Resilience of China's Economy

According to the data released by China's General Administration of Customs on January 14, 2022, the scale of China's import and export of goods trade in 2021 reached a new level, exceeding 6 trillion US dollars for the first time (see Fig. 7.1), and presented many features such as stable growth in import and export with major trading partners, further optimization of trade patterns, and effective stimulation of the vitality of foreign trade operators (see Table 7.4 for details).

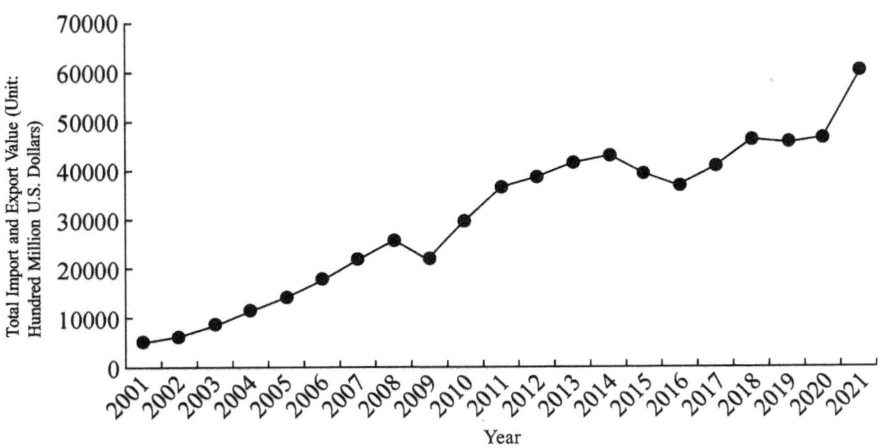

Fig. 7.1 China's merchandise trade import and export volumes since its accession to the WTO (as of 2021). Data source: Ministry of Commerce of the People's Republic of China

Table 7.4 Import and export volume and growth rates between China and its top five trading partners in 2021

	ASEAN	EU	USA	Japan	Korea
Import and export (trillion yuan)	5.67	5.35	4.88	2.4	2.34
Growth rate (%)	19.7	19.1	20.2	9.4	18.4

Data source: China Customs

The main reason for such a great achievement is that China's economic development has maintained its leading position in the world. The deeper reason is that China's position as the hub of the global industrial chain and supply chain has been consolidated to a certain extent, rather than being subjected to the so-called rupture that was feared by outsiders after repeated shocks from the epidemic. The deeper reason is that, when the global economy was hit by the epidemic and the major developed countries failed to respond properly, resulting in a large-scale "lack of oxygen" in the normalized operation of the world economy and trade system, China ensured that the guarantor of the global economy and trade system did not fall out of position with the soundness of its domestic economic system, its resilience and its highly responsible international actions. China has ensured that the guarantor of the global economic and trading system has not been left out of the picture as a result.

Despite the adverse currents, the deepening momentum of globalization has proved to be unstoppable. The international economic and trade system has been highly integrated for a long time, and the normal development of trade among countries greatly depends on the security and stability of regional and even global industrial chains and supply chains. Therefore, in the face of repeated impacts of the epidemic, countries to stabilize foreign trade, first of all, we need to short and medium-term, macro and micro policy combinations to play a role; secondly, stabilizing expectations is a prerequisite for the policy investment is to save the emergency, stabilize the industrial chain, supply chain is a guarantee, stabilize the overseas market is the core of the key links to stabilize foreign trade.

After the global spread of the epidemic, "beggar-thy-neighbor" and narrow national egoism immediately rose, based on a variety of so-called "security" reasons for trade protectionism is increasing, which requires the international community to have the strength and responsibility to participate in the main body in the cooperative game. On the basis of cooperative game, hand in hand to deal with the great challenges posed by the epidemic. But unfortunately, some developed countries not only did not take the initiative to assume the responsibility of stabilizing the industrial chain and supply chain, but also used various excuses to destabilize the global industrial chain and supply chain. What's more, they intentionally create and magnify differences in ideological fields, artificially create breaks in the international industrial chain, and cause international trade to show fragmentation and bloc tendencies such as regional localism and national egoism.

Under such circumstances, China's economy, in the face of internal and external challenges, including all kinds of difficulties and even provocations from the West, has demonstrated sufficient strategic strength, and has not been disoriented because of the complexity and change of the international environment and the uncertainty of the foreign trade situation. We have always been focusing on ensuring the stability and smoothness of the industrial chain and supply chain internally and the global industrial chain and supply chain externally.

China has played a dual role in the upstream, middle and downstream links of the global industrial chain. In addition to holding nearly one-third of the global supply of intermediate goods, with its commitment to move toward the middle and high end of the global value chain in recent years, China has increasingly played a central role in the global industrial chain, thus building a more dynamic internal and external economic linkage system. In the past 2 years, China has, on the one hand, made full use of the stabilization of the economic order brought about by its correct and decisive anti-epidemic policy to resume production, activate export production capacity, and ensure the smooth flow of the core industrial chain and supply chain. On the other hand, we have given full play to the global resource allocation capacity formed in the "Belt and Road" to promote global connectivity, and taken the initiative to assume the responsibility of safeguarding the global industrial chain and supply chain through bilateral and multilateral coordination during the extraordinary period, effectively filling the gap between global supply and demand. In the face of the global spread of the epidemic, China has made every effort to ensure that the global supply of anti-epidemic materials is not out of line, which also fully reflects China's reform and opening up for more than 40 years to enhance the resilience of the economic system and the resilience to deal with emergencies.

China's foreign trade to continue to maintain a high rate of growth on the basis of the existing high base, obviously difficult to face the uncertainty, instability, imbalance factors will also increase significantly. Coupled with the economic development is facing demand contraction, supply shocks, expectations of the weak triple pressure, as well as from the world's "value depressions" export capacity to enhance the competitive squeeze and developed countries to gradually repair the export capacity of the impact of the impact of the effect of the next few years, China's foreign trade in order to further stabilize and rise, but also need to effectively deal with the relevant uncertainties from both inside and outside. Factors.

However, the growing resilience of the economic system, the long-term positive fundamentals and the rich experience accumulated in dealing with major external shocks will help China to activate the business endowment and innovation vitality of the micro-entrepreneurs with precise policy inputs in a counter-cyclical state.

Chapter 8
The Economic Logic Loop of High-Standard Reform and Opening-Up

The Opening-Up of the Capital Market on All Fronts Urgently Requires Enhanced "Financial Capabilities"

Fang Xinghai, Vice Chairman of the China Securities Regulatory Commission (CSRC), stated on May 29, 2018, that a fully open Chinese capital market has been established from the perspectives of products, investors, intermediaries, capital flows, and other aspects. As the capital market continues to open up in depth and breadth, it is particularly necessary to enhance our ability to anticipate significant international financial and economic risks, increase the intensity of cross-border regulatory cooperation, and strengthen international regulatory collaboration. Concurrently, we must expedite the development and attraction of regulatory professionals who are knowledgeable about both domestic and international business practices.

Since 2018, China has markedly accelerated the opening of its capital market to the global arena, primarily by easing access to the capital market and reinvigorating its own capital market, as well as by hastening the integration of the domestic capital market with international markets. These liberalization measures have been met with positive responses from key players in the international capital market. Examples include the Securities and Futures Commission (SFC) permitting foreign entities to hold up to 51% of the shares in joint venture securities and fund companies for the first time, the inclusion of the first batch of 234 A-shares in the MSCI indexes, and the launch of the highly anticipated "Shanghai-Lunan Tong" products. These developments signify that China, as a super-emerging market brimming with development opportunities, is opening up across various levels. China, as a super-emerging market with abundant development opportunities, is expediting the effective alignment with the capital markets of the US and Europe, enhancing the competitiveness of China's capital market in the process of opening up and development. Against the backdrop of RMB internationalization, it is expected that global financial capital will increasingly allocate to RMB-denominated assets, thereby

Y. Zhang, *Addressing Uncertainty*, Understanding China,
https://doi.org/10.1007/978-981-92-2692-4_8

deeply integrating China's financial system into the global market system. Ensuring the resilience and stability of the financial market, and preventing various financial assets, including stocks, bonds, loans, and derivatives, from forming price bubbles, will be a challenging task.

The modern capital market is an extremely complex systemic entity, encompassing the knowledge and exploration of its nature and form by financial scientists and economists, as well as market participants. This not only fosters the development of the capital market itself but also involves the design of numerous financial products, including various high-risk financial derivatives and derivative markets. Even the designers of these financial products may sometimes lack effective strategies to mitigate the risks associated with them. This phenomenon is not confined to the United States and the United Kingdom, where the financial industry is highly advanced. In China, for instance, the rapid economic growth following its accession to the WTO is largely attributable to the country's opening up and the swift advancement of its financial system. However, on the flip side, China's grasp of the adverse effects of excessive financial deepening, particularly the intricacies of the capital market, remains incomplete and challenging to fully comprehend, as demonstrated by the significant market fluctuations that have recurred over the past decade.

Indeed, the development and popularization of microfinance in China lag behind those of financial superpowers such as the United States and the United Kingdom. Consequently, China's capital market maturity remains low, despite the construction of a vast capital market system in less than 30 years—a feat that took centuries in the United States and the United Kingdom. Therefore, there is an urgent need to establish a basic policy environment conducive to the orderly functioning of a mature capital market. This includes efficient and orderly financial regulation, a robust financial system, and a supportive institutional framework. Specifically, there is a need for transparent and effective contract law and enforcement, a sound accounting system and practices, a well-established corporate governance structure, and a reliable payment and settlement system, among others. Some of these measures are being implemented gradually, while others are still in progress. The challenge lies in respecting the laws of capital market development and fostering a competitive mechanism to create a healthy ecosystem for capital growth. It is evident that we must promptly cultivate and develop a highly responsive team of regulatory specialists and a cadre of investment bankers on par with their U.S. and European counterparts. This will enable us to build a financial talent pool capable of participating in all facets of the global financial division of labor and leading the domestic capital market's development.

Financial regulation is a field that demands highly specialized knowledge. It requires not only rigorous academic training for regulators but also extensive market experience. Regulators must have a forward-looking perspective on the development trends of both domestic and international capital markets, a skillful command of financial management tools, and, naturally, the appropriate qualities to effectively engage in domestic and international regulatory cooperation. Moreover, it is essential to prevent the "capture" of regulators by vested interests. In essence, modern financial regulation is a synthesis of keen financial insights, grounded in a precise understanding of market operations and the effective identification and timely resolution of risks. Specifically, anticipating major international financial risks, ensuring the stability of domestic financial markets, and coordinating cross-border regulatory efforts require not only the continuous updating of financial market infrastructure but also the diligence and expertise of international regulatory professionals.

Over an extended time horizon, the primary challenges that China's financial system may encounter in the first half of the twenty-first century are expected to arise from three main sources. Firstly, there is the ongoing strain on financial stability posed by systemic risks that have accumulated within the existing financial framework over time. Secondly, China's economy, which is now deeply intertwined with the global system, faces a significant test from the potential onset of the next global financial crisis. Thirdly, there is a contradiction between China's global responsibility as a key supporter of the international financial system and the continuous provision of risk prevention capabilities, especially after the Renminbi high degree of internationalization. Consequently, it is imperative to define the relevant indicators for financial services that support the real economy, delineate the boundaries of economic financialization, consistently bolster the competitiveness of the real economy, and establish a robust financial system capable of withstanding global economic competition in the twenty-first century, thereby ensuring the fundamental security of the financial landscape.

Strategic financial talents represent specialized human capital that embodies a wealth of implicit financial knowledge and experience. While education and training at universities and research institutes are merely the initial steps, market experience and management understanding are paramount. The enhancement of "financial skills" is not only an endogenous requirement of capital market development for regulators but also a behavioral self-awareness of regulators. Just as a great soccer goalkeeper must invest countless hours of hard work and continuously refine his judgment of the incoming ball to achieve success, the continuous improvement of the "financial skills" of Chinese financial industry professionals should also adhere to this principle.

40 Years of China's Foreign Trade: Steadily Moving Toward the Middle- and High-End of the Global Value Chain

Forty years is merely a drop in the ocean of human time. However, within the history of China's and global trade transformations, these four decades from 1978 to 2018 have witnessed the transformation of the largest developing country, which was once on the periphery of the global trade value chain, into a significant participant in international trade and a system builder.

Through reform and opening up, China has found an interface to participate in the global production and trade division of labor. By joining the WTO, it has established a path that allows China to adapt to flexible business rules, rely on endogenous technological progress, and continuously improve the competitiveness of its products and the added value of its exports. Consequently, China steadily moves towards the middle and high end of the global value chain, within the logical framework of global economic integration and trade liberalization. This also represents the challenge facing China's foreign trade.

Establishing Special Economic Zones to Open the Door to Foreign Trade

In 1978, China, which was in need of opening its doors to foreign trade, issued a clear call for "a great development of foreign trade" in the government's work report of the First Session of the Fifth National People's Congress held in February of that year, which was responded to by Shanghai, the province with the most industrial and technological strength in China. -Shanghai was the first to respond, and other provinces followed suit. In that year, China's exports reached 9.745 billion U.S. dollars, an increase of 28.6% over the previous year; imports reached 10.893 billion U.S. dollars, an increase of 51% over the previous year. Although China's total import and export volume of 20.638 billion U.S. dollars accounted for only 0.77% of the global share, the significance of the indicator is very obvious. In terms of imports, China in that year in one fell swoop signed the Baosteel and other 22 introduction of advanced technology and complete sets of equipment projects, involving tens of billions of dollars. This figure even today has considerable significance, not to mention that the purchasing power of the dollar at that time was far greater than today's purchasing power of the dollar. All this shows that a big country, which has ended its turbulence and is in its initial stage, is eager to integrate into the world economy and trade system, and is eager to narrow the gap with the world's advanced level by opening up to the outside world.

Indeed, in 1978, despite China's total economic output ranking ninth in the world, the overall economic and technological level was significantly behind that of developed countries. The magnitude of this gap was so profound that it deeply shocked the then Vice Premier of the State Council, Gu Mu, during his delegation's visit to five Western European countries (France, Switzerland, Belgium, Denmark, and West Germany) from May 2 to June 6. The delegation was struck by the fact that, after 30 years of post-war development, Western countries had taken a leading position globally. The technological advancements and management reforms in the West were deemed worthy of emulation, while China's economic development was notably out of sync with the international community. Upon returning to China, the delegation reported their observations and insights to the Central Committee and proposed numerous valuable suggestions. Subsequently, the central government held a retreat lasting over 2 months, during which most leaders acknowledged the economic disparity between China and the rest of the world. With the revolutionary and reformist spirit of a true leader, Comrade Deng Xiaoping made a critical assessment: continuing to build in a nearly closed environment would not only prevent the realization of the "Four Modernizations" but would also widen the gap with the

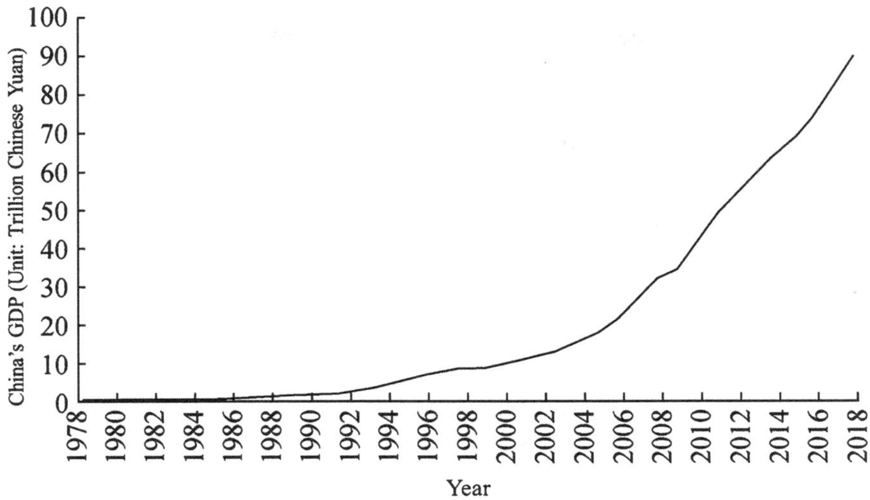

Fig. 8.1 Changes in China's GDP over 40 years of reform and opening-up. Data source: National Statistical Office

world's advanced levels. Comrade Deng Xiaoping made a resolute decision: "If you don't reform and open up, you're dead." This marked the logical starting point for the significant transformation in China's foreign trade pattern. (See Fig. 8.1 for the changes in China's GDP in the 40 years following the reform and opening up, specifically from 1978 to 2018.)

The beginning of everything is challenging, and at that time, China's foreign trade faced severe damage: it could not scale production with the international "comparative advantage" of manufactured goods, there was a serious lack of talent familiar with the rules of international trade, the number of enterprises engaged in import and export trade was small and their systems rigid, the main body of foreign trade lacked vitality, and foreign exchange was extremely scarce. Although the international context of the U.S.-Soviet rivalry was favorable for China to conduct business with the governments and enterprises of Europe, America, Japan, and other developed countries, under these conditions, China gradually unleashed its enthusiasm for foreign trade, while also striving to find a breakthrough in the expansion of foreign trade, leading to Deng Xiaoping's subsequent two major diplomatic initiatives.

Deng Xiaoping, then Vice Premier of the State Council, paid an 8-day visit to Japan from October 22 to 29, 1978, and gained a deep and intuitive impression of Japan's modernization, which directly contributed to the breakthrough development of Sino-Japanese economic, trade and technological cooperation; and Deng Xiaoping's ice-breaking trip to the United States from January 28 to February 5 of the following year not only fully displayed his vision and foresight as one of the most important strategists of the twentieth century, but also strengthened his determination to narrow the gap between China and developed countries by opening up to the outside world through visiting advanced manufacturing bases in the United States. The establishment of Special Economic Zones (SEZs) is not only an important testing ground for China's opening-up, but also a key lever for promoting foreign trade.

In April 1979, Deng Xiaoping first proposed the opening of "special export zones". In July of that year, the CPC Central Committee and the State Council agreed to set up special export zones in Shenzhen, Zhuhai, Shantou and Xiamen on a trial basis, and in May 1980, the "special export zones" were formally renamed as "special economic zones", which were modeled after the operation of the world's free port zones, with preferential measures such as tariff reductions and exemptions. By means of preferential measures such as tariff reduction and exemption, the Special Economic Zone has been developed into a bridgehead of export-oriented economy through the creation of favorable investment and business environment, encouragement of foreign investment, undertaking of international industrial transfer, introduction of advanced or sub-new technologies and management methods, and the adoption of special economic policies and management system. The nationally recognized "Shenzhen Speed" and the "Shenzhen Miracle", which has an important position in the history of global urban development, are the direct results of the establishment of the Special Economic Zone. Today, Shenzhen not only has a complete and efficient manufacturing industry chain, which is extremely rare in the world, but also creates 1/10th of the country's foreign trade import and export with the strength of a single city, and is the core supporting force of the super bay area, Guangdong, Hong Kong and Macao.

Subsequently, similar bridgeheads have continued to emerge. Among these, the official launch of the development of Shanghai Pudong in 1990, while slightly later, has had a significant international impact. In the history of China's foreign trade, Pudong has left several indicative marks: the birth of the country's first financial and trade zone—the Lujiazui financial and trade zone, the first bonded zone—the Waigaoqiao Free Trade Zone, and the first pilot free trade zone—the China (Shanghai) Pilot Free Trade Zone, among others. It can be said that the development of Pudong has directly reactivated Shanghai's long-dormant business potential and trade "genes".

Just as economic reform is composed of a series of events, so too is the development and reform of China's foreign trade. The list of events is too extensive to detail here. In summary, through reform and opening up, particularly by establishing special economic zones and implementing a series of significant opening-up policies, China has created an interface for its enterprises to engage in the global division of labor in production and trade.

Achievements in China's Foreign Trade over the Past 40 Years

The development achievements of China's foreign trade in the 40 years from 1978 to 2018 are manifested by the fact that China's ranking in global trade in goods jumped from the 30th to the 1st place in that year, and its share in global imports and exports increased from 0.77% in that year to 10%; and the deep strategic value is that China has promoted the upgrade from a manufacturing and trade power to an industrial and capital power through the continuous expansion of opening up and continuous embedding in the global trade value chain; and explored a good institutional design to promote a new round of opening up of the economy, and provided an industrial and capital power through the globalization of high-quality production capacity allocation. The deeper strategic value is that, by continuously expanding opening-up and continuously embedding itself in the global trade value chain, China has promoted the upgrading from a manufacturing and trade power to an industrial and capital power; and explored the promotion of a new round of opening-up of the economy with a good system design, providing replicable business model design through global allocation of high-quality production capacity, the establishment of regional and globalization of financial services, as well as the enhancement of the related international coordination and mobilization, and combining with the internationalization of the RMB to continuously release the dividends of the economy's opening-up and the development of foreign trade, which will bring about the development of foreign trade. Combined with the internationalization of the RMB, the dividends of economic openness and foreign trade development have been released continuously, and China has thus built a more dynamic internal and external economic linkage system. (The major events of China's foreign trade in the 40 years of reform and opening up are shown in Table 8.1.)

In terms of time series, the development history of China's foreign trade over the 40 years from 1978 to 2018 can be roughly categorized into three stages.

In the first phase, from 1978 to 1992, China adhered to the basic national policy of reform and opening up and partially restored the attributes of enterprises as market players. First of all, with the reform of the foreign trade management system, the introduction of foreign capital, technology and management, and the cultivation of the manufacturing capacity of domestic enterprises, China was able to participate in the global economic cycle (what is known today as the global value chain). Though the famous "Three Lies and One Supplement" has gradually become a historical

Table 8.1 A chronology of major events in China's foreign trade during 40 years of reform and opening-up

1978	Explicit call for "A major expansion of foreign trade"
July 1979	The Central Committee of the Communist Party of China and the State Council agreed to set up special export zones in Shenzhen, Zhuhai, Shantou and Xiamen on a trial basis
May 1980	"Special export zones" were officially renamed "Special Economic Zones"
1986	China's request for reinstatement of its legal status under the General Agreement on Tariffs and Trade (GATT)
1990	Official launch of the development of Pudong, Shanghai
2001	China's accession to the World Trade Organization (WTO)
2012	China overtakes U.S. as world's top trading nation for the first time

term in today's view, it was of considerable value to China at that time in sharing the dividends of international industrial transfer and in establishing the export system in the coastal areas. Secondly, with the continuous promotion of state-owned enterprise reform and the gradual liberalization of private capital in domestic related industries, it has greatly activated the long-term business endowment of China's market players, the rapid development of processing trade, and the export of mainly labor-intensive products. Although China's foreign trade in the global value chain benefits to a lesser extent, the export-oriented foreign trade policy has injected considerable vitality into the economic development. In addition, as a founding member of GATT, China formally submitted the Memorandum on the Foreign Trade System of the People's Republic of China to the organization in July 1986, requesting the restoration of China's legal status. This was version 1.0 of China's foreign trade reform and development.

The second stage was from 1993 to 2001. During this 8-year period, China established the reform objective of establishing a socialist market economic system, the market began to play a fundamental role in resource allocation under the State's macroeconomic control, and State-owned enterprises moved towards the reform of the modern enterprise system in the process of transforming their operating mechanisms. What is particularly important is that, through China's accession to the WTO, it has not only embedded itself in the international economic and trade value chain at an unprecedented speed, but also guided the further opening up of the domestic market through the expansion of opening up and started to explore the construction of a competitive market system. The scale of China's import and export in these 8 years has crossed the 200 billion dollars, 300 billion dollars, 400 billion dollars and 500 billion dollars mark; foreign exchange reserves also jumped from less than 20 billion dollars in 1992 to 212.1 billion dollars in 2001, an increase of nearly 10 times. More indicative is that China's "accession to the WTO", not only do not have to fight for the so-called "most-favored-nation" treatment every year as in the past, but also squarely integrated into the global trading system (although this system is the leading developed countries to design), China has been quite a complete manufacturing system through technological advances and the design of the system. China's already quite complete manufacturing system through technological progress and the extension of the trade value chain, but also to a certain extent to improve China's position in the global division of labor. This is the 2.0 version of China's foreign trade reform and development.

The third stage is the period from 2001 to 2018. During this period, on the basis of continuously improving the socialist market economic system, China has gradually established a new concept of the scientific concept of development, and in the process of comprehensively participating in the global economic competition, the size of its economy has jumped from US$1.3 trillion in 2001 to US$18 trillion in 2017, making it the only two economies in the world with a GDP of more than US$10 trillion; the total volume of its foreign trade has exceeded US$6 trillion, and the international competitiveness of trade in services has also been increasing. The international competitiveness of trade in services is also increasing. The Economist magazine in the United Kingdom published an article as early as 2012, that China in 2012 for the first time overtook the United States to become the world's largest exporter of goods in the achievement of the Qing Dynasty Emperor Qianlong's legacy.

Although in December 2016, the United States, Europe, Japan and other major economies refused to recognize China's market economy status on the occasion of China's formal accession to the WTO for 15 years. Japan even deliberately amplified the decibel of this refusal, but as the world's largest trading body of China, obviously has a strong adaptability to the rules, better know how to use the rules, and then on December 12 that year, the United States and Europe on China's anti-dumping "substitution of countries" practice has put forward a WTO dispute settlement mechanism under the consultation request, and officially launched the WTO dispute settlement process. Formally launched the WTO dispute settlement procedures. At that time, even the British "Financial Times" could not stand, published an editorial calling on the United States, Europe and Japan to rationally resolve differences with China.

On June 28, 2018, the Information Office of the State Council published a white paper on China and the World Trade Organization, which elaborated in four aspects how China has deeply participated in economic globalization over the past 40 years since its reform and opening up, especially since its accession to the WTO in 2001, and how it has actively put into practice the concept of trade liberalization, comprehensively fulfilled the commitments made upon accession, and substantially opened up its markets to achieve wider mutual benefits and win-win results; it also explained to the It has also explained to the world that China, as an important beneficiary and defender of the established international economic system, resolutely upholds the core position of the World Trade Organization (WTO) as the multilateral trading system, and actively seeks to work with the relevant responsible economies to abide by and safeguard the WTO rules, support an open, transparent, inclusive and non-discriminatory multilateral trading system, and fully participate in the work of the WTO. This is the 3.0 version of China's foreign trade reform and development.

The Path Toward Ascending the Middle- and High-End of the Global Value Chain

Summarizing China's achievements in the development of foreign trade since its accession to WTO, it can be found that, thanks to the improvement of the terms of trade, the transfer of global industries and the comparative advantage of the cost of labour for a certain period of time, China has rapidly grown into the world's number one exporting and manufacturing country, accumulated huge foreign exchange reserves, and achieved a relatively stable return in the division of labour in the global value chain. China is also regarded as one of the few countries in the world with a relatively complete industrial chain of high, medium and low manufacturing industries.

However, trade liberalization, by its very nature, has never been a pseudo-proposition, and the promotion of trade facilitation is the stage-by-stage goal pursued by all countries. Nowadays, in the international economic and trade game still dominated by the Western industrial and financial powers, China has steadily built up its bilateral and multilateral trade system by adapting to international trade rules, expanding the scale of trade and enhancing the competitiveness of its products, and the added value of its export commodities has also been increased, and the position of its export manufacturing industry in the industrial chain has gradually risen.

However, a fact that can not be ignored is that since China's "accession to the WTO", in the economic strength and global trade map of the status of the promotion, to some extent, can be said to exceed the expectations of developed countries, including the United States, Europe and Japan, and the actual control of the border, and has always had the institutional advantages and arrogant mentality of their heart is very difficult to identify with China's development model. development model. Even in the view of some Westerners, after China has completed its initial industrialization and built a relatively perfect trade and financial services system, its demand in the reform of the international economic order may not only be a passive adaptation, but also based on the existing economic power, actively seeking to participate in the construction of the international economic discourse system or even rebuild the discourse system, including the provision of public goods to the world, and challenge the existing international economic and trade order.

Thus, irrespective of China's willingness, it is evident that this represents the established order of dominant high-value strategic objectives. This includes the strategic blockade of China's increasingly powerful high-end manufacturing system, compelling China's second "accession," and China's development situation within the U.S.-led framework of the established order.

Objectively speaking, for an emerging economy with a great lack of independent brands and little control over pricing power, China, despite the halo of the world's first (and sometimes second) exporter, but when you do the math, its strategic value is not as great as one might think. Take the trade structure between China and the United States as an example, on the surface, China is the biggest beneficiary, but in fact it is a real wage earner. Chinese textile exporters to the U.S. average profit margin of only 2–3%. Even the bulk of elector-magnetically exports are mainly processing trade-based, but also by the U.S. investment in China by the production of enterprises. Anyone with a discerning eye knows that transnational corporations such as Boeing, Apple, General Motors, Ford, IBM, Intel, Procter & Gamble, Coca-Cola, etc. are the biggest profit makers. For example, the industrial chain constructed by Apple in China highlights the embarrassing position of China's related industries in the international division of labor. China has become the largest and most important manufacturing base in Apple's industry chain, but at the same time, it also has the least say because the profit margin of this huge manufacturing base is insignificant. For example, Apple's iPhone profits are ridiculously high, but Foxconn, the famous OEM giant, only benefits from less than 2% of the iPhone value chain.

At present, a considerable portion of China's export manufacturing products is still concentrated in low value-added areas, and the vast majority of industries are still at the middle and lower ends of the industrial chain in the international division of labor. Whether they belong to the labor-intensive manufacturing industry or high-tech industries, to varying degrees, the following situation: the lack of core technology and core products, local enterprises rely heavily on foreign technological innovation, profitability level is limited and squeezed. In some advanced manufacturing fields, transnational corporations, through the vertical division of labor within the product chain, invest in China for the production of low value-added parts and the assembly of the whole machine, while importing high value-added components that condense the essence of technology, and most of the profits are taken away by foreign investors. The result is the emergence of serious industrial hollowing out phenomenon, that is, technology-intensive industries have no core technology, the formation of technical dependence on transnational corporations; the consequence is that when the deterioration of the terms of trade in the international arena, will be technologically constrained by others. Therefore, although the so-called trade imbalance between China and the United States can be analyzed simply in terms of figures, it should be analyzed from the perspective of value gain, and it is clear that the United States is the real winner.

The great achievements made by China's economy after its accession to the WTO are in themselves the result of China's adherence to the basic laws of the market economy and to the liberalization and facilitation of trade. The author does not deny that a certain degree of state intervention still exists in China's economic operation, but market players, including China's top decision makers, have been taking positive actions over the years to promote the early completion and perfection of the mechanism for the market to play a decisive role in resource allocation. Respect for the laws of the market, respect for the market, and the promotion of trade liberalization has been the broad consensus of the major market players, including the Chinese government. Moreover, China has long been an important participant in the reconstruction of regional and even global trade rules with considerable trade countermeasures capability. Subsequently, China and Europe, the United States, Japan and other countries or regions will be around the market economy status and the maintenance of the multilateral trading system to carry out a number of rounds of games, including cooperative games and passive non-cooperative games. However, no matter what, China, as an important beneficiary of economic globalization and trade liberalization and a stabilizing force in the system, will steadily improve its position in the global trade value chain on the basis of exploring the construction of an effective benefit-sharing mechanism with its major trading partners.

The Economic Logic of China's High-Standard Opening-Up

President Xi Jinping announced at the second Belt and Road Summit Forum on International Cooperation in 2019 that China will take a series of major reform and opening-up initiatives, strengthen institutional and structural arrangements, and promote a higher level of opening-up to the outside world. He highlighted the specific opening-up initiatives to be launched in the following five areas: expanding market access for foreign investment in a wider range of areas, strengthening international cooperation in intellectual property protection with greater vigor, increasing imports of goods and services on a larger scale, implementing international macroeconomic policy coordination more effectively, and attaching greater importance to the implementation of the opening-up policy, among others.

The initiatives for opening up in the five areas mentioned form a comprehensive system that addresses the fundamental elements of a country's strategy for economic engagement with the global community.

Integrating into Global Value Chain and Advancing Openness

First of all, China's economy, which has been deeply integrated into the international economic system, especially the global value chain system, cannot realize further upgrading of the industrial chain without the improvement of the supply capacity of local enterprises based on independent innovation and technology, as well as the in-depth participation of powerful external participants, or foreign investors. As a matter of fact, China has already implemented the management mode of pre-access national treatment plus negative list, including continuing to significantly reduce the negative list, promoting the opening up of modern service industry, manufacturing industry and agriculture to the outside world on all fronts, as well as permitting foreign holding or wholly-owned operation in more important fields such as financial services and high-end manufacturing industry, which is the policy expression of the logic of this opening up.

Furthermore, the initiatives for opening up are also evident in the establishment of several new pilot free trade zones, expanding upon the existing ones. There is also an acceleration in the exploration of constructing free trade ports and a hastening of the formulation of supportive policies. These efforts aim to ensure the rigorous enforcement of the Foreign Investment Law, providing institutional, technical, and legal frameworks for global investors to enter China's market with confidence. Concurrently, measures have been introduced to bolster international cooperation in the protection of intellectual property rights.

Secondly, to increase imports of goods and services on a larger scale is a natural logical extension of China's progress from a large manufacturing country and a large exporter to an industrial and capital powerhouse, and then to develop into an important guarantor of the global economic system. Because since China's accession to the WTO, thanks to the "accession" dividend, global manufacturing transfer dividend and demographic dividend, China's manufacturing industry in the scale of successively more than Germany, Japan, and in 2010 more than the United States jumped to the world's first. This is the United States since 1895 for the first time to give up the global manufacturing industry leading position (if measured by technology, brand and benefit from the degree of indicators, the United States is still the world's first manufacturing power). According to the World Bank statistics, the

United States manufacturing value-added accounted for the proportion of GDP fell from 16.1% in 1997 to 11.6% in 2017, while China's real economy accounted for more than 30% of GDP in 2017.

Today's China is not only the world's largest production capacity "factory," but also hosts the world's largest middle-income group. It is accelerating consumption upgrading and has enormous potential for consumption growth, making it a true "world market." Increasing imports of goods and services on a larger scale is not only a fundamental need to balance economic relations between China and its major trading partners but also a structural arrangement to improve the quality of consumption.

Finally, China will more effectively implement international macroeconomic policies and place greater emphasis on the execution of its open-door policy. This will help prevent the "fallacy of composition" in the foreign economic policies of powerful global actors and mitigate the effects of "beggar-thy-neighbor" policies, unilateralism, and protectionism on the global economic and trading systems. This represents China's commitment to global economic growth and sustainable development as a responsible emerging economy.

The author has analyzed that the reasons why globalization, trade liberalization, and multilateralism have faced protectionist obstruction in recent years are, to a considerable extent, due to the fact that the United States has not been sufficiently motivated to continue promoting globalization and trade liberalization, or, when it has refrained from accelerating, has not found effective alternatives to allow other engines to enter the existing power system.

In other words, as the most important promoter and the biggest beneficiary of globalization and trade liberalization, the United States, when it finds that the trend of globalization, trade liberalization and multilateralism and the explicit and implicit benefits they have brought about are increasingly beyond the boundaries of the United States' ability to control, and that the United States' willingness and ability to foot the bill for them are inevitably declining, the rise of isolationism, "anti-globalization", becomes the stage expression of the State's behaviour. The rise of "anti-globalization" isolationism becomes a stage expression of state behavior. This window of time occurs at the end of 2015, when the United States has basically completed its repair of the financial crisis, made great efforts to consolidate the competitiveness of its domestic manufacturing industry, and initiated interest rate hikes.

Therefore, if we observe from the perspective of global economic competition and pattern change, the tide of globalization, or that the global multilateral and bilateral openness has appeared to a certain extent at the national level willingness to decline, because the developed countries, which in the past played the most important driving force of economic globalization, in the face of the growth of the strength of the emerging economies as well as the enhancement of the willingness to participate in the change of the global economic governance and the ability to perform a certain degree of discomfort. And since the industrial revolution, the United States and Europe have long been proud of being the global industrial and financial capital, when it found that the transnational capital from emerging economies has become more and more important to participate in the main body of the global resource allocation, the same show a certain degree of maladaptation.

Classical Trade Theories Stand the Test of Time and Space

All rational market players should understand that trade liberalization, openness to the outside world, comparative advantage, competitive advantage, market economy, global economic integration, saving transaction costs, and the relationship between the State, the market and the enterprise have been the masterpieces of a series of theories and policies in the course of global economic development and economics since the seventeenth century. Nowadays, although the trend of global economic, trade and financial integration has been blocked, no artificial barriers can be put in place to technological advancement, especially the rapid advancement of big data technology and artificial intelligence, which makes the expansion of markets and the redistribution of wealth on a global scale unavoidable. The endogenous momentum of globalization based on the free flow of factors and the saving of transaction costs is very difficult to curb. In other words, whether it is the United States, Europe and other developed countries, or China and the vast number of developing countries, there is no party that can disregard the industrial chain, supply chain, service chain and even the value chain of the inter-linkage, and there is no capital force and national power can be constructed through the construction of a variety of barriers to block the reasonable flow of global factors.Classical trade theories not only stand the test of time and space, but also tend to have historical inheritance because they are the crystallization of human wisdom. Studies have shown that China's open-door practice based on trade liberalization and comparative advantage actually coincides to a certain extent with a series of classical trade theories of Western economists such as Smith, Ricardo, Eli Heckscher and Bertil Ohlin. For example, as early as more than two thousand years ago, the Chinese "Shiji—Cargo Shik Lianzhuan" and "Huainanzi—Qi custom training" have already used the "with all the more easy to all the fresh", "with all the easy to all nothing", "with all the work easy to all the clumsy" The logic of economics has already been expressed in a condensed form in the following words. In his English book Chinese Economic Thought Before the Seventeenth Century, Mr. Hu Yixing, a great master of the history of economic thought, gave a theoretical and logical exposition of the interconnections between Chinese and Western economic thought.

It is evident that trade liberalization and openness to the outside world, which serve as significant catalysts for global economic expansion, urgently require further internationalization and facilitation in the allocation of global resources through concrete actions by competent participants. As a major beneficiary of globalization, trade liberalization, and openness, China also bears the historical mission of being a promoter. A series of major reform and opening-up initiatives that China plans to undertake, including the strengthening of institutional and structural arrangements and the promotion of a higher level of openness to the outside world, are indeed in line with the concept of a socialist market economy that is continuously being improved. To date, there is no universally accepted definition of a market economy, and there are significant discrepancies in economic theories.

However, as a competitive economy, the market economy is, after all, a historical form of human civilization, and therefore must have its own inherent social order, i.e., a set of rules of conduct on market competition. From the point of view of existing theoretical studies and relevant legal provisions, some common aspects can be summarized, including whether the role and behavior of the government are standardized; whether the rights and behavior of enterprises are liberalized; the degree of marketization of factors of production, including whether the prices of factors are determined by the market; whether the costs of enterprises are real; the degree of fairness of the terms of trade; and the rationalization of financial parameters, etc. The core issue lies in whether the market economy is a competitive economy, which is a historical form of human civilization, and therefore must have its own internal social order, that is, a set of rules of conduct on market competition. The core issue lies in judging the efficiency of resource allocation and market competition in terms of the relationship between the government, the market and enterprises, especially the degree of freedom of market access and market pricing, and the degree of autonomy of enterprise behavior.

All these concepts are highly consistent with the core logic of China's efforts to strengthen institutional and structural arrangements to promote a higher level of opening up to the outside world, indicating that after establishing the basic framework of a market economy, China has already realized or is in the process of realizing changes in the way of resource allocation, changes in the way of macro-intervention by the government, and changes in the ownership and property rights system of enterprises, including changes in the structure of the ownership system and changes in the degree of freedom of competition of enterprises, to clarify the relationship between the government, the market and the rule of law, clearly position the boundary between the government and the market, and lay the institutional foundation for a higher level of opening up to the outside world.

Benchmarking Global Standards: Accelerating Shanghai's International Financial Center Development

February 14, 2020, the People's Bank of China, the Banking and Insurance Commission, the Securities and Futures Commission, the Foreign Exchange Bureau, the Shanghai Municipal People's Government jointly issued the "on further accelerating the construction of the Shanghai International Financial Center and financial support for the integrated development of the Yangtze River Delta views", around the implementation of the CPC Central Committee, the State Council on the expansion of financial reform and opening-up of the deployment of the introduction of 30 specific measures. From the point of view of the specific content of the measures, each of which has a strong practical relevance and policy objectives pointing to the intention of accelerating the promotion of a wider range of Shanghai, a higher standard, a higher level of market openness, business innovation, factor agglomeration and the rules of convergence, and strive to achieve the basic construction of Shanghai with China's economic strength and the international status of the RMB international financial center compatible with the goal.

As a key player in the development of international financial centers, the Shanghai Municipal Government is committed to advancing the construction of such centers. On January 15, 2020, the Shanghai Municipal Government released the "Implementation Plan for Accelerating the Construction of Shanghai's Financial Technology Center," outlining 25 innovative and practical initiatives across five key areas. The goal is to transform Shanghai into a globally competitive financial technology hub within 5 years. The plan aims to establish Shanghai as a globally competitive fintech center over the course of 5 years.

In the face of national tasks, historical missions and established time nodes, Shanghai, which has always been leading China's financial reform and open development with high standards of early and pilot implementation, should not only benchmark the advanced management experience and international operation rules of major international financial centers, such as New York and London, but also work diligently and in the spirit of working from day to night. Of course, because the construction of an international financial center is an extremely complex systematic national project, relying on the efforts of the local government is far from enough, but we also need to have the ability to communicate and coordinate and implement the systematic support to ensure the implementation. Therefore, whether the People's Bank of China has assumed an important coordinating role, or as an important participant in the Banking and Insurance Commission, the Securities and Futures Commission, the Foreign Exchange Bureau, as well as holding the relevant resources to support the ability of the Development and Reform Commission, the Ministry of Science and Technology, the Ministry of Industry and Information Technology and the Ministry of Finance and other ministries and commissions, we must coordinate the implementation of the unprecedented sense of urgency to accelerate the promotion of the construction of the Shanghai International Financial Center. From the coordination and implementation level, the Action Plan for the Construction of Shanghai International Financial Center (2018–2020), which was introduced on January 17, 2019, clearly stipulates that the action plan was agreed by the State Council and jointly issued by eight departments, including the People's Bank of China, and promoted in a coordinated manner. This reflects the coordination at the central government level and the respective roles of the relevant participants.

On the other hand, in terms of the reform and development of the global financial system and the competition pattern of international financial centers, the construction of international financial centers has long been not limited to a country's domestic affairs, but requires the in-depth involvement of relevant international market players and win-win cooperation. In other words, whether Shanghai can be built as an international financial center in line with China's economic strength and the international status of the RMB as scheduled depends not only on the upgrading of China's economic development and the progress of RMB internationalization, but also on whether the world's top financial capitals, such as Goldman Sachs, Morgan Stanley, UBS and BlackRock, etc., will regard Shanghai as the most important platform for sharing China's economic development, as well as whether the international industrial capitals will take Shanghai as the most important platform for the development of China's economy, and whether the international industrial capitals will take Shanghai as the most important platform for the development of China's economy.

At present, more than 2 trillion U.S. dollars of foreign capital in China's territory to create profits of hundreds of billions of dollars a year, which is the attraction of China's global industrial chain center. Of course, international financial capital is also concerned about the huge market opportunities brought by China's gradual emergence as a global wealth center. In fact, in the global economy, trade and finance encountered a lot of uncertainty in 2019. JP Morgan, Nomura, UBS and other representatives of international financial capital are generally optimistic about the Chinese market, obviously accelerated the business layout in Shanghai. With the inclusion of A-shares in the MSCI index and FTSE Russell Emerging Markets Index, and the inclusion of China's bond market in the Bloomberg Barclays Global Aggregate Index, the net increase in foreign investors' holdings of domestic bonds and equities in 2019 will be as high as 128 billion U.S. dollars. The official launch of the Shanghai-London Stock Connect (HLCC) on June 17, 2019 marks the effective docking of the financial trading systems of the two major cities in the East and the West, namely Shanghai and London, and signifies that there is a vast market for the HLCC. It also signifies that China, with its vast market space and huge demand for financial services, is accelerating the release of reform and development dividends to developed countries, including the United Kingdom.

The United Kingdom, which is densely covered with financial genes, has been making every effort to promote the construction of London as the offshore center of RMB in Europe in recent years. This is for the United Kingdom after the departure of the European Union, is a national development strategy to grasp the opportunity. As the old financial "aristocrat", Britain has a few advantages that emerging economies can not reach: London is the world's most historical top financial center and primary products pricing center; in the international financial market, London's level of service has long been ranked first in the world; London's position as the world's most important foreign exchange center has been for many years, no one can be shaken; London is the world's most important foreign exchange center. Can be shaken; London is also the world's top financial expertise and financial creativity of the concentration of the area. All these are undoubtedly very important overseas resources. In the process of moving towards an international financial center with global influence and competitiveness, Shanghai needs to pay special attention to absorbing the historical experience of the construction of old international financial centers such as London and make up for the short boards of relevant systems and elements. At the same time, Shanghai should look forward to the new opportunities and possible new variables in the competition and development of international financial centers in the twenty-first century, and rooted in the basic conditions of China as the world's largest emerging economy, take the establishment of a RMB-denominated global wealth allocation center and asset pricing center as a breakthrough, and continue to push for the enrichment and improvement of the supply system of global financial public products. The British have always been extremely sensitive to changes in the trend of the British also understand that the internationalization of the RMB is very difficult to stop the trend, in fact, London is the world's first offshore foreign exchange trading center of the RMB and the world's second largest offshore RMB clearing center.

If one day, high-tech companies from the United States, Europe, and Japan can be listed on Shanghai's Science and Technology Innovation Board, similar to how Alibaba is listed on NASDAQ, it will signify that Shanghai has essentially established its position as the center for financial asset allocation and wealth management in Asia.

How Chinese Enterprises Can Avoid New "Pitfalls" in Internationalization

On August 3, 2022, Fortune magazine released its list of the world's top 500 companies. As the world's top two economies, the United States and China have more companies on the list than all other countries combined, demonstrating the positive correlation between the size of a country's economy and the number of multinational corporations it hosts.

Since this list came out in 1995, the enterprises that have occupied the list for a long time are mainly from the United States, Japan and European economic powers, and Chinese enterprises have long been in a supporting role. For example, in 1995, the U.S. and Japan had 151 and 149 companies on the list, while China had only

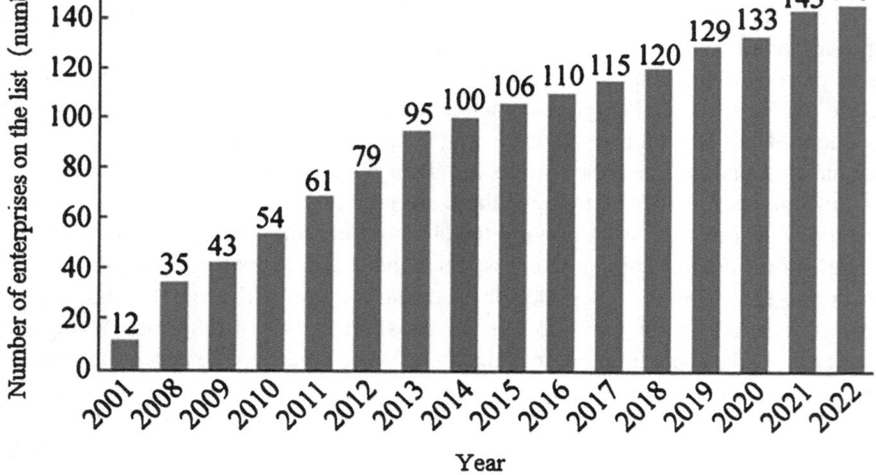

Fig. 8.2 Number of Chinese enterprises entering the fortune global 500 list. Data source: Fortune

three; 6 years later, in 2001, when China joined the WTO, China had 12 companies on the list; 10 years later, in 2011, as the size of China's economy surpassed that of Japan, the number of Chinese companies on the list also surpassed that of Japan. Today, Chinese companies are the absolute dominant players in this list (See Fig. 8.2).

This change underscores the significant progress achieved by Chinese enterprises through their active engagement in the global division of labor and resource allocation since joining the WTO. It also reiterates the importance of economic globalization, the effective integration of domestic and international markets, and the ongoing expansion of openness for emerging economies and developing nations.

Examining the timeline, from the inception of reform and opening up in 1978 to China's entry into the WTO in 2001, it took 23 years to establish the groundwork for China's participation in the global economic division of labor and the internationalization of its enterprises. With accession to the WTO serving as the logical starting point for opening up interfaces for two-way linkages between Chinese enterprises and the international market, China subsequently underwent three stages of development.

The first stage was the transition period of "WTO accession," which spanned from 2001 to 2006, during which Chinese enterprises experienced rapid growth in a relatively favorable international environment.

Domestic enterprises, on the one hand, have stepped up their efforts to familiarize themselves with international rules, especially commercial and legal rules, and have gradually raised their awareness of risks; on the other hand, they have seized the enormous opportunities for development brought about by WTO accession, and have given full play to the comparative advantages of the export processing industry that have been accumulated over the years, and have made every effort to expand their exports to developed markets and emerging markets. Manufacturing enterprises have also significantly improved their international competitiveness and continued to expand their international market share by accepting the dividends of international industrial transfer and absorbing more advanced technologies and combining them with independent research and development. China's financial industry, represented by its banks, has also made full use of the window of time given for reform during the transition period, introduced international strategic investors, accelerated equity reforms and established a modern corporate governance system, thus greatly narrowing the gap with its international counterparts.

The second stage is marked by the outbreak of the U.S. subprime mortgage crisis from 2007 to 2012, during which the world emerged from the turbulent recessionary quagmire. Chinese enterprises withstood the international financial crisis, particularly enduring the severe test posed by fluctuations in the export market.

Under the country's strategic plan of actively expanding domestic demand and promoting Chinese enterprises to "go out" to seek global resource allocation, Chinese enterprises with the conditions to seek to expand their overseas market share through the knowledge they have acquired since their accession to the World Trade Organization (WTO), and by accumulating experience in competition with their counterparts in the U.S.A., Europe and Japan, are actively seeking to build a regional and even global resource allocation system by laying the material and technical conditions for the construction of a regional and even global resource allocation system. They are actively seeking to expand their overseas market share and laying down material and technical conditions for the construction of a regional and even global resource allocation system. This stage is not only the golden period of effective division of labor and cooperation between China and the major economies of the world, but also one of the fastest periods of improvement in the internationalization capability of Chinese enterprises. During this period, China has successively released development dividends to the outside world, continuously opened up its domestic market, and become one of the most important participants in global direct investment.

The third stage is marked by the 18th National Congress of the Communist Party of China (CPC), held in 2012. This event heralded a new period for Chinese enterprises to deeply participate in the international division of labor and assume key roles in the global value chain, industrial chain, and supply chain.

On the one hand, China is restoring the rebalancing of the domestic economy through supply-side structural reforms, and on that basis, it is committed to building and improving a modernized economic system through high-standard opening-up in all directions, at multiple levels and in a wide range of fields. On the other hand, it has been promoting regional and global trade and investment facilitation and connectivity with unprecedented efforts, and implementing the Belt and Road Initiative, which is a global public good, into concrete actions through mutually beneficial cooperation between Chinese enterprises and enterprises of countries along the Belt and Road Initiative. Through mutually beneficial cooperation between Chinese enterprises and enterprises in countries along the Belt and Road, China has put the Belt and Road initiative, which is a global public good, into concrete actions, and thus become one of the important forces in maintaining and leading globalization. Many world-class Chinese enterprises with global competitiveness have grown up during this period.

Regrettably, since 2017, the power preference of major developed countries to promote globalization has obviously declined, and protectionism and unilateralism have become serious constraints on global financial stability, trade and investment facilitation as well as enterprises' pursuit of optimal allocation of global resources, resulting in the fact that Chinese enterprises, which have been deeply integrated into the global economic system and have played an important role in the economic life of all countries around the world including the developed countries, are facing a major "trap" in internationalization since "accession to the WTO". As an important beneficiary of globalization, Chinese enterprises have encountered all kinds of tangible or intangible protectionist obstacles when they try to return the development dividends brought by globalization, and the international living and development environment has become much worse than before, and they even face the risk of being subject to a global resource optimization and allocation system. The international environment for survival and development has been greatly weakened, and even faces the danger of "semi-globalization". The so-called "semi-globalization" refers to the belief that the world may be divided into two sets of markets and technology systems, and that Chinese enterprises are unable to fully participate as equal market players. Clearly, this has become one of the most serious challenges to globalization in the twenty-first century.

However, where there is danger, there is opportunity. If we approach the situation with calmness, we will realize that despite the growing uncertainty in the world order today, which may even seem somewhat ominous, even the most brutal and non-compliant countries cannot suppress the trend of globalization indefinitely. The Chinese and foreign enterprises listed in the Fortune 500 will continue to be the pillars of globalization. Those at the helm of truly global enterprises with an entrepreneurial spirit also understand better that the inherent momentum of globalization, based on the free flow of factors and the reduction of transaction costs, can hardly be halted. In today's world, no country or enterprise can artificially obstruct the industrial chain, supply chain, and value chain. They should not attempt to prove that they are more astute than the market-driven free economic order.

Maximizing the promotion and facilitation of the rational flow of capital, technology, and related factors, constructing a wide range of benefit-sharing mechanisms between Chinese and foreign enterprises, as well as between Chinese enterprises and global service recipients or consumers, and continuously releasing the internationalization dividends of Chinese enterprises are key strategies to overcome the new internationalization "trap".

RCEP: A New Paradigm for Regional Free Trade in an Era of Competition and Cooperation

At a time when the supply of regional and global public goods is experiencing insufficient momentum due to the impact of protectionism and unilateralism, the signing of RCEP is a pivotal move to inject elements of predictable growth dividends into the uncertain world economy.

An editorial in the international mainstream financial media indicated that at a time when the benefits of trade liberalization are being questioned and concerns about globalization are escalating globally, the signing of the RCEP holds not only strong symbolic significance but also serves as a reminder to the world that trade liberalization is the optimal path to achieve greater prosperity.

Indeed, as the capitalist world, which has long championed trade liberalization and reaped numerous benefits from it, has recently begun to exhibit a tendency to resist trade liberalization, it is especially crucial for the international community to demonstrate robust support for trade liberalization and the facilitation of trade and investment through practical actions. The Regional Comprehensive Economic Partnership (RCEP), encompassing the most dynamic economies in the Asia-Pacific region, stands as the quintessential testament to economic globalization and regional economic integration.

With regard to the national conditions, economic development levels and institutional cultures of the 15 members of RCEP, the fact that a high-standard trade agreement could be negotiated and finalized in less than 10 years is in itself a masterpiece that unites the wisdom and collective intelligence of the members. As we all know, since Smith's inception of modern economics, trade liberalization, as one of the core concepts of classical economics, has played an important role in promoting global economic growth and enhancing the well-being of the people of all countries, and has been an important driving force for global economic prosperity. However, since 2017, global trade has been disturbed by factors with some strong policy preferences, and trade frictions between major economies have been intensifying, so that global trade volume declined in 2019 for the first time in 10 years. The WTO, which is widely regarded as the world's most important public good in the field of trade, is facing a crisis of survival, indicating that the "unethical behavior" of individual countries is undermining the cornerstone of trade liberalization, and that the global trading system in the post-Bretton Woods era is facing major challenges.

Fortunately, with the advancement of digital technology, the trade in services has become the most dynamic segment of international trade. According to the World Trade Report 2019 released by the WTO, global trade in services experienced an average annual growth rate of 5.4% from 2005 to 2017. This trend is anticipated to persist over the next two decades. China stands as a significant contributor to the expansion of global trade in services, a testament to the developmental benefits it has shared with its trading partners worldwide, as evidenced by its per capital GDP, which has surged to $10,000.

Looking at all 20 chapters of RCEP, although the content is very rich and even some provisions are complicated, the most obvious feature is the reduction of tariffs. For example, the number of zero-tariff products in the trade of goods as a whole exceeds 90%, the level of liberalization of trade in services and investment is significantly higher than that of the original "10+1" FTA, and the FTA between two pairs of important economies, namely, China, Japan and Japan and South Korea, has been added. In particular, the tariff reduction arrangement between China and Japan, as the second and third largest economies in the world, will greatly promote the economic integration of East Asia. The liberalization and harmonization of rules of origin for intra-members' trade in commodities, i.e., the harmonization of rules of origin, will be very conducive to the promotion of a more extensive Free Trade Area of the Asia-Pacific (FTAAP) process. People familiar with the import and export business know that when exporters only need a certificate of origin to trade with any member of RCEP, its strategic value is not only the facilitation and saving transaction costs related to institutional arrangements, but also to maintain the regional industrial chain, supply chain security and stability of the important guarantee.

China now plays a dual role in the upstream, midstream and downstream segments of the Asia-Pacific and global industrial chain. China is not only the largest provider of global intermediate goods, but also plays a central role in the global industrial chain. China has not only gradually climbed up to the middle and high end of the global value chain in the fields of information, high-end equipment manufacturing, etc., but also formed an international pattern of division of labor in the middle and low end of the global industrial chain, with China as the upstream country and Vietnam and other regional manufacturing centers as the downstream countries. As a result, China has built a more dynamic internal and external economic linkage system. Under the framework of RCEP, China's foreign-funded enterprises will build a new community of interests based on the industrial and technological division of labor, which is a very beneficial structural arrangement for Chinese enterprises to expand the global industrial chain, and for regional members to release resource allocation and related development dividends from China.

It should be noted that the division of labor and cooperation within the industrial chain between China and the major global economies, as well as China's pivotal role in the global industrial and supply chains, are underpinned by an inherent economic logic. This logic is characterized by the cyclical and phased nature of changes in the global industrial production and industry patterns, as well as by stability within these cycles.

Around 2010, China became an emerging economy with a complete industrial chain of high, medium and low industries in the global manufacturing industry, and it is since then that China has become the most important force for global economic growth, and has been releasing growth dividends from China to the region and the world. The release of this wave of dividends, the future will be based on the upgrading of the manufacturing industry, a high level of openness and the internationalization of finance, etc., and the timely signing of the RCEP and the implementation of the landing, may make the release of the dividends of growth for 30 years. Obviously, this will constitute a new impetus for economic globalization and further trade and investment facilitation in the first half of the twenty-first century.

In the era of competition, the RCEP members in the Asia-Pacific region, with significant disparities in economic and social development levels, have concluded a high-standard trade liberalization agreement. This agreement not only effectively counters the prevalent trade fragmentation, protectionism, and nationalism at the national level in recent years but also is expected to provide a new development paradigm for the replication and promotion of new types of multilateral trade and investment agreements in the global market through the subsequent implementation on the ground.

Regulating Foreign Investment to Safeguard Security for Higher-Standard Opening-Up

The National Development and Reform Commission (NDRC) and the Ministry of Commerce (MOFCOM) issued the Measures for Security Review of Foreign Investment on December 19, 2020, to which some foreign media have paid "unusual" attention, deliberately linking it to protectionism. In fact, those who are familiar with international investment rules and territorialized management know clearly that the security review system for foreign investment is a common practice in developed countries or regions such as the United States, Europe, Japan, Australia and so on, and is not original to China. From the point of view of institutional arrangements or government regulation to regulate foreign direct investment, China's promulgation and implementation of such a provision has no special objective, but is precisely a move to comply with the law.

Over 40 years of reform and opening up, China has evolved from a weak participant in international trade to the world's second-largest recipient of foreign investment. A significant reason for this is China's continuous expansion of openness, which has optimized the business environment and subsequently unleashed successive waves of dividends. Statistics indicate that from 2020 to 2022, China's annual absorption of foreign investment amounted to $149.3 billion, $173.4 billion, and $189.1 billion, respectively. Even with the new crown epidemic, a major external variable that has seriously impacted international trade and investment, the objective reality of China remaining one of the world's most sought-after investment destinations has not changed.

As one of the two economies in the world with an economic size exceeding 10 trillion dollars, China's stock of foreign investment stands at 2.4 trillion dollars, with an annual investment income amounting to hundreds of billions. As China progresses towards becoming the world's largest economy and largest import market, the benefits it releases to the international market extend beyond the sharing of general market opportunities. They also encompass the systematic products of "high quality at appropriate prices" and the substantial dividends of the internationalization of the RMB.

Smart international investors pay particular attention to studying China's major development strategies. In their view, China's continued opening up and effective acceptance of the dividends associated with economic globalization are the fundamental reasons why it has become one of the world's most important manufacturing and trading centers. China's Foreign Investment Law, which came into force on January 1, 2020, effectively strengthens the protection of the legitimate rights and interests of foreign investments, relaxes market access, and optimizes the business environment with the authority and enforceability of law, aiming to achieve an effective interface between China and developed countries in terms of market access and intellectual property rights protection from the perspective of system design and implementation.

As China approaches the completion of its industrialization and is dedicated to establishing itself as an industrial and financial powerhouse, it will persist in optimizing the environment for foreign investment. The country is committed to further opening up to enhance its international competitiveness, thereby releasing the benefits of reform and development to both domestic and foreign participants within its vast market space and continuously expanding service demand.

But there is no such thing as an open and unregulated market, otherwise it would be a sort of "tragedy of the commons". Smart international investors will not stay in that kind of "commons" for long. In fact, in today's world, there is no country that does not attach importance to the construction of national economic security system, including industrial security, financial security and so on. Whether as the world's largest foreign capital absorber of the United States, or an important participant in the international market in Germany, Japan, Britain, France and so on, all so. Only individual Western powers in recent years, deliberately distorting the use of its, often national security reasons for foreign investment into their own markets set up heavy obstacles and even sanctions, resulting in protectionism, unilateralism has become a major threat to the facilitation of international trade and investment. During the "14th Five-Year Plan" period and for a long time to come, China will be based on good institutional design and high level of opening up to the outside world, to promote global trade and investment trade facilitation, and lead the development of a new round of economic globalization. In the next decade or so, as long as we maintain an average annual growth rate of about 5%, we will become the world's largest capital exporter and the largest consumer market in 2035. In this process, how to promote and protect foreign investment with a market-oriented, rule-of-law and internationalized business environment, how to effectively safeguard national economic security while connecting to the internationally accepted trade and investment rules, and how to ensure the sustained and healthy development of China's economy are not only the list of tasks in front of the Chinese government, but also China's international responsibility as an important guarantor of the global trade and investment system in the twenty-first century.

The International Political Economy Logic of China's High-Standard Opening-Up

Repairing the global economic, trade, and technological systems that have been disrupted, as well as the financial ecosystem that has degraded, is easier said than done in the short term. Addressing the dysfunction of the economic system, or economic ecosystem, will be the foremost priority for all nations.

For China, injecting a stabilizing factor into an uncertain world through a high level of openness to the outside, and then promoting and leading the facilitation of trade and investment on a regional and even global scale, is the mission entrusted to China, as the world's second-largest economy, by history.

China's Longstanding Commitment to Opening-Up

The 2020 Central Economic Work Conference held in December 2020, when deploying the work for the opening year of the "14th Five-Year Plan", put forward specific requirements for building a high-standard socialist market economic system, opening up to the outside world at a high level, and promoting the mutual reinforcement of reforms and opening up, including relaxing market access, promoting fair competition, protecting intellectual property rights, building a unified market, creating a market, rule of law and international business environment;

actively considering joining the CPTPP; improving macroeconomic governance, strengthening international macroeconomic policy coordination, and creating a market, rule of law and international business environment. protection of intellectual property rights, building a unified market, and creating a market-oriented, rule-of-law, internationalized business environment; actively considering joining the CPTPP; and attaching importance to the application of internationally accepted rules to safeguard national security in the process of improving macroeconomic governance and strengthening international macroeconomic policy coordination. To summarize, China, which has become a global mega-market, has not only not tightened its pace of opening up to the outside world due to the interference or even suppression from external economic conservatism, but also insisted on implementing opening up to the outside world in a wider scope, broader fields and at a deeper level.

As we all know, China's opening up to the outside world was initiated, explored, and gradually deepened in the absence of an existing reference system. If we examine the timeline, starting from 1978, when the Third Plenary Session of the Eleventh Central Committee formally decided to open up to the outside world, to 2013, when the Third Plenary Session of the Eighteenth Central Committee of the Communist Party of China (CPC) adopted the Decision of the CPC Central Committee on Several Major Issues Concerning the Comprehensive Deepening of Reforms, a full 35 years have elapsed since then. All these years have been dedicated to preparing for the implementation of China's opening up to the outside world at high levels today.

Because from the past 30 years of China's economic growth of the constituent elements, it is thanks to the government of the private economy management system reform deepening, the development of the private economy environment has been significantly optimized, China's private business endowment has been suppressed for a long time has been stimulated, coupled with the continuous expansion of opening up to the outside world to promote the inflow of FDI and the efficiency of the private, foreign-funded enterprises and the competition, the state-owned enterprises itself, the continuous improvement of operational efficiency, together constitute the driving force of China's economic growth. Together with the continuous expansion of open-door policy to promote the inflow of FDI and the efficiency radiation and competition among private and foreign enterprises, the state-owned enterprises themselves have been improving their operational efficiency, which together constitute the driving force of China's economic growth.

Since 2013, the economic strength of developed countries has relatively declined, leaving them with less capacity to drive economic globalization and provide global public goods. This has led to a collective trend of "involution," exposing structural deficiencies in the guardians of the global economic and trading system. Additionally, there has been a noticeable increase in national-level egoism, and trade liberalization development has intermittently faced a "lack of oxygen" situation. Consequently, the global economic and trading system's guarantors are grappling with structural issues, national-level egoism is on the rise, and trade liberalization is experiencing periodic challenges.

In this period of uncertainty, China has seized the 40th anniversary of its reform and opening-up as an opportunity to introduce a series of liberalization measures that have exceeded expectations. It has been continuously shortening the negative list for foreign investment access, accelerating the construction of free trade zones, and actively seeking bilateral or multilateral trade and investment agreements with regional and globally significant economies to establish a permanent and stable market access mechanism.

On the other hand, during this period, China has also launched the BRICS New Development Bank, the Asian Investment Bank and other investment and financing public products that have gathered the greatest common denominator in the world, which fully reflects that China, as an important beneficiary of globalization, is fulfilling its commitments in terms of market access, trade in goods, trade in services, intellectual property rights protection and transparency through continuous opening up at a time when the multilateral trading system and the logic of global economic integration are being challenged in an unprecedented manner, providing important impetus to the new round of globalization. China's continued openness in fulfilling its commitments in market access, trade in goods, trade in services, intellectual property protection and transparency will provide an important impetus to the new round of globalization. Facts have shown that the more uncertain the global economy is, the more China further integrates into and even leads economic globalization through in-depth opening up, thus providing the most important impetus for global economic growth. This is evidenced by the fact that China's average contribution to world economic growth in recent years has exceeded 30%.

Addressing the "Samuelson's Concern" Through Concrete Actions

As a significant external factor, the novel coronavirus pandemic was the primary cause of the severe global economic downturn in 2020 and the widespread resurgence of "depression economics." Given the challenge of identifying a baseline scenario for the pandemic-related shocks, the global economy experienced a precipitous decline, severely affecting the resilience of economic systems worldwide, particularly the stability and resilience of the global industrial and supply chains.

In addition to the impact of the epidemic, the global economy has also been dragged down by protectionism, unilateralism and hegemony, which are characterized by strong national interests. Despite being the first to be hit by the epidemic, the East Asian countries represented by China, Japan and South Korea have, on the whole, demonstrated a strong ability to cope with the impact of the epidemic in a comprehensive manner. China, in particular, has been able to stabilize its economic fundamentals in a relatively short period of time and become the only country among the world's major economies to achieve positive growth in 2020, which will become the most valuable sample of a large country in the history of global disaster economics.

With the signing and gradual implementation of RCEP, East Asia and Southeast Asia are expected to become an important source of global investment and trade growth. With the anticipated resurgence of multilateralism to some extent, if major economic powers can maintain stability in the economic and trade spheres and initiate negotiations to join the CPTPP, a stabilizing factor will be introduced into the global economic and trade system, which was previously expected to be in a state of significant uncertainty.

In today's world, no country or enterprise can overlook the connections between industrial chains, supply chains, and value chains. Neither capital nor national power can obstruct the rational flow of global factors by erecting various barriers. In other words, despite its imperfections, globalization—though not Pareto-optimal—is an indispensable pathway for fostering effective global economic growth and achieving human well-being.

Against this backdrop, China's launch of a new round of high-standard opening-up not only reflects the integration of its open economy, with a size exceeding 18 trillion U.S. dollars, a stock of foreign investment reaching up to 3.12 trillion U.S. dollars, and imports and exports surpassing 6.3 trillion U.S. dollars, into the process of leading global economic, trade, and financial system changes through more active and open institutional arrangements. It also releases benefits to the international market and, to some extent, alleviates Samuelson's Concern. The image of a responsible major country has, to some extent, addressed "Samuelson's Concern" through concrete actions.

The so-called "Samuelson's Concern" originates from a paper titled "Globalization in the Eyes of Mainstream Economists," published by Paul Samuelson in the summer 2004 issue of the Journal of Political Economy (JPE), an American economics journal. Against the backdrop of the economic rise of China and India, the paper contends that the United States has gained a competitive edge by making innovations in certain fields. However, once latecomer countries achieve comparable productivity through borrowing and learning, the United States' competitive advantage will disappear, and its national interests could be permanently compromised. In essence, Samuelson's article has influenced the international trade policy perspectives of United States policymakers.

As China continues to advance technologically, its position in the global industrial and supply chains will continue to rise. While China will pay attention to the maintenance of national economic security to ensure the sustained and healthy development of the Chinese economy, while interfacing with internationally recognized rules of trade and investment, the economic complementarities between China and the major developed countries will persist for a long period of time in the first half of the twenty-first century.

Global economic development, trade facilitation, and financial stability all necessitate that major economic powers transcend their differences. They must collectively foster the free movement of goods and capital, share the benefits, and enhance the global economic governance system to actively promote effective global economic growth. This logic underpins China's strategy of high-standard opening-up to the world in the realm of international political economy.

Chapter 9
How to Achieve Effective Growth and Coordinated Development in the Economy

Grasping the Economic Growth Mechanism and Development Pulse of a Distinct Emerging Economy

In the coming period, while increasing its investment in human capital, China should lead the overall upgrading of its industrial structure with forward-looking technological inputs and high-quality technological transformation. At this stage, on the basis of undertaking international technology transfer, certain enterprises with relative competitive advantages should all the more improve the security of Chinese enterprises in the global value chain through independent innovation. On the other hand, China should strive to enhance its professional service capabilities in financial markets, research and development design, and system integration, strengthen its financial services, technology supply and operation management functions, especially its ability to manage the global value chain, and increase its investment in key technologies in strategic emerging industries, in order to expect a breakthrough in core technology bottlenecks in key industrial sectors that are crucial to China's future position in the international division of labor.

The global economy is being abducted to some extent by what appears to be irrational trade protectionism underlying national competitive strategies, and thus faces a delicate window of new growth uncertainty. It is particularly important for China, as a unique emerging power, to maintain stable economic growth and development momentum, and to continue to lead the new round of globalization and trade liberalization order changes.

Y. Zhang, *Addressing Uncertainty*, Understanding China,
https://doi.org/10.1007/978-981-92-2692-4_9

China's Great Contribution to the World Economy and the Development of Economics

Since March 2018, the biggest variable in the global economy has originated in the world's number one economic power, not from endogenous and exogenous variables in the economic sense, but rather from the policy preferences of individual leaders and strong uncertainty of expectations.

For the world's second largest economy, China's economy in 2018 achieved a growth rate of 6.6%, contributing 30% incremental growth for the global economy, and this figure is the conclusion of the IMF after measurement. The IMF's *World Economic Outlook Report*, released on April 9, 2019, revised China's 2019 economic growth forecast to 6.3%, up 0.1 percentage point from the January estimate. China was the only one of the major economies to have its economic growth forecast raised. Data from China's National Bureau of Statistics also showed that China achieved an economic growth rate of 6.4% in the first quarter of 2019, which exceeded expectations, thanks to tax reforms, effective fiscal policies and the expression of related measures aimed at boosting consumption. As the OECD chief said at the time, even if the growth rate slows down, it is expected that China's economy will still maintain a growth rate of more than 6% in 2019 and 2020, continue to be the main driving force of world economic growth, and continue to catch up with developed countries. The OECD even predicted in the recently released *China Economic Survey* that by 2030, China's share of world GDP will be as high as 27%, and its contribution to world economic growth will exceed that of OECD members.

China's reform and opening-up has made remarkable achievements without a ready reference. Relevant studies have shown that many successful explorations in the process of China's economic reform and development have not only partially changed the general conclusions of existing economics, but have also gradually become the subject of research and the focus of attention of mainstream economics. For example, the reform of the economic system centered on the reform of state-owned enterprises has, in a sense, proved the feasibility and rationality of gradual reform, as well as distilled the logic of property rights reform in countries in transition. China's reforms have taught the world that, while clear property rights are very important, they are not the only arrangement for promoting economic development, nor is it the most important institutional arrangement. The property rights system is an endogenous institutional arrangement, and it is only when other systems of the market economy have been improved accordingly that the endogenous nature of property rights will be clarified, thus further promoting economic development. Under the guidance of an effective government, SOEs can not only adapt to marketization, but also construct new advantages in market competition.

It can be said that China's economic reforms, characterized by gradual reforms, provide a valuable research sample for related reforms around the world. The study of this sample has enriched the research perspectives of modern economics. In fact, the development experience of major economies shows that important reform junctures faced by countries are important opportunities for breakthroughs in economic research and economic policy revolutions. The stagflation dilemma facing the U.S. economy in the 1970s provided a rare opportunity to develop Lucas's New Classical Macroeconomics. After Clinton came to power, faced with the George H.W. The Bush administration left a pile of economic problems, he asked many big-name economists for advice, and then neutralized Keynesianism, Monetarism, Supply-side economics and Rational Expectations School, and established a set of both opposed to complete laissez-faire and opposed to excessive intervention of the Clinton economics, which in turn created the golden eight years of the United States after World War II in the history of the economy, so that a lot of Americans are still nostalgic about the Clinton's administration of that period of good times.

Similarly, although China's reform and opening-up has lasted for more than 40 years and more than 1600 reform programs have been introduced, reform is always on the way. The many complex issues facing China's reform and opening-up process today also provide excellent research samples for responsible Chinese economists, such as the establishment of a sound market economic system.

How to Initiate the Next Cycle of Prosperity in the Chinese Economy?

After gradually bidding farewell to the demographic dividend, the "WTO accession" dividend and the international industrial transfer dividend, China's future economic growth momentum will face more uncertainty. Some Western economic analysts have asserted that China's economy is about to collapse, which is a typical bearish argument. However, we don't need to pay too much attention to it. If we look at it from a different perspective, this is not a bad reminder that we should look at economic fundamentals and medium to long-term growth risks. Of course, the author doesn't agree with the judgment of some optimists, based on Kondratiev Cycle Theory, that China will be able to achieve an average annual economic growth rate of 8% until 2030 by adjusting its economic growth tools. This is because, leaving aside the question of whether or not the supporting conditions are sufficient to achieve the above-mentioned growth targets, the solution of such a serious economic problem requires not only long-term follow-up studies but also a full estimation of the complexities that may be faced in the future.

Studies have shown that China's economic growth is highly dependent on the established path. Once the established momentum declines and the alternative momentum is underdeveloped, it will mean a decline in economic growth. Therefore, the next boom cycle of China's economy must come from the deep-seated reform of the economic system, that is, how to shift the engine of economic growth to be driven by effective consumption and technological progress. The author has put forward three judgment perspectives on China's economic growth cycle switching: first, the "handover" cycle of the old and new growth engines and its smoothness;

second, the effective docking degree of the government's behavioral boundaries and the market's behavioral space; and third, the distribution of micro-entrepreneurs' vitality in the industry and the region and its performance. The so-called "handover" does not mean that new dynamics completely replace the functions of traditional growth dynamics, but rather that efforts must be made to cultivate and solidify the dominant dynamics that support long-term economic growth.

The strategic competition among the world's major economies is increasingly characterized by the competition for the dominance of core technologies and industries, especially the underlying technologies and pricing ability, which has become an important symbol of a country's ability to enter the high-end segment of the global value chain. As a unique emerging country, China, in the process of moving from a manufacturing and trading power to an industrial and capital power, urgently needs to make up for its shortcomings in basic research, industrialization and application, and global resource allocation, so as to strengthen the supply of independent technologies in important industrial fields, and thus enhance the level of benefits in the global market.

At present, the output value of China's manufacturing industry is roughly comparable to that of Germany, the world's fourth-largest economy, and the share of high-end manufacturing in the total value-added of industry is comparable to that of the United States, the European Union and Japan, indicating that the impetus for economic growth based on technological progress has been relatively strong. However, foreign capital plays an important role in China's high-end manufacturing output, and even dominates in some areas. Some key technical shortcomings can never be eliminated overnight. China has long emphasized applied research and experimentation and ignored the status quo of basic research has not yet undergone a fundamental change. The United States basic research accounted for nearly 20% of all R&D investment, while China less than 6%, the gap is quite obvious. Long-term large and stable investment in basic research is a prerequisite for breeding revolutionary technological breakthroughs. Innovation in the true sense of the word is large-scale creative destruction, which requires not only the groundbreaking expression of strong accumulation of basic research, but also the conscious development of relevant behaviors, especially open-mindedness, willingness to take risks, industriousness, fun, and a mindset that dares to challenge technological authority, to be widely formed in the whole society.

In other words, to change China's passive situation in the field of general-purpose computer CPUs and basic software as well as integrated circuits and chips with high degree of dependence on foreign countries, which seriously affects the security of the industry, a large amount of R&D investment is certainly an indispensable condition, but the key also lies in the full respect of the law of basic research, tolerance of innovation failure, attaching great importance to the endowment of human resources for innovation, and the highest priority protection of property rights, especially intellectual property rights, and elimination of impatience, and so on. The key lies in full respect for the law of basic research, tolerance for innovation failure, great attention to the innovation endowment of talents, the highest priority for the protection of property rights, especially intellectual property rights, and the elimination of impetuous mentality. There is a particular need to change the ossified administrative-led resource allocation model, to create a favorable innovation ecosystem, and to change the government's position in the innovation system. In the medium and long term, a fundamental change in education philosophy and a breakthrough in the education and research system are also needed.

The history of economic development has proved that in order for any economy to achieve high-quality development, it must first achieve high-quality growth. The prerequisite for realizing high-quality growth is to ensure the incremental returns to scale caused by knowledge innovation, technological progress and human capital as the core endogenous variables. The endogenization of technological progress is forcing China in the twenty-first century to continue to increase its investment in human capital, promote the rational mobility of labour factors and raise total factor productivity. If we can transform the technology and business model of traditional industries through artificial intelligence, big data, and "Internet Plus", increase R&D investment in forward-looking technologies and industrialization, continue to open up, and widely activate the business and innovation endowment of the private economy, endogenous growth based on a significant increase in total factor productivity will be the most important foundation for supporting high-quality development. The most important foundation for high-quality development.

From the policy level, China's supply-side structural reform should not only accomplish market clearing and the cultivation of new dynamics and new driving forces, but also attach great importance to the forward-looking study of market instability and economic complexity, especially external uncertainty and complex economic and financial systems, within the logical framework of global economic integration.

For this reason, in the coming period, while increasing its investment in human capital, China should lead the overall upgrading of its industrial structure with forward-looking technological investment and high-quality technological transformation. At this stage, certain enterprises with relative competitive advantages should, on the basis of undertaking international technology transfer, improve the security of Chinese enterprises in the global value chain through independent innovation. On the other hand, China should strive to enhance its professional service capacity in financial market, R&D and design, system integration, etc., strengthen its financial service, technology supply and operation management functions, especially its ability to manage the global value chain, and increase its investment in key technologies in strategic emerging industries, with a view to breaking through the bottlenecks of core technologies in the key industrial fields concerning China's future position in the international division of labor, and forming a high-end industrial cluster at an early date to support the next growth cycle of China's economy. In order to break through the core technology bottlenecks in the key industries related to China's future position in the international division of labor, and to form a high-end industrial cluster that can support China's economy in the next growth cycle.

No unilateral or even multilateral force can easily cut China's core value chain, and no unilateral or even multilateral force can easily shorten China's economy and interrupt its economic development cycle. China and the world's major powers around the trade disputes and industry and the rules of control of the struggle will certainly start many rounds of strategic games. To this end, China must transcend its past inertia, master the logic of dealing with uncertain competitors, and improve its early-warning capabilities to stabilize development expectations.

Grasping the Shifts in Global Technology Hubs and New Trends in Talent Mobility

Behind science and technology is a collection of elements such as economic strength, R&D foundation, micro-entrepreneurs, organizational and institutional systems, decision-making leadership, and the research environment. In 2022, China's R&D investment has reached the scale of 440 billion U.S. dollars, accounting for 2.55% of GDP, which is comparable to the average level of the European Union. Both the growth rate of R&D investment and the growth rate of R&D personnel are the most outstanding among the major economies. Today, China has made major breakthroughs in basic research, experimental and applied research, and the construction of mega-engineering projects that combine the accumulation of cutting-edge technologies and complex management capabilities, such as 5G mobile communications, quantum communications, high-temperature iron-based superconductivity, manned spaceflight, deep-space and deep-ocean exploration, smart grids, nuclear power plants, etc., and is moving towards becoming a mega-innovative country in the twenty-first century.

In the past, the West has always preferred to look at China's economic development and scientific and technological achievements with a more static perspective. to China's scientific and technological development presents a "blowout" situation, although there are still significant discomfort, but in the face of China's great achievements in the field of science and technology one after another to stand up to scrutiny, even the most critical of Western science and technology observers, also have to recognize the unique advantages of China's organization and leadership in the field of cutting-edge science and technology and comprehensive management capabilities. Even the most critical Western science and technology observers are forced to recognize China's unique advantages and comprehensive management capabilities in organizing and leading cutting-edge science and technology. Among the top ten scientific discoveries in 2020 announced by *Nature* magazine through its official website, China's FAST telescope[1] is among the top ten scientific discoveries in terms of fast radio bursts. In fact, this achievement is a systematic project organized and implemented by the National Astronomical Observatories of the Chinese Academy of Sciences (CAS) aiming at the frontiers of scientific research to achieve major original breakthroughs, reflecting the leadership of Chinese scientists in this field.

[1] FAST, with China's independent intellectual property rights, is the most powerful single-antenna radio telescope with the largest aperture that has been built in the world, and its design comprehensively reflects China's high-tech innovation capability.

Just as China's economic reforms have begun and will continue to change the general conclusions of mainstream economics, China's progress in the field of science and technology is leading to the emergence of Beijing, Shanghai and Shenzhen as one of the world's major science and technology centers.

Correspondingly, the United States, Europe, Japan and other developed countries or regions of scientists and even top scientists have accelerated the flow to China in recent years. In particular, in Japan, which is close to China, more than 1000 top scientists have sought to develop in China in recent years. Statistics from Japan's Ministry of Education, Culture, Sports, Science and Technology (MEXT) show that the number of Japanese researchers who stayed in China for less than a month was about 18,460 in 2018, an increase of about 25% from 2014. The growing attraction of China to Japanese scientists, in addition to the increasing constraints of the domestic research and development environment in Japan, is also due to the significant improvement in the research base and capabilities of Chinese research institutes in recent years, and the return of hundreds of thousands of returnees to China to set up their own businesses, which has made it possible for researchers from both sides to have a smooth interface between research and technology.

It is generally believed that China's breakthrough progress in the field of science and technology and its attraction to talents from all over the world is attributed to the deepening of the reform of the science and technology management system by the Chinese government, which has significantly optimized the environment for the development of private science and technology enterprises, and stimulated the latent endowment of research and development and innovation of the Chinese civil society, which has led to the rapid development of the private science and technology enterprises. Together with the efficiency radiation of private and foreign enterprises and market competition, the continuous improvement of mission-driven innovation and industrialization efficiency of R&D carriers represented by colleges and universities, scientific research institutes, central enterprises and local state-owned enterprises, etc., together constitute the driving force of China's scientific and technological "blowout" in recent years. Another element that cannot be ignored is that China has been committed to innovation drive in recent years, and has made efforts to create an innovative ecological environment, which has gradually formed a solid soil that can nurture original achievements and industrialized applications, both in the developed coastal areas and in the central and western regions. For example, Guizhou, located in the western region of China, despite its relatively backward level of economic development, is realizing a turnaround in big data and applications under the leadership of a new round of technological revolution. Guizhou is not only China's first national-level big data comprehensive pilot zone, but its capital Guiyang is also focusing on building a nationwide platform for arithmetic services, transaction services, security services and talent services, and will form three major industrial clusters of data centers, electronic information manufacturing, and software and information technology services.

Looking at the current trend of global scientific and technological development, some super enterprises with strong R&D strength or seemingly small but innovative enterprises that are closely connected to the technology and market will lead the trend of scientific and technological and industrial changes to a large extent.

Correspondingly, some strategic talents who master the core technology will largely determine the degree of autonomy and control of a country or region in the field of key core technology. The history of global economic development has shown that the prerequisite for any economy to achieve high-quality development in the face of fierce international competition is to ensure increasing returns to scale caused by endogenous variables centered on knowledge innovation, technological progress and human capital. The endogenization of technological progress is forcing China to continue to increase its investment in human capital, promote the rational mobility of labour factors and raise total factor productivity.

From this point of view, China has reached or is close to the world's first-class level of colleges and universities and research institutions, the flow of its stock and incremental talent will, to a certain extent, affect the competitiveness of China's economy, technology and industry in the international arena. What should be done in the current and future period is not only to continue to expand international exchanges and cooperation in the field of education in the context of opening up to the outside world at a high level, but also to absorb and learn from the experience of leading international innovation and technology parks and enterprises, to continue to create a sense of belonging to the environment of teaching, scientific research and results incubation that can cultivate first-class talents, produce first-class scientific research results, and provide first-class industrial applications, and to form a sense of urgency and a systematic output mechanism for the construction of an innovation-oriented country by the whole society.

Digital Transformation as a Driving Force for Shanghai's First-Mover Advantage

Shanghai, which already has rich experience in the field of mega-city governance, has proposed in recent years to comprehensively promote the city's digital transformation, with the goal of creating an international digital capital with world influence. Shanghai, which has been newly positioned as a "central node of the domestic cycle and a strategic link between the domestic and international cycles", is pursuing its transformation and development with a spirit of urgency, with a view to realizing its vision for the 14th Five-Year Plan period and up to 2035, and to creating an endogenous mechanism that can ensure leapfrog development. In the process of realizing its vision for the 14th Five-Year Plan period and up to 2035, Shanghai is seeking to develop an endogenous driving force that will ensure leapfrog development.

Why is Shanghai proposing a digital transformation of the city as a whole? To what extent will Shanghai's strategic design lead the city's industrial transformation and development? How can Shanghai, in the midst of digital transformation, establish its competitive advantage in the first half of the twenty-first century through deep self-revolution and forward-looking grasp of future development trends based on the pulse of the world's industrial and technological development? These are not only major issues in front of policy makers and executives, but also realistic propositions that concern every market participant and the general public.

From the perspective of Shanghai's transformation and development dynamics, the COVID-19 pandemic, as an external variable, does not constitute an endogenous driving force for the city's digital transformation, but city managers have deeply felt the urgency of accelerating digital transformation and the huge development opportunities through the practical exploration of coping with the epidemic. Shanghai's experience in epidemic prevention and control shows that Shanghai has been able to achieve effective operation of the city while accurately managing and controlling risks, which not only reflects Shanghai's high capacity of big data screening based on the "One-stop Online Services" and "Unified Online Governance" and the terminal emergency response module, but also shows that Shanghai's rapid switching of economic development mode, including various new business forms, new models and new scenarios based on digital transformation, has greatly activated the city's self-repairing and balancing ability as an economic and social ecosystem. In a nutshell, the fact that Shanghai, with its highly export-oriented economy, can achieve an economic growth rate of 1.7% in 2020, the year of the outbreak of the new crown epidemic, is closely related to the timely complementary position of the new generation of information technology output value growth of 6.2%.

From the viewpoint that Shanghai is vigorously promoting the construction of "five centers" (international economy, finance, trade, shipping and scientific and technological innovation) and comprehensively strengthening the endogenous nature of "four major functions" (global resource allocation, scientific and technological innovation, high-end industry leadership and open hub and gateway), digital transformation is not only the basic condition for promoting the construction of "five centers" and strengthening the "four major functions", but also a key move for Shanghai to gain a leading edge in the competition for digital survival and development in global or regional cities such as New York, London, Tokyo and Singapore.

In recent years, the United States, Japan, Germany, the United Kingdom, France, Singapore and so on have put forward the digital development picture and given a specific roadmap, especially the United States, Singapore is making every effort to enhance the competitiveness of the digital economy. A research report of the Shanghai Academy of Social Sciences pointed out that China maintains a leading trend in digital industrial competitiveness, but there are shortcomings in digital innovation and digital governance. 2020, Shanghai, as the leading city in the Yangtze River Delta region, the digital economy totaled more than 2 trillion yuan, accounting for about 54% of the proportion of GDP. Throughout the 13th Five-Year Plan period, the average annual growth rate of Shanghai's digital economy industry will exceed 20%.

Specifically, Shanghai is accelerating the construction of the international economic center, international trade center, international shipping center, international financial center, as well as a scientific and technological innovation center with global influence, cannot be separated from the big data, artificial intelligence as the basic conditions of digital technology and related industries support. In recent years, Shanghai has accelerated the in-depth integration of new-generation information technology and manufacturing industry, as well as the synergistic innovation of "5G+AI+Industrial Internet" and the "two-network penetration" of Industrial

Internet and Consumer Internet to form a number of leading industrial scenarios, and to provide a platform for the integration of healthcare, finance, transportation, and other industries in the future. We will promote the popularization and application of new AI products and technologies in key fields and application scenarios for the integrated development of healthcare, finance and transportation. In addition, more than 200 companies have already been listed on the KEM Board of the SSE, indicating that policy makers not only hope to provide reasonable and effective valuation and financial support for high-potential companies including high-tech and strategic emerging industries through the system design and implementation of the KEM Board, but also hope to give birth to a new model of "Silicon Valley+Wall Street"—style of "Technology Grafting to Capital" in Shanghai. Obviously, the successful operation of the Science and Technology Innovation Board, combined with the new Lingang District's new breakthroughs in the formation of a full-chain "smart port" driven by "science and technology innovation + high-end industries", is expected to forge a mega digital industry concentration zone from Lujiazui to Lingang District, and thus enhancing Shanghai's global competitiveness in the first half of the twenty-first century. As for the accelerated development of digital trade due to the COVID-19 pandemic, it is also expected to become an important area for the new Lingang area to gain competitive advantage in the new round of global trade division of labor. Until now, the container throughput of Shanghai port has been the world's first for 13 consecutive years, the accumulation of a large number of industrial data, trade data and financial data, if the integration of the data platform, through big data, cloud computing, artificial intelligence to be utilized, will soon form a digital trade facilitation system, thus laying a solid foundation for a bigger and stronger digital trade industry cluster.

Finally, from the point of view of the level of Shanghai's economic development, in accelerating the formation of a new development pattern with the domestic macro-cycle as the main body and the domestic and international double-cycle promoting each other, how to take the digital transformation of the city of Shanghai as an opportunity to be more open-minded, more forward-thinking, and more sensitive to the technical judgment ability, and on the basis of keeping the pulse of the world's industrial development, to seek for the second with the deep-seated self-revolution, it is a strategic proposition to seek a major breakthrough in the development of secondary and tertiary industries with a deep-seated self-revolution and to cultivate a number of pillar industries at the level of hundreds of billions of yuan or even trillions of yuan. Based on this, Shanghai urgently needs to accelerate the promotion of the new generation of information technology and the deep integration of manufacturing industry.

Shanghai should combine its professional service advantages in the financial market, especially in RMB asset allocation and pricing, R&D and design, high-end manufacturing, system integration, global value chain management capabilities, etc., and strive to nurture a batch of unicorns that attach great importance to the future consumption experience of human beings and carry out forward-looking R&D and testing, and make efforts to create an innovative ecological environment in order to form a solid soil that can give rise to great companies in large quantities.

Chapter 10
Preventing and Resolving Systemic Economic and Financial Risks

Addressing Regulatory Gaps in China's Financial Supervision through Forward-Looking Expectations Management

The most important goal of China's financial regulation should be to maximize the liquidity support and wealth appreciation effect of finance as the blood of the real economy under the premise of ensuring that no systemic financial risk occurs. As a unique emerging country, the great challenge facing China's financial regulation is how to enhance its early warning capability of financial crisis and block the transmission of financial market risks with forward-looking expectation management by constructing an effective system of leading indicators and maintaining sharp intuition, without any reference system for reference.

Can financial crises be predicted? If a new financial crisis breaks out, are there sufficiently accurate early warning indicators? These are extremely difficult propositions, and it is really hard to give accurate answers in the real world.

As 2018 marks the tenth anniversary of the global financial crisis, in-depth investigations into the causes of the financial crisis have appeared in the press one after another, including the lamentations of those who experienced the crisis about whether Lehman Brothers should have been rescued, which still evokes from time to time the world's painful memories of the "Darwinian" shock caused by the crisis. Rouriel Roubini, known as "Dr. Doom," wrote an article in 2018 warning that the next financial crisis could erupt in 2020. Moreover, unlike in 2008, policymakers will have limited tools at their disposal in the event of a new financial crisis; in other words, the constraints on fiscal policy due to high debt leverage and the conflict between possible bailout packages and populism will make the policy tools, if offered at all, ineffective.

Recently, heavyweights, including China's key financial policymakers and mainstream economists, have been focusing their attention on how China can enhance its financial competitiveness with a more open financial temperament and forward-looking expectation management in an increasingly uncertain domestic and

Y. Zhang, *Addressing Uncertainty*, Understanding China,
https://doi.org/10.1007/978-981-92-2692-4_10

international economic and financial environment, in order to ensure economic growth and financial stability. Among them, how the Financial Stability and Development Commission of the State Council (FSDC) can establish an effective communication mechanism with the financial market and listen to the voices of the financial market more extensively, how to play the role of experts and scholars better in financial decision-making, and in particular how to stabilize the market expectations are all important propositions before China's financial policy makers and reformers. Financial policy makers and reformers have a difficult task ahead of them. As Yi Gang, the governor of the People's Bank of China, said, the opening up of China's financial market, in general, is still mainly a "pipeline" opening up, the depth and breadth of the financial market is insufficient, convenience needs to be improved, the international competitiveness of the financial industry still needs to be strengthened, and the degree of convergence of the financial system environment with the international community needs to be upgraded, and the business environment for foreign financial institutions needs to be further improved. All these problems cannot be solved without the in-depth liberalization of the financial industry, especially the forging of the overall competitiveness of the financial industry in the process of liberalization.

The author has said earlier that the major tests faced by China's financial system in the twenty-first century will come from three aspects: firstly, the long-term accumulation of systemic risks in the existing financial system will be a constant test of the financial levee; secondly, the next global financial crisis that may break out in the future will be a major test of China's economy, which has already been deeply integrated into the global system; and thirdly, the high degree of internationalization of the RMB will lead to a contradiction between the global responsibility China should fulfill as a guarantor and the continuous supply of risk prevention capacity. Based on this, clarifying the relevant indicators of financial services for the real economy, controlling the boundaries of financialization of the economy, and continuously consolidating the competitiveness of the manufacturing industry should be the fundamentals of constructing a resilient financial system adapted to the competition of the global economy in the twenty-first century, so as to prevent the occurrence of systemic financial risks.

It should be noted, however, that although China has rich experience and strong financial tools in preventing systemic financial risks, the important characteristics of financial crises lie in the uncertainty of the time of their outbreaks, the high sensitivity of the transmission mechanism and the depth of their damage to the economic system. Therefore, even the United States, which has the largest number of Nobel Prize winners in economics in the world, has shown inaccurate forecasts, the fermentation of panic and insufficient confidence in repairing financial crises, among other things, in the face of financial crises. The international financial crisis of 2008 has proved and will continue to prove that, with the deepening of the financialization of the global economy, the two sides of financial innovation and development have become more and more obvious. If a country's financial deepening is excessive and even economic growth is mainly supported by credit expansion, the outbreak of a financial crisis will be unavoidable when the performance of the real economy fails to improve at the same time.

Debt arrangement is not only an important promoter of economic growth, but also a tumor that breeds crises, and any market entity that is "uncomfortable without debt" will ultimately be eroded by the tumor of debt and will not be able to heal itself. It has been said that the animal spirits of entrepreneurs drive the financial cycle, and as long as the animal spirits remain unchanged, financial crises will not disappear from the face of the earth, and financial crises can only be transferred but not eliminated, and it is unrealistic to expect to develop a prevention and control system to eliminate the virus of financial crises. However, just as there are indicators for doctors to observe in judging the physical condition of their patients, the "credit gap" or "credit-output gap" benchmark has been recognized over the years by the Basel Committee on Supervision and the Bank for International Settlements as a useful early warning indicator of financial crises, measuring the extent to which corporate and household debt-to-GDP ratios have deviated from their long-term trend values, and from which differences between current and historical borrowing patterns can be observed. Existing studies on the subprime mortgage crisis in the United States in 2008 and the European debt crisis in 2010–2012 show that, in the context of middle- and high-income countries where household consumption accounts for more than 50% of GDP, before the crisis broke out, the private-sector credit gaps of the countries concerned were significantly above the early warning value (10%), that is to say, in the case of credit gaps greater than 10%, the probability of a banking crisis in the United States and Europe is 72% in three years. Therefore, a credit gap of more than 10%, summarized on the basis of this empirical evidence, is regarded as an early warning signal that an important crisis may break out. The Bank for International Settlements in a study in 2016 that China's "credit gap" in March of that year, once more than 30%, far more than 10% of the value of the concern. The reason didn't trigger systemic financial risks, authors believe that this is mainly due to China's central government's fiscal position is quite healthy, and can timely target risk points accurate demolition of bombs.

Of course, another key indicator that should not be ignored is the macro leverage ratio, which measures the ratio of total debt to GDP. By the end of 2022, China's macro leverage ratio was 281.6%, 9.6 percentage points higher than the previous year. In the first quarter of 2023, it was 8 percentage points higher than the end of the previous year, at 289.6%. For this reason, it is necessary to conduct a comprehensive inventory of the non-performing loan ratios of state-owned and private enterprises as soon as possible to confirm the amount of problem loans, and those problem loans removed from the balance sheets of banks must be counted as non-performing loans to confirm the true non-performing loan ratio, so that more credit resources can be allocated to enterprises with higher economic efficiency and innovation-driven development industries, thus maintaining the relative stability of the macro leverage ratio.

In terms of the historical interpretation of the global financial crisis, neither the United Kingdom, once a super financial power, nor the United States, which has been occupying the top tier of the financial division of labor since 1944, has been able to insulate itself from the financial crisis, which makes forward-looking expectation management and maintaining a keen intuition of the financial market particularly important today. In fact, the Basel Committee, which has an important mission, placed special emphasis on macro-prudential regulation and liquidity regulation in its final proposal for international financial regulatory reform in the post-crisis era, released in December 2017. Important indicators such as the liquidity coverage ratio (LCR), which reflects the ability of commercial banks to respond to liquidity needs for at least the next 30 days under stress scenarios, and the net stable funding ratio (NSFR), which reflects an indicator of the stock of medium- to long-term liquidity, are increasingly emphasized and put into supervisory practice in major economies. Just as the internationally recognized benchmark that strategic oil reserves should reach at least 90 days has become an important reference point for China's oil security, China needs to accumulate long-term experience and technical safeguards in the process of constructing a unique regulatory paradigm for emerging powers that can adapt to the global financial competition and industrial changes, whether it is to pay close attention to the margins of safety of systematic financial institutions, or to the control and monitoring system of core financial information, or even to the rapid response to unexpected financial events. And how to achieve effective coordination of financial policy and fiscal policy, industrial policy, to prevent inconsistency between different sectors in the policy objectives, to avoid regulatory arbitrage in different industry institutions, to correct the regulatory policy in the implementation and transmission of the bias, is the construction of the financial regulatory system of a large country is the most important thing.

Finally, the widespread activation of the innovation endowment of micro-entrepreneurs is an important hedge against systemic financial risk. In a sense, this is also an important foothold of expectation management. It can be said that today China's economy and financial system facing a number of complex problems, not only is the disease of the past development model of the disease expressed one after another, but also the economy has not been able to make a delay in the strategic transition to pay the marginal cost. All market players who understand the mechanism of economic development should understand that investment has only instrumental value in economic growth, that there is no such concept as "consumption-driven growth" in the economic sense, and that imports and exports are in fact an exchange of resource endowments between economies. The only sustainable and effective economic growth is that which is knowledge-based and driven by technological innovation or technological revolution. In the medium to long term, China must gradually leave the debt-driven growth model.

Managing Financial Risks Through Prudent Regulation

The *Systemically Important Banks Assessment Methodology,* which came into effect on January 1, 2021, has made reference to the global SIB assessment methodology and the *Domestic Systemically Important Banks Framework* issued by the Basel

Committee on Banking Supervision in 2012, and has adjusted the assessment indicators in light of the actual situation in China. It is generally recognized that banks with domestic assets of RMB 1 trillion and above will be included in the list of systemically important banks. As the lender of last resort, the Central Bank has taken the lead in formulating the *Additional Regulatory Provisions for Systemically Important Banks* (Trial), reinforcing supervisory requirements in such areas as liquidity, large risk exposures, risk data aggregation and risk reporting, and carrying out monitoring and analysis as well as stress testing, so as to practically enhance the operational soundness of systemically important banks. Among them, through the quantitative scoring of the four primary indicators and 13 secondary indicators of the selected systemically important banks, supplemented by the qualitative evaluation of supervision, it will provide the basis for the subsequent formulation and implementation of differentiated special supervisory requirements and disposal mechanisms, which also marks the entry of differentiated supervision into the substantive stage of operation, and at the same time, it also provides the basis for the issuance of the relevant assessment and implementation rules for systemically important insurance institutions and systemically important securities institutions.

Against the policy background of keeping the bottom line of no systemic financial risks as one of the most important tasks of economic work in the current and future period, comprehensive testing of the financial systems of banking, insurance and securities and identifying gaps or mismatches between supervisory capabilities and risk exposures, and benchmarking the requirements of high-quality development of the financial system with precise scrutiny and management on the basis of categorized supervision are not only endogenous requirements for China's sustained and stable economic development, but also arrangements for injecting stability into the global economy and financial system from China.

In recent years, under the unremitting efforts of local governments and regulators, China has made remarkable achievements in preventing and resolving systemic financial risks, with stable low growth rates helping the corporate sector to reduce leverage and local governments to resolve hidden debts; precise bomb disposal, smooth and orderly disposal of high-risk financial institutions, and timely containment of the spread of major financial risks; vigorous efforts to rectify the financial order, and the special rectification of Internet financial risks such as online lending and loans, which have achieved remarkable results, and illegal capital-raising activities have been severely cracked down, and various types of illegal trading venues have been brought under control, with the financial market as a whole showing a smooth operation.

However, the work of preventing and resolving systemic economic and financial risks in China is extremely arduous, and supervision cannot be relaxed for a moment. There are still "outstanding risk points" in the financial system, mainly in the areas of high-risk financial institutions, key financial holding groups, shadow banking, Internet lending and illegal fund-raising. Although the incremental risks in these areas have basically been brought under control, the stock of risks still requires a high degree of vigilance. In addition, in view of the booming development of financial technology has given rise to many new forms of financial business, greatly increasing the difficulty of financial regulation, the future direction of financial laws and regulations to improve the transition from treating the symptoms to treating the root cause of the problem, and the pace of making up the shortcomings of the system needs to be accelerated. In the new stage, in order to win the battle of preventing and resolving systemic economic and financial risks, the central bank and the CBI need to continue to make comprehensive efforts.

Mr. Yi Gang, the governor of the central bank, has written an article in the magazine *Qiushi* that the central bank has set up a specialized department for macro-prudential management, and is strengthening the macro-prudential management of systemically important financial institutions and financial holding groups, so as to curb the diversion of finance from the real to the virtual and to guide the flow of financial resources to the real economy, especially to the weak segments. In the key points that may trigger systemic risks, the central bank will make precise efforts to fulfill the lender of last resort's duties; at the same time, it will also strengthen the macro-prudential policy, pressurize the responsibilities of all parties, and gradually expand the coverage of macro-prudential management and improve the organizational structure of macro-prudential management in the future. Governor Yi Gang has actually given a roadmap and operational plan for China's financial deepening and regulatory reform in the current and future period.

Indeed, as the world's largest mega-economy in terms of financial assets, how China manages and allocates 300 trillion yuan of financial assets is a difficult proposition in itself. Today, China's financial system accounts for 7.8% of GDP, and the trend of financial deepening will continue. (2011–2022 China's financial system accounted for the proportion of GDP, see Fig. 10.1) In addition to being a major manufacturing country, China has also become a major global economic and financial country of systemic importance, so it is necessary to stand in the stability of the global economic and financial system and the country's economic and financial security from a strategic perspective to examine the nature of the financial system, which is an extremely complex system. As the financial system continues to expand

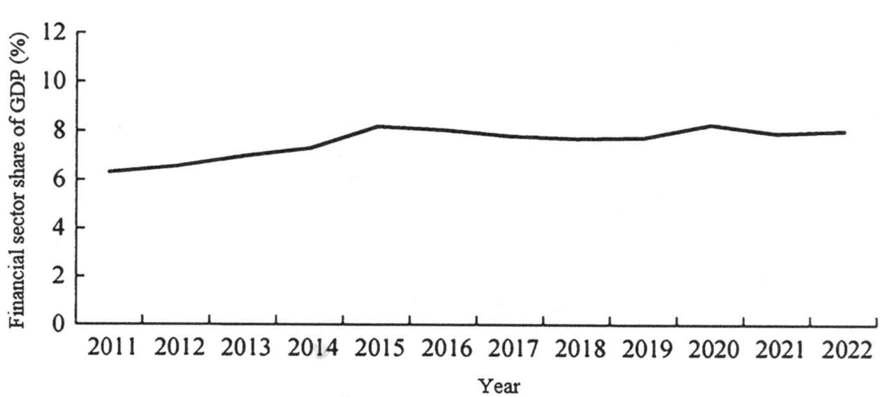

Fig. 10.1 The Share of China's Financial Sector in GDP, 2011–2022. Data source: *China Statistical Yearbook* (various years)

and increase in complexity, problems such as hidden guarantees, credit gaps, local debts and high leverage of enterprises are becoming more and more prominent, and localized risks or individual risks of micro-entities are emerging from time to time. Therefore, we can no longer just look at modern finance from a static perspective, nor can we simply apply the relevant international theories on financial innovation and financial regulation, including the modern monetary theory that has been prevalent in recent years, to guide or judge China's financial reform and development.

In today's world, any open economy must maintain sufficiently sharp risk intuition and precise prudential management in financial deepening and financial innovation in order to stabilize economic development expectations in the increasingly uncertain global economic and financial ecology. Although systemically important financial institutions (SIFIs) and financial holding groups (FHGs) are already "too big to fail" in the overall economic situation, an important reflection of the 2008 international financial crisis for regulators and the economics community is that it was the mismatch between these SIFIs in terms of their risk-pricing capabilities in complex financial products and financial institutions, as well as the over-confidence of the regulators, that magnified the risks, and therefore missed the window of time to make up for them. China, with its huge financial assets, should not only pay attention to the continuous improvement of the performance of the real economy, but also find the optimal solution between risk and control to promote the high-quality development of finance.

How Can the Financial Security System Address Uncertainty in Expectations

As a major exogenous variable, COVID-19 has brought direct or indirect shocks to the global financial system, and the unlimited quantitative easing policy of the United States, which has been completely reckless, although to a certain extent it has had the short-term effect of stabilizing the economy and the financial situation, the successive emergence of its side effects has been particularly worrisome.

Regulators, who have always had a keen intuition of financial risks, have warned that the unprecedented unlimited quantitative easing policy of the United States, in an international monetary system dominated by the United States dollar, is in fact also depleting the creditworthiness of the United States dollar and eroding the foundation of global financial stability, which will have unimaginable negative impacts. Emerging economies may face multiple pressures such as imported inflation, shrinking foreign currency assets, exchange rate and capital market shocks. Worse still, the world could once again be on the brink of an international financial crisis.

The economic sense of the "synthetic fallacy" in the countries to deal with the new crown epidemic in the policy put, once again get the fullest expression, especially as the global economy and financial stabilizer of the Federal Reserve, in order to avoid the U.S. economy by the epidemic pandemic triggered by a major recession washed out, almost out of the monetary policy toolbox of all kinds of tools, infinite quantitative Easing policy not only the past as a non-mainstream modern monetary theory directly endorsed for the mainstream monetary theory, but also simple and brutal, no instrumental rationality.

In the short term, the Federal Reserve not only has no intention of withdrawing its currency, but will further relax its monetary policy by continuing to buy Treasury bonds and mortgage-backed bonds at a rate of about $120 billion a month. Recently, the U.S. dollar index has been showing a downward trend, some market participants are concerned that if the dollar continues to depreciate, not only will the global economy continue to slump, and it may even trigger the second financial crisis that Dr. Roubini has been warning of the doomsday. In fact, even the Federal Reserve officials also recognized that the ongoing public health crisis will be in the short term to economic activity, employment and inflation under severe pressure, and in the medium term on the economic outlook poses considerable risk.

Although few people in the real world can accurately predict when financial crises will break out, macroeconomics has long proven that recessions and financial crises are inherently linked to significant declines in the productivity of labor and the return on capital. If large amounts of credit and money creation continue to be used to purchase stock assets rather than for productive investment and technological research and development, the next round of financial crises will not be far away.

With the deepening of the financialization of the global economy, the two sides of financial innovation and development have become more and more obvious. If a country's financial deepening is excessive and even economic growth is mainly supported by credit expansion, the outbreak of a financial crisis will be unavoidable if the performance of the real economy fails to improve at the same time.

The overall operation of China's financial system is stable, but some potential risks remain large. As the person in charge of the relevant departments pointed out, China's financial risks face the problem, first, the stock of risk has not yet been completely dissolved; second, non-performing assets to increase the upward pressure, the risk is likely to accelerate the emergence of the third is the background of the capital side of the easy rebound in the market chaos; fourth, the new crown epidemic to speed up the adjustment of global economic and financial patterns, uncertainty, uncertainty and increased risk of external inputs, and so on. To summarize, how to ensure the safety of China's financial assets of more than 400 trillion yuan, is the urgent task facing China.

Important progress has been made in China's financial reform and the internationalization of the renminbi, but the maintenance of financial security, especially the security of the financial transaction system, is one of the most urgent tasks at present.

At present, China urgently needs to consider economic growth, monetary policy, exchange rate system reform, international capital flow control and financial system opening and innovation as a whole from the perspective of safeguarding the country's financial security, and to build a three-dimensional regulatory and early warning system. China should not only adhere to the bottom line and principles, but also show appropriate flexibility to prevent "derailment" and "decoupling" from the financial, technological and trade systems of the major financial powers, and make efforts to strengthen cooperation and win-win zones with its major trading partners in the important links of the global value chain. It is recommended to continue to expand the scale of local currency swap agreements between the People's Bank of China and the central banks of important investment and trade target countries; make full use of the opportunities arising from the establishment of a wholly-owned Chinese legal entity of SWIFT and the acceptance of the RMB by SWIFT, and strive to continuously increase the proportion of the RMB in the settlement of global transactions. It will also push forward the construction of the "Belt and Road" and the construction of new RMB clearing channels, vigorously develop the capacity of RMB market-making and clearing and settlement services in the global market; accelerate the research and development of the digital currency system and its application, enhance the preference of RMB cross-border payment system for overseas use, and build a digital RMB system for the global bank settlement system.

The Economic and Financial Logic of Building a Modern Central Banking System

The People's Bank of China released the *China Monetary Policy Execution Report for the Second Quarter of 2021*, which re-emphasized the construction of a modern central banking system. The 53rd meeting of the State Council's Financial Committee held in July 2021 pointed out that it was necessary to strengthen the research on strategic, forward-looking, fundamental and targeted issues in the financial field, including the construction of a modern central banking system.

The construction of a modern central banking system is one of the major core propositions put forward by the decision-making level in leading economic and financial work. The Fourth Plenary Session of the 19th CPC Central Committee called for the construction of a modern central banking system in the process of promoting the modernization of the national governance system and governance capacity; the Fifth Plenary Session of the 19th CPC Central Committee emphasized the establishment of a modern fiscal, taxation and financial system, the construction of a modern central banking system, the improvement of the mechanism for regulating the supply of money, the steady advancement of the research and development of digital currencies, and the improvement of the mechanism for the formation of market-based interest rates and the mechanism for the transmission of interest rates; and so on. Subsequently, the construction of a modern central banking system and the improvement of the mechanism for regulating the money supply were included in the Fourteenth Five-Year Plan, indicating that the central government attaches great importance to the construction of a modern central banking system in the new historical period.

What is a modern central banking system? According to Yi Gang, a modern central banking system is the sum of a modern monetary policy framework, a financial market infrastructure service system, a system for preventing and resolving systemic economic and financial risks, and a governance mechanism for international financial coordination and cooperation. In his view, the goal of building a modern central banking system is to establish a central banking system and mechanism that can help realize the four major tasks of currency stability, full employment, financial stability, and balance of payments, manage the monetary floodgates, provide high-quality financial market infrastructure services, prevent and resolve systemic economic and financial risks, control external spillover effects, and promote the formation of a fair and reasonable pattern of international financial governance.

In the author's view, the above definition not only summarizes the essential attributes and functional arrangements of the modern central banking system, but also stands in the perspective of international economic and financial governance, including the People's Bank of China and other major central banks around the world, the international responsibilities of the relevant definition. In this sense, major Western central banks, including the Federal Reserve, the European Central Bank, the Bank of England, the Bank of Japan, the Swiss Central Bank, etc., have also been exploring the soundness and development of their own central banking systems. Especially in the COVID-19 pandemic as a major external variable under the impact of the central bank's monetary policy and balance sheet have undergone significant changes, the central bank in the country in an extraordinary period not only to play the role of lender of last resort, but also to some extent to play a role in support of employment and even with the Ministry of Finance to join hands with the role of direct assistance to low-income people.

In fact, this is the central bank's function of unlimited amplification of the immediate behavior, after all, the orderly operation of the economy and society ultimately relies on the development of the real economy, rather than relying on monetary policy to play a leading role in the long term. People note that in recent years, at the G20 or G7 central bankers meeting, many central bankers have warned: central bank balance sheet as a counter-cyclical tool has far exceeded the role of the previous expectations, fiscal deficit monetization is not a long-term solution; central banks must ensure that in the future there is enough policy space to implement quantitative easing to deal with the subsequent potential crisis. In addition, the rapid development of technology, especially digital technology, and changes in the form of money have also prompted central banks to reflect on their own role in the national and social coordinate system, and to prevent the trend of "decentralization" from becoming a real threat and thus shaking the foundations of central banks.

In China's case, the history of China's central bank in the modern sense is not very long. If we take China's accession to the WTO in 2001 as the beginning of the opening up of the banking sector to the outside world and the internationalization of finance as the symbol, the history of the PBOC's exploration of the establishment of a modern central banking system is only 22 years. If we take the outbreak of the international financial crisis in 2008 and the subsequent G20 Washington Summit as the point in time when the PBOC became deeply involved in international financial stability and coordinated and cooperative governance, the relevant history is only 15 years. And from the domestic important time nodes, in July 2017, the central government announced the establishment of the State Council Finance Committee, marking China's formal entry into a new era of building a modern central banking system. The purpose of the establishment of the Financial Committee is to strengthen the People's Bank of China's macro-prudential management and systemic risk prevention responsibilities, and to strengthen the regulatory responsibilities of financial supervisors to ensure financial security and stable development. Since then, the Fourth Plenary Session of the 19th CPC Central Committee has raised the construction of a modern central banking system to a new height; the Fifth Plenary Session of the 19th CPC Central Committee has made a strategic plan for the construction of a modern central banking system based on the promotion of high-quality development and the integration of development and security; and so on. All these indicate that the State's understanding of the construction of a modern central banking system is deepening, the path is becoming clearer and the strategic pattern is improving.

From the perspective of system design and improvement, any system construction is aimed at solving the stock of problems and realizing the medium- and long-term development goals. Looking through the list of challenges before China's financial reform policymakers in recent years, the construction of a modern central banking system has the following difficult propositions to be solved: Firstly, in the increasingly uncertain domestic and international economic and financial environments, how to make China's existing monetary policy framework sufficiently elastic to ensure the stability of the currency? How to improve the benchmark interest rate system? Where is the reasonable boundary for the degree of monetization of the Chinese economy? Second, how to build a resilient and stable financial system that can withstand counter-cyclical shocks, including the banking system, the securities system, the insurance system, the asset management system, and the new financial system driven by new technologies? How to enhance the loss-absorbing capacity of the financial system as a whole, hedge against systemic risks accumulated over time, as well as the impact of possible outbreaks of overseas financial risks on China's economy and financial system, so as to ensure economic growth and financial stability? Thirdly, how to cultivate financial forces that can actively participate in international competition and super financial institutions or intermediaries that can compete with international financial capital through building a high-standard financial market system? Fourth, how to open up channels for financial services to the real economy, give full play to the People's Bank of China's window guidance role in optimizing the structure of the financial market, promote the orderly conversion of savings and investment, and effectively solve the financing difficulties and problems of private enterprises, small and medium-sized enterprises and micro-enterprises? Fifth, how to give full play to the asset pricing and wealth appreciation role of finance as an important core competence of the country, while steadily pushing forward the marketization of interest rates, exchange rates, the opening up of the capital market, and the strengthening of cross-border cross-border supervision of capital, and ultimately grasping the experience of managing complex financial systems? Sixth, how to establish and improve effective communication mechanisms with domestic and foreign financial markets in the context of high-standard financial liberalization? In the process of promoting the internationalization of the RMB and the construction of Shanghai as an international financial center, how to take the pulse of the internationalization of the RMB and play an important international role in international financial governance? This is also the historical mission that the PBOC must fulfill in promoting the implementation of the modern central bank system.

Establishing Policy Benchmarks for the Prevention and Resolution of Systemic Financial Risks

On December 31 2021, the People's Bank of China (PBOC) issued the *Macro-prudential Policy Guidelines (Trial Implementation)* (hereafter referred to as *the Guideline*). In terms of implementation, this is a direct deployment by the PBOC to implement the major decision of the 19th CPC National Congress to "improve the two-pillar financial regulation of monetary policy and macroprudential policy" since the Fifth National Financial Work Conference explicitly requested the PBOC to be the lead organization for the establishment of a macroprudential management framework. In terms of policy objectives, under the current increasingly complex domestic and international economic and financial situation, the financial regulators, on the basis of summarizing domestic and international financial regulatory experience, have established policy benchmarks for preventing and resolving systemic economic and financial risks, so as to achieve a clear and comprehensive policy and "move the gate forward", and to promote macroprudential policy in a comprehensible, grounded, and operable manner, so as to effectively improve China's ability to prevent and resolve systemic economic and financial risks. In order to effectively improve China's ability to prevent and resolve systemic economic and financial risks. {The Guidelines} consist of nine chapters and 38 articles. The content reflects that China's financial regulators have been able to match high-standard theoretical research with forward-looking policy design in terms of accurately grasping the macroprudential policy framework, and also reflects that after recent years of supervisory practice and exploration, and after firmly guarding the bottom line of not incurring any systemic risk, China's financial regulators are still scrutinizing and responding to all kinds of risk that may arise in the domestic and overseas financial system at any time, with a twelve-percent sense of urgency and a high sense of responsibility. As the head of the relevant department of the People's Bank of China pointed out in his reply to a reporter's question on \textit{\textit{the Guidelines}}, the concept and practice of macroprudential policy is a new field, and the understanding of macroprudential policy in various circles is still deepening, and the practice of major economies is still evolving. This means that there are still many blind spots in the knowledge, identification, early warning and prevention, and resolution of systemic risks in the economic and financial fields among powerful participants, including major central banks and major international economic organizations, which means that there is a need to continue learning, exploring, and summarizing in order to solve the problem of insufficient competence that has long been troubling financial regulators.

Finance is the core and bloodline of the modern economy and an essential prerequisite for the operation of the real economy and the participation of market players in international competition. Since the advent of modern finance, human production and life, especially trading activities, have been difficult to find an optimal solution between financial innovation and risk prevention, despite the fact that they have benefited from the many conveniences brought about by financial deepening and innovation and have enjoyed the wealth-enhancing effects that come with them. In fact, judging by the characteristics of the two global crises that have broken out since the twentieth century, financial crises have repeatedly plagued mankind because of the uncertainty of the time of their outbreak, the high sensitivity of the transmission mechanism, and the great destructiveness to the economic and financial system. Can financial crises be predicted? Has mankind so far found sufficiently accurate early warning indicators? It is difficult to find precise answers to these difficult propositions in the real world. As a matter of fact, even the United States, which has the most developed financial industry and the highest level of financial science, showed its inability to make accurate predictions, panicked, and lost its way in the face of the once-in-a-century international financial crisis that erupted in 2008. This, coupled with the fact that financial crises can only be diverted, not eliminated, makes concerted action the only way for countries to work together to overcome the many challenges they pose. However, in the real world, "beggar-thy-neighbor" policies are often the norm in many countries in the face of financial crises, thus highlighting the importance and necessity of developing and implementing macroprudential policy frameworks at the global and national levels.

The international financial crisis that erupted in 2008 and the subsequent accumulation of systemic risks in the international monetary and financial spheres have shown the world that, with the deepening of the financialization of the international economy, the duplicity of financial innovations has become more and more obvious. If the financial deepening of major economies is excessive, and even if economic growth is supported mainly by credit expansion or increased debt leverage, then, in the absence of a corresponding improvement in the competitiveness of the real economic system, it is unlikely that a worldwide financial crisis will be triggered by the outbreak of systemic economic and financial risks.

In the case of China, the systemic economic and financial risks that need to be guarded against come mainly from within the economic system. As pointed out by the People's Bank of China in \textit{\textit{the Guidelines}}, great importance must be attached to the procyclical accumulation of systemic financial risks, as well as cross-institutional, cross-industry, cross-market and cross-border contagion, and only by effectively improving the resilience and robustness of the financial system can we enhance our ability to withstand the financial crisis. In the decade or so since the 2008 international financial crisis, as the scale of China's financial assets has continued to expand, the trend of risk concentration in the banking sector and debt financing has become more and more obvious. As we all know, the macro leverage ratio is the first issue related to financial stability. From an international comparative perspective, although China's overall macro leverage ratio is lower than the average level of developed countries, it is still necessary to focus on stabilizing systemic risks in the domestic economic system and pay close attention to the exposure to domestic financial risks.

At the same time, in the process of preventing and resolving systemic economic and financial risks, China must be very vigilant against the overlapping effects of external risk transmission and internal risk intertwining. Although the People's Bank of China and other financial regulators have accumulated rich experience in preventing and resolving systemic economic and financial risks, and the policy toolbox is rich in relevant tools, China's ability to manage complex financial systems still needs to be strengthened. Against the backdrop of a high level of financial market liberalization, the overall competitiveness of China's financial industry has yet to be improved, and the degree of international integration of the financial system environment has yet to be upgraded, so it is easier said than done for macroprudential policies to be "macro, countercyclical, and contagion resistant".

Enhancing the vitality of micro-entrepreneurs and the competitiveness of the real economy is a prerequisite for preventing and resolving systemic economic and financial risks, and in order to effectively prevent and resolve systemic financial risks, it is necessary to achieve a high level of policy implementation and coordination of regulatory policies. Preventing and resolving risks is an important guarantee for realizing macroeconomic policy objectives rather than the ultimate goal. Economically speaking, the most important goal of China's financial regulation is to maximize the liquidity support and wealth appreciation effect of finance as the blood of the real economy on the basis of the bottom line of not incurring systemic financial risks. To this end, after establishing the policy benchmark of preventing and resolving systemic economic and financial risks, China should further clarify the relevant indicators of financial services for the real economy, control the behavioral boundaries of financialization of the economy, continue to consolidate the competitiveness of the real economy represented by the manufacturing industry, especially the advanced manufacturing industry, strengthen the control and monitoring system of the core financial information, enhance the rapid response capability to deal with unexpected financial incidents, and achieve effective coordination between financial policy and development planning, fiscal policy, credit policy and industrial policy, to form policy synergy, and to correct the deviation of macroprudential policy in implementation and transmission in due course. All these should be the basic elements for enhancing the implementation capacity of macroprudential policies.

Part IV
Establishing a Better Development Economics

Chapter 11
Urgent Need for the Reform of Mainstream Economics

In Extraordinary Times, the West Turns Again to "Nationalization"

In 2020, the COVID-19 pandemic, as a major "black swan" event, suddenly disrupted the global economy pulse. Leaders of major countries in Europe and the U.S. faced various extent of the "protecting the economy" challenge, and the severity of the situation forced them to quickly open the crisis response toolbox of previous decision-makers at that time and restructure their operational systems. Among these, nationalization represents a classic policy remedy, with some European media even discussing whether it could be the lifeline for the European economy when facing the pandemic, despite the fact that during times of economic prosperity, financial and economic leaders, market participants, economists, and even some media in Europe and the U.S. had much criticism of nationalization.

In the two most capitalist countries, the UK and France, when the authorities realized that the existing measures were insufficient to withstand the large-scale trial-and-error of the COVID-19 pandemic, they quickly turned back to "nationalization". For example, in 2020, to prevent the UK's railway transport group from collapsing due to the impact of the pandemic, the UK government announced the suspension of railway franchise agreements, and the railway system was immediately placed under nationalization. Just earlier, the French Finance Minister stated that the government would take all necessary measures to support France's large enterprises. If needed, the government would support nationalizing companies, including the two major car manufacturers. Furthermore, the wealthy German government not only unveiled a €750 billion stimulus and rescue package but also warned foreign investors against making hostile acquisitions of top German companies like Daimler, Volkswagen, and BMW. The German government pledged to fully assist domestic companies if necessary.

As for the world's largest economy, the United States, where the economic fundamentals still rank relatively well among major capitalist countries, in response to

Y. Zhang, *Addressing Uncertainty*, Understanding China,
https://doi.org/10.1007/978-981-92-2692-4_11

the financial shock triggered nationwide by the COVID-19 pandemic, it not only declared a national emergency until the end of April 2020, but also passed a $2 trillion stimulus package. This legislation allocated $500 billion in aid to businesses hit by the pandemic, such as airlines.

When faced with the massive systemic risk posed by the COVID-19 pandemic, governments in the US and Europe once again embraced nationalization at a critical moment. The policy logic and operational methods behind this move closely resemble those seen during the 2008 global financial crisis. If we extend the time spectrum back to 1933, over the past 90 years, whether under Franklin Roosevelt, or the administration of George W. Bush and the Trump, when the national economy was during extraordinary times on the brink of collapse, each government unexceptionally set aside the dogma of free-market capitalism and resorted to the "nationalization" tactic, which had repeatedly proven to be the most effective, motivating, and executable solution in times of crisis. Even though these measures during critical times were at odds with the free-market principles they usually publicized—essentially a form of self-contradiction—they were implemented without hesitation.

If the neoliberal economist Milton Friedman were still alive, he would undoubtedly launch a fierce critique against the U.S. government's blatant violation of the principles of a laissez-faire capitalist market. If Friedrich August von Hayek, an unwavering opponent of central planning, had lived to witness the financial crisis of 2008, he would have undoubtedly stomped his feet in frustration and condemned the Bush administration—despite its professed commitment to free-market capitalism—as a complete chameleon in economic policy. If the two central figures of the famous "Great Debate on Socialism" of the 1930s, Ludwig von Mises (see Fig. 11.1) and Oskar Lange (see Fig. 11.2), were to return to the world, Lange might have

Fig. 11.1 The Economist Ludwig Von Mises

Fig. 11.2 The Economist Oskar Lange

written to Mises, proposing a sequel to their grand debate on Socialist Economics and mocking him: "You may win an argument for a time, or even for a period, but you cannot win forever."

The 300-year evolution of capitalism has repeatedly proven that a purely free market economy has largely been a false proposition—an assumption that holds perfectly only in the realm of theoretical economics. Economic policy, especially in extraordinary times, fundamentally serves political ends or, more precisely, is guided by national interests. Whether in the United States, home to the most Nobel laureates in economics, or in Europe, the stronghold of classical capitalism, policymakers who routinely criticize the "flaws" of nationalization or state-owned enterprises in times of stability often turn to nationalization as a "white knight" when crises arise, viewed as the ultimate savior.

This is a form of state rationality. After all, in times of crisis, no politician would dare to stand idly by while strategically vital and systemically important enterprises face the threat of sudden collapse.

Comrade Xiaoping Deng once pointed out: "A planned economy is not equivalent to socialism—capitalism also has planning; a market economy is not equivalent to capitalism—socialism also has markets. Planning and markets are both economic tools."[1] This profound insight remains historically illuminating today. France, a nation that has especially long advocated freedom, holds a unique perspective on the value of nationalization. The French Constitution of 1946 explicitly stated: "All wealth and enterprises that already serve or will serve the public interest, or that have or will have a de facto monopoly nature, must become the property of society

[1] Selected Works of Xiaoping Deng (Volume III), People's Publishing House, 1993, p. 373.

as a whole." Even today, France continues to implement, in a sense, a form of "planned market economy," with the state-owned economy component playing a significant role in key industries such as manufacturing and finance, which are crucial to the national economy and public welfare.

Likewise, after World War II, successive U.S. governments have consistently sought to find a balance between state intervention and laissez-faire policies. For example, when Keynesianism failed after hitting the wall of stagflation, New Keynesianism emerged in response. Although Milton Friedman's monetarism had a significant impact, it could not curb the government's inherent instinct and impulse to intervene in the economy. The fusion of monetarism and the rational expectations school gave rise to New Classical macroeconomics, which introduced distinctive theories on the relationship between unemployment and inflation, economic cycles, and government policies. However, President Bill Clinton, known for his adept policymaking, believed that the most pragmatic approach was to integrate elements of Keynesianism, monetarism, supply-side school, and the rational expectations school. As a result, the Clinton administration opposed both complete laissez-faire and excessive intervention, leading to a period of significant economic prosperity in the U.S. Subsequent administrations, including those of George W. Bush, Barack Obama, Donald Trump, and the current Biden administration, have also continuously sought the optimal balance between the two approaches.

During the extraordinary period when the COVID-19 pandemic severely impacted the economy, developed countries in the U.S. and Europe once again embraced nationalization. Although their primary goal was to rescue the market and safeguard the lifeline of capitalist economies, this move, as has happened more than once in history, once again legitimized the very concept of "nationalization"—an economic remedy they have repeatedly stigmatized. At least for now, they are unlikely to be in a hurry to label nationalization as unfair competition.

How Can the World Avoid a Return of Depression Economics?

The economic recession caused by the impact of the COVID-19 pandemic has almost pushed the collective wisdom of global macroeconomists to the limit.

Unlike the global economic recession caused by the 2008 global financial crisis, the shock brought by the COVID-19 pandemic has almost no baseline scenario to reference. In other words, major economies had no time to prepare response plans before being immediately hit by a paralyzing external shock. The virus's impact on human survival, production, and daily life vividly illustrated the dual-risk spiral formed by lethal threats and panic, simultaneously shocking both the supply and demand sides of various nations.

The then U.S. President Donald Trump had been boasting about the unemployment rate dropping to its lowest point in the past 50 years. However, after the outbreak of the pandemic, he was forced to face the dilemma of nearly 40 million people applying for unemployment benefits.

Statistical data show that in April 2020, the U.S. unemployment rate soared to 14.7%, the highest since the 1930s. Additionally, retail sales plummeted by 16.4%, and the industrial production index dropped by 11.2%, both marking the largest single-month declines on record. These catastrophic economic figures were something Trump could not conceal, no matter how hard he tried.

The Eurozone experienced its worst recession since 1999. Even in Japan, where the pandemic was relatively mild at the time, the government's economic pessimism reached to the highest level in the past 10 years. Meanwhile, China, one of the earliest countries hit by the pandemic, made nationwide efforts to resume work and production. However, its GDP still contracted by 6.8% year-on-year in the first quarter of 2020. This marked China's first quarterly negative growth since it began publicly reporting quarterly GDP data in 1992.

In 2020, amid great uncertainty, China's top leadership elevated the assessment of economic difficulties to the highest level. As for small and medium-sized economies with weaker resilience, especially the least developed countries, they faced even greater suffering.

A slight consolation is that this global economic recession was not caused by a significant deterioration in global economic fundamentals or financial imbalances. This also means that as long as the pandemic can be controlled to a certain degree, the recovery to economic normalcy will not take too long. In fact, many experts are even anticipating a subsequent rebound-driven growth.

In Extraordinary Times, Distributing Money Is the Hard Truth

Since the global spread of the pandemic, the monetary and fiscal response measures implemented by the U.S., Europe, and other countries have largely fallen into the following essential categories: (1) Injecting liquidity to stabilize market sentiment. (2) Providing direct assistance or even taking over enterprises facing bankruptcy due to the pandemic's impact. (3) Directly aiding the lower-income population.

Regarding the first measure, if the Federal Reserve had not urgently injected large-scale liquidity in March 2020, the U.S. stock market might have already been halved in value. As for the second type of rescue measure, while it deviates significantly from textbook economic principles, a government standing idly by when its key enterprises are on the brink of bankruptcy would be nothing short of political incompetence. Concerning the third initiative, although mocked by some wealthy representatives in the U.S., the general American public has a low preference for savings. This makes them highly vulnerable to the massive wave of unemployment caused by the pandemic. At such a time, direct cash payments from the government are the only pragmatic solution.

On the other hand, the absence of preemptive plans meant that government responses across different nations were inevitably imprecise, with some policies even exhibiting strong interest-driven biases. In the post-industrial era, economic confidence has become heavily reliant on credit expansion. The greater the role played by monetary authorities in developed countries, the more debt risks continue to accumulate.

The 2008 global financial crisis delivered a harsh lesson: If a country persistently deepens its financial sector without a corresponding improvement in the real economy, and if economic growth is primarily sustained by excessive credit expansion, the eventual result will be irreparable damage to the economic system.

Yet, in recent years, the global economy's actual growth, industrial development, and technological progress have been insufficient to offset the accumulation of financial bubbles and risks. As a result, many major economies have fallen into a debt-driven growth trap.

Macroeconomic theory has long demonstrated that economic recessions and financial crises are fundamentally linked to declines in labor productivity and significant reductions in returns on capital. If massive credit and monetary creation continues to flow into existing assets rather than productive investments and technological research and development, the arrival of the next financial crisis will only be a matter of time.

Returning to the Path of Endogenous Economic Growth

As a major public health crisis, the pandemic will eventually pass. However, the excessive monetary expansion resulting from the Federal Reserve's issuing massive bailout and stimulus checks will not be easily reversed. The same applies to other major economies. Just like the human body, an economic system or economic ecosystem cannot be frequently and excessively stimulated—especially on a large scale—without causing functional imbalances.

Visionary economic policymakers are well aware of the historical significance of Paul Romer's endogenous growth theory, which earned him the 2018 Nobel Prize in Economics. Romer's research highlights that the most critical drivers of economic growth are knowledge innovation, technological progress, and the enhancement of human capital. Real-world economic practices have proven that Romer's new growth theory not only explains many economic growth phenomena but also promotes the transformation of economic growth in many countries and regions.

While policy recommendations from endogenous growth theory may seem too slow to meet urgent needs amid an immediate crisis like the pandemic, the facts have shown that the global economic recovery from 2008 to 2014 was inherently filled with uncertainties. Major developed countries did not start the new round of economic growth by reviewing the shortcomings of their existing growth models and increasing investment in technological R&D as well as human capital improvement, but primarily relied on credit expansion to create a superficial sense of prosperity.

In the long run, economic growth must be driven by technological endogenous progress and substantial improvements in human capital. Economy financialization and debt arrangements are always double-edged swords—they are not true engines of economic growth.

Just as economic crises are triggered by a chain of events, the economic recovery that nations are hoping for also requires a series of major events to activate. The key challenge for global policymakers in the post-pandemic era is how to implement precise policies that unleash the entrepreneurial potential and innovative dynamism of microeconomic actors.

Supply-Side Reform as Empirical Support for Development Economics

China's supply-side structural reform aims not only to achieve market clearance and foster new drivers and new momentum, but also to place significant emphasis on the proactive study of market instability and economic complexity within the logic framework of global economic integration, especially for complex economic and financial systems. Such an endeavor necessitates surpassing the neoclassical economics of equilibrium optimization in order to establish a market economy model that both effectively constrains the self-interested behavior of "economic man" and maintains an appropriate level of market intervention. This model seeks to promote economic growth driven by core endogenous variables such as technological progress and human capital development. By doing so, it may be possible to establish a growth mechanism that sustains long-term economic vitality.

A research report released by the International Monetary Fund (IMF) suggests that if China can effectively address the issue of "zombie enterprises," its long-term economic growth rate could increase by 0.7 to 1.2 percentage points annually. The report highlights that dealing with unviable zombie enterprises is one of the key challenges China currently faces. Around the same time, during the IMF-hosted Fifth Statistical Forum, experts paid close attention to China's significant advancements in digital transformation. Some market analysts view China as a unique case in global digital transformation. As the world's largest mobile internet market, China's world leading position in e-commerce and mobile payments is expected to help it become a trend leader.

Comprehensive information, accurate data, and a scientific analytical framework are prerequisites for rational judgment. Whether in economic research or economic policy analysis and research, it is difficult to reach sound conclusions without an analytical framework based on information extraction and data processing. From a global perspective, China is a uniquely emerging economy in modern economic development history, with no readily available reference model for its economic reform and development. The rationale behind China's large-scale supply-side structural reform is clear: to eliminate deep-rooted economic development problems, absorb the impact of previous stimulus policies, and establish the next phase of economic growth on a new logic foundation of structural balance. The reform progress achieved thus far suggests that as supply-side structural reform advances, China may undergo a relatively significant optimization reallocation process of capital and labor resources. Whether state-owned, private, or foreign capital, all will seek market opportunities within this dynamic optimization process. Total factor productivity—driven by technological advancement, organizational innovation, specialization, and productivity improvements—will be the primary source of China's sustainable economic growth in the future.

As a super-emerging economy still in the process of industrialization, China's economic growth exhibits a strong dependence on existing development paths. If the current growth drivers weaken while alternative drivers remain underdeveloped, economic growth will inevitably slow down. The next cycle of economic prosperity in China will undoubtedly stem from deeper economic system reforms, that is, how to shift the engines of economic growth toward effective consumption and technological progress.

Since the launch of supply-side structural reform in 2015, significant progress has been made, especially with the ongoing implementation of capacity reduction plans in the coal and steel industries. New supply has become a major driving force for China's economic growth. The expansion of traditional industrial clusters, represented by heavy and chemical industries, is gradually slowing down, while emerging industrial clusters—represented by high-end manufacturing and modern services—are rapidly growing. Driven by government-led negative list reforms, the "Mass Entrepreneurship and Innovation" initiative, and increasing R&D investment, microeconomic actors have unleashed greater innovative vitality, continuously stimulating economic growth potential. The rise of unicorn companies under the wave of the "Mass Entrepreneurship and Innovation" initiative is gradually providing strong support for China's participation in the next round of global economic and technological competition.

A prevailing consensus is that China's economy is gradually moving away from an era of government investment-led, heavily chemical characteristics, extensive growth model. The economic structure and development stage are undergoing significant changes, moving toward a consumption-driven new development phase. In 2016, China's service sector accounted for 51.6% of GDP (The changes in the proportion of China's service sector in GDP are shown in Fig. 11.3). From January to October 2017, total retail sales of consumer goods increased by 10.4% year-on-year, surpassing the 7.5% year-on-year growth in fixed asset investment. Meanwhile, the digital economy is expanding rapidly, with booming developments in the sharing economy, internet information economy, artificial intelligence, and service-oriented economic sectors. China is quickly catching up with developed nations such as the United States in advanced manufacturing, achieving a series of major breakthroughs one after another in research and development as well as construction of quantum communication, high-temperature iron-based superconductors, manned spaceflight, civil aviation, deep-sea exploration, smart grids, and nuclear power station, accumulates relevant cutting-edge technologies and continuously

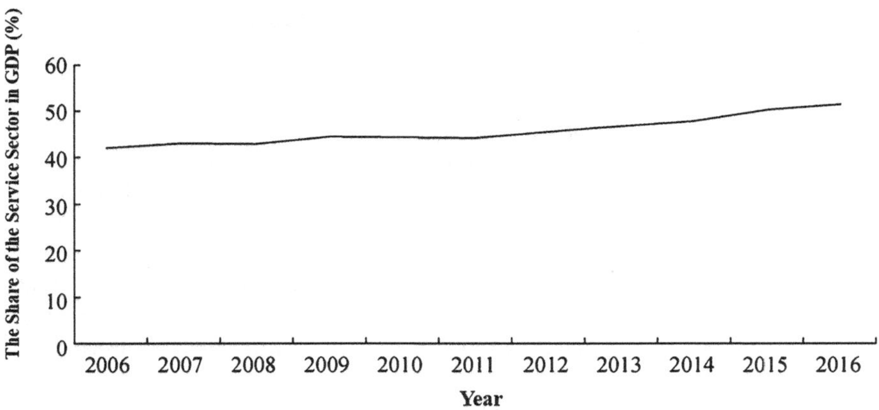

Fig. 11.3 Changes in the share of China's Service Sector in GDP. Data Source: National Bureau of Statistics of China

improves complex management capabilities, leading to the emergence of enterprises with strong market potential. In the first three quarters of 2017, the net profit of China's listed manufacturing companies accounted for 25.8% of total listed company net profits, increasing by 3.53 percentage points from 2016. The net profit growth rate of listed manufacturing companies reached 47.28% year-on-year, suggesting that the achievements of supply-side structural reform have long been reflected in the real industry. The trend of existing funds shifting from the real economy to the virtual economy is undergoing a change, and the financial system is gradually returning to its fundamental role of serving the real economy.

Theory both originates from practice and transcends it. Therefore, in a sense, under the guidance of the new development philosophy, the progress made in supply-side structural reform during this critical period, as well as its future reform priorities, have provided and will continue to provide valuable research samples and empirical support for development economics. China must gradually move away from a debt-driven growth model through deep-level reforms, demonstrating that financial deepening and financial innovation are, more often than not, auxiliary existence serving the real economy rather than absolute dominant forces. Furthermore, by deepening economic analysis and research on China's transformation, and fully considering economic imbalances, China aims to explore a market economy model suited to its economic development.

After more than 70 years of development, developing countries have undergone profound economic and social transformations. A common characteristic and trend among them are the diversification of development models and the unevenness of development processes. China's unique development path and trajectory provide a crucial practical foundation and theoretical source for enriching and innovating traditional development economics.

Toward China's Emergence as a Creation Hub for Modern Economic Thought

The Third Plenary Session of the 19th Communist Party of China (CPC) Central Committee proposed to resolutely eliminate institutional and systemic barriers that hinder the market from playing a decisive role in resource allocation while enhancing the government's role, center on promoting high-quality development and building a modern economic system, adjust and optimize government functions, rationally allocate the responsibilities of macroeconomic management departments, deepen the streamlining of administration and delegation of power, improve market regulation and law enforcement systems, reform natural resource and ecological environment management systems, enhance public service management mechanisms, strengthen interim and ex-post supervision, improve administrative efficiency, comprehensively enhance government effectiveness to build a service-oriented government that satisfies the people. Clearly, as China marked the 40th anniversary of reform and opening-up, these measures served as crucial preparations for launching a new round of major reforms.

In the long course of human history, 40 years is but a fleeting moment. However, the four decades from 1978 to 2017 stand as a remarkable chapter in China's economic reform and development. As American investment guru Warren Buffett put it, human potential has been fully demonstrated in China's development—China has achieved in 40 years what took the United States 200 years. Today, a vast majority of developing countries openly acknowledge that China has accomplished the greatest economic achievement in human history. Since the beginning of the twenty-first century, China has rapidly surpassed developed economies such as the United Kingdom, France, Germany, and Japan, becoming the only country besides the United States to expand its economy beyond $10 trillion while continuously narrowing the economic gap with the U.S. British scholars predict that, with ongoing economic growth and the internationalization of the renminbi, China is highly likely to create the greatest dividend in the history of global economic and monetary transformation in the first half of the twenty-first century. China is likely to generate the most significant economic and monetary transformation in the first half of the twenty-first century. The United Kingdom, with its unique financial culture and international geographical advantage, must seize this rare historical opportunity tightly. Over the past 40 years, China's economic reforms and institutional transformations have either drawn on the experiences of developed market economies, including the United States, or remained deeply rooted in China's national conditions to relentlessly explore in key areas such as state-owned enterprise (SOE) reform, economic transition, and the relationship between the market and the government.

Today, an increasing number of mainstream Western economists recognize that China has a long history of commerce and trade, with family businesses and marketplaces existing for a long time. Moreover, China adopted paper currency far earlier than the West—an indisputable historical fact. As a result, in its pursuit of a market economy, China has not only drawn lessons from Western institutional experiences but has also looked inward, seeking cultural roots in its development history of rich commercial traditions. Nowadays, China's market-oriented reforms are still ongoing. In the process of building a modern economic system, China must ensure that the market plays a decisive role in resource allocation. While there has never been a single universal model for a market economy benchmark, current theoretical discussions, relevant international legal regulations, and global economic practices indicate that today China has developed a quite profound understanding of the five key elements widely regarded as essential for a mature market system and is continuously implementing these elements through reforms. The five elements are: Whether the role and behavior of the government are properly regulated, whether enterprises enjoy freedom in their rights and operations, the extent of marketization in production factor (including whether factor prices are determined by the market and whether business costs are true), the fairness of trade conditions, the rationalization of financial parameters and so on.

Since the reform and opening-up, a key insight gained by economists from China's economic reforms is that stimulating the market vitality of microeconomic entities is the best recipe for growth. However, activating market vitality evidently requires the government to significantly improve standards in microeconomic and macroeconomic regulation. This necessity, in turn, pressures the marketization reform of factor prices to achieve breakthrough progress as soon as possible, urges state-owned enterprises, which hold the most economic resources, to expedite their transformation into market-oriented entities, and calls for the elimination of institutional and systemic barriers that hinder economic transformation. This is precisely the rationale behind the emphasis of the Third Plenary Session of the 19th CPC Central Committee on resolutely removing institutional and systemic obstacles that restrict the market from playing a decisive role in resource allocation while enhancing the role of the government.

Of course, markets are limited, and the efficient market hypothesis has been proven to be blackboard economics with a strong classical economic influence. Market failures are the norm in the real economic world, and even limited markets are not necessarily efficient. The government should strive to create conditions that expand the scope for businesses to operate within the market. Experience has long proven that economic behaviors made by businesses and households based on market signals are often more prudent than government decisions. The role of the government is not within the market but outside of it—to define and protect property rights and ensure contract enforcement.

China's economic growth and development transformation provide a highly valuable research sample for global economists, including Chinese scholars. Research on the above issues will not only enrich existing perspectives in economics but also has the potential to change the general conclusions of existing mainstream economics.

From the perspective of historical development logic, after China has essentially achieved modernization and become a strong industrial and capital power, a complete set of macroeconomic theories will emerge to explain China's economic development and institutional changes, especially the endogenous mechanisms of China's economic growth. This will, in turn, become an important part of global mainstream economics. In this regard, I strongly agree with the viewpoint of Li Daokui, Director of the China and World Economy Research Center at Tsinghua University: The Chinese economic academia must have a sense of urgency. We must tell China's story well and develop Chinese theories. If we fail to develop a solid theoretical foundation or present a coherent argument, we will suffer disadvantages internationally, in policy development issues forever.

From the perspective of the trend in historical logical evolution of economic development, the economic theory that has gradually formed in China, rooted in its great economic practices, has reached the point where it should be transformed into a theory with certain international applicability and paradigm influence and able to compete with Western mainstream economic theories over a trend. China's continuous advancement and deepening of economic reforms have already provided, and will continue to provide, verification and support for exploring feasible development paths for unique emerging major nations. This, in turn, lays the foundational conditions for the formation and development of a vibrant intellectual market. As China becomes the power center of the global economy, it will inevitably also become the center for the creation of modern economic thought.

Looking Forward to China's New Position in the Twenty-First Century Economic System

In May 2021, WTO Director-General Ngozi Okonjo-Iweala appointed four trade experts from China, the United States, France, and Costa Rica as new Deputy Directors-General. This appointment was widely seen as closely aligning with the landscape and trend evolution of current international trade. Moreover, it reflects the WTO's significant expectations for China as the world's largest trading nation.

From a time-series perspective, since joining the WTO in 2001, China has leveraged its continuous expansion of opening-up and facilitating the effective alignment and deep integration of Chinese and global industrial and supply chains. In less than 20 years, it has become one of the most significant participants in global trade. This transformation not only holds special practical exploratory value in the history of global trade evolution but also has even greater research value as a sample of a major economy from an economic perspective. The United Nations Conference on Trade and Development (UNCTAD) once commented that China's economic development might be one of the most unprecedented stories in modern history. For instance, in the late 1970s, China's share of global trade was less than 1%, whereas by 2020—40 years later—its share had surged to nearly 15% (See Fig. 11.4 for China's share of World Trade Volume, 2000–2020).

Why is China's openness and development valuable as a case study of a major economy from an economic perspective? This is because, in the process of

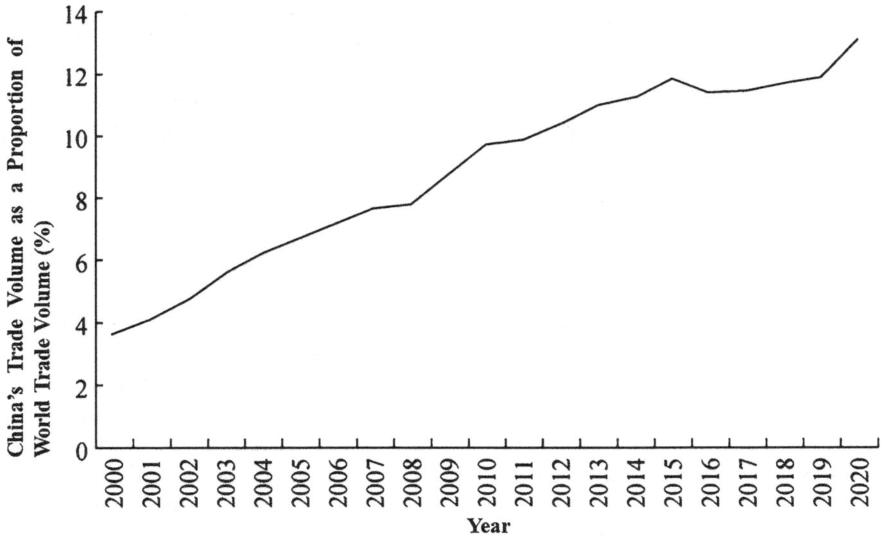

Fig. 11.4 China's share of World Trade Volume, 2000–2020. Data Source: National Bureau of Statistics of China; WTO

high-level opening-up, China has placed greater emphasis on the external release of development dividends, particularly international coordination of macroeconomic policies. It has also attached greater importance to the effective implementation of its opening-up policies, striving to prevent globally capable participating entities from adopting beggar-thy-neighbor policies, unilateralism, and protectionism in foreign economic policy, which could disrupt the global economic and trade system. This reflects China's role as a responsible emerging major power, an international commitment to global economic growth and sustainable development.

Although the trend of global economic, trade, and financial integration occasionally encounters obstacles, technological progress will not stagnate due to artificial barriers. In particular, the rapid advancements in big data technology and artificial intelligence make global market expansion and wealth redistribution inevitable. The endogenous driving forces of globalization, based on the free flow of factors and the reduction of transaction costs, are difficult to suppress in the long term. Whether for developed countries such as the U.S. and Europe or a wide range of developing countries like China, no party can ignore the enormous sunk costs caused by large-scale disruptions in industrial, supply, service, and even value chains. Moreover, no capital or national power can block the rational flow of global factors by erecting various barriers.

Leading international economists studying China's economic reform and development have long recognized that China has achieved remarkable success in its reform and opening-up without a ready-made reference model. Many of China's successful explorations in economic reform and development have not only challenged certain conclusions of modern macroeconomics but are also gradually becoming research topics and focal points in mainstream economics. Including the highly focused area of State-Owned Enterprise (SOE) reform, China's practical explorations have drawn significant attention from Western economic academia. The issue of SOE reform has always been a challenging problem widely faced by countries around the world. China's successful practices demonstrates that while clearly defined property rights are crucial, they are not the sole determinant of economic development. The endogenous nature of property rights will only become clarified only when other market economy institutions are well-developed, further driving economic development. Moreover, under the guidance of an effective government, SOEs can not only adapt to marketization but also build new advantages in market competition. This requires establishing clear government regulations, a reasonable equity structure, sound corporate governance, a sustained spirit of innovation, and granting SOE executives the necessary decision-making autonomy while defining the principles for allocating residual claims. It is essential to clarify SOEs' true identity as market entities, delineate their role in both the market and society, and prevent the reinforcement of SOEs' interest demands as a special group in the increasingly entrenched interest structure, in order to resolve the "moral hazard" difficult issue that has troubled SOE reform for many years.

China will continue to deepen reforms and promote high-level opening-up to build and improve a modern economic and financial system that can effectively support high-level economic development. This will provide a highly valuable research sample for the development of twenty-first-century macroeconomics and will also lead to the formation of a groundbreaking framework for the development of macroeconomics.

Chapter 12
How Can the Global Economy Move toward Steady Growth?

More Innovative Entities Are Needed to Inject New Momentum into the Global Economy

In its 2019 World Economic Outlook, the International Monetary Fund (IMF) expressed concerns about global economic growth for that year, forecasting a decline in the global economic growth rate to 3.5%, which was 0.2 percentage points lower than the previous World Economic Outlook forecast. According to the IMF, global growth faced downside risks, with several evident uncertainties negatively impacting global economic expansion. In response, the IMF recommended that countries strengthen cooperation to resolve differences, implement measures to boost potential output growth, enhance inclusivity, and strengthen fiscal and financial buffers, particularly in an environment of heavy debt burdens and tightening financial conditions.

As an international economic organization with significant responsibility for global economic and financial stability, the IMF's concerns about global economic growth largely reflect the urgent need to address certain structural issues in the current international economic landscape. While its policy recommendations for national economies may not be particularly novel, they are challenges that finance ministers and central bank governors must confront. However, as the saying goes, "easier said than done." If the IMF were truly tasked with managing a country's economy, its management effectiveness might not necessarily be better—though this organization, which brings together numerous renowned economists and financial leaders, may not necessarily agree.

The author is particularly focused on the IMF's advice to governments regarding measures to promote potential output growth, which is a high-quality recommendation deserving of significant attention from all countries. Generally speaking, the potential output growth rate refers to the growth rate of GDP that can be achieved when all resources in the economy are fully utilized. Therefore, the potential output growth rate refers to the growth rate of potential aggregate supply, assuming that the

Y. Zhang, *Addressing Uncertainty*, Understanding China,
https://doi.org/10.1007/978-981-92-2692-4_12

potential of production factors is fully realized. For example, according to the relevant views presented in the 2019 Economic Blue Book, jointly published on December 24, 2018, by the Economic Division of the Chinese Academy of Social Sciences, the Research Bureau of the Chinese Academy of Social Sciences, the Institute of Quantitative Economics and Technical Economics, and the Social Sciences Academic Press: since China's labor supply began to decline in 2012, the total factor productivity growth rate has remained low in recent years, and the growth rate of capital stock has also decreased as fixed asset investment growth has slowed. Due to these factors, which are difficult to change in the short term, China's GDP potential growth rate is expected to decline slightly within an appropriate range in 2019. However, the author believes that, in addition to the factors mentioned above, the reasons behind China's actual GDP growth rate being lower than the potential output growth rate and the widening output gap also include: China's economy is gradually losing its comparative advantage, yet it has not yet built a solid competitive advantage. Additionally, the lag in economic rebalancing continues to cause significant mismatches between supply and demand in the short term, and the pace of supply-side structural adjustments is not keeping up with the changes in demand-side structures, among other factors.

It is precisely because of the relevant constraints on China's economic growth that Jizhe Ning, who was the head of the National Bureau of Statistics at the time, argued for a stronger counter-cyclical policy adjustment to promote the continuous, healthy, and high-quality development of the Chinese economy. He put forward six key suggestions, including focusing on deepening innovation-driven strategies and promoting the transformation and upgrading of the manufacturing industry. The author believes that this is a crucial step for promoting the growth of China economy's potential output. In fact, this focus on innovation is not limited to China. Governments and enterprises in developed countries such as the United States, Japan, Germany, the United Kingdom, and France place particular emphasis on R&D investment and innovation-driven growth, especially during economic downturns. This was also the case during the 2008 global financial crisis. At that time, despite the world being ravaged by a once-in-a-century financial crisis, Microsoft, Apple, Google, and other U.S. technology companies generally increased their investment in research and development. According to a survey conducted by the European Commission on R&D investments of 2500 major companies across 46 countries or regions for the 2017 fiscal year, the 2018 EU Industrial R&D Investment Scoreboard showed that U.S., EU, Chinese, Japanese, and South Korean companies were the main players in industrial R&D investment. Among them, Samsung ranked first with €13.437 billion in R&D spending, followed by Alphabet (Google's parent company), Volkswagen, Microsoft, Huawei, Intel, Apple, and Roche, in that order. Moreover, 96% of the companies in the top 50 R&D investment rankings were from the U.S., Europe, and Japan. This demonstrates that the main technological drivers of global economic growth still come from the super enterprises of developed countries.

However, global economic growth and the prosperity of developed countries cannot be built on the widespread underdevelopment of developing nations. The global economy urgently needs more innovation-driven entities to lead growth and prosperity, including emerging economies and relatively underdeveloped developing countries. In 2018, the "Global Innovation Index" (GII), jointly released by Cornell University, The European Institute of Business Administration (INSEAD), and the World Intellectual Property Organization, covered 126 countries. The study highlighted that despite remarkable innovation achievements in Sub-Saharan African countries such as South Africa, Kenya, Rwanda, Madagascar, Malawi, and Mozambique—where science and technology and skilled labor have enhanced competitiveness, attracted more foreign direct investment, and increased corporate revenue streams—most countries in the region still ranked beyond the top 100 in innovation index. Similarly, progress in some Latin American countries had also stagnated. The biggest constraints in these regions include insufficient financial investment, a lack of feasible policy support, poor market ecosystems, and the need for improved engineer training.

It is encouraging to see that with the continuous development of innovation activities in BRICS countries and South Korea, global technology and knowledge are showing a trend of two-way flow. In particular, as Chinese and South Korean companies increase their investment in cutting-edge technology research and development, the positive spillover effects on traditional developed countries are gradually becoming apparent.

From a technological perspective, there are three main dimensions to assess whether the global economy will enter a new economic cycle at some point in the future: The first one is whether the endogenous factors supporting global economic development are stable. The second one is whether new global growth drivers are strong. The third one is whether the markets of microeconomic entities based on technological progress and financial innovation are vibrant.

In the current context of slowing global economic growth, rising uncertainty and potential risks, countries must not only maintain multilateral cooperation to ensure the relative stability of existing rules and systems but also possess sufficient risk awareness and keen intuition. Moreover, they must adjust domestic policies to broadly activate the innovative capabilities of microeconomic entities, increase investment in research and development in key industries and forward-looking technological fields, and accelerate the industrial application process. This will help establish effective global economic growth on a foundation driven by the collective efforts of more innovation-driven entities.

Developed Countries Must Remember the Responsibilities of "Prosperity First"

There is a significant divide between developed countries, led by the United States, and developing countries, represented by China, India, and others, regarding WTO reforms. The most prominent disagreement centers around whether to maintain or reduce the "Special and Differential Treatment" (SDT) granted to developing countries within the WTO framework. The United States has proposed that WTO members meeting certain criteria—such as being classified as a high-income economy by the World Bank, being an OECD member, being part of the G20, or having a global trade share of over 0.5%—should no longer be considered developing countries. This proposal aims to strip developing countries of their entitlements under WTO, including the Most-Favored-Nation (MFN) principle, the non-discrimination principle, formulating the multilateral framework for rule-making, and special and differential treatment. As a result, it has been strongly opposed by developing countries like China, India, and South Africa.

This leads to a commonly discussed question in economics: What defines a developed country? As is well-known, thanks to the exploration of generations of economists, modern economics has developed a series of foundational theories over the past 300 years, often referred to as "models" and "theorems". These foundational theories are not direct descriptions of the real world but are often idealized concepts that cannot be fully realized in practice, representing "textbook economics." However, they provide benchmarks or reference points for analyzing real-world problems and offer important analytical perspectives. In fact, since 1944, economists from institutions such as the World Bank, IMF, WTO, and OECD have conducted a large amount of rigorous and solid research on defining concepts like developed countries, developing countries, and least developed countries, as well as the relevant criteria for classification. Based on this, they have provided numerous valuable policy recommendations for international organizations with missions centered around poverty reduction and promoting development, playing a certain role in narrowing the North-South divide.

The author believes that the classification of concepts such as developed countries, developing countries, and least developed countries carries both symbolic and substantive meaning. More importantly, these concepts themselves are largely the result of industrialization, which has caused significant changes in global division of labor and led to unfair resource allocation.

In a certain sense, developed countries and early industrialized countries refer to the same concept. Since the Industrial Revolution, European and American countries, represented by the United Kingdom, France, Germany, Italy, the United States and so on, were the first to complete industrialization through technological advancements and human capital accumulation rate. While completing the initial accumulation of wealth, they rapidly expanded their resource allocation power both regionally and globally. Japan in East Asia also completed industrialization through the Meiji Restoration, quickly catching up with the Western powers, and thus joining the ranks of the most advanced capitalist countries. As is widely known, the G7 is a club formed in the 1970s by the seven most industrialized countries in the world.

From the perspective of G7 countries, history and their absolute power have endowed them with the role of guarantors of the global political, economic, and security systems. Among them, the United Kingdom, as the first country to implement industrialization, became the world's first superpower ahead of the United States. In the nineteenth century, it was the true guarantor of the global system and an early representative of financial imperialism. The British pound standard once dominated the global financial system for a long time. Even after World War II, the UK, relying on imperial inertia and astute national strategies, continued to play the role of a global economic and financial system guarantor alongside the United States. The reason the UK and the US became global system guarantors was not only due to their industrial and trade systems that were superior to those of other countries but also because of some other special advantages, such as the globally distributed maritime power projection and strike systems, flexible commercial interventions, and intangible financial control systems.

As a superpower, the United States established a tightly organized mechanism of hegemony after World War II. The so-called "mechanized hegemony" refers to the order paradigm the U.S. created by influencing a series of international organizations, mechanisms, and alliances. Through its dominance of institutions like the World Bank and IMF, the U.S. controlled the power and discourse of setting international financial rules, the hegemony of determining financial market price levels, and creative decisions regarding various financial instruments and titles. Wall Street, the G7, various elite clubs, globally dominant financial expert certification and registration agencies, and so on are all symbols of the U.S.'s control over the world financial order.

Since its establishment in 1913, the Federal Reserve quickly integrated with the U.S. Treasury and the vast commercial and investment banking system, collectively serving the national interests and strategic goals of the United States. From an economic perspective, U.S. national interests are first and foremost reflected in maintaining its position in the global financial division of labor, followed by the low-cost acquisition of foreign resources through the dollar standard or the external projection of economic costs. At the time, the Soviet Union attempted to replace the U.S. as the world's leading superpower, using military power as its primary tool. However, Soviet leaders forgot one key thing: while the Soviet Union had many advantages over the U.S., such as natural resources and strong mobilization capacity, there was one crucial thing the Soviet Union could never match the U.S. in: the ruble. Although the ruble seemed strong at the time, it was confined to the Soviet sphere of influence, whereas the dollar could be used to allocate resources worldwide. Thus, both engaged in the arms race, the Soviet Union could initially hold on, but gradually found it difficult to sustain. The U.S., on the other hand, had no such concerns, because it could spend only a portion of its own money and resources, with much of the spending coming from other countries' money or low-cost acquisitions of foreign resources.

Times change, and so do circumstances. The once "empire on which the sun never sets" is no longer capable of maintaining its former strength. The United States, once the sole superpower, is increasingly finding it difficult to serve as the sole guarantor of the global economy. The Western world has come to realize that the global landscape is evolving in the following way: the United States, as the hegemonic power, still holds a leadership position, but is gradually losing its absolute dominance; multiple secondary economic and military centers are rapidly emerging; several reserve currencies coexist; the responsibility of protecting the global commons has shifted from one country to multiple nations, and competition and instability have become the new normal. As the *Financial Times* has pointed out, for the United States and other wealthy or developed countries, accepting this shift in global dynamics does not seem to be an easy task.

Some developed countries, represented by the United States, seem to have forgotten how they became "developed" in the first place. They are increasingly unwilling to bear the obligations and responsibilities of promoting global development and are instead focused solely on safeguarding their own existing interests. Emerging countries such as China, Russia, India, and Indonesia, despite achieving remarkable progress in economic growth, technological advancement, international trade, and even finance, still lag significantly behind developed nations like the United States in most key indicators. They remain, without a doubt, developing countries.

One of the original purposes behind economists' classification of developed, developing, and underdeveloped countries was to promote the principle of "those who become prosperous first should help others prosper" and achieve common development. Developed countries must not forget this initial intent. They should not fall into the paradigm of "as a developed country, I must always maintain an absolute lead," nor should they seek to monopolize prosperity while denying other nations the opportunity to grow. Even worse, they must not go so far as to hinder other countries' right to development as a means of maintaining their dominance.

Where Lies the Path to Effective Growth of Global Economy under Stimulus?

In 2020, due to the impact of the COVID-19 pandemic, the global economy had actually entered a recessionary zone without a baseline scenario. People's expectations for economic recovery were as anxious and urgent as patients longing for a vaccine, making the situation particularly complex. At that time, the pressing task for the global economy was not only to prevent major countries from experiencing a free-fall recession but also to stabilize the economic fundamentals while paving the way for recovery and effective growth.

For the monetary and fiscal authorities of various countries, already exhausted from coping with challenges, the pandemic was like a heavy blow, instantly disrupting the policy framework for 2020. With saving lives, stabilizing markets, supporting businesses, and ensuring people's livelihoods becoming top priorities, liquidity injections and fiscal subsidies have been continuously effective as primary response tools. For governments worldwide—especially the financial authorities of major economies—that are paradoxically both short on and flush with money, the response has been unprecedented. In just two months since March 2020, they rolled out over $8 trillion in comprehensive measures, an extraordinary action rarely seen since the establishment of the Bretton Woods system. The Federal Reserve, traditionally the lender of last resort, swiftly transformed into the lender of first resort as the pandemic spread. It directly purchased commercial paper, mortgage-backed securities, and corporate bonds from both primary and secondary markets. Moreover, it nearly exhausted the entire arsenal of monetary policy tools accumulated over its 107-year history, both existing and newly introduced. As a result, by the week of April 22, 2020, its balance sheet had ballooned to $6.6 trillion. At the same time, large corporations in the U.S. and Europe borrowed money at record speeds or turned directly to their governments for assistance. The economic downturn was vividly reflected in the empty streets of major cities across the U.S. and Europe.

The *Financial Times* has depicted the economic aftermath of the COVID-19 pandemic, including a sharp decline in output, widespread business closures, rising unemployment, and mounting fiscal deficits. The world's wealthiest nations are expected to experience a rapid decline in wealth, face heavier debt burdens, and implement stricter border controls. This scenario is not an exaggeration; countries must take it seriously and adopt effective countermeasures.

In 2020, when economic production was severely contracted and development expectations were still surrounded by significant uncertainty, discussing economic recovery might seem a bit unrealistic. However, as a global public health crisis, the pandemic is, in the long span of human survival and development, a relatively short-term external shock. The economic development of various countries and the global economy will not be permanently stalled due to the large-scale impact of the pandemic. While globalization and its trends have been affected to some extent, they will not come to a standstill.

The G20, which brings together the world's major developed countries, regions, and emerging economies, pledged to provide support in the fields of health and medicine to countries in need after the outbreak of the pandemic. They also agreed that the world's poorest countries could suspend debt repayment from May 1, 2020, to the end of 2020. This reflects the G20's sense of international responsibility as the world's key economic forces during a critical period. The reason the G20 did not directly commit to debt relief was primarily because these countries or regions themselves were also facing significant fiscal pressures and growth gaps. The United States, as the world's largest economy, also faces a series of serious issues caused by excessive stimulus. The Federal Reserve's decision to open the monetary taps was not a particularly difficult move; however, the real challenge lies in how to reverse the massive liquidity expansion, a process known as 'quantitative tightening.' While this may sound simple, it is difficult to execute, and for the majority of countries heavily reliant on the dollar system, it becomes a painful process.

The world should remember that Paul Volcker (See Fig. 12.1), the former Chairman of the Federal Reserve, who was praised by Alan Greenspan as "the father of American economic vitality over the past two decades," made a pivotal decision in the early 1980s during the U.S. recession. He chose to abandon control over the money supply of the U.S. dollar and instead used interest rates as a tool to regulate the macroeconomy. From then on, the U.S. increasingly relied on debt-driven economic growth. Greenspan, who carried the aura of an "economic czar," went even further than his predecessor in injecting liquidity into the markets. However, since 2008, the United States, which carries significant responsibility for

Fig. 12.1 Economist Paul Volcker

global economic growth and financial stability, has seen its marginal contribution decrease overall. In the context of global real economic growth and technological progress over the past decade failing to effectively offset asset bubbles and the accumulation of risks, the global economy's recovery from 2009 to 2014, and its growth from 2015 to 2019, relied increasingly on debt leverage. In contrast, the total factor productivity driven by technological and human capital accumulation has not seen significant progress over the past decade. This has led to economic recovery and growth being inherently unstable to a large extent.

The lessons from history repeatedly demonstrate that no country's economy can continue to operate in a high-leverage zone over the long term without eventually facing a debt crisis. Moreover, the more unstable the economic environment and the more complex the financial system, the more likely a financial crisis is to erupt. For macroeconomics, with its mission in mind, there are always unsolved problems, but never a perfect final answer. The many stimulus policies implemented by countries so far have, to some extent, served as emergency measures to stop the bleeding. However, to avoid repeating the mistakes of the previous crisis response, there is an urgent need for macroeconomic policies to focus more on the real economy and industrial development, as well as people's welfare, especially the replacement, upgrading and improvement of the public health and safety system. Based on this, G20 members should take the lead in aligning financial development to serve the real economy as a collective action plan of all countries. They should discuss, formulate, and implement an actionable policy framework for financial services that supports the real economy, to prevent credit expansion from continuing to be used for large-scale purchases of existing assets or primarily directed towards large corporations. At the same time, while maintaining appropriate policy flexibility, countries should increase investments in technological research and development and industrialization, effectively enhancing the competitiveness of manufacturing and restarting endogenous economic growth models.

Safeguarding the WTO as the "Guardian of Free Trade"

The WTO, with a history spanning over 70 years, is now caught in the historical dilemma typically faced by global public goods.

After the departure of Roberto Azevêdo, who was originally charismatic and had international ambitions, the WTO launched the selection process for a new Director-General. On February 15, 2021, the WTO officially appointed Nigeria's candidate, Ngozi Okonjo-Iweala, as the seventh Director-General, with her term starting on March 1, 2021. The arrival of the "new helmsman" provided the WTO, which had been facing a suspension of its dispute settlement mechanism for more than half a year, with an opportunity to reshape its image and revive the vitality of its mechanisms.

As an upgraded version of the GATT, the WTO is a product of institutional changes brought about by economic globalization and trade liberalization. Since its official operation in 1995, it has made historic contributions in advancing fair competition in the trade sector, ensuring the effectiveness of the multilateral trade system, and facilitating trade and services among members in an equal competitive environment and so on. As a result, the WTO, alongside the World Bank and the IMF, is recognized as one of the three major global public goods in the economic realm and is often referred to as the "Economic United Nations."

However, just as finding the optimal solution for free trade in the real world is a difficult challenge, the WTO, despite its glorious past and the strong support it once received from the free trade-promoting U.S. and Europe, has found it increasingly difficult to maintain its neutrality. As emerging economies have joined the WTO and become more integrated into the global trade system, developed countries have begun to change their stance toward the WTO. This has made it harder for the organization to maintain its balanced approach. In particular, the United States, one of the key architects of the WTO, has become increasingly dissatisfied with the organization in recent years, even threatening to withdraw multiple times.

The United States has accused the existing WTO mechanisms of causing international trade to fall into a state of market failure and stagnation, claiming that judges of the WTO dispute settlement mechanism's Appellate Body frequently "overstep their authority" and "abuse" powers that are not granted to them under WTO-related laws and regulations during their interpretation of WTO legal provisions. The U.S. has repeatedly stated that it will use all available means to ensure WTO reforms regarding the status of developing countries, aiming to prevent nations that "self-declare" as developing countries but lack the appropriate economic indicators from enjoying the flexibility of special and differential treatment in WTO negotiations. Using this as a pretext, the U.S. government, acting unilaterally, effectively crippled the WTO's dispute settlement mechanism—the Appellate Body—at the end of 2019 by delaying and obstructing the appointment of new judges, rendering the mechanism incapable of reviewing trade disputes between WTO members. As a result, the global multilateral trade dispute resolution system has been actually left in a state of brain paralysis.

It now appears that the United States is taking a step back to advance its agenda by paralyzing or even completely shutting down the WTO dispute settlement mechanism to weaken support for the multilateral trading system. At the same time, it is using the strategy of drawing in certain emerging economies as a breakthrough point, enticing some members to follow its lead. The ultimate goal is the only one: to reshape the WTO according to the will of the United States.

There is no doubt that the WTO is one of the most important institutions for safeguarding free trade. With the rapid development of the digital economy, the WTO urgently needs to establish international standards for digital trade. This is the driving force and urgency behind the WTO's need for self-reform to adapt to technological advancements and trade development. The outbreak of the COVID-19 pandemic has significantly accelerated the digitalization of global trade. It can even be said that, to some extent, it has established the dominant position of digital trade. In the era of digital trade, the WTO clearly has a broad scope for action in accelerating e-commerce negotiations, strengthening the digitalization of cross-border goods and services trade, bridging the "digital divide," enhancing privacy protection, and ensuring a fair competitive environment.

Even if the cold winds of protectionism and unilateralism arise from time to time, even if the fragmentation and bloc-based competition of global trade rules severely hinder the process of global economic integration and significantly increase bilateral or multilateral trade frictions and transaction costs, the WTO has no reason to marginalize itself.

At this critical moment when WTO reform is at a standstill, China, as a responsible emerging major power, should make every effort to unite other members and work together to advance WTO reform in a positive and constructive direction. To this end, we can explore ways to integrate China's three fundamental principles and five proposals for WTO reform with the reform propositions and demands of developed economies such as Europe and Japan, as well as those of emerging economies and the broader developing world. On the other hand, while resolutely countering any economic and trade bullying by the United States, we should also demonstrate appropriate flexibility to prevent China-U.S. economic and trade relations from falling into a comprehensive "derailment" and "decoupling" driven by some hawkish factions in the U.S. towards China. It is also worth exploring possible areas of cooperation between China and the United States within WTO reform, such as tariffs, non-tariff barriers, and technology transfers, where constructive dialogue can be carried out.

After all, zero-sum games are harmful and unproductive. The achievement of global economic governance goals "inherently" requires WTO members to demonstrate a sense of international responsibility in the process of cooperative games, aiming to eliminate differences and promote the free flow of goods and capital, so that they can benefit from sharing and jointly safeguard the WTO's image as the "guardian of free trade."

Will Economic Conservatism See a Period of Retreat?

After the world has endured the most challenging year of this century in 2020, looking ahead to the trajectory of economic conservatism in the "post-pandemic era" is a necessary premise for judging the medium- and long-term development trends of the global economy.

In April 2020, Kristalina Georgieva, the Managing Director of the International Monetary Fund (IMF), who bears significant responsibility for global financial stability, warned that although the resilience of the global financial system was sufficient to withstand the impact of the COVID-19 pandemic, policymakers should not take financial stability for granted. She emphasized the need for swift action to restore economic growth and prevent widespread financial distress. Georgieva's concerns were primarily expressed from a technical perspective, without delving deeply into political factors beyond the economic sphere.

It is widely acknowledged that any major economic issue is, to some extent, also a political issue. In fact, in recent years, global economic development has been affected not only by major external shocks such as the COVID-19 pandemic but also by economic conservatism, which is heavily influenced by national interests. At the same time, the immense uncertainty stemming from certain economic conservatism policies has made it difficult even for the most market-savvy analysts to predict outcomes accurately, let alone identify optimal responses within the conventional policy framework. The development of the global economy depends not only on technological advancements, human capital accumulation, and the reduction of transaction costs but also on optimistic expectations and rational foresight from governments, businesses, and consumers worldwide.

In summary, the greater the uncertainty facing the global economy, the more countries must avoid the "fallacy of composition" in economic policy to enhance their resilience against external shocks. This principle underlies China's ongoing efforts to expand openness and promote trade and investment facilitation at both the regional and global levels.

Following the outbreak of COVID-19, voices emerged suggesting that the pandemic would prompt more multinational corporations to reconsider their reliance on China's supply chains and even accelerate the process of "decoupling" between China and developed countries in terms of industrial and supply chains. However, an examination of the supply and demand sides of global pandemic response materials reveals that the United States, which has been the loudest proponent of "decoupling," actually benefited the most from the global circulation of such materials. According to official Chinese statistics, as of November 22, 2020, China had exported approximately 39.43 billion masks, 800 million surgical gloves, 650 million protective suits, and 46.76 million goggles to the United States.

Complete information and accurate data are prerequisites for rational decision-making. These statistics indicate that in today's world, no country or political force can ignore the deep integration of industrial, supply, and value chains; no national power can artificially block the rational flow of global production factors by erecting various barriers; and no economy can easily replace China's crucial role in global supply chains. More importantly, despite its control over key segments of global industrial supply chains, China has not implemented any form of economic conservatism toward other countries.

It is commendable that Japan and South Korea, as China's close neighbors and G20 members with deep industrial and supply chain ties to China, strongly supported China's fight against COVID-19 in its early stages, hoping for a swift economic recovery to maintain the smooth operation of East Asia's supply chains. Subsequently, China, Japan, and South Korea not only strengthened cooperation in pandemic prevention and control and jointly took on the responsibility of ensuring regional economic stability and supply chain security but also worked together to resolve differences and accelerate regional economic integration. The successful signing of the Regional Comprehensive Economic Partnership (RCEP) is a landmark achievement of China, Japan, South Korea, and ASEAN countries in creating a mutually beneficial regional public good. It also demonstrates that the agreement's members are taking concrete steps to repair the global economic system, which has been severely disrupted by protectionism and unilateralism. The ongoing China-Japan-South Korea free trade agreement (FTA) negotiations are expected to accelerate further due to RCEP. If these three economies, with a combined GDP exceeding $20 trillion, eventually reach an FTA agreement, it will serve as the strongest reinforcement of RCEP's achievements.

As the world's second-largest economy, China took action within two weeks of signing RCEP to expedite its implementation, highlighting its sense of international responsibility in upholding free trade and seeking regional and global cooperation for mutual benefit. At the same time, China has proactively engaged with the Comprehensive and Progressive Agreement for Trans-Pacific Partnership (CPTPP) after a careful evaluation. This move reflects China's strong confidence in its economic reforms and openness, the significant overlap between RCEP and CPTPP in terms of zero-tariff coverage on goods trade, and an optimistic outlook for its medium- to long-term development goals under the 14th Five-Year Plan and the 2035 vision. In other words, under the irreversible trend of global economic integration, China, guided by the goal of building a high-standard socialist market economy, not only does not need to shy away from high-standard FTAs but can also seize the opportunity to deeply integrate into the global economy, actively promote the free movement of production factors, facilitate trade and investment, and further reduce transaction costs. It is also noteworthy that the new political cycles underway or beginning in some countries, along with the policy rationality demonstrated by most G20 members since 2020 in advancing economic globalization, create a potential window for the retreat of economic conservatism.

Grasp the Pulse of Green Finance Development and Global Industrial Transformation

After the central government and national authorities defined achieving carbon peaking and carbon neutrality as a broad and profound systemic transformation of economic life—and incorporated it into the overall framework of ecological civilization development—green finance, which has gained significant attention due to the carbon neutrality goals, has become not only the hottest and most challenging topic in the financial sector but also an essential threshold that regulators and all market participants must cross.

In March 2021, when discussing green finance, People's Bank of China Governor Yi Gang highlighted both the potential impacts of climate change and the green transition on existing financial assets and financial system stability, as well as the central bank's urgent commitment to practicing green development and advancing green finance. Under the constraints of carbon neutrality, China's financial development, industrial structure, and technological transformation will undergo fundamental changes. The scale of green investment and financing—encompassing green loans and green bonds—is projected to expand from RMB 13 trillion at the end of 2020 to a multi-trillion level. The substantial investment gap clearly necessitates a mature and well-established market system to bridge it. How to establish a green financial standard system that is both rigidly enforced and adaptable while ensuring seamless alignment between domestic and international standards remains a complex challenge. Meanwhile, as carbon emissions trading is promoted, reducing the cost of clean energy usage or energy consumption per unit of GDP through technological progress and the modernization of social governance presents not only a significant opportunity for Shanghai in its medium- to long-term development during the 14th Five-Year Plan period and beyond to 2035 but also signals that Shanghai and major global financial centers will, for the first time, compete on an almost equal footing in this new race.

Fundamentally, this represents a paradigm shift for all economic and market participants, even challenging existing economic theories. China is actively creating favorable conditions to achieve its carbon peaking and carbon neutrality targets. For instance, China has established world-class digital infrastructure and possesses advanced industrial digitalization capabilities, allowing for the efficient allocation and optimization of energy and resources within a green development framework. China's proactive efforts in formulating and implementing green standards have also provided the country with a leading advantage in green finance development. Furthermore, the accelerated establishment of a primary carbon trading market—especially the official launch of carbon emissions trading—will help foster a broad and conscious commitment among market participants to facilitate a low-carbon transition within the overarching framework of ecological civilization development.

From an economic perspective, in today's world, carbon emission rights are essentially a scarce, valuable economic resource. The fact that they can be traded highlights their strong financial attributes, yet such rights also reflect an unequal

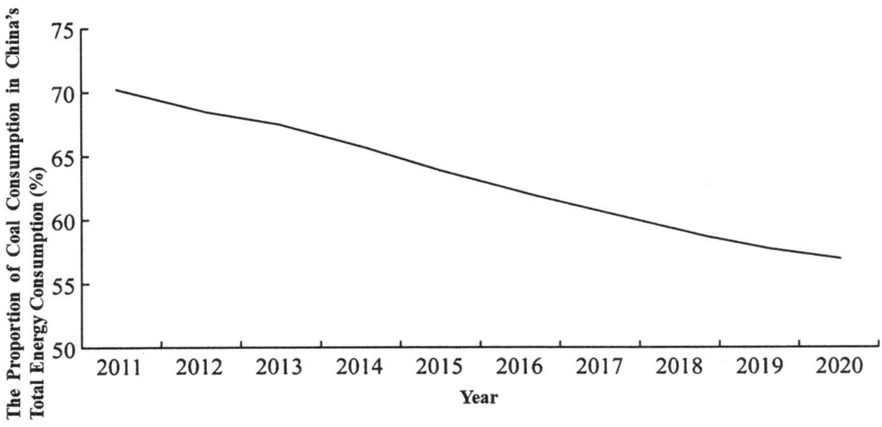

Fig. 12.2 Proportion of coal consumption in China's total energy consumption, 2011–2020. Data Source: National Bureau of Statistics of China

division of labor and trading system, particularly for developing countries. A crucial constraint is that under the rigid requirement to achieve carbon peaking before 2030, industries and enterprises heavily reliant on fossil fuels with high costs for technological upgrades will face a "race against time" to meet emission reduction targets. In 2019, coal consumption accounted for 58% of China's total energy consumption (as shown in Fig. 12.2, illustrating China's coal consumption as a proportion of total energy consumption from 2011 to 2020), while China's total carbon emissions made up 29% of the global share. China's per capita carbon emissions were 46% higher than the global average, and its energy consumption per unit of GDP was approximately three times that of the OECD average. Although there is considerable potential for energy conservation, for China—where per capita GDP has only recently surpassed the $10,000 threshold—achieving carbon peaking requires first assessing the vast industrial manufacturing system and then taking action toward emissions reduction, restructuring, or shutdowns. While the 30-year period from carbon peaking to carbon neutrality may seem lengthy, in practice, it means that after 2030, China's carbon emissions must decline rapidly every year. This is necessary to achieve the expected target by 2060, where over two-thirds of the country's energy supply will come from clean electricity, and about one-fifth of energy consumption will be offset through carbon capture methods. Essentially, there is no buffer period in this transition.

For the financial industry, as Governor Gang Yi stated, the development goals of carbon peaking before 2030 and carbon neutrality before 2060 impose new and higher requirements on financial work. These goals not only demand massive investments but also impact financial stability and monetary policy. In particular, the green transition may lead to a decline in the value of high-carbon-emission assets, affecting the asset quality of enterprises and financial institutions. Under the roadmap of carbon neutrality, modern finance is increasingly becoming an effective integration of a nation's technological innovation, output, creativity, green development, capital pricing power, and international coordination and leadership. How to accurately grasp the pulse of green finance development and global industrial transformation, steadily advance the green transition of financial assets, actively strive for pricing power in green financial assets, and achieve high-quality economic development under this new developmental path will constitute the core theme of China's macroeconomics for the next 40 years.

With a well-structured plan in place, during the 14th Five-Year Plan period, China must prioritize the improvement and perfection of the green financial system while accelerating the establishment of a high-standard financial market system. Currently, China's green financial standard system has entered an institutionalized and systematic phase, aligning with leading international countries and regions. We must seize this rare opportunity to strengthen international coordination and actively promote the global recognition of China's green financial standards, particularly in ensuring the uniformity, comparability, and transparency of data standards, which are crucial for establishing a sustainable global data standard framework. On the other hand, in the process of accelerating the development of a green financial market trading system, Shanghai—China's most resource-efficient city—must leverage market mechanisms to direct financial resources toward carbon neutrality. This involves expanding the depth and breadth of green financial products, prioritizing the listing and financing of green industrial enterprises aligned with carbon neutrality goals, encouraging commercial banks to enhance green credit services, and establishing a robust green finance market system encompassing bonds, insurance, funds, trusts, and asset management, all guided by green development principles. As China's most important carbon emissions trading market, Shanghai enjoys unique advantages in developing carbon finance and encouraging the trading of carbon-related financial products such as forwards, futures, and options. Coupled with the city's continuous progress in building an international financial center, Shanghai has the potential to become a globally influential carbon market pricing hub.

Finally, the green technologies and their industrial applications driven by carbon neutrality goals will decouple energy and power development from carbon emissions and separate economic and social growth from carbon dependency, ultimately leading to a low-carbon or even zero-carbon energy revolution. Given the ongoing acceleration of digital transformation in Shanghai and across the country, China is well-positioned to break free from carbon lock-in on schedule and rapidly transition its economic development path toward a green, low-carbon, circular, and sustainable trajectory.

Chapter 13
The Foundation of China's High-Quality Economic Development

New Development Philosophy Opens a New Chapter for China's Economic Growth

In terms of the time spectrum, 2017 served as a crucial transitional year leading up to the milestone of China's 40th anniversary of reform and opening-up. It is considered a pivotal year for two main reasons. First, the globally watched 19th National Congress of the Communist Party of China explicitly put forward the "Two-Step" strategy for fully building a modern socialist country, advancing the goal of basically achieving modernization by 15 years. This strategy not only provided a clear framework for the aspirations of the entire Party and the people of all ethnic groups in China but also outlined specific micro-level objectives, offering a long-term development roadmap for the country. Second, 2018 marked the 40th anniversary of China's era-defining reform and opening-up. Over these four decades, China transitioned from the initial "crossing the river by feeling the stones" approach to establishing and continuously refining the socialist market economy system since the 1990s. Since the 18th National Congress, China has actively contributed to global public goods, shared the benefits of its economic growth, and participated in global economic governance. These efforts have shaped a unique Chinese development paradigm and strategic approach amid shifts in the global economic landscape, reflecting the nation's wisdom in adhering to economic development principles and policy logic. China's proposal of a new development philosophy—centered on "innovation, coordination, green development, openness, and shared growth"—aims to balance key economic relationships, including government and market, supply and demand, fairness and efficiency, economic growth and environmental protection, and domestic development with global integration. This philosophy provides a Chinese policy framework for international competition and cooperation in a rapidly evolving global landscape.

Development, of course, is best illustrated with data. In 2017, China's GDP grew by 6.9%, and large-scale industrial enterprises saw an impressive 21% increase in

Y. Zhang, *Addressing Uncertainty*, Understanding China,
https://doi.org/10.1007/978-981-92-2692-4_13

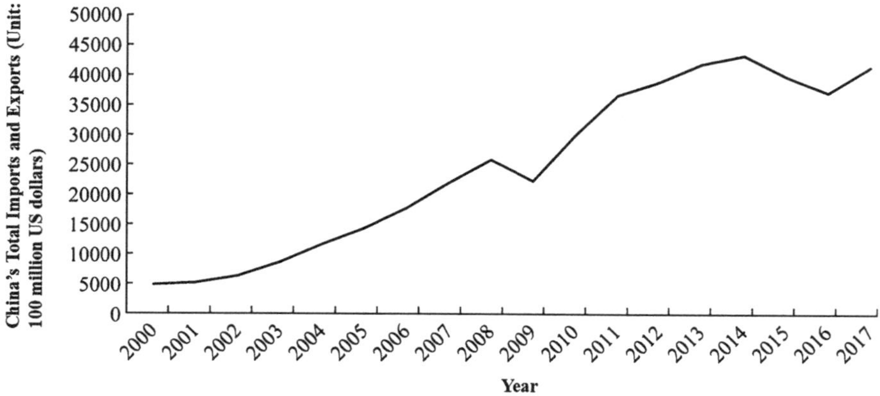

Fig. 13.1 Changes in China's Total Import and Export Volumes, 2000–2017. Data Source: National Bureau of Statistics of China

profits. Particularly, state-owned enterprises experienced a remarkable 45.1% profit growth, strongly supporting the ongoing state-owned enterprise (SOE) mixed-ownership reforms. That year, despite geopolitical risks and trade protectionist measures from certain countries, the first synchronized economic expansion among major global economies in a decade contributed to a moderate recovery in global investment and trade. This external support helped China's exports rebound by 10.8% year-over-year after two years of decline, with total foreign trade exceeding the $4 trillion mark once again. (See Fig. 13.1 for the changes in China's total imports and exports from 2000 to 2017.) Additionally, expectations of a one-sided RMB depreciation were successfully reversed, leading to the stabilization and recovery of foreign exchange reserves. Fiscal revenues, a key concern for governments at all levels, also showed a promising outlook, achieving a growth rate of 7.4%, providing solid financial support for various national initiatives.

Overall, with the steady progress of supply-side structural reforms and the improvement in investment and export conditions in 2017, China's economy, after gradually bidding farewell to its "most difficult period," was preparing to embrace the arrival of a new economic cycle, driven by the next round of reforms.

When discussing development, it is essential to assess existing problems, particularly risk evaluation and early warning systems. If we were to choose the key issue of China's economic operation in 2017, it would undoubtedly be "ensuring that systemic financial risks are prevented." Both the 19th Party Congress report and the Central Economic Work Conference highlighted maintaining this baseline as a priority for economic and financial work. From the very beginning of the establishment of the Financial Stability and Development Committee (FSDC), it was announced that its focus would be on shadow banking, the asset management industry, internet finance, financial holding companies, and other areas, seeking to identify risk points and strengthen risk prevention mechanisms.

Indeed, concerning the debt ratio, there can be no room for relaxation. By the end of 2016, China's macro-leverage ratio was at 247%, with the corporate sector leverage reaching 165%. Notably, some state-owned enterprises exhibited significant debt risks, and the market clearing of "zombie enterprises" was slow. Although local government debt risks were generally controllable, the Ministry of Finance's report indicated that some local governments still resorted to illegal leverage practices through financing platform companies, public-private partnerships (PPP), government investment funds, and various "equity debt" schemes. The warning from past lessons is clear: no economy has managed to operate in a high-leverage debt zone for an extended period without facing debt crises or even systemic financial crises. Clearly, this baseline cannot be crossed.

To achieve high-quality development, China must focus on development that adapts to, guides, and enhances demand. This requires establishing a multi-level, diversified resource allocation mechanism to discover, adapt to, and guide demand. Therefore, China must carry out a fundamental restructuring of its economic structure based on the benchmarks of effective economic growth. Specifically, this includes deepening reforms to improve market mechanisms, enhancing the legal system supporting these mechanisms, accelerating government system reforms, strictly controlling the risk exposure of local government debt, and enhancing the resilience of financial market participants. Governments at all levels and relevant market entities must especially prepare for adjustments in economic policies and shifts in growth drivers under the new normal, promptly clearing the longstanding economic issues and establishing the new growth logic for China's economy in this context: creating an endogenous economic growth model through significant advancements in technology and specialized human capital accumulation driven by continuous and effective R&D investments.

From a longer-term development perspective, China's exploration of development concepts and growth models, as well as the substantial progress already made, hold a certain paradigm value in the history of global economic thought and modern economic development. China's economic reform and development not only provide a unique experimental ground for the theoretical application of socialism with Chinese characteristics but also offer a valuable research sample for constructing a new economic growth model that balances both universal theoretical applicability and distinct Chinese characteristics. Clearly, the New Development Concept has defined the new growth logic of China's economy.

The Upgrading and Transformation of the Economic System to Redefine New Global Competitive Coordinates

Building a modern economic system is a comprehensive and complex task, representing both a major theoretical proposition and a significant practical challenge. It requires in-depth exploration through the integration of theory and practice.

Constructing a modern economic system is a strategic goal for China's development, as well as an urgent requirement for transforming the economic development model, optimizing the economic structure, and shifting the economic growth drivers. Only by forming a modern economic system can China better adapt to the trends of modern development, gain an advantage in international competition, and provide strong support for modernization in other fields. China has elevated the construction of a modern economic system to a strategic height that concerns the country's future and destiny, because facing international competition requires building a systematic national competitive advantage.

Over 40 years ago, China's economic reform was initiated without a ready-made international benchmark, which made it an extremely difficult exploration for a populous developing country, filled with uncertainties and risks. At that time, China could "feel its way" through the process, experimenting with reforms in specific regions and sectors to find replicable and scalable models. Looking back, these accumulated reform examples have provided rich materials for the study of transition economics and development economics, and have further attracted international mainstream economics to focus on China's economic reforms and development. For example, Nobel laureates such as Michael Spence (see Fig. 13.2) and Joseph E. Stiglitz (see Fig. 13.3) have increasingly focused on China's economic reforms over the last decade. The work "China's Long-Term Development and Transformation: Perspectives and Recommendations from an International View," co-authored by Spence and Lin Chonggeng, is a wise contribution from international economists observing China's economic reforms and development trends. Many of Spence's suggestions regarding China's economic reform have, to some extent, been adopted by Chinese policymakers. Stiglitz, from the 1980s

Fig. 13.2 Economist Michael Spence

Fig. 13.3 Economist Joseph Stiglitz

onward, has offered advice on numerous important issues, including the choice of reform models and paths, clarifying the relationship between government and market, state-owned enterprise reform, financial market regulation, capital account opening, income distribution, and the construction of new public goods. These forward-looking suggestions have had a significant impact on China's reform policies. The contributions of international economists like Spence and Stiglitz, along with domestic scholars and reform practitioners like Wu Jinglian, Li Yining, Lou Jiwei, and Guo Shuqing, have transformed into valuable decisions for China's overall economic reform and goal-setting.

Forty years later, it is no longer possible for China to "feel its way forward" during deep reforms, as it did in the past. After all, China is no longer the closed economy it once was; it is deeply involved in global economic integration, and in many ways, it is leading the emerging economies of globalization. In fact, China's actions are directly influencing the process of globalization. In other words, while the fact that China doubled its GDP between 2010 and 2017 is a remarkable achievement, what should be presented to the world today is not just a series of stunning economic data, but the economic logic and paradigm behind these figures—what kind of system and driving force allowed China to achieve sustained economic development? And are these systems and forces sustainable? In the international market environment, does the economic system and growth model that China has built over the past 40 years of reform and opening up have lessons for other countries?

If we look at the growth logic and development paths of leading industrialized countries, it is clear that, apart from the United States—whose system based on technological advancement and financial hegemony has allowed its economy to maintain long-term growth, making it the first super-economy to surpass a $10 trillion GDP—no other developed country has reached the same level of development. Japan, which once had aggressive development momentum, saw its economy reach two-thirds of the United States' size in the mid-1980s, but after the collapse of its bubble economy, the gap with the U.S. continued to widen, and for over 20 years its economy has been stuck around $5 trillion. Today, Japan's economy is less than a quarter of the size of the U.S. economy. Europe, as a key global economic region, is large enough to compete with the U.S., and its development ideas are noteworthy. However, in today's world where countries are still the most important players in global economic competition, such horizontal comparisons have limited practical significance. Perhaps from the U.S. perspective, Germany is the only major competitor that deserves extra attention. This is because Germany not only has a larger economic scale and greater competitiveness in Europe but also has been the most successful European country in economic governance since the 2008 global financial crisis. In a sense, Germany's economic system is the most adaptable model in Europe for global competition. Germany's focus and investment in the real economy, particularly advanced manufacturing, is unmatched in Europe. Its significant progress in Industry 4.0, precise understanding of the relationship between finance and the real economy, high-level investments in education, healthcare, and social security, relentless pursuit of quality improvements in export products, and the expansion of national soft power are the fundamental reasons why Germany leads Europe.

Therefore, from both domestic and international experience, the construction of a modern economic system is both a systematic summary and refinement of China's economic transformation and upgrading, which was proposed over 20 years ago, and a strategic design and execution path for the future development of the country's economy, after crossing the $10 trillion economic scale, in the context of global economic competition in the twenty-first century.

Building a modern economic system means focusing on developing the real economy, establishing a modern industrial system, and improving the socialist market economic system. Specifically, it involves accelerating the construction of a manufacturing powerhouse, revitalizing the manufacturing industry, and implementing the "Made in China 2025" plan; developing a modern internet industry system, deeply implementing the "Internet+" action plan, encouraging large manufacturing enterprises to build an open, internet-based innovation platform that gathers global resources and intelligence to serve manufacturing; accelerating the development of modern service industries, promoting the specialization and value-chain extension of productive services, and the refinement and high quality of consumer services.

Thus, behind the modern economic system is not only a series of improved institutional designs and economic structure optimization but also a concrete manifestation of national philosophy in the economic domain. It can be said that China's push for supply-side structural reform, progress in key areas of "Made in China 2025," comprehensive checks on systemic financial risks, risk control, and a series of strategic steps to promote innovation-driven and balanced development—all of these are preparations for building a modern economic system.

Just as there is no single optimal corporate governance model in the world, there is no unified benchmark for the reform and reshaping of national economic systems. In an era where delaying reform may increase the marginal cost of transformation, no government with a mission can afford to be complacent.

Aligning Capital and Innovation Efficiently: How Can Shanghai Take this Step?

In 2018, to implement the national commitment to establish the Sci-Tech Innovation Board (STAR Market) at the Shanghai Stock Exchange and pilot the registration-based IPO system, relevant departments in Shanghai launched a call for potential companies to list, requiring the recommended companies to have a significant global or domestic industry position, emphasizing R&D investment as a percentage of revenue and the number of authorized invention patents. The companies were not limited to profitable ones but should have a certain scale of revenue. Relevant working groups were formed, with a focus on nurturing and recommending high-quality science and technology innovation enterprises and establishing a "white list" mechanism for listing on the Sci-Tech Innovation Board. Other provinces and cities took similar actions, organizing the recommendation of backup enterprises for the Sci-Tech Innovation Board. According to venture capital institutions involved in the recommendations, the companies being recommended were concentrated in industries encouraged by the state, such as aerospace, military, big data, cloud computing, and biomedicine, with the most favored being the "hidden champions" in these sectors.

As we know, among China's current four-tier capital market structure, the most influential markets are the main boards of the Shanghai and Shenzhen Stock Exchanges, the Small and Medium-Sized Enterprise Board, and the Growth Enterprise Market, while the New Third Board has faced some developmental bottlenecks in recent years. With technological advancement and economic development, especially the need to establish a modern economic system, new requirements have been placed on the design and reform of the capital market. The timely introduction of the registration-based IPO system is a natural extension of the development of the capital market. On February 17, 2023, the full implementation of the registration-based IPO system officially began, marking a milestone in the reform and development of China's capital market.

Given the current situation of China's capital market, building a mature Sci-Tech Innovation Board similar to NASDAQ is easier said than done. It requires good institutional design and operating mechanisms, especially the establishment of a relatively mature market discovery mechanism. This includes new systems for issuance, trading, delisting, investor suitability, securities company capital constraints, and introducing long-term capital and other supporting measures. The pilot program should proceed incrementally, with new funds and pilot progress matching each other, achieving a balance of investment and financing, first and second markets, and the interests of new and old shareholders of companies on the Sci-Tech Innovation Board, while also promoting the formation of positive expectations in the existing market. Clearly, this is a complex systemic project.

Today's global technological and industrial development is changing in ways not entirely based on government planning; however, governments must play a more important role than ever before in driving technological and industrial progress. Governments must create an "actively non-interventionist" innovative environment while providing precise services to align technological changes with market trends, helping innovative enterprises with great potential that are constrained by financing to find an accelerator for breakthrough development.

Looking back at the history of NASDAQ, it was a chance innovation on Wall Street that ignited the enthusiasm of Silicon Valley scientists and adventurous young people for innovation and wealth creation, resulting in the emergence of leading American high-tech companies such as Intel, Microsoft, Apple, Amazon, and Google. This led to the creation of market returns exceeding a trillion dollars, as seen with Apple and Amazon. It can be said that NASDAQ, with only a 52-year history, has perfectly interpreted the performance of the Silicon Valley model in the capital market, and has been a key support for the development of the U.S. high-tech industry.

China needs to build an efficient, transparent, well-structured, and safe multi-level capital market, and naturally, a mature exchange like NASDAQ for financing high-tech enterprises cannot be missing. The reason companies like Tencent and Alibaba chose to list on the Hong Kong Stock Exchange and NASDAQ is partly due to the underdevelopment of relevant domestic markets in China. As the global wealth allocation center and asset pricing center shift eastward, and as China's enterprises increase R&D investment and face growing financing needs, Shanghai, as the capital market hub of an emerging economy with a scale of over $10 trillion, has both the responsibility and the conditions to provide more convenient listing conditions for both domestic and foreign high-tech enterprises. This includes creating conditions for Chinese concept stocks to return and accelerating the formation of leading companies in the new economy sector. The internationalization of the Shanghai Stock Exchange will gradually be achieved through the establishment and development of the Sci-Tech Innovation Board.

Chinese entrepreneurs have never lacked business acumen, and scientists have never lacked innovative drive, but what is needed is an environment that can activate these elements. To a large extent, the business environment can be understood as a competitive market system that activates business acumen and entrepreneurial enthusiasm in a fair and orderly manner. As for the innovation environment, it requires not only efficient and orderly service from administrative departments but also a high degree of recognition of innovation from all participants, a certain tolerance for innovation failure, and of course, an awareness of risk prevention.

From the perspective of global economic and financial development, whether it is the internationalization of currency and capital markets or the upgrading of financial centers, it is impossible without the government's deep cultivation of the financial ecosystem. However, the key internal elements are still sufficient competition among market participants and a high concentration of financial elements, especially the deep participation of global enterprises. Only on this basis, with the formation of a financial element aggregation platform and financial temperament widely recognized internationally, can a country's financial development goals be naturally achieved.

Modern finance is a comprehensive "extraction" of a country or region's technology, output, creativity, and especially wealth allocation and asset pricing capabilities. Finance and innovation are not only an important support for Shanghai's leap in development capabilities but also key areas that need to strengthen competitiveness as Shanghai moves towards becoming a global core city. How to base itself on institutionalization and marketization, attract high-quality companies to list on the Shanghai Stock Exchange, maximize the activation of innovation potential, and achieve an efficient connection between capital market services and technological innovation needs, is what both domestic and foreign markets are keenly watching as Shanghai takes this step.

Promoting the High-Quality Development of the Financial Industry and Forging China's "Financial Capital Strength"

In February 2019, General Secretary Jinping Xi, while presiding over a collective study session of the Political Bureau of the CPC Central Committee on improving financial services and preventing financial risks, emphasized that finance is an important core competitiveness of a country. He called for a deeper understanding of both domestic and international financial situations, the correct grasp of the essence of finance, and a balanced approach to stabilizing growth and preventing risks. He also made strategic deployments for deepening the financial supply-side structural reform, enhancing financial services for the real economy, and resolutely combating and resolving major risks, including financial risks, to promote the healthy development of China's financial industry.

Through Jinping Xi's series of discussions since the 18th National Congress of the Communist Party of China on the essence of finance, financial reform, and the prevention of systemic financial risks, it becomes clear that in the context of the irreversible trend of global economic integration, as China transitions from a phase of rapid economic growth to one of high-quality development, and as China moves toward the construction of a modern economic system, China must view the essence of finance from a strategic perspective, considering its important role in national development and the international economic system. It must not be viewed with a static mindset, nor should international theories on financial innovation and regulation be directly applied to China's financial reform and development.

The construction of Shanghai as an international financial center is a major national strategy proposed by the Party Central Committee and the State Council from a holistic perspective. According to Shanghai's "14th Five-Year Plan," by 2025, the capability of Shanghai as an international financial center will significantly improve, solidifying its position as a center for the allocation of RMB financial assets and risk management. This will lay a solid foundation for the goal of becoming a globally influential international financial center by 2035.

In 2022, the total transaction volume in Shanghai's financial markets reached 293.298 trillion yuan, a year-on-year increase of 16.8%. Significant breakthroughs in financial reform and innovation were made. In the insurance sector, the construction of an international reinsurance business platform was initiated; in the securities market, support for expanding "Shanghai-London Stock Connect" to major European markets such as Switzerland and Germany was provided; new financial products such as the CSI 1000 index futures, SSE 50 index options, and CSI 500 ETF options were launched. During the same period, 52 new licensed financial institutions were added. As a major gateway to connect with international financial markets, Shanghai is both the primary interface for the input of international financial risks and bears the important responsibility of financial risk management.

Recently, the effects of the banking crises in the US and Europe have become evident, with the bankruptcy of Silicon Valley Bank and the acquisition of Credit Suisse. Non-bank financial institutions, insurance companies, and funds are experiencing various "chain reaction". This shows that even in highly developed financial sectors like the US and Europe, there are many blind spots in recognizing, identifying, and preventing systemic financial risks, and it is difficult to find the optimal solution between financial innovation and risk prevention.

How Shanghai can more actively explore and establish a financial risk prevention and control system compatible with the construction of an international financial center and the fine management of a megacity is an urgent task to strengthen financial risk management in the city.

A review of the reform challenges faced by China's financial industry in recent years reveals several difficult issues to address: First, in the increasingly uncertain domestic and international economic and financial environment, how can China enhance its financial competitiveness through deeper financial opening and ensure economic growth and financial stability? Second, how can a flexible and resilient financial system be built, including banking, securities, insurance, and new financial systems driven by new technologies? Third, how can China cultivate financial tools capable of actively participating in global competition, such as super financial institutions or intermediaries that can compete with Wall Street's financial capital? Fourth, how can the channels through which finance serves the real economy be improved to prevent financial misconduct? Fifth, how can the financial sector maximize its asset pricing and wealth-enhancing effects as a core national competitiveness, while ensuring that systemic financial risks do not occur?

Each of the issues above is a high-difficulty proposition with many constraints, and they represent obstacles that China must overcome as it moves toward becoming a strong industrial and capital country. As for potential solutions, they rely on the continuous accumulation of financial regulatory and reform experience, which leads to improved financial capabilities. They also come from establishing effective communication mechanisms between the decision-making bodies, such as the Financial Stability and Development Committee of the State Council, and the financial markets, listening more broadly to the voices of the financial market, and better utilizing the expertise of scholars in financial decision-making. Just as the People's Bank of China cannot rely on the Federal Reserve to teach them how to stabilize the exchange rate and respond to international financial crises, China, which lacks a reference system for financial reform and regulation, must primarily rely on its own strength and wisdom to solve the complex problems emerging from the financial system. Moreover, even the US, with the most Nobel Prize-winning economists globally, has shown shortcomings in its ability to predict financial crises, leading to panic and insufficient confidence in crisis recovery. Although internal reports from the US Securities and Exchange Commission (SEC) in 2006 identified many of the risks that led to the financial crisis, the overly confident SEC did not use its regulatory power to guide financial institutions in reducing risks. Everyone who understands the mechanisms behind financial crises knows that they are closely related to significant declines in labor productivity and capital returns. As global financialization deepens, the dual nature of financial innovation and development becomes more evident. If a country excessively deepens its financial system and economic growth relies mainly on credit expansion, it is inevitable that a financial crisis will erupt unless performance in the real economy improves synchronously. Therefore, while early warning systems for financial crises are essential, the true stabilizing mechanism lies in: moving away from a debt-driven growth model, breaking the cycle of using credit expansion to support economic confidence, broadly activating the innovative potential of microeconomic entities, and realizing endogenous economic growth. In short, by improving capital returns and reinforcing existing financial stability mechanisms, long-term financial stability can be achieved.

On the other hand, in this era of global economic integration, China's financial industry, which is deeply integrated into the global financial system, must also stay vigilant against pressures and shocks from both internal and external markets. So far, China's financial system faces significant challenges in several areas: first, the enormous impact of systemic risks accumulated within the existing financial system if they were to explode on a large scale; second, the potential shock from the next global financial crisis to China's economic system; third, the potential conflict between China's responsibility as an important guarantor in the global financial system and its ability to continue supplying risk prevention measures as the renminbi becomes increasingly internationalized.

Finance, as the highest level of global division of labor, is not only a "national instrument" and one of a country's most important core competitive strengths, but also an area where systemic risks, which are highly destructive, are likely to arise. To transition from a major manufacturing and trading country to an industrial and capital strong nation, China urgently needs to deepen financial supply-side structural reforms, establish a high-quality financial industry built on solid manufacturing competitiveness, rising trade value chains, and the proactive management of financial security. This will forge a "financial capital strength" capable of maintaining China's economic dominance and proactive influence in the changing international financial order.

In terms of financial regulation, whether it's closely monitoring the safety margins of systemic financial institutions, managing core financial information, coordinating monitoring systems, or responding quickly to sudden financial events, long-term experience accumulation and technical support are still necessary. Moreover, how to effectively coordinate financial policies with fiscal policies and industrial policies, prevent inconsistencies in policy objectives between different departments, avoid regulatory arbitrage behaviors among various industry institutions, and correct deviations in regulatory policies during execution and transmission are all key tasks in building a modern financial regulatory system in China.

As for financial services to the real economy, it is not enough to simply implement moderately loose credit policies; rather, appropriate industrial regulation reforms through supply-side structural reforms should be implemented to lower the entry barriers for private capital in industrial development, improve resource allocation efficiency, and enhance companies' profitability and investment returns. At the same time, the indicators for financial services to the real economy should be clarified, the boundaries of financialization of the economy should be controlled, and manufacturing competitiveness should be continuously strengthened. This is the foundation for building a resilient financial system that can adapt to twenty-first-century global economic competition and prevent systemic financial risks.

Finally, during this period of global financial reshuffling, China urgently needs to summarize past financial development experiences, learn from the financial crises in the US and Europe, and proactively analyze the future ecosystem of global financial competition. This will help China become a key player in the global top-level financial division of labor. To this end, China's market-oriented financial reforms, while steadily advancing interest rate liberalization, exchange rate marketization, capital market opening, and strengthening cross-border capital regulation, should focus on cultivating the core competitiveness of the banking and securities markets, thereby developing and producing a group of strategic financial talents who understand international economic and financial rules, are proficient in global financial management tools, and are capable of expressing China's positions internationally. This will enhance China's ability to allocate capital on a global scale. In the current and upcoming period, it is especially important to cultivate the reputation mechanism of the renminbi (RMB) in international markets, focusing on enhancing the preference of foreign market participants for holding and using the RMB. Efforts should be made to guide the RMB to deeply integrate into global multi-level asset pricing and trading systems, forming the RMB as a core financial symbol and generating combined influence through market-driven operations, known as "financial capital strength."

Leveraging the STAR Market to Drive High-Quality and Comprehensive Development of China's Economy

On June 13, 2019, the Science and Technology Innovation Board (STAR Market), which holds significant symbolic meaning in the history of China's securities market development, was officially launched at the highly influential Lujiazui Forum. The launch of the STAR, from its announcement to the gathering of domestic and international wisdom to improve the reform plan and finally its official opening, took only about 200 days. This sends a clear message to the world: China is advancing new initiatives and reforms with a sense of urgency, fulfilling its commitment to further opening up the capital market.

The central government entrusted Shanghai with hosting the China International Import Expo (CIIE) because of its trust in Shanghai's strong ability to connect with advanced concepts, products, technologies, and services, given Shanghai's position as the most developed region in China's modern industrial civilization. It also recognizes Shanghai's unique international character as a mega-city and its rich experience in hosting large-scale international events, particularly its strong comprehensive mobilization capacity and excellent city governance. Regarding the three major policies announced by General Secretary Jinping Xi at the first CIIE to support Shanghai's further opening and development, all of them reflect the central government's high expectations for Shanghai's role in the new round of high-level opening up and high-quality development. From the perspective of global economic competition and industrial changes in the first half of the twenty-first century, Shanghai, as the vanguard of China's new round of reform and opening up, especially as a pioneer in participating in international top-tier division of labor, will carry the national mission and serve as a model for high-quality development, which will drive the city's self-reform.

Since the beginning of the twenty-first century, economic competition between major global economies has increasingly been about the control of industries and the high-end segments of trade and financial value chains. Modern finance today is no longer just a typical capital good; it is a systemic existence that deeply influences the direction of the real economy and is a never-sleeping trading activity.

In fact, since the introduction of the "Opinions on Accelerating the Construction of a Globally Influential Science and Technology Innovation Center" by Shanghai in May 2015, the achievements in building Shanghai into a science and technology innovation hub have attracted worldwide attention. Relevant data shows that Shanghai has made significant contributions to the six major technological achievements listed in the report of the 19th National Congress of the Communist Party of China, including Jiaolong (Deep-sea submersible), Tiangong (Space station), Beidou (Navigation system), Tianyan (Arecibo radio telescope), Mozi (Quantum communication satellite), and the C919 (Large passenger aircraft). In cutting-edge global technology, Shanghai hosts the largest, most comprehensive, and most powerful photon scientific facility group. In 2017, the ultra-strong and ultra-short laser device achieved 10 petawatt laser amplification, setting a world record for peak pulse power. In 2018, the world's first cloned monkey from somatic cells and the first eukaryotic cell with a single linear chromosome were created. From 2014 to 2018, Shanghai participated in 11 of the 50 major national scientific breakthroughs. On the economic and social front, the C919 large aircraft took to the skies, strategic products such as integrated circuit advanced packaging and etching machines were exported, and high-end medical imaging equipment filled domestic gaps, reflecting the increasing influence of industrial innovation. Today, Shanghai's R&D investment accounts for 4.2% of its GDP, with about 40 high-value invention patents per 10,000 people. Shanghai's comprehensive technological progress index has remained in the top two nationwide, and the contribution of technology to economic development is steadily increasing.

The construction of the science and technology innovation center essentially supports Shanghai's goal of becoming an international financial center. Shanghai aims to become a global center for wealth allocation and asset pricing, denominated in RMB. Achieving this strategic goal would not only represent a leap in Shanghai's development capabilities but also position the city as a critical strategic pivot in China's progress toward becoming an important guarantor in the global economic and financial system.

From the perspective of its functional positioning and mission, the establishment and development of the Shanghai Science and Technology Innovation Board aims to provide an optimal platform for the birth and growth of great companies through well-designed systems and appropriate access thresholds, effectively combining innovative potential with capital markets. This will offer institutional support and relevant incentives for cultivating great companies. For example, by truly implementing the information disclosure-based securities issuance registration system, establishing a regulatory concept centered on information disclosure, improving market incentive and restraint mechanisms, holding intermediaries accountable, actively promoting judicial supply, increasing the cost of violations, and severely cracking down on false disclosures and fraudulent issuance, the board aims to purify the market ecosystem.

In recent years, China has made substantial progress in advancing cutting-edge technological development, economic transformation, and fostering an innovative ecological environment, gradually creating fertile ground for the batch production of great companies. Global economic development history has shown that for any economy to achieve high-quality development, the prerequisite is to ensure scale returns driven by endogenous variables such as knowledge innovation, technological progress, and human capital. The endogenous nature of technological progress is forcing China to continue increasing investment in human capital, promoting the rational flow of labor, and improving total factor productivity. By transforming traditional industries' technology and business models through AI, big data, and the "Internet+" approach, increasing investment in the R&D and industrial application of cutting-edge technologies, and activating the business and innovation potential of private enterprises, endogenous growth driven by significantly improved total factor productivity will form the most important foundation for supporting high-quality development.

From this new height, the opening of the Science and Technology Innovation Board is not only a significant reform breakthrough in the design and execution of China's securities market system, but it also opens the channel for the circulation and interaction of technology, capital, and the real economy. It provides strong support for high-quality economic development, creating an innovative ecological environment, and stimulating the economy's ability to maintain strong innovation and competitiveness.

How Does "Carbon Neutrality" Reshape Paradigms in the Banking Sector?

On December 28, 2021, the Ministry of Industry and Information Technology, together with seven other departments, jointly issued the 14th Five-Year Plan for the Development of Intelligent Manufacturing. The plan sets out that by 2025, the majority of manufacturing enterprises above designated size will have achieved digital and networked operations, with leading enterprises in key industries beginning to apply intelligent technologies. By 2035, digitalization and networking will be fully adopted across large-scale manufacturing enterprises, and intelligent transformation will be basically realized among key industry leaders. This development plan for the intelligent transformation of the manufacturing sector is not only a crucial step in China's overall economic digitalization but also a technical preparation for the core sectors of the real economy to meet the goals of "carbon peaking" and "carbon neutrality." As the lifeblood of the modern economy, the financial sector now faces a critical question: under the framework of serving the real economy, how can it improve the green finance system with the goal of carbon neutrality, while also achieving a comprehensive transformation of its own development? This has become an important challenge facing millions of financial professionals.

Both domestic and international studies have shown that, based on currently mature green and low-carbon technologies and commercial operating systems, China is expected to reduce carbon emissions by approximately 70% from 2020 levels by 2050, and achieve net-zero carbon emissions before 2060. As a sector highly sensitive to market changes, the banking industry has in recent years actively shifted toward green finance. According to data released by the People's Bank of China, since the issuance of the Guidelines for Establishing a Green Financial System in 2016, the domestic green finance market has expanded continuously. By the end of 2020, the balance of green loans in China reached RMB 11.95 trillion, ranking first in the world. Among these, RMB 8.08 trillion in loans—accounting for 67.6% of the total—were directly or indirectly invested in carbon reduction projects. The six major state-owned banks alone held green loan balances totaling RMB 6.27 trillion, representing more than half of the national total. Among joint-stock commercial banks, financial institutions such as Industrial Bank, China Merchants Bank, and Shanghai Pudong Development Bank have significantly increased their investments in green credit in recent years. To improve the quality of information disclosure, some banks have also begun to adopt the Environmental, Social, and Governance (ESG) framework to report on their corporate social responsibility initiatives. In terms of green bond issuance, by the end of 2020, China ranked second in the world, just behind the United States, in total outstanding green bonds. In 2021, China issued USD 68.2 billion in green bonds, compared to USD 83.5 billion issued by the U.S., reflecting the strong determination and concrete actions of Chinese financial institutions and real economy enterprises in pursuing green and low-carbon transformation.

Judging from the progress of cooperation between the People's Bank of China and the central banks of the EU, Germany, the UK, and France, both China and Europe have been working toward aligning their green investment classification standards. By the end of 2021, the two sides had implemented a mutually recognized environmental qualification taxonomy for enterprises, helping to establish a well-regulated green definition framework within the region. With the establishment and continuous improvement of global carbon trading markets, it is anticipated that an increasing share of global capital will flow into low-cost sectors such as wind power, solar energy, and biofuels, while investments in high-cost fossil fuel projects will decline. This shift aims to support the realization of global net-zero carbon emissions.

For China's banking sector, which holds over RMB 300 trillion in total assets, the economic transition driven by the goal of carbon neutrality presents tremendous business opportunities. However, on the other hand, the construction of a green transformation and green finance system is a systematic and long-term endeavor. Banks both domestically and internationally still face capability gaps in this regard, commonly encountering challenges such as insufficient expertise. Within the framework of carbon neutrality, China's banking industry is expected to face at least three major challenges:

The first challenge lies in the identification, assessment, and disclosure of risks related to high-carbon assets. Although banks in China have in recent years strengthened efforts to build teams of professionals dedicated to green transition, and some leading banks have established research groups focused on environmental risk analysis and assessment—even exploring the use of AI to monitor corporate environmental performance—it remains extremely difficult to identify how much of their vast asset portfolios are high-carbon, and what specific risks loan or investment targets may face in the foreseeable future. This is partly due to a lack of unified green standards and mandatory disclosure requirements, and partly due to bottlenecks in talent transformation and a shortage of professionals specialized in green finance.

Second, there are challenges related to innovation in green finance business and transformation support, as well as the ability to match the demand for green investment and financing with sufficient resource supply. From the disclosure of green finance development in the banking sector, although the proportion of new loans allocated to green sectors continues to increase—such as strengthening support for energy-saving and environmental upgrades, technological advancements, and clean energy projects in traditional industries, as well as limiting loans to high-carbon emission sectors—the banking industry still faces a series of challenges in completing the low-carbon transformation of existing financial assets and ensuring the high-quality operation of incremental financial assets. These challenges include how to participate in the design of low-carbon transition plans or instruments, innovate and develop green finance services, and provide sufficient credit funding.

Third, the challenge of risk pricing and international cooperation capabilities under the trend of global convergence of green finance standards. As China's banking sector undergoes green transformation in the context of a country that has not yet fully completed its industrialization, many financial institutions are still in the mid-stage of asset accumulation and business capability enhancement. In contrast, financial institutions in traditional financial powerhouses such as the UK and the US maintain a global leadership position in green finance development, especially in the area of ESG. China's banking industry, however, holds certain advantages in investments related to renewable energy and materials. In the coming period, China's banking sector urgently needs to enhance its understanding and implementation of international green finance standards, while strengthening its capabilities in risk pricing and international cooperation.

China's commitment to achieving the Sustainable Development Goals and implementing the Paris Agreement has led to the pledge of "peaking carbon emissions before 2030 and striving for carbon neutrality before 2060." This signifies that during the 14th Five-Year Plan period and the following 40 years, China will undergo a broad and profound systemic transformation of its economic life. For China's banking sector, which currently holds assets exceeding RMB 300 trillion, the carbon neutrality goal presents not only enormous business opportunities in the first half of the twenty-first century, but also external variables that introduce significant uncertainty regarding the risk exposure of existing assets and their potential revaluation. China's banking sector must, in the course of supporting the green transformation of the economy, rapidly develop the capabilities necessary for green finance development—including risk identification, assessment, and information disclosure; innovation and transformation support for green financial services; the capacity to align green investment and financing needs with resource supply; and the ability to price risks and engage in international cooperation under the global trend of green finance standard integration.

Strengthening Central SOEs' Corporate Governance to Build Endogenous Competitive Advantages

In May 2021, the General Office of the CPC Central Committee issued the "Opinions on Strengthening the Party's Leadership in the Improvement of Corporate Governance of Central State-owned Enterprises," calling for further strengthening of the development of a modern enterprise system with Chinese characteristics, reinforcing Party leadership in improving corporate governance, and accelerating the building of world-class enterprises.

With total assets now exceeding 80 trillion yuan, central state-owned enterprises (SOEs) serve as the core pillars supporting national economic stability, people's livelihoods, and the development of strategic industries. They are also a critical foundation for China's participation in global division of labor and its enhancement of global resource allocation capabilities. Since the mid-1980s, the reform of state-owned enterprises, including central SOEs, has long been at the core of China's economic system reform. This is not only because China possesses the world's largest system of state-owned assets and enterprises, but also because SOE reform has long been a highly complex challenge commonly faced by countries around the world. Major developed economies such as the United States, Japan, Germany, France, and the United Kingdom have all recognized the value of state-owned enterprises. Should China achieve significant breakthroughs in this area, it would have profound implications not only for the country's economic governance and development logic but also carries significant economic implications. Over the past two decades, Chinese and international economists have increasingly focused on the theoretical study of China's SOE reforms, striving to offer explanations with paradigm-setting value.

We know that corporate governance is a product of the constrained boundaries of managerial possibilities that arise after the separation of ownership and control. In the real world, company founders often find it relatively manageable to oversee assets worth 500 million yuan, but as the enterprise grows and reaches 5 billion yuan in assets, management becomes more challenging. When managing assets at the level of 50 billion or even hundreds of billions, more modern institutional designs become necessary. The concept of modern corporate governance was introduced by Nobel Prize-winning economist Oliver Williamson (see Fig. 13.4) in 1975. Before that, scholars such as Berle, Means, Jensen, Meckling, and Coase had already made landmark contributions to the establishment of corporate governance theory. Since then, with the development of theories of the firm, property rights economics, game theory and information economics, new institutional economics, and financial economics, corporate governance has not only achieved continuous theoretical breakthroughs but has also become one of the key elements for the survival and growth of modern enterprises.

Theoretical research and practical exploration of modern corporate governance in China began in the late 1980s, coinciding with China's economic reform, which shifted from rural to urban areas and initiated the reform of state-owned enterprises. During this process, generations of economists and reform practitioners, in light of China's national conditions, continuously introduced, digested, absorbed, and innovated upon modern corporate governance theories and models. They put forward new ideas, new paths, and new models in the field of corporate governance, including state-owned enterprises, thereby contributing to the global development of research and practical exploration in corporate governance reform.

The production, living, and trading activities of humans over thousands of years have proven that humans are boundedly rational and extremely complex behavioral

Fig. 13.4 Economist Oliver Williamson

individuals. Due to the bounded rationality and opportunistic nature of individual economic behavior, contracts are almost always incomplete, and more often take the form of relational contracts. Although all rational market participants understand that a world without contracts is unimaginable, even the most rational market participants may still have impulses to violate the spirit of contracts and conceal core information. Therefore, optimal contract design is often a false proposition in the real world. The reason people expect such optimal contract designs is to maximize the reduction of transaction costs and promote economic and social development under conditions of as much information symmetry as possible. On the other hand, with the development of agency theory and practice, the question of who should represent shareholders to optimize the management of enterprises, prevent 'insider control' and 'unethical behavior,' and strengthen corporate social responsibility, has led to the need for a complete and continually improving modern corporate governance system. This applies equally to both domestic and foreign enterprises.

As the world's second-largest economy and the country with the most Fortune 500 companies, China's economic growth, enterprise development, and internationalization provide a valuable research sample for global economists, including Chinese scholars. Research on the above issues will not only enrich existing perspectives in economics and management studies but also has the potential to change prevailing conclusions in mainstream economics and modern management theory. From a historical development perspective, after achieving its first "centenary goal," China will develop a comprehensive macroeconomic theory that explains its economic development, institutional changes, and the endogenous mechanisms of China's economic growth. This will undoubtedly give rise to a forward-looking and adaptable corporate governance theory and practical framework, emerging from the exploration of modern corporate governance practices by Chinese enterprises, including central state-owned enterprises, and ultimately becoming an integral part of the global corporate governance system.

Great eras are bound to give birth to great enterprises. In 1995, when Fortune magazine first released the Global 500 list, China had not yet joined the WTO, which was founded that same year. At that time, Chinese enterprises were far behind those from the United States, Japan, and European capitalist countries in terms of their position on the global economic map. However, thanks to the continuous expansion of opening-up and the ongoing integration into global industrial, supply, and value chains, China has, 28 years later, become one of the most important hubs for industries and supply chains in the world.

Regarding the reform and corporate governance development of central state-owned enterprises (SOEs), after two stages of reform—'delegating power and sharing profits' and establishing the 'modern enterprise system'—the reform of SOEs has entered a new phase. The goal of this new phase should be: under a clear government regulatory framework, to cultivate and develop enterprise clusters with a reasonable ownership structure, effective incentive and constraint mechanisms, and that truly adapt to a market-oriented environment and global resource allocation competition. This process requires not only rigorous theoretical research and practical exploration but also a large group of strategic entrepreneurs with an international perspective, global operational awareness, and innovative thinking, who can skillfully navigate global management tools. Therefore, it is essential to enhance supervision and constraints while also providing central SOE leaders with the necessary operational space and distribution principles. It is important to clarify the true identity of central SOEs as market players, define their boundaries of behavior in the market and society, and eliminate the long-standing "moral hazard" issue that has troubled state-owned enterprise reform for years, in order to foster a new era of Chinese entrepreneurial spirit and enhance the intrinsic competitive advantages of central SOEs.

Pudong's Timely Ascent as a Global Resource Allocation Hub

Shanghai Pudong will strive to launch and operationalize a series of high-level financial functional platforms as soon as possible.

According to Hang Yingwei, Deputy Secretary-General of the Shanghai Municipal Government and District Mayor of Pudong New Area, in order to implement the "Opinions on Supporting the High-Level Reform and Opening-Up of Pudong New Area and Building a Leading Area for Socialist Modernization Construction" issued by the CPC Central Committee and the State Council in April 2021 (hereinafter referred to as the "Opinions"), in the financial sector, Pudong will focus on promoting key projects such as an international financial asset trading platform, a national bulk commodity warehouse receipt registration and depository center, and a private equity and venture capital equity transfer platform.

Regarding the construction of a series of high-level financial functional platforms, the "Opinions" first mentioned leveraging the active role of the Shanghai Insurance Exchange to build a world-class reinsurance center.

"Pudong is the core area of Shanghai's international financial center, and it is timely for the central government to position Pudong as a leading area in global resource allocation," I explained in an interview with Jiemian News in 2021, interpreting the profound significance and development path behind Pudong's efforts to strengthen its global resource allocation capabilities, including building an international financial asset trading platform, a world-class reinsurance center, a private equity and venture capital equity transfer platform, and the market-making system of the Sci-Tech Innovation Board.

The following is the transcript of the interview, compiled by Jiemian News:

The Perfect Timing for Pudong to Establish itself as a Global Hub for Resource Allocation

Jiemian News: On July 29, 2021, the Lujiazui Administration released the *Measures for Implementing the Central Government's Guiding Opinions on Building a Core Functional Zone for a Global Asset Management Center*, with the aim of further enhancing its global resource allocation capabilities and better serving the establishment of a new development paradigm. Could you share your thoughts on how Pudong can strengthen its global resource allocation capacity? Are there any international experiences in this area that Pudong could learn from?

Yugui Zhang: From an economic perspective, global resource allocation capability can be summarized in twelve Chinese characters: global platform, market-based pricing, and cost efficiency. It refers to the ability to optimize the allocation of global resources—such as capital, technology, information, and talent—within an open and competitive market system, under the backdrop of global economic integration. The development of this capability is not something that can be achieved overnight; it requires continuous exploration, practice, and evolution.

As for Pudong's foundational strengths in the global financial resource allocation landscape, the area currently hosts 13 financial factor markets and infrastructure platforms. It is home to over 1100 licensed financial institutions, both domestic and international. Pudong has become one of the most comprehensive, active, and dynamic regions in the world for financial factor markets.

It can be said that Pudong is the core area of Shanghai's development as an international financial center. The central government's decision to position Pudong as a leading zone for participating in global resource allocation is both timely and strategic.

After more than 30 years of development and opening-up, Pudong has become not only a pioneer in Shanghai's integration into the global value chain, but also a vital driving force in upgrading the regional economy. Under the new development paradigm, the Yangtze River Delta urban cluster—led by Shanghai and powered by Pudong as a "leverage point" and "bridgehead"—is set to operate under the highest international standards of openness. Pudong is expected to leverage its strengths in financial markets, R&D and design, high-end manufacturing, systems integration, and global supply chain management to become a large-scale platform for attracting international high-end industries and financial capital. This will support the national strategy of building a strong industrial and financial power and ultimately enable China to allocate resources on a global scale.

Historically, improving global resource allocation capabilities has never relied solely on the efforts of a single country or region. It requires the deep involvement of international market players and a win-win approach to cooperation. In other words, Pudong's ability to significantly enhance its global resource allocation capacity depends not only on China's economic advancement, the internationalization of the renminbi, and Shanghai's high-level reforms and openness, but also on whether global financial capital views Pudong as the key platform to continuously benefit from China's economic growth and the renminbi's global rise. Moreover, it hinges on whether international industrial and financial capital are willing to establish their Asia-Pacific—or even global—value chain management headquarters in Shanghai without hesitation.

The United Kingdom, deeply embedded with financial DNA, has in recent years made a concerted effort to establish London as Europe's offshore renminbi center. For the UK, especially post-Brexit, this represents a strategic opportunity for national development. As a long-standing financial powerhouse, the UK still holds several competitive advantages: London is one of the most historic global financial centers and a key hub for commodity pricing; it has consistently ranked as the top provider of financial services in international markets; it remains the world's most important foreign exchange trading center; and it is a global magnet for top financial talent and financial innovation. All of these are invaluable international resources.

As Shanghai moves toward becoming a global financial center with international influence and competitiveness, it must pay close attention to the historical experiences of mature financial hubs like London and work to address gaps in its institutional systems and market infrastructure. Pudong, as the most financially concentrated area in China, should root itself firmly in the reality of China being the world's largest emerging economy. It should aim to become a global center for wealth allocation and asset pricing, denominated in renminbi, as a key breakthrough in the next phase of development.

Jiemian News: According to the *Guiding Opinions*, the central government supports the establishment of an international financial asset trading platform in Pudong. How can Pudong build an international financial asset trading platform with global influence?

Yugui Zhang: The central government's support for establishing an international financial asset trading platform in Pudong is a critical step in accelerating the development of Shanghai as an international financial center—especially in building a global asset management hub.

According to the *Opinions on Accelerating the Development of Shanghai as a Global Asset Management Center* issued by the Shanghai Municipal Government, the city aims to speed up the construction of a global asset management hub by building an international financial asset trading platform centered on the global allocation of renminbi-denominated assets. The key term here is "renminbi assets," which signals that Shanghai will anchor this development on renminbi-denominated financial products. By constructing a market-oriented platform, it seeks not only to solidify its role as a domestic financial asset trading center, but also to meet the growing demand from foreign investors for renminbi asset allocation through more efficient and accessible trading arrangements.

In terms of operations and implementation, Pudong is expected to expand the types, scale, and level of renminbi asset trading along two dimensions and across two markets. This will enrich the full-function trading ecosystem of renminbi assets, gradually positioning Shanghai as a global center for pricing and allocating renminbi-denominated assets. In turn, this would enhance international investor preference for renminbi assets and strengthen China's influence on global financial asset pricing.

The "two dimensions, two markets" approach refers to drawing appropriate lessons from the development and trading mechanisms of the global U.S. dollar asset system, while leveraging Shanghai's role as a key node in the Belt and Road Initiative and as a leader in high-level reform and opening-up. It involves including both standardized financial products—such as renminbi-denominated stocks, bonds, foreign exchange, futures, insurance, and bills—and non-standardized financial products—such as trust assets, asset management products, and debt financing instruments—into the scope of tradable international financial assets. These assets would be traded on platforms that either already possess international connectivity or can establish interfaces with global markets. The ultimate goal is to achieve a two-way integration of onshore and offshore renminbi assets, and a high degree of interaction between domestic and international markets.

Jiemian News: Among these reform measures, which areas will be the key focus moving forward? What are the main considerations behind these priorities?

Yugui Zhang: In terms of overseas investors' demand for allocating renminbi-denominated assets, the steady recovery of China's economic fundamentals and its prudent monetary policy have made renminbi assets stand out among major global currency assets. Renminbi assets have not only acquired certain safe-haven characteristics but are also increasingly demonstrating strong investment value and potential for medium- to long-term returns.

Data from Crédit Agricole and the Hong Kong Bond Connect program show that in 2020, foreign investors' holdings of Chinese stocks and bonds rose to approximately USD 806 billion—USD 678 billion in bonds and USD 128 billion in equities—up from USD 570 billion the previous year. This reflects a significant increase in foreign central banks' and institutional investors' preference for holding and trading renminbi assets, driven by China's high-level financial opening and the benefits of its sustained economic growth.

To build a multi-tiered and influential financial asset trading platform, Pudong will focus on several areas. These include steadily improving the liquidity and stability of the bond market while strengthening cross-border bond trading platforms; promoting the issuance of depositary receipts under the Shanghai-London Stock Connect to attract more high-quality foreign enterprises to raise funds in Shanghai; and, when conditions are right, introducing streamlined financing mechanisms in A-shares for qualified foreign enterprises. Additionally, Pudong will work on establishing renminbi asset management product trading platforms and financial derivatives trading platforms that cater to both domestic and international investors, and so on.

The "Three-Pronged Approach" to Building a World-Class International Reinsurance Center

Jiemian News: The phrase "leverage the role of the Shanghai Insurance Exchange to build a world-class international reinsurance center" stands out as the only part of this major policy document that specifically highlights "insurance" as a development priority. Looking at international financial centers, all of them have well-developed insurance and reinsurance markets. So, for Pudong, how can it go about building a world-class international reinsurance center?

Yugui Zhang: From the experience of building and developing international financial centers, a world-class insurance and reinsurance hub is an essential supporting element.

From a technical standpoint, reinsurance is the most internationally integrated insurance system, often referred to as the "insurance for insurance." It is the product of an insurance market that continues to evolve and aligns closely with a country's high-level financial market openness.

Shanghai is the birthplace of China's modern insurance industry and bears the historical mission of building a twenty-first-century international insurance center. The central government's explicit support for leveraging the Shanghai Insurance Exchange's role in building a world-class international reinsurance center is not only an acknowledgment of Shanghai's capability as an influential international insurance hub, but also a historical mission to empower the Shanghai Insurance Exchange as a national-level financial infrastructure, providing essential leadership and platform support in the construction of Shanghai as an international reinsurance center.

Building a world-class international reinsurance center requires deep participation from both domestic and foreign reinsurance market entities, such as reinsurance companies, captive insurers, and insurance brokers. It also depends on the digital empowerment of reinsurance registration, clearing, and settlement platforms, as well as the broad recognition of Shanghai's international reinsurance center capabilities by leading global reinsurance institutions and their executives.

Pudong has already become the region with the highest concentration of reinsurance institutions in China. It currently hosts eight reinsurance companies, including one foreign reinsurance legal entity and four foreign reinsurance branches, with foreign reinsurance institutions accounting for more than 60% of the total number of foreign reinsurance institutions in China. Actuarial companies, rating agencies, and professional law firms, all highly connected to the reinsurance industry, are also gathering in the area. Pudong should make full use of the reform opportunities granted by central government documents, actively enhancing the technical and trading settlement capabilities of the Shanghai Insurance Exchange, strengthening digital infrastructure, and improving the communication and coordination functions of international reinsurance conference mechanisms.

Pudong is Expected to Open the Second S-Fund Trading Platform in China

Jiemian News: The *Opinions* propose establishing a private equity and venture capital equity transfer platform in Pudong. What is the significance of this? Are there any experiences to draw from?

Yugui Zhang: As Shanghai accelerates the development of its international financial center and a globally influential science and technology innovation center, the private equity and venture capital equity transfer platform plays an indispensable role.

With the segmentation of the financial market and the development of the venture capital market, China's private investment industry (including private equity and venture capital, hedge funds, and secondary share transfers) has grown rapidly, especially with the remarkable development of the venture capital market.

In the most developed private investment hubs—Beijing, Shanghai, and Shenzhen—the introduction of relevant institutional frameworks and transfer platforms will greatly support the allocation of financial market resources to innovation and entrepreneurship activities.

In April 2021, the Beijing Equity Exchange issued business rules regarding the transfer of equity investment and venture capital shares, providing standards and guidelines for the first time for the transfer of fund shares (S-Fund), filling a gap in the domestic S-Fund transaction rule system.

In June 2021, the Beijing Local Financial Regulatory Bureau and other departments jointly issued the *Guiding Opinions on Promoting the Pilot Work of Equity Investment and Venture Capital Share Transfers*, the first-ever domestic guidance on fund share transfer transactions (S-Fund). This document encourages existing parent funds to adopt S-strategies and participate in the transfer of high-quality fund shares or equity in invested projects through the share transfer pilot at the Beijing Equity Exchange.

With Pudong set to launch the second S-Fund trading platform in China, and considering the ongoing development of innovation centers in areas like Zhangjiang, along with the introduction of offshore renminbi trading on the Sci-Tech Innovation Board, this may create a "Wall Street + Silicon Valley" effect, potentially fueling a significant transformation.

The Sci-Tech Innovation Board (STAR Market) Welcomes New Policy Benefits, Including QFII (Qualified Foreign Institutional Investors) and Market Maker Reforms

Jiemian News: What is the significance of allowing Qualified Foreign Institutional Investors (QFII) to use renminbi in participating in the Sci-Tech Innovation Board (STAR Market) stock issuance and trading, as stated in the *Opinions* pilot program?

Yugui Zhang: This pilot policy sends three major signals to international investors.

First, the Sci-Tech Innovation Board (STAR Market) represents the systematic presence of China's top-tier technology companies in a renminbi-denominated capital market. The valuation and investment potential of these companies on the capital markets are rare investment targets for internationally savvy investors.

Second, over 20 stocks from the Sci-Tech Innovation Board have already been included in the Shanghai-Hong Kong Stock Connect, and the MSCI has incorporated the Sci-Tech Innovation Board index into its global index system. The Sci-Tech 50 ETF has been listed in the U.S., U.K., Japan, and other regions, indicating that the STAR Market has already gained preliminary recognition from the international market, especially from institutional investors. Since 2021, the proportion of foreign capital in Sci-Tech Innovation Board stocks has significantly increased. This not only shows that foreign investors' preference for high-quality renminbi assets is rising, but also that they have gained substantial returns by holding stocks on the board.

Third, from a technical standpoint, allowing Qualified Foreign Institutional Investors (QFII) to use renminbi for participating in the issuance and trading of Sci-Tech Innovation Board stocks means that the growing offshore renminbi will enter the STAR Market through officially recognized market entities like Renminbi Qualified Foreign Institutional Investors (RQFII). This not only expands the investment channels for foreign capital but also enriches the types of investors in the STAR Market and increases international participation in A-shares. Most importantly, allowing offshore renminbi to enter the Sci-Tech Innovation Board through compliant channels benefits the repatriation of offshore renminbi, improves the competitive market pricing system of the STAR Market, and significantly boosts its internationalization, thereby advancing the construction of Shanghai as a global renminbi asset allocation center.

Jiemian News: The introduction of the market maker system on the Sci-Tech Innovation Board (STAR Market) involves qualifications for market makers, market regulation, and other aspects, which require the development of supporting system rules. The China Securities Regulatory Commission (CSRC) has previously stated that relevant departments and units are making preparations. What efforts are needed from all parties to implement the market maker system? How can financial institutions provide support?

Yugui Zhang: Currently, China's Shanghai and Shenzhen stock markets operate under an auction trading system. The market maker system has already been introduced in the New Third Board, and operational practice has shown that stocks with market makers in the New Third Board experience relatively active trading.

From the perspective of market development and the needs of the Sci-Tech Innovation Board itself, introducing the market maker system to the Sci-Tech Innovation Board will help address issues like insufficient market liquidity caused by high investor thresholds. It will improve market liquidity, promote the formation of a professional and rational pricing mechanism for the Sci-Tech Innovation Board, and, through the market makers' relatively stringent bid-ask spreads, counterbalance institutional investors and capable individuals who might manipulate stock prices. This will promote the healthy development of secondary market trading.

From the overall performance of Sci-Tech Innovation Board listed companies, over 500 companies are now listed. However, there is clear market segmentation, with some popular stocks showing strong trading volumes and rising prices, while others see sluggish trading. The overall market vitality still needs improvement.

Since securities firms and large financial institutions are the main participants in the market maker system, an important responsibility of regulators is to ensure that these powerful market participants do not use their market maker status to access sensitive information, abuse their authority, or manipulate the market.

Furthermore, to prevent the market maker system, which is internationally recognized, from being distorted in Sci-Tech Innovation Board stock trading, regulators must design and adapt the system properly. Specifically, they need to clarify the Sci-Tech Innovation Board's positioning as a platform for financing "hard tech" companies, maintain high standards for information disclosure, and prevent unethical behavior by market makers; It's also important to strengthen the responsibilities of intermediaries such as securities firms, accounting firms, and law firms, and guide market participants to fulfill their duties; Additionally, regulators should actively research and improve the new stock issuance pricing mechanism, strengthen performance guidance, and emphasize growth expectations, while reinforcing government regulation and market oversight.

New Changes in Capital Market May Support a New Financial Economics Revolution

The speech delivered by Huiman Yi, Chairman of the China Securities Regulatory Commission (CSRC), at the opening ceremony of the 60th Annual Meeting of the World Federation of Exchanges in September 2021, has been widely regarded as a high-quality address filled with substantial insights. Through this speech, China's financial regulators not only conveyed to global market participants and their overseers the country's strong commitment and determination to further open up its capital markets, but also raised a series of major issues worthy of in-depth study in response to the regulatory challenges posed by new technologies, business models, and developments that have emerged in global capital markets in recent years. This reflects the increasingly sharp market intuition, risk awareness, and strategic thinking of China's financial regulatory authorities within the broader framework of global economic integration.

It is well known that the capital market is a product of industrialization, which in turn is a result of technological revolutions—driven by scientists and inventors. The logical connections among them are tightly interwoven, reflecting not only the general laws of human economic and social development, but also profoundly shaping the way human societies produce and live. Today, the impact of capital markets on open economies is greater than at any point in history.

Since 2008, I have consistently warned of the following risk: in the post-industrial era, credit expansion has increasingly become a primary technical tool used by major economies to counter economic downturns, leading to a pattern of habitual dependence. The heavier the role assumed by monetary authorities in developed economies, the more debt risks accumulate, increasing the likelihood of a systemic crisis. A profound lesson from the 2008 global financial crisis is that if a country continues to push for financial deepening—especially when improvements in real economic efficiency fail to keep pace—and relies heavily on massive credit expansion to sustain economic growth, it can ultimately inflict irreversible damage on its economic system.

Therefore, although financial factor markets—including capital markets—are playing an increasingly important role in both normalized and non-normalized economic environments, it remains essential that policymakers, market participants, and responsible economists do not overlook the study of certain strategic and foundational issues critical to the long-term sustainable development of capital markets. In particular, it is vital to identify effective approaches for balancing financial risk prevention with the need to serve the real economy.

From the perspective of financial economics, Wall Street has witnessed two major financial revolutions since the 1950s. The first was the introduction of Harry Markowitz's portfolio selection theory in 1952 (see Fig. 13.5), and the second was

Fig. 13.5 Economist Harry Markowitz

Fig. 13.6 Economist Fischer Black

Fig. 13.7 Economist Myron Scholes

the emergence of the option pricing theory developed by Fischer Black (see Fig. 13.6) and Myron Scholes (see Fig. 13.7) in 1973. These two financial revolutions largely arose in response to the pressing real-world challenges posed by the development of capital markets and the demand for more effective wealth allocation, to which economists responded with adaptive theoretical innovations. In recent years, the growth of mathematical finance, combined with the widespread application of computer and information technologies, has significantly reshaped the financial trading ecosystem and investor behavior. For instance, the well-known "retail investor movement" in the United States, the impact of special purpose acquisition companies (SPACs) on IPO models in certain overseas markets, as well as the market volatility and risks triggered by the abuse of quantitative and high-frequency trading, have all posed major and practical challenges to contemporary financial economics research.

As stock trading costs continue to decrease, it becomes evident that the primary beneficiaries are increasingly concentrated among institutional investors, particularly large, well-capitalized asset management companies. At the same time, with the ongoing expansion of algorithmic trading in financial markets and the gradual fragmentation of market information flow, the "clustering" of retail investors poses an ever-growing challenge to market regulation and risks to investors themselves. If SPACs are viewed as Silicon Valley's alternative resistance to the rigid cost regulations of traditional IPOs, then as regulators of capital markets and financial trading platforms, should there not be adaptive reforms and responses to the changes in business models brought about by technological and industrial development? Clearly, regulators must maintain both forward-looking warning capabilities and sufficient market discipline, ensuring they are not led astray by endless financial innovations or financial adventurism.

Finally, in terms of the practical demands for the development of financial economics and its theoretical foundation, the new changes in capital markets are indeed an unavoidable reality that must be addressed through sustained and in-depth research. Whether it is the new challenges brought by the coupling of high technology and advanced finance, the management of risk assets in the era of big data, or the effective control of various trading risks, all of these require systematic research on underlying assets, pricing systems, trading structures, trading behavior, and risk assessment. Financial economics will continue to develop in this process and provide theoretical support for the development and reform of capital markets.

Empirical Research to Support the Stable Development of China's Securities Market

The 2021 Nobel Prize in Economic Sciences was awarded to David Card, Joshua D. Angrist, and Guido W. Imbens for their pioneering contributions to natural experiments and causal relationship analysis methods. This award not only highlights the Nobel Committee's longstanding focus on original academic contributions, but also sends an important signal to the global economics community and market participants that economic research is increasingly emphasizing real-world issues.

It is well known that a rigorous economist must not only be proficient in the mechanisms and methods of theoretical economics but also face the economic phenomena and issues in the real world. When necessary, they must offer policy recommendations during times of significant economic crises at both the national and global levels. This is exemplified in the life of John Maynard Keynes, who is widely regarded as one of the greatest economists of the twentieth century. Keynes not only played a crucial role in addressing the Great Depression of 1929–1933, but also demonstrated the wisdom and strength of an economist and a representative of the British government during the construction of the Bretton Woods system.

Since the twenty-first century, especially after the 2008 global financial crisis, facing the severe realities of persistent economic stagnation, high unemployment, growing inequality, and deepening social conflicts in capitalist countries, many Western mainstream economists have increasingly focused on these economic phenomena and social issues in the real world. One of the most representative figures in this regard is the French economist Thomas Piketty. In his book *Capital in the Twenty-First Century*, Piketty not only analyzes the economic logic behind the apparent issues of capitalism but also uses extensive data to prove that the level of inequality in major developed countries, especially in the United States, has reached or exceeded historical highs. He argues that unchecked capitalism has exacerbated the unequal distribution of social wealth and that this inequality will continue to worsen. The publication of this book immediately attracted widespread attention and ongoing discussion in the international academic community.

Clearly, both Keynes and Piketty place great emphasis on causal analysis, which is not in conflict with Eugene Fama's *Efficient Market Hypothesis* (EMH) research paradigm (see Fig. 13.8). Why is this the case? Because the premise of the *Efficient Market Hypothesis*, namely that "in a society full of information exchange and information competition," is a necessary condition for academic research itself.

Fig. 13.8 Economist Eugene Fama

Anyone who understands basic economic principles knows that a real economic world cannot exist with perfectly symmetric information and perfect competition. Therefore, Fama's statement that "as long as the market fully reflects all available information, market prices represent the true value of securities, and such a market is called an efficient market" is, in essence, causal analysis. However, the constraints for the market to achieve efficient operation are numerous, which is why economists hope that governments will strive to create an institutional and legal environment conducive to the efficient functioning of securities markets. The reason the *Efficient Market Hypothesis* is criticized is not because the theory itself is flawed, but because Western governments, when faced with a group of profit-driven financial oligarchs, mistakenly treated economic assumptions as the basis for formulating economic policies, allowing financial liberalization and neglecting the proactive role of governments as maintainers of market order!

In the context of securities markets, an ideal securities market would, of course, be one where information is as symmetrical as possible and competition is fully present, with an effective price discovery mechanism that achieves optimal resource allocation. However, this is merely the aspiration of market participants and regulators. As we all know, securities trading involves decision-making behavior for intertemporal capital allocation in an environment of uncertainty. The costs and returns of securities investment decisions are distributed over time, and neither the decision-makers nor anyone else can clearly know the outcome of the transaction in advance. Even with the highly developed technology of computers and big data today, it is impossible to achieve expected management of the trading behaviors and decision-making changes of millions of individual participants at the same time. The questions of how individual participants' decisions affect the overall behavior of the securities market, how the prices of securities assets influence resource allocation, how to effectively price risky securities, how to identify and prevent financial risks, and how to maintain market stability and orderly functioning, are all highly challenging issues. Therefore, securities trading and market regulation are considered among the most complex and unpredictable economic activities in human history.

In terms of the institutional design and operation of China's securities market, after more than 30 years of reform and development, China has not only become the second-largest securities market in the world, following the United States, but has also made significant progress in establishing the basic conditions necessary for building a mature securities market. These include an effective price discovery mechanism and supporting market regulation, a sound financial system and institutional environment, transparent and effective contract law and enforcement systems, robust accounting standards and practices, improved corporate governance systems, reliable payment and settlement systems, and a market accountability system, among others.

In this process, not only has the wisdom and strength of securities market designers, regulators, market intermediaries, and other participants been consolidated, but it has also relied on the research and exploration of financial researchers from several generations regarding the essence, functions, operating systems, risk management, and other theoretical and practical issues of China's securities market. For example, how to establish a more effective stock issuance mechanism; how to conduct effective asset pricing; how to create a truly competitive stock market system; how to effectively leverage the securities market to support the real economy; how to achieve a high level of openness and high-quality development of the securities market in the context of global economic integration; how to improve the modern financial regulatory system, strengthen the three pillars of macroprudential, microprudential, and conduct regulation, and safeguard against systemic financial risks—these securities market reforms and practices, which are driven by strong problem awareness, have attracted a continuous stream of responsible researchers with keen market intuition to push the theoretical frontier, focus on international comparisons, identify the logical issues, and provide solutions. Although the nature of social sciences (finance) makes random control experiments highly challenging, researchers have continued to explore how to adopt more effective methods to conduct forward-looking or supplementary research on the securities market, leading to increasing emphasis on empirical analysis.

Today, with the Nobel Prize in Economic Sciences placing significant emphasis on experimental economics and the study of real-world economic issues, it can be expected that natural experiments and causal relationship analysis methods will not only continue to be applied in research on issues such as labor and employment markets but will also quickly be applied and developed in the related research on capital market reform and regulatory practices. An increasing number of researchers, driven by a strong sense of problem awareness, will focus on the challenges in the operation and development of China's securities market. Through constructing suitable experimental research methods and applying statistical analysis to sift through vast amounts of financial data to identify high-confidence key data, they will continuously improve their causal analysis capabilities and provide rigorous research conclusions and policy recommendations, helping to drive the steady and long-term development of China's securities market.

Building a Population and Talent Support System for High-Quality Economic Development

Recently, discussions and policy measures regarding China's population issues have garnered significant attention. These include topics such as birth rates, population structure, and a series of policies implemented by the central and local governments to address the challenges of low birth rates and an aging population. It is clear that both the government and society are increasingly approaching and addressing population issues from a strategic and sustainable development perspective.

Although many people were surprised by the data showing that the national birth rate dropped below 1% for the first time in 2020, researchers who have long observed China's population growth trends view this as an inevitable issue. The public is particularly concerned about this problem because it largely indicates that China's demographic dividend is decreasing and may eventually disappear at some point in the future. The demographic dividend is extremely important for the medium- and long-term development of China's economy. As is well known, China's economy has been able to maintain an average annual growth rate of over 8% for more than 40 years since the reform and opening-up, mainly due to the market vitality and related development dividends released by the reforms, especially the support from the three major dividends: the demographic dividend, the "WTO accession" dividend, and the international industrial transfer dividend.

Relevant research shows that the effective growth of China's economy has largely been the result of endogenous choices based on resource optimization, especially with China's accession to the WTO, which significantly activated the entrepreneurial capabilities of market participants and their enthusiasm for participating in global resource allocation. Combined with the push from foreign direct investment (FDI) and the efficiency spillover from the private sector and foreign-funded enterprises, the ongoing reforms of state-owned enterprises (SOEs) and state-owned capital have led to continuous improvements in operational efficiency and the enhancement of state capital capabilities. These factors together have formed the most important support for China's sustained economic growth since the twenty-first century. Recent research further indicates that China's economic growth increasingly relies on scale economies generated by knowledge, information, data, research and development (R&D), and innovation, as well as the driving forces of core endogenous variables such as technological progress and human capital growth.

However, among the aforementioned endogenous variables, population and talent remain irreplaceable fundamental elements, which is why both the government and society are highly focused on issues such as birth rates, population aging, and population quality. In fact, the data from the Sixth National Population Census already indicated the severity of the population aging problem. According to the census, the total population aged 60 and above in mainland China was 178 million, with the level of population aging reaching 13.26%, an increase of 2.93 percentage points compared to the 2000 census. Among this group, the population aged 65 and above accounted for 8.87%, an increase of 1.91 percentage points from the 2000 census. The data from the Seventh National Population Census has raised the severity of the aging problem to a new critical point: the population aged 60 and above exceeds 260 million, accounting for 18.7% of the total population, with those aged 65 and above exceeding 190 million, or 13.5% (See Fig. 13.9 for details). The direct result of the declining birth rate is a reduction in net population growth. However, China can still benefit from the diminishing demographic dividend. With the true arrival of the "Lewis turning point", China's economy must undergo a thorough transformation of its growth model, focusing on enhancing human capital accumulation and total factor productivity to offset the gaps caused by the decline of the demographic dividend.

Another unavoidable fact is that China entered the process of capital deepening while its per capita income was still at a lower-middle level. It failed to fully utilize the relatively abundant labor resources from the late twentieth century to the early twenty-first century to more effectively develop labor-intensive industries, and there

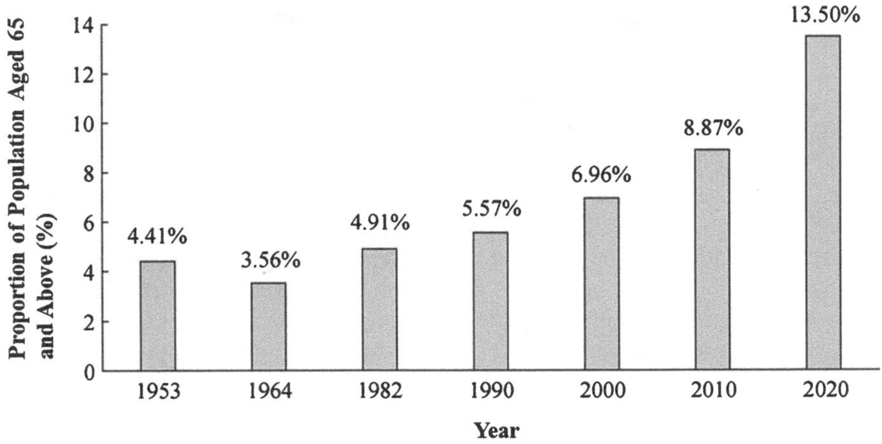

Fig. 13.9 Proportion of Population Aged 65 and Above in the Seventh National Population Census. Data Source: National Bureau of Statistics of China

has been relatively slow progress in technological advancements and applications, leading to a lack of significant improvement in total factor productivity since 1995. For example, a key indicator of capital allocation efficiency, the Incremental Capital-Output Ratio (ICOR), has shown a downward trend in recent periods. Moreover, while overall labor productivity has seen substantial improvement in recent years, it is still relatively low compared to international leading levels. In 2018, China's overall labor productivity (calculated using the 2018 average exchange rate) was $17,529, which is 1.79 times its per capita GDP. In contrast, the overall labor productivity of the United States was $132,344, which is 2.11 times its per capita GDP, making the U.S. labor productivity 7.55 times that of China. Even in China's most developed city, Shanghai, overall labor productivity was only $36,948, which is 28% of the U.S. level. Of course, if measured using the World Bank's purchasing power parity (PPP) GDP data, in 1952, U.S. labor productivity was 66.5 times that of China, but by 2018, this gap had narrowed significantly to 4.03 times, indicating a major reduction in the disparity between China and the U.S. Overall, there is still significant room for improvement in the value creation ability of Chinese workers.

Optimistically, after China implements the "three-child" fertility policy and various regions adopt distinctive support and protective measures, it is expected that by the end of the "14th Five-Year Plan," a uniquely Chinese "welfare economics" will take shape. This includes a significant increase in national income, the establishment of a high-quality education and social security system, continuous upgrades in basic public services, widespread coverage of public resources with enhanced service capabilities, the extension of urban public services to rural areas, and improved urban-rural coordination. These developments will, in turn, promote the coordinated development of material civilization, spiritual civilization, and ecological civilization at a higher level, effectively supporting sustainable economic growth.

China aims to transition from an element-driven rapid growth phase to an innovation-driven high-quality development phase during the "14th Five-Year Plan" period. This transition requires maintaining an appropriate investment scale and high capital accumulation, as well as prioritizing investments in human capital. It is essential to promote the reasonable flow of labor elements, ensure the continuous supply of high-quality human capital, and address the disconnect between general human capital and specialized human capital, particularly focusing on improving the accumulation of specialized human capital. Today, the "Talent Power" strategy has become a national strategy. Local governments are exploring talent work mechanisms suited to both domestic and international talent development, improving talent policy systems, establishing and perfecting an open, equal, competitive, and merit-based talent resource allocation mechanism, and implementing policies conducive to talent aggregation. By creating a comprehensive support system for high-end specialized talents, the resulting activation of innovation and business capabilities will, along with other factors of production, contribute to the creation of a growth mechanism that maintains economic vitality.

Strengthening Shanghai's Strategic Advantages in Economic Development Capacity from Four Dimensions

Based on the development experience of mature international economic and financial centers, enhancing Shanghai's capacity for global resource allocation and asset pricing depends not only on the continued advancement of China's high-quality development and high-level opening-up, but also on aligning with the highest international standards of openness and market operations. To build competitive advantages in areas such as factor markets, R&D and design, high-end manufacturing, system integration, and global supply chain management, it is also essential to strengthen Pudong's leading role as a large-scale platform for attracting international high-end industries and financial capital.

Shanghai is China's Trump Card in Participating in High-Level Global Division of Labor

As China's largest economic center, Shanghai has steadily advanced high-quality economic development and high-level opening-up since the start of the 14th Five-Year Plan. In recent years, Shanghai's economy has shown steady improvement and strong resilience. Although there are still some gaps compared with international metropolises such as New York, London, and Tokyo in terms of key economic and financial indicators, the city has maintained strong growth momentum. Notably, significant progress has been made in the development of an international financial center, with Shanghai essentially establishing a financial hub that aligns with China's economic strength and the international status of the renminbi, laying a solid foundation for future growth.

Shanghai has received strategically significant policy support from the Party and the central government in the new round of development, as outlined in the *Guiding Opinions* issued in April 2021. These *Opinions* not only reaffirm Shanghai's already critical strategic position within the overall work of the Party and the country, but also, from the perspectives of goal-setting, policy rationale, and operational guidance, designate Shanghai as the "principal vanguard" representing China in participating in top-tier global division of labor during the first half of the twenty-first century.

Shanghai's position and influence within regional, national, and even global economic landscapes depend not only on the enhancement of its absolute economic strength during the 14th Five-Year Plan period and the long-range vision through 2035, but also on its comprehensive competitiveness as China's most internationally oriented megacity—built upon the strengthening of its "four core functions" and the development of the "five types of economy."

Objectively speaking, from the perspective of economic scale and structural transformation, Shanghai's early-mover advantages are, in some respects, diminishing under the growing competitive pressure from other regions across the country, while its new sources of competitive strength are still in the process of cultivation and formation. Economically and fiscally, for instance, in 1983, Shanghai's total industrial output accounted for one-ninth of the national total, its fiscal revenue made up one-sixth of the national total, and its per capita GNP approached USD 1500—far ahead of other provinces. By 2020, however, Shanghai's GDP was less than one twenty-fifth of the national total, amounting to just 38% of Guangdong's, the largest provincial economy. That said, Shanghai's fiscal revenue in 2020 remained among the highest in the country, trailing only Guangdong, Jiangsu, and Zhejiang. More importantly, Shanghai maintains a strong edge in areas that are difficult for most other provinces to match—such as strategic industries, R&D and design, advanced technology and high-end manufacturing, the factor market system and resource allocation capacity, as well as systems integration and global supply chain management. Particularly notable is its capacity to align with the world's highest standards and rules. This is precisely why the central government entrusted Shanghai with the mission of building a globally influential science and technology innovation center—it recognizes Shanghai's comprehensive competitive advantage in these domains.

From the perspective of the development stages of global metropolitan centers, Shanghai is currently at a critical juncture where it is focused on advancing high-end services and advanced manufacturing, while also accelerating its digital transformation to enhance its overall urban capacity and core competitiveness. As Pudong continues to yield fruitful outcomes in its pioneering role as a leading area for socialist modernization, and with substantial progress anticipated in the internationalization of the renminbi and the development of Shanghai as an international financial center during the 14th Five-Year Plan period and through to the 2035 long-term vision, the city is poised to significantly elevate its strategic position in global industrial, trade, and financial networks. This will be further supported by its emergence as a world-class hub for industrial innovation and a leader in institutional reforms aligned with high international standards, as well as a strong base for top-tier talent.

Shanghai's Economic Capacity and Strategic Advantages Still Need to be Strengthened

Shanghai's share of national GDP has declined from its peak of one-tenth to less than one-twenty-fifth of the total, which is both a natural extension of China's industrialization, urbanization, and the growth of its service sector, and a reflection of the country's transition to high-quality economic development marked by a more balanced and diversified economic landscape. Nevertheless, as the ace of China's economy, Shanghai must continuously elevate its economic capacity in order to achieve corresponding improvements in both scale and quality—especially in terms of influence. In short, by 2035 and even looking ahead to 2060, Shanghai must not only lead the way in transitioning under the "dual carbon" goals, but also identify the endogenous drivers and strategic leverage points that will enable its economy to reach levels of $1 trillion, $2 trillion, or even higher.

From an international comparative perspective, among the world's top ten cities, New York and Tokyo each have an economic output of around $1 trillion, placing them in the first tier. Los Angeles, ranked third, has a GDP of approximately $750 billion, about $100 billion ahead of third-tier cities such as London, Paris, and Chicago, and roughly $200 billion higher than Shanghai, which ranks eighth. Cities ranked seventh, eighth, and ninth—Houston, Shanghai, and Beijing—have GDP differences of about $40–50 billion among them. According to Shanghai's 14th Five-Year Plan development targets, the city's economic output is expected to approach $800 billion by 2025, with per capita GDP exceeding $30,000.

Of course, to turn static plans into reality in the real world of economic development, a series of constraints must be addressed. The long-term development of Shanghai's economy is constrained by factors such as the rigid limitations of land and spatial layout, rising business costs, and the hollowing-out of some industries. Moreover, significant challenges include the aging population and the competitive pressure on human capital advantages. From both domestic and international perspectives, whether Shanghai can truly become the central node of the domestic circulation and a strategic link in the dual circulation of domestic and international markets depends not only on the maturity and vitality of Shanghai's urban competitive system, which is formed through the integration of various factors like economic development, research and development, urban governance, living conditions, social culture, education, healthcare, and transportation, but also on its ability to enhance factor aggregation and allocation through large-scale platforms in finance, technology, data, and trade. Among these, population and talent are the most important variables and will always be the key focus for Shanghai as it continues to optimize the economic and social development environment and overcome development bottlenecks.

From now until the mid-twenty-first century, economic competition among major global economies will increasingly focus on the control of core industries and cutting-edge technologies, high-end segments of trade and financial value chains, and the competition for strategic talent. As China's "official pioneer" in high-quality development and high-level openness, especially in participating in the global top-tier division of labor, Shanghai's national mission and its role as a leading example of emerging global core cities will serve as the intrinsic driving force for Shanghai's ongoing efforts to enhance its development capabilities and strengthen its strategic competitive advantages.

Strengthening Shanghai's Comprehensive Competitive Advantage in Four Dimensions

Existing research in macroeconomics has shown that the most important drivers of economic growth are knowledge innovation, technological progress, and the enhancement of human capital. Practical experience in the real world has long demonstrated that long-term economic growth must rely on endogenous technological progress and significant improvements in human capital. As for the elements that support endogenous economic growth, issues such as financial transactions and asset pricing, trade and investment facilitation, research and development (R&D) and advanced manufacturing capabilities, smooth supply chains and transaction cost savings, and the establishment of the rule of law and dispute resolution mechanisms, are critical core issues that must be highly prioritized and addressed in the formulation and implementation of a country's or region's medium- and long-term economic development plans.

Shanghai is one of the few cities in the world today that integrates manufacturing, finance, trade, technology, shipping, and other sectors, while also having highly developed land, sea, and air transportation systems. It is an important power center with a superior geographic location, expansive strategic hinterland, and deep commercial and cultural heritage. In its progress toward becoming one of the world's most competitive international cities, Shanghai should strengthen its core leadership role in the development of the Yangtze River Economic Belt and the integration of the Yangtze River Delta. It should solidify its position as the national center for strategic industry operation and management, gradually serve as an "anchor" in the Asia-Pacific economic landscape, and become a super-large platform that absorbs international high-end industries and financial capital. In particular, Shanghai should become a "lever of power" and "bridgehead" in actively participating in global top-tier division of labor, thus contributing to the national development strategy of building a modern socialist strong country.

Firstly, by deepening reforms in core elements that promote endogenous economic growth, such as technology and education, Shanghai should align itself with the development logic of global super cities that hold a competitive advantage in the division of labor. Drawing from Shanghai's pioneering experiences in science and technology innovation and education reform, the city should precisely understand the pulse of technological development in its digital transformation. Through deep self-revolution and keeping pace with or even leading future development trends, Shanghai can build new advantages in science, technology, and education for the first half of the twenty-first century. To achieve this, Shanghai needs to create an innovative ecosystem and educational environment that can nurture cutting-edge technological achievements. On one hand, it should continue to activate the innovation and entrepreneurial capabilities of micro entities; on the other hand, it needs to drive fundamental changes in educational philosophy and breakthrough reforms in the research system. This can be achieved by fostering innovative thinking through experiential education and demonstration, gradually liberating relatively introverted cultural traits, and forming broad support from both the government and society for innovative practices. Furthermore, it should create a culture of tolerance for innovation failure, effective protection of talent innovation enthusiasm, the highest priority protection of property rights, especially intellectual property and so on.

Secondly, by deeply understanding the trends of global industrial changes and providing precise services that align with technological advancements and market shifts, Shanghai should solidify its position as the national strategic industry operations center. Historically, the industrial revolutions that have shaped humanity were initiated in Europe and the United States. However, in today's era of big data and artificial intelligence, China, with the world's largest information infrastructure, the largest consumer market, and a rich array of digital application scenarios, holds certain competitive advantages in aerospace technology, quantum communication, AI manufacturing, and new energy sectors. Additionally, China is breaking through the bottlenecks restricting the development of the information industry and information services, addressing the gaps in the integrated circuit industry, and accelerating the cultivation of enterprises with core technological advantages, thereby entering the global high-level competition in both economics and technology. In this process, Shanghai carries the mission of building a globally influential science and innovation center and an industrial innovation hub. It should adopt a more dynamic and rational perspective to assess its position in global and Chinese industrial landscapes and competition. Shanghai must fully leverage its comprehensive advantages in research and development foundations, financial services, industrial support, new technology industrialization, taxation, and international talent management, particularly its ability to coordinate and manage world-class projects. By enhancing system integration across design, production, and services, Shanghai can foster a group of unicorn enterprises and create opportunities for their value to be re-evaluated in the capital market.

Thirdly, by leveraging the high-level reform and opening-up in Pudong to create a leading area for socialist modernization, Shanghai should focus on strategic institutional supply and high-quality implementation. By aligning with international high-standard trade and economic rules, Shanghai can attract the aggregation of high-end domestic and foreign elements and talent. This will help cultivate Shanghai as a high-quality example of trade and investment facilitation, achieving the optimal allocation of global resources such as capital, technology, information, and talent.

The issuance of the *Opinions* marks the best window of opportunity for a new round of development in Pudong, and also signifies that the Lingang New Area of the Shanghai Free Trade Zone has reached the forefront of global economic, industrial, and financial competition. From an operational and execution perspective, the central government's strategic positioning and development goals for Pudong in China's economic layout indicate that Pudong and the Lingang New Area will enhance their capabilities in resource allocation and industrial innovation in two dimensions and markets. These two dimensions and markets refer to, on the basis of aligning with international high standards in trade, economic, and financial rules, combining Shanghai's role as a hub serving the "Belt and Road" initiative and as a leading area for high-level reform and opening-up. This will strengthen Pudong's role as a platform for absorbing international high-end industries and financial capital, achieving the dual connection between onshore and offshore RMB assets, and facilitating high-level linkage between domestic and international markets. With the successful operation of the STAR Market and the driving force of "technology innovation + high-end industries" in the Lingang New Area, Pudong will continuously make breakthroughs in forming a full-chain "Smart Manufacturing Port." It is expected to create a concentrated zone for large-scale digital industries and financial technology applications, stretching from Lujiazui to the Lingang New Area. This will nurture a group of innovative enterprises that focus on future human consumption experiences and conduct forward-looking research and testing. Ultimately, by creating an innovation ecosystem, Shanghai aims to form a fertile ground capable of producing great enterprises in large numbers, achieving the goal of nurturing pillar industries worth hundreds of billions or even trillions of RMB.

Fourth, in the process of becoming a globally influential and competitive international financial center, Shanghai needs to not only pay attention to the historical experiences of building mature international financial centers but also deeply root itself in China's basic national conditions as the world's largest emerging economy. Shanghai should use the establishment of a global financial resource allocation center and an asset pricing center for capital denominated in RMB as a breakthrough, continuously promoting the enrichment and improvement of the global financial public goods supply system, and further strengthening Shanghai's urban temperament as an international financial center.

From the general development logic of global economic and financial powers, both the internationalization of currency and the upgrading of financial centers, although deeply reliant on government efforts to cultivate the financial ecosystem, fundamentally depend on the sufficient competition of market players and the high-density aggregation of financial elements, particularly the deep involvement of international financial capital. Therefore, Shanghai should be regarded as the most important platform for continuously sharing the dividends of China's economic development and for allocating both Chinese and global financial assets. In the current and near future, Shanghai should continue to improve its financial market system, strengthen its service capabilities, and showcase its open-mindedness and exceptional business environment.

Finally, finance, as a manifestation of the highest level of global division of labor, is one of the most important core competencies of a nation, and fully leveraging its role in the modern market economy relies on the consolidation of manufacturing competitive advantages, the continuous enhancement of trade value chains, and the ongoing improvement of systemic risk prevention capabilities. In this regard, Shanghai undoubtedly possesses vast operational space and a solid foundation for continuously improving its development capabilities.

Overcoming Shanghai's Population and Talent Bottlenecks through Forward-Looking Strategic Design

At present, the population and talent bottlenecks facing Shanghai are major practical challenges that must be urgently addressed in the implementation of the 14th Five-Year Plan and the realization of the city's 2035 long-term development goals. Shanghai must not only act with a strong sense of urgency and adopt precise measures to stabilize the natural population growth rate, but also prioritize population and talent issues in its medium- and long-term strategic planning.

Shanghai urgently needs to strengthen top-level design and improve major policy systems to respond to population aging in a timely, scientific, and comprehensive manner. It must fully leverage talent as the primary driving force behind the creation of new development miracles in the new era. Through forward-looking strategic design and integrated reforms, Shanghai should aim to transform its population structure. This requires elevating population and talent development to a strategic priority and advancing in five key areas: establishing a baseline security system to support three-child families, promoting talent attraction alongside building world-class talent hubs, optimizing spatial planning to support new population dynamics, and enhancing the foundational role of education and investment in human capital. A coordinated effort across these five dimensions will be essential to overcoming the city's population and talent bottlenecks.

The Population Issue Is a Major Real Problem We Currently Face

The population issue, particularly the challenge of aging, was one of the key topics of discussion among delegates at the 2022 National People's Congress and Chinese People's Political Consultative Conference. Many delegates submitted related proposals, reflecting the deep concern across all sectors of society regarding population aging.

In 2022, the State Council issued the *14th Five-Year Plan for the Development of the National Aging Undertaking and Elderly Care Service System*. This plan represents a key measure for implementing the national strategy of actively responding to population aging and for promoting the high-quality development of the elderly care service system. It also serves as a concrete follow-up and supporting implementation at the national level of the *July 2021 Decision on Improving Birth Policies to Promote Long-term Balanced Population Development*.

Since the second half of 2021, local governments across China have gradually introduced region-specific "three-child" birth policies and supporting measures. Among them, the approaches taken by Beijing and Shanghai are particularly representative. On February 9, 2022, the Beijing Municipal Party Committee and Municipal Government issued the *Implementation Plan on Optimizing Birth Policies and Promoting Long-term Balanced Population Development*, which introduced 22 measures aimed at encouraging childbirth and providing related support. Similarly, on December 3, 2021, the Standing Committee of the Shanghai Municipal Party Committee reviewed and approved the *Implementation Opinions on Optimizing Birth Policies and Promoting Long-term Balanced Population Development in Shanghai*. The document outlines concrete plans for implementing national directives, aligning with Shanghai's demographic realities, adapting to population development trends, improving birth-related policies, and ensuring coordinated efforts between fertility policies and broader socio-economic policies.

According to statistics, by 2022, a total of 25 provinces across China had completed revisions to their Population and Family Planning Regulations. Several provinces and municipalities have already formulated and begun implementing plans to optimize birth policies, and a fertility-friendly social environment is gradually taking shape nationwide.

Undoubtedly, the accelerated implementation of the "three-child" birth policy and supporting measures by provinces across China—including Beijing and Shanghai—reflects that population issues have become urgent and significant challenges that local governments must address during the 14th Five-Year Plan period. China has now entered a period of negative population growth. According to data from the National Bureau of Statistics, the natural population growth rate (birth rate minus death rate) in 2022 was only −0.60‰, compared to 3.34‰ in 2019—a clear and concerning downward trend (see Fig. 13.10 for details). The net population growth figures are equally alarming: from 2019 to 2021, China's net population increases were 4.67 million, 2.04 million, and 0.48 million respectively. In contrast, the population in 2022 decreased by 850,000 compared to 2021. It is evident that the country must intensify efforts to fully implement the three-child policy and stabilize the birth rate.

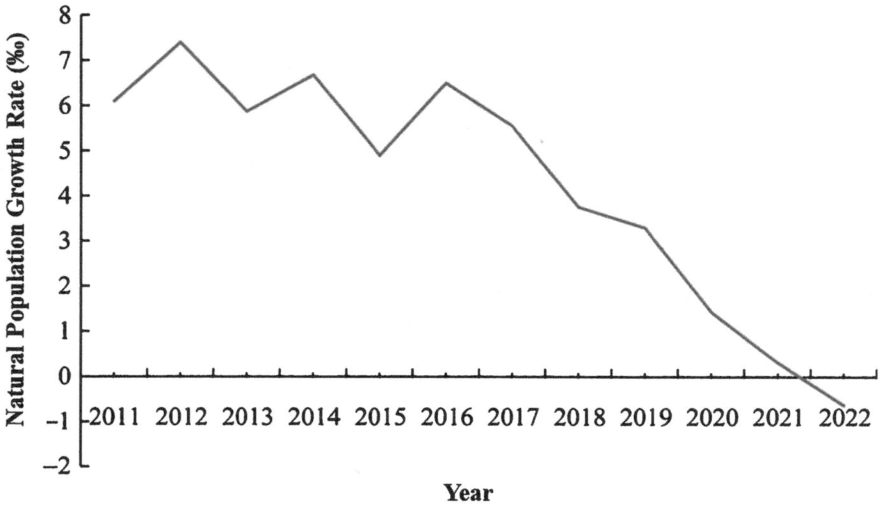

Fig. 13.10 Changes in China's Natural Population Growth Rate from 2011 to 2021. Data Source: National Bureau of Statistics of China

Shanghai's Primary Goal Is to Stabilize the Natural Population Growth Rate

In the case of Shanghai, the core reason why its total population is unable to maintain the previous rapid growth is not primarily due to the strict implementation of policies to control the population size of mega-cities in recent years, but rather stems from the following three aspects: the birth rate of registered residents has remained low, resulting in a negative natural growth rate of the registered population for consecutive years; the entire society has entered a stage of deep aging, with the dependency ratio approaching 50%, signaling the imminent end of the demographic dividend; and the widely discussed trend of declining birth rates has not been reversed by the full implementation of the "three-child" policy.

Regarding the first aspect, according to data from the Shanghai Municipal Bureau of Statistics, from 1993 to 2011, the natural growth rate of the registered population in Shanghai was negative for 19 consecutive years. Although the natural growth rate of the registered population turned positive in 2012, reaching 0.26‰—an increase of 0.94 percentage points from the previous year's − 0.68‰—this was primarily due to cyclical generational continuation rather than endogenous fertility drivers. In fact, from 2013 to 2018, the natural growth rate of the registered population in Shanghai was positive only in 2014 and 2016, while the other four years showed negative growth. In 2020, Shanghai's permanent resident population had 127,600 births, a decrease of 41,400 compared to the previous year. Of these, 68,100 were born to registered residents, a drop of 24,000 from the previous year. Since the registered population accounts for nearly 60% of Shanghai's permanent resident

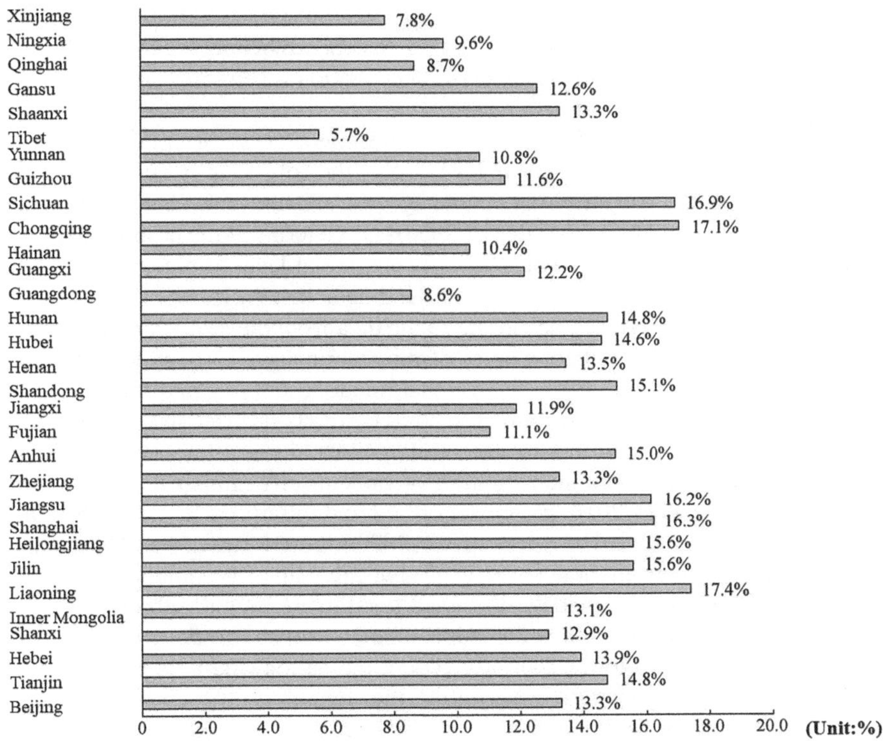

Fig. 13.11 Proportion of Population Aged 65 and Above by Province/Municipality in the Seventh National Population Census. Data Source: National Bureau of Statistics of China

population, one of the key population bottlenecks Shanghai must overcome at this stage is to reverse the decline in the birth rate and natural growth rate of the registered population, providing the foundational conditions for sustainable economic and social development.

Regarding the second aspect, according to internationally recognized standards, if the proportion of a country's or region's population aged 65 and above reaches or exceeds 7%, it indicates that the country or region has entered an aging society. If this proportion reaches 14%, the country or region is considered to have entered a stage of deep aging. According to the data from the seventh national census, in 2020, the proportion of the population aged 65 and above in Shanghai's permanent resident population reached 16.3%, and among the registered population, those aged 65 and above accounted for more than 24%. This clearly indicates the characteristics of a deeply aging society (as shown in Fig. 13.11 for the proportion of populations aged 65 and above in various provinces and municipalities). On the other hand, the number of elderly people aged 65 and above in the non-local permanent resident population has been increasing rapidly over the past decade, further accelerating the pace of deep aging. The deepening of aging directly increases the overall dependency ratio. Statistical data shows that Shanghai's overall dependency ratio was 31% in 2010, rising to 49.7% by 2020, nearly reaching the 50% threshold in economic terms. When the overall dependency ratio exceeds 50%, it signifies the end of the demographic dividend period.

Existing research shows that among the four major cities—Beijing, Shanghai, Guangzhou, and Shenzhen—Shanghai is not only the "oldest" city but also the one aging the fastest. The proportion of people aged 65 and above in Shanghai is twice that of Guangzhou and five times that of Shenzhen. In terms of the proportion of the population aged 0 to 14, Shanghai is the only provincial-level administrative unit in the country with a share of less than 10%, standing at just 9.8%.

Regarding the third aspect, according to the data from the seventh national census, China's total fertility rate for women of childbearing age is 1.3, which is already at a relatively low fertility level. In Shanghai, the total fertility rate for women of childbearing age has long been below 1 and has currently dropped to 0.7, indicating that the concepts of "unwilling to have children" or "having fewer children" are firmly entrenched. Although the national government fully implemented the "two-child" policy in January 2016, its impact on improving fertility levels in Shanghai has been limited. It only led to a peak of 129,200 births among the registered population in that year, the highest since 1995, but after that, the numbers began to decline, indicating that the widely discussed trend of declining birth rates has not been reversed by the full implementation of the "two-child" policy. As for the immediate and medium-to-long-term effects of the nationwide implementation of the "three-child" policy starting in May 2021, they remain to be observed. The intertwined phenomena of declining birth rates and deep aging are the two major challenges Shanghai faces in the short term.

The Demographic Dividend from Population Size Is the Prerequisite for the Dividend from Population Quality

Shanghai is the largest city in China in terms of population size and has a highly developed higher education system. By the end of 2020, it had a permanent resident population of 24.89 million and 64 regular higher education institutions. According to the data from the seventh national census, Shanghai has the highest number of people with a high school education per 100,000 people in the country. The population with a university degree reached 8.42 million, and compared to 2010, the number of university-educated individuals per 100,000 people rose from 21,893 to 33,872, an increase of 55% over the decade, second only to Beijing in the country. Among Shanghai's working-age population (ages 16 to 59), 46.4% have a university education, a 20.2% increase from 2010. This reflects Shanghai's achievements in placing a high emphasis on both basic and higher education, as well as attracting outstanding talents from both domestic and international sources. The continuous improvement of Shanghai's population's educational quality and the ongoing accumulation of talent dividends have, to some extent, offset the adverse effects of population aging, making them key factors supporting Shanghai's implementation of the 14th Five-Year Plan and its 2035 long-term development goals.

However, for Shanghai, which bears the core mission of building the "Five Centers" and leading the integration of the Yangtze River Delta, while consolidating the already-formed demographic quality dividend (including the talent dividend) is undoubtedly important, it must not be assumed that the importance of the demographic quality dividend has surpassed that of the demographic size dividend. If the demographic size dividend continues to diminish, the vitality of the city will inevitably be impacted, potentially affecting the sustainable and high-quality development of both the economy and society.

In fact, Shanghai's permanent resident population grew at a significantly slower pace between 2010 and 2020: during the period of the sixth national census (2000–2010), Shanghai's permanent resident population increased by 6.61 million, whereas in the seventh national census cycle, the increase dropped to 1.85 million, making the "ceiling effect" of population size more apparent. In contrast, Shenzhen, the youngest megacity in China, with an area of 1997.47 square kilometers—less than one-third of Shanghai's size—saw its population grow by 7.14 million over the same 10 years, reaching a total population of 17.66 million, approximately 70% of Shanghai's population. Since April 2011, Shenzhen has launched talent programs such as the "Peacock Plan" to attract a large number of high-level overseas talents, which has significantly boosted the city's economic development. The talent dividend effect has been very notable, demonstrating Shenzhen's strong emphasis on both the demographic size and quality dividends.

Advancing with "Five Forces" to Break through Shanghai's Population and Talent Bottlenecks

According to Shanghai's 2035 vision goals, by the end of the '14th Five-Year Plan' period, Shanghai will have essentially become a socialist modern international metropolis with global influence and a core leading city within the world-class Yangtze River Delta urban cluster. Its comprehensive economic strength will rank among the top global cities. High-quality development will be achieved first, and high-quality living will be widely enjoyed. The city will build a higher-level healthcare system, ensuring full-cycle, all-encompassing health services for its people. Shanghai will become an important window for the construction of a socialist modern nation and a benchmark city.

First, placing population and talent development as strategic priorities. For Shanghai, which has already entered a stage of deep aging, to achieve a shift from an "aging" population structure to a "vibrant" one, it is essential not only to stabilize the natural population growth rate but also to prioritize population and talent development as key strategic objectives.

Shanghai has had a low fertility rate for many years, and the reasons are multifaceted, with industrialization and urbanization having a significant impact on residents' views on childbearing. On one hand, as the most economically developed city in China, Shanghai has always had a high labor force participation rate among women of childbearing age, and the trend of late marriage and late childbearing has become increasingly common. On the other hand, in recent years, the proportion of single, unmarried, and childless individuals has risen, coupled with constraints on housing conditions and the high cost of raising children. As a result, the issue of "having fewer children" or even "unwillingness to have children" has become a prominent problem. The immediate and even medium-to-long-term effects of the nationwide implementation of the "three-child" policy starting in May 2021 may require 3 to 5 years of data accumulation to assess accurately. Based on observations of the implementation effects of the "two-child" policy in the past, the realization of positive medium-to-long-term effects will require support from many accompanying conditions, which involves the organic combination of overall strategic design and the execution of supporting policies.

In summary, for Shanghai to fully implement its optimized fertility policy and achieve the strategic goal of long-term population balance, policy design should not be limited to the scope of the "three-child" policy. Instead, it should be framed within the context of the "dual carbon" goals, with a focus on planning and designing population development with an eye toward the 2035 vision and even the 2050 timeframe. This planning should encompass population size, structure, quality, as well as the coordination and integration of natural, environmental, and socio-economic development.

From a time-series perspective, there are less than three five-year plans remaining until 2035, and just over a generation's time until 2050. This marks a critical time point for observing and assessing the medium-to-long-term effects of the "three-child" policy, and possibly the full liberalization of fertility policies in the future. Relevant observation indicators include the birth rate, total fertility rate of women of childbearing age, and natural population growth rate. For Shanghai, achieving a total fertility rate for women of childbearing age above 1 and turning the natural population growth rate from negative to positive are crucial interim goals. From the perspective of ensuring generational replacement, a fertility rate of 2 or above is considered healthy.

As for the talent development strategy, it is based on an overall design that considers the size, structure, and quality of both the existing and incremental population. Of course, a key challenge is how to break the long-standing duality between population policies and talent policies, and establish an adaptable mechanism for connecting population and talent management. This is also a crucial element in maintaining the competitive vitality of the city.

To achieve the transformation from an "aging" population structure to a "vibrant" one, it is essential to address the issue of upgrading the physical fitness structure of the existing population. The "14th Five-Year Plan" for Shanghai explicitly outlines key measures for "actively responding to population aging," including further enhancing the quality of life and life expectancy of the elderly, actively developing elderly human resources, and promoting the concept of "aging with purpose." To achieve these goals, it is necessary not only to increase investment in healthcare and sports infrastructure but also to rely on widespread societal awareness and active participation.

Second, take the lead in establishing a baseline security system for "three-child" child-rearing. From both the government and societal perspectives, the implementation of the "three-child" fertility policy primarily involves revising relevant regulations, ensuring an orderly transition between old and new policies, improving the population service system, enhancing population monitoring and situation analysis, raising the level of prenatal and postnatal care services, developing and optimizing universal childcare services, and addressing how to reduce the costs of childbearing, child-rearing, and education. For instance, the 22 related fertility incentives and supporting measures introduced by Beijing are representative, offering detailed implementation guidelines and a clear roadmap, emphasizing reform and innovation under the guidance of clear objectives. Shanghai should promptly improve its "three-child" fertility policy measures, focusing on aligning fertility policies with related economic and social policies for coordinated action.

However, for local governments, promoting long-term population balance is much more challenging than driving economic growth. In terms of economic growth, the government has a wide range of tools at its disposal, and there is a strong proactive approach. But when it comes to promoting population growth, especially raising the fertility rate and implementing the "three-child" policy, the space for action is much smaller. This is because the mechanisms of population reproduction are fundamentally different from those of economic production. Since the reform and opening up, research on population issues in China has formed a relatively complete theoretical system, which provides explanations for phenomena like low fertility rates and ultra-low fertility rates. Some scholars have even proposed a "baseline standard" for the minimum living requirements of the population, including the minimum needs for housing space, distance, and ecological balance. All of this constitutes the theoretical foundation for promoting population growth. However, population reproduction, especially the implementation of the "three-child" policy, is carried out by couples of childbearing age, the micro-level actors in reproduction. This largely depends on couples' willingness to have children, their ability to raise them, and their comprehensive evaluation of the future life and happiness balance after having multiple children. According to sample data gathered in my research, the post-1985 and post-1995 generations in Shanghai, who are at their peak fertility age, generally have cautious expectations regarding the "three-child" policy. However, a significant number of couples of childbearing age remain optimistic about the future of a "five-person family."

Therefore, to address the issue of low birth rates that will affect Shanghai's medium- to long-term development, the key is to strengthen top-level design and further improve the "three-child" fertility policy. This top-level design goes beyond the usual reforms in areas like tax reductions, maternity insurance coverage, universal childcare services, prenatal and postnatal support, as well as basic education and healthcare services. It should be framed at the height of the great rejuvenation of the

Chinese nation and strategically plan and design Shanghai's role as the nation's "ace" in the population and talent fields, aiming to establish a multi-dimensional support system for encouraging childbirth. Particularly in the two core areas that are of utmost concern to childbearing couples—housing and education—Shanghai can, drawing on experiences from overseas cities such as Singapore, strategically plan and design solutions that suit local circumstances. Of course, in order to solidify the implementation of the "three-child" policy, an important starting point is to establish a baseline security system for "three-child" child-rearing. Shanghai must take the lead in forming a "three-child family" survival and development baseline, creating a foundation for worry-free childbirth.

Third, Shanghai must advance both the inclusive development of its population and the construction of a high-level talent hub in parallel. To gradually reduce Shanghai's overall dependency ratio and maintain the population dividend, it is necessary not only to leverage the "key variable" of the "three-child" policy, but also to rely on further innovation and bold breakthroughs in population and talent policies. This requires Shanghai to move forward with both the inclusive development of its population and the creation of a high-level talent hub simultaneously.

From international experience, for aging cities to restore their original population vitality and maintain international competitiveness, it is a highly complex and long-term systemic project. There are three main paths to achieve this: First, implement a flexible residency admission system, primarily by attracting young external populations, thereby injecting vitality into the urban population system; Second, activate the endogenous motivation for childbearing among the existing eligible population through high-level welfare investments; Third, attract and retain international talent by offering top-tier urban competitiveness and living environments, ensuring that they can establish long-term roots and development within the city.

In the case of Shanghai, achieving a gradual reduction in the total dependency ratio and maintaining the population dividend before 2035 largely depends on the "key variable" of the "three-child" fertility policy. In comparison with international experiences, Shanghai has already implemented a series of related policies to actively address aging and enhance the vitality of the urban population and its international competitiveness. These policies include reforms to the settlement policies for recent graduates and efforts to actively promote the construction of a talent hub, with a focus on attracting and cultivating five major categories of talent: international talent, returning overseas talent, local talent, specialized talent, and young talent. The positive effects of these policies are gradually becoming apparent.

However, for Shanghai to truly establish the strategic position of talent as the driver of urban development and form a talent system with attractiveness and international competitiveness, it needs further innovation and bold breakthroughs in its population and talent policies. In particular, there must be breakthrough reforms in attracting and retaining domestic and overseas young talent that is suited to the development of the "Five Centers." It is recommended to conduct high-level research to gather sufficient information and accurate data, with a long-term perspective, to precisely assess the challenges faced by young professionals, especially innovative talents, in settling and developing in Shanghai. This will help in designing talent policies that reflect foresight and adaptability. If Shanghai can attract over a million competitive domestic and international young talents in the next decade, it will not only significantly enhance the city's diversity and population vitality, but also bring cutting-edge technology and innovative ideas. The multiplier effect of talent aggregation will be highly beneficial in addressing the population aging issue.

Fourth, optimizing spatial development to serve the new population growth. In this regard, Shanghai has already made relevant plans and taken actions. For example, in its "14th Five-Year Plan," Shanghai proposed a new spatial development pattern characterized by "centralized radiation, dual-wing development, new city empowerment, and north-south transformation." In 2021, the Shanghai Municipal Government released the *Implementation Opinions on Accelerating New City Planning and Construction* during the 14th Five-Year Plan Period, which outlined the phased and long-term goals for the planning and construction of five new cities: Jiading, Qingpu, Songjiang, Fengxian, and Nanhui. By 2025, the total resident population of these five new cities is expected to reach approximately 3.6 million, with the GDP of these districts reaching 1.1 trillion yuan. These new cities will have essentially formed independent urban functions and be on their way to becoming comprehensive node cities. By 2035, each of the five new cities will have a resident population of around 1 million, and will be built into comprehensive node cities in the Yangtze River Delta with radiating and driving effects.

From the perspective of urban and regional planning, Shanghai's new spatial development strategy—particularly the strategic planning and design of the five new cities—marks a transition from a single-core model centered around the main urban area to a multi-centered, progressively balanced metropolitan development pattern. This shift facilitates the rational flow and optimal allocation of key elements such as population, talent, capital, and technology, positioning Shanghai to become a new driving force for advancing new urbanization by 2035. If the construction of the five new cities successfully integrates traditional characteristics with innovative practices to form localized and distinctive "urban spaces," it will greatly enhance Shanghai's ability to attract and retain population. Furthermore, it will expand Shanghai's spatial and functional capacity as the core leading city for high-quality integrated development in the Yangtze River Delta, ultimately boosting the city's overall vitality and attractiveness.

From the perspective of more optimized spatial planning, Chongming District—an area roughly twice the size of Singapore but currently with a population of less than 700,000—will serve as a strategic hinterland for Shanghai in achieving its dual carbon goals and mid- to long-term development objectives. Chongming not only has a relatively vast land area but is also known as a longevity region in China and a national ecological demonstration zone, offering an exceptionally livable environment. It also functions as a key hub connecting Shanghai's main urban area with Nantong. Nantong, as an important city in the Yangtze River Delta integration strategy, has experienced rapid economic development in recent years and is projected to exceed 1.5 trillion yuan in total economic output by 2025. As high-quality integration of the Yangtze River Delta progresses, Chongming's strategic pivot role will become increasingly evident. In alignment with Chongming's long-term goal of becoming a globally leading ecological island and a carbon-neutral demonstration zone of international influence, it is recommended to further optimize spatial planning, upgrade transportation models, accelerate infrastructure development and support systems, and strategically deploy green industries and R&D bases that align with twenty-first-century development principles.

Fifth, strengthen the leading role of education and investment in human capital. To consolidate and continuously enhance the population quality dividend and achieve a leading position in global human capital competitiveness among major cities, Shanghai must leverage the pioneering role of education. At the same time, aligned with the need for specialized human capital accumulation driven by the development of the "Five Centers," the city must continue to increase investment in human capital.

Ideally, for Shanghai to maintain and enhance its international competitiveness, it must retain both the demographic dividend from population size and the quality dividend from population structure. However, for a city already in deep aging, this is clearly a highly challenging goal. Of course, high difficulty does not mean it's impossible. As previously discussed, if Shanghai can establish a multidimensional support system that promotes active childbearing—particularly by offering optimized solutions to the two core concerns of prospective parents: housing and education—it will significantly improve the willingness of individuals to follow through with the three-child policy. As early as 2014, Shanghai was designated a national pilot region for comprehensive education reform, implementing reforms across the entire life cycle from early childhood to elder education. Through pioneering education reform initiatives, the city has accumulated valuable experience. In 2021, Shanghai was again appointed as a national experimental zone for basic education reform, with new missions that include promoting the accessible, safe, and high-quality development of preschool education and ensuring balanced, high-quality development in compulsory education. Therefore, Shanghai can fully leverage its existing educational resources by increasing investment in an inclusive childcare system, optimizing the allocation of compulsory education resources across districts, and achieving equitable access to quality educational resources. It can also address the educational access barriers faced by children of migrant workers, thereby providing a more stable and reassuring education outlook for prospective parents.

On the other hand, it is essential to continue advancing a fundamental transformation in educational philosophy and achieving breakthrough reforms in science, education, and governance systems. This includes fostering broad-based support from the government and society for innovative education, vigorously cultivating an innovation ecosystem and educational environment capable of nurturing cutting-edge scientific achievements, and significantly increasing investment in human capital and vocational education. It is also crucial to enhance the efficiency of labor resource utilization and place greater emphasis on strengthening the accumulation of specialized human capital. Swiftly addressing the disconnection between general and specialized human capital will help ensure a sustained supply of highly qualified talent and lay a solid foundation for leveraging the advantages of the population quality dividend.

The Underlying Meaning of China's Economic Growth Indicators Is Undergoing Positive Changes

In 2022, China's economy achieved a growth rate of 3.0% despite being impacted by multiple complex domestic and international factors. Objectively speaking, this fell short of the static expectations set at the beginning of the year. However, macroeconomic forecasting has always been one of the most complex and challenging tasks—it relies not only on comprehensive information and accurate data but is also influenced by constantly changing internal and external conditions, especially non-economic factors.

In 2022, China's economy faced at least three major constraints: First, effectively coping with the multidimensional shocks caused by the 'triple pressures'; second, finding a balance between pandemic control and economic development; and third, minimizing the impact of rising commodity prices and localized supply chain disruptions amid heightened uncertainties brought about by geopolitical conflicts.

From the perspective of actual performance, it was no easy task for China to stabilize the macroeconomic fundamentals in 2022, especially with some key indicators showing signs of recovery. If a series of expectation-stabilizing policies could be effectively implemented in the fourth quarter—particularly in generating tangible work output and boosting effective investment—combined with the gradual recovery of domestic demand, then it is entirely possible for the overall economy to achieve meaningful growth for the year, guided by the primary goals of stabilizing employment and prices.

Evaluation of China's Economic Performance since the COVID-19 Pandemic

Analyzing China's economic situation requires placing it within the context of the medium- and long-term economic cycle, as well as scientifically analyzing the distribution and performance of microeconomic entities' vitality across industries and regions. Additionally, it is essential to conduct a comprehensive assessment of the multidimensional and repeated shocks brought to the macro and microeconomy by the pandemic, which is a significant variable. For governments around the world, ensuring the healthy operation of economic activities is a major test of their capacity limits. The outbreak of the Russia-Ukraine conflict in 2022, along with the resulting financial market turmoil, rising commodity prices, and the increased risk of stagflation, has significantly heightened the difficulty for governments to stabilize the macroeconomic fundamentals.

For China, as the first economy to be impacted by the COVID-19 pandemic, although the economy contracted by 6.8% in the first quarter of 2020, it quickly rebounded in the second quarter, achieving a 2.3% growth for the entire year, making it the only major economy in the world to achieve positive growth in 2020. In

2021, China achieved an 8.1% economic growth rate, ranking second among major global economies, contributing 25% to global economic growth that year. More significantly, in 2021, China's total GDP, converted at the average exchange rate of the year, reached 17.7 trillion USD, accounting for 18.5% of the global economy, with per capita GDP surpassing the world average.

China's economy withstood the impact of the COVID-19 pandemic in 2020 and 2021, demonstrating characteristics such as strong economic resilience, robust domestic demand, ample room for maneuver, comprehensive industrial support, and strong fiscal sustainability, compared to other major economies. This is reflected in key economic indicators: the incremental economic output in 2020 and 2021 increased by 3 trillion USD, and China's share of global goods exports saw a significant rise. In 2020, the shares of China, the United States, Germany, and Japan in global goods exports were 14.7%, 8.13%, 7.84%, and 3.64%, respectively, further widening the gap with the second-ranked economy. In 2021, China's annual import and export volume, measured in USD, surpassed the 6 trillion USD mark for the first time, with a year-on-year growth of 21.4%.

Research shows that over the past decade, there has been a strong correlation between global economic growth and China's export volume, as well as a positive correlation with China's export growth rate, highlighting the importance of China as a central hub in the global industrial and supply chains for global economic growth. Data shows that China's manufacturing value added increased from 16.98 trillion yuan in 2012 to 31.4 trillion yuan in 2021, with its global share rising from 22.5% to nearly 30%, maintaining its position as the world's leading manufacturing power.

The reason China was able to quickly stabilize its economic fundamentals in the face of the pandemic shock and mitigate the impact of external uncertainties to some extent is due to its policy response logic: when micro-market entities face survival crises due to external shocks, the government immediately plays the role of market order maintainer and even the "lender of last resort" in critical times. On one hand, the government remains highly vigilant about potential liquidity shortages in the market; on the other hand, it connects market and enterprise pain points through policy transmission mechanisms, directly intervening to ensure that macro policies do not "suffocate" during implementation. This approach not only focuses on rescuing "too big to fail" enterprises but also ensures the survival and development of small and medium-sized enterprises from the perspective of people's livelihood, demonstrating the responsibility of a proactive government.

The Underlying Meaning of China's Economic Growth Indicators Has Undergone Positive Changes

In recent years, under the backdrop of China's visible economic indicators moving away from the high-growth phase, core indicators such as employment and prices have undergone positive changes. This indicates that China, as a super-economy with a GDP level of trillions of yuan or one that will soon enter the 20 trillion-dollar club, is adapting to a moderate growth rate of 4%—5%, and is gradually achieving macroeconomic goals that previously required a growth rate of 8%—9%.

As for employment, the most important goal, during the long period from 2000 to 2013, one of the key considerations for the Chinese government in setting an annual GDP growth target of around 8% was to meet the urban employment demand of 12 to 15 million new jobs each year. During this period, for every 1 percentage point of GDP growth, the number of jobs created ranged from 1 million to 1.7 million. For instance, from 2009 to 2011, the number of jobs created for every 1 percentage point of GDP growth was between 1.1 million and 1.2 million, while from 2012 to 2013, it was between 1.6 million and 1.7 million, showing an overall upward trend with some fluctuations.

With the adjustment of China's economic structure, especially the accelerated development of the service industry, the service sector, which is the largest absorber of employment, has become key to stabilizing the employment base and maintaining market entities. According to reports from the National Bureau of Statistics, from 2013 to 2018, the service sector maintained a growth rate of 4.4%, creating an average of 13.75 million jobs annually. By the end of 2018, employment in the service sector reached 359.38 million people, accounting for 46.3% of total employment, making it the largest industry for job absorption. In 2019 and 2020, more than 70% of young people aged 16 to 24 were employed in the service sector. Meanwhile, from 2013 to 2019, the employment-generating capacity of the secondary industry continued to decline, with a total reduction of nearly 20 million jobs over six years, indicating a continuous increase in labor productivity in the industrial sector.

In recent years, the correlation between China's economic growth rate and employment rate has been changing. For example, from 2014 to 2015, each 1% increase in GDP led to about 1.8 million jobs. From 2016 to 2017, it led to about 1.9 million jobs, and in 2018 and 2019, it led to approximately 2.03 million and 2.22 million jobs, respectively. The continued rise in the number of jobs generated per unit of GDP indicates that China's economy is shifting towards a path of high-quality growth. In 2020, the year the pandemic broke out, China's economic growth was 2.3%, but the country added 11.86 million urban jobs, exceeding the annual target. In 2021, with an economic growth rate of 8.1%, 12.69 million new urban jobs were created, again surpassing expectations. In 2022, with a 3.0% economic growth, 12.06 million new urban jobs were added, demonstrating that the strong correlation between economic growth and employment rate in the past is being replaced by uneven employment drivers due to economic structural changes. This also provides evidence that China has developed an industrial support system and microeconomic foundation capable of achieving full employment under uncertain conditions (See Fig. 13.12 for the changes in China's nominal GDP growth and urban employment from December 2011 to June 2022) Furthermore, the more than 160 million market entities today are not only a solid foundation for maintaining economic resilience and vitality, but also the key pillar for absorbing employment.

Of course, due to the pandemic's impact on the service industry exceeding expectations, the number of new jobs provided by the service sector in 2020 and

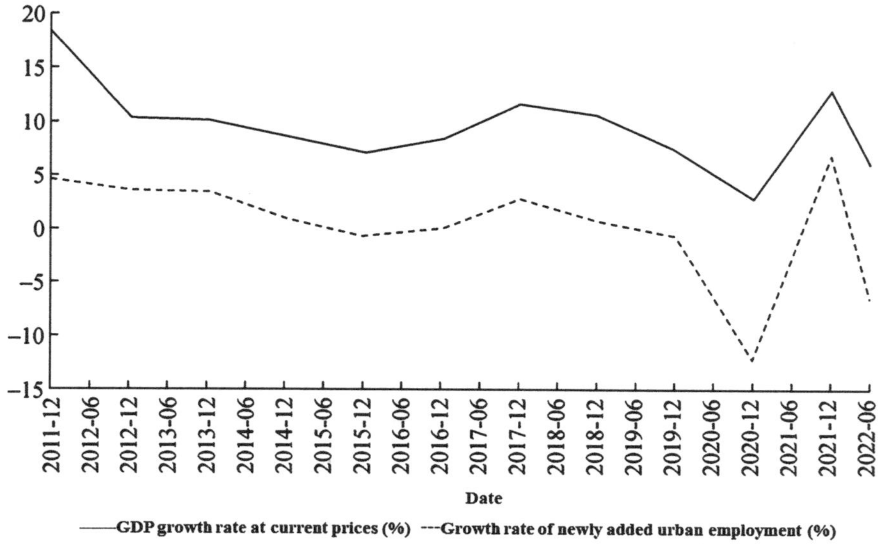

Fig. 13.12 Changes in Nominal GDP Growth and Urban New Employment from December 2011 to June 2022. Data Source: National Bureau of Statistics of China, Ministry of Human Resources and Social Security of China

2021 increased by only 3.07 million, far lower than before the pandemic. In contrast, the number of new jobs in the secondary industry increased by 4.8 million, primarily because the overseas supply chain restrictions increased foreign demand's reliance on China's manufacturing production. In the first half of 2022, the service sector was severely impacted by the pandemic, leading to the actual unemployment rate being higher than the natural unemployment rate. This indicates that, with the slowdown in economic growth, employment and other livelihood issues have become the primary goals of macroeconomic operations.

Another positive change in the connotation of China's economic growth indicators is the ability to maintain overall price stability amid a complex international economic environment. The effectiveness of a country's economic growth largely depends on whether the government can achieve full employment and control inflation while promoting economic growth. In mature market economies, there is a "333" barometer to measure whether the economy is operating healthily. This means that the economic growth rate should not be lower than 3%, the unemployment rate should not exceed 3%, and the inflation rate should not exceed 3%. If any one of these indicators or multiple indicators deviates significantly, it indicates that the economy has slipped out of a healthy trajectory.

Since the 2008 global financial crisis, unemployment and inflation have been two major issues troubling the U.S. and Europe. Particularly since 2022, inflation in the U.S. and Europe has intensified. Both overall inflation and core inflation are significantly higher than the target levels, and in the short term, no turning point is in sight.

Against this backdrop, China has been able to maintain stable prices, with only slight and moderate fluctuations, indicating that the country's macroeconomic fundamentals are robust and its monetary policy, particularly in terms of managing expectations, has reached a high level. According to data from the National Bureau of Statistics, in 2021, the Consumer Price Index (CPI) rose by 0.9% year-on-year; in 2022, under the pressure of imported inflation, the CPI increased by 2.0%, while the Producer Price Index (PPI) for industrial producers rose by 4.1% year-on-year.

China's ability to maintain relatively stable prices is due to both the stabilizing role played by its comprehensive and independent industrial system in ensuring supply and stabilizing prices, as well as the government's experience in supply-demand adjustment, strengthening market regulation, improving risk warning mechanisms, and enhancing expectations management. These factors have collectively laid a solid foundation for controlling inflation expectations.

Medium- and Long-Term Challenges and Economic Development Trends

Of course, the short-term difficulties and medium- to long-term development bottlenecks of the Chinese economy should not be overlooked. Currently, China's economy is facing some prominent contradictions, including high debt among real estate companies, excessive risk exposure of small and medium-sized banks, risks at the micro level, and increasing employment pressures. From an international perspective, if external markets remain unstable, especially with persistent high inflation and weakening external demand, it will significantly increase the difficulty for China to maintain its economy within a reasonable range. In a certain sense, China is currently facing the "risk triangle" dilemma proposed by the Bank for International Settlements, which includes slowing growth or declining productivity, rising leverage, and narrowing macroeconomic policy space. Therefore, while the central government adheres to the general policy of seeking progress while maintaining stability, it is focusing on promoting high-quality economic development, ensuring that the economy remains stable, that development is secure, and especially safeguarding the bottom line of safety in all aspects, consolidating the trend of economic recovery, and guiding the economy to operate within a reasonable range.

The author believes that from now until 2035, China's economic development will face at least three external challenges:

First, in an increasingly uncertain world, major external shocks like the pandemic may become a regular, recurring threat. It is essential to enhance early warning capabilities for major crises and strengthen the ability to respond quickly. By adopting rational and endogenous development methods, along with a deep respect for natural ecology and biodiversity, the likelihood of "black swan" events can be reduced. In the context of the pandemic causing a retreat in globalization and disruptions to supply chains and industrial chains, it is crucial to promptly conduct a comprehensive review of national public health security, industry, technology, and financial safety, generate high-quality inspection reports, maintain control over national security, and ultimately achieve high-quality development.

Second, based on historical experience, as China moves towards becoming the world's largest economy, it will be difficult to maintain its status as both the largest producer and the largest consumer for an extended period. With the acceleration of China's industrial and financial capital seeking global resource allocation and the continuous increase in the internationalization of the renminbi, China may face significant challenges such as industrial hollowing out and the "Triffin dilemma" around 2035. At that time, issues like "reindustrialization," "manufacturing reshoring," and how to avoid falling into a debt-driven economic trap will be urgent matters in the economic field.

Third, as China deeply integrates into the global industrial division of labor system and remains highly connected with international markets, the challenge will be how to promote further opening up through sound institutional design and alignment with the highest global standards of the twenty-first century. China must explore ways to continuously unlock the dividends of economic openness and foreign trade development through global allocation of high-quality capacity, provision of replicable business models, and other strategies. In doing so, China can offer more public goods to support global economic trade and financial development, contribute to global economic rebalancing, and foster sustainable development. This represents both a significant international mission for China in the twenty-first century and a test of its ability to cultivate mechanisms for international prestige.

From the perspective of growth base, after China's economy surpassed the $10 trillion mark in 2014, it has maintained an annual economic increase of about $1 trillion, which is the absolute growth capacity only possessed by a giant economy at the $10 trillion level. Based on the recent trends of China's economy and factors such as fluctuations in the exchange rate between the yuan and the US dollar, it is expected that China's nominal GDP will exceed $20 trillion in the later stages of the 14th Five-Year Plan (2025–2030) and surpass the $30 trillion milestone before 2035.

In terms of growth drivers, during the 13th Five-Year Plan period, China's economy was in a crucial phase of transitioning its growth drivers, constrained by structural, institutional, and cyclical issues accumulated in the past, and further impacted by the pandemic. This led to a decline and instability in growth momentum. However, overall, China's economy maintained a medium-to-high growth rate of 5.8% annually during the 13th Five-Year Plan. In the 14th Five-Year Plan period and the long-term development cycle up to 2035, the structural and institutional constraints on China's economic growth will gradually diminish. However, cyclical shocks, as well as the impacts of population aging, declining birth rates, and reduced fertility, will significantly increase the uncertainty of economic growth. This calls for a focus on technological progress and human capital improvement, combined with a new round of technological revolution and industrial transformation, to reshape China's economic structure. The goal is to promote the development of new productivity in the digital economy era, foster and strengthen a number of new, high-quality, fully integrated modules, effectively countering the impact of the diminishing functions of traditional production factors. Furthermore, new drivers of growth should emerge in key scientific fields such as artificial intelligence, quantum information science, biotechnology and manufacturing, green energy, and new materials. This will aim to ensure that China's economic growth operates at a high-quality, reasonable range of 4%–5% over the next 15 years.

From the theoretical support for economic growth, China is one of only two economies in the world with a GDP exceeding $10 trillion. From the historical development logic, as China moves toward its second centenary goal after essentially achieving modernization, it will develop a complete set of economic growth theories that explain its own development and institutional changes. China's economic reform and development provide a highly valuable research sample and substantial validation support for global economic growth theories and practices.

In the process of promoting high-quality economic development and accelerating the realization of Chinese-style modernization, on one hand, China needs to pay great attention to the proactive study of market instability and economic complexity, especially the complex economic and financial systems. Based on deepened research, China should gradually transcend the new classical macroeconomics of equilibrium optimization, with the aim of establishing a market economic model that effectively restrains the self-interested behavior of the "economic man" while maintaining appropriate government intervention in the market, allowing the government to truly play the role of the "night watchman."

On the other hand, it is essential to cultivate a sharp sense of risk awareness among managers at all levels and market entities, and to establish and improve a forward-looking expectations management mechanism. To achieve early warning and effective response after a crisis occurs, it is crucial to emphasize the broad activation and cultivation of risk awareness among microeconomic entities. This requires fully leveraging the roles of an effective market and a proactive government, creating conditions that promote economic growth driven by core endogenous variables such as technological progress and human capital growth, and establishing a healthy development mechanism that allows China's economy to continuously maintain vitality and operate within a reasonable range.

Important Functions and Strategic Thinking of Computing Power in Economy Development

Since the twenty-first century, the core drivers of global economic growth have increasingly relied on endogenous technological progress and the enhancement of human capital. The new wave of technological and industrial transformation, represented by the "digital revolution," is accelerating the digital transformation of economies and societies across countries. The construction of new infrastructure, primarily focused on digital infrastructure (referred to as "new infrastructure"), is becoming a new platform for countries to respond to economic competition in the twenty-first century. The digital economy, formed by the industrial application of digital technology and the digital transformation of traditional industries, has surpassed the traditional field of information and communication, bringing revolutionary changes to human production, life, trade, and even national and global governance. It is gradually becoming the key core area for major economies to build new competitive advantages.

As the core driving force and indispensable supporting element of digital economy development, the emergence of computing power and the booming development of the computing power economy are the results of humanity's continuous exploration of technologies such as computers, big data, cloud computing, artificial intelligence, and blockchain, and their industrial applications. This also represents a global confirmation of Comrade Deng Xiaoping's important statement in 1988 that "science and technology are the primary productive forces," as it manifests in the twenty-first century. Computing power, as a new form of productive force in the digital economy era, is increasingly becoming an important benchmark for measuring a country's or region's perception of cutting-edge technologies and their industrial applications. With the upgrading and iteration of digital technologies, represented by computing power, deeply integrating with the real economy and continuously empowering it, economies worldwide are accelerating their shift toward digital transformation. This shift is guiding global capital, both stock and incremental, to increase investment in computing power infrastructure construction. Coupled with the optimization of computing power resources and the enhancement of application efficiency, this is increasingly becoming a key variable driving high-quality economic development.

As the world's second-largest economy and the largest developing country, China has placed significant emphasis on investment in digital technologies and their industrial applications in recent years, elevating the development of the digital economy to a national strategy. General Secretary Jinping Xi's important discussions on the digital economy have become an integral part of Jinping Xi's Thought on Socialism with Chinese Characteristics for a New Era, guiding the direction of high-quality digital economy development. As the engine of the digital economy, computing power is bound to profoundly influence the trajectory of the new round of technological revolutions and industrial transformations, reshaping the global economic structure and driving the economic and industrial transformation of countries worldwide.

Computing Power Drives Profound Structural Changes in China's Economy in the New Era

Since the reform and opening up, China has maintained over 40 years of continuous and stable growth, with its total economic output steadily reaching new milestones. Especially since 2016, China's GDP has consecutively surpassed the thresholds of 70 trillion, 80 trillion, 90 trillion, and 100 trillion yuan, making China one of the only two economies in the world with a GDP exceeding 10 trillion USD. The structure of China's economy has also undergone profound changes as innovation-driven and transformation-based development has deepened: Since the 18th National Congress of the Communist Party of China, with the rapid development of the digital economy, China has not only consolidated its position as the world's largest manufacturing power but has also accelerated the modernization of its economic structure. The value added of the service sector exceeded 50% of GDP for the first time in 2015, indicating that China is driving its economy toward high-quality development by advancing the sophistication of its service sector, with technological progress and industrial transformation as key drivers.

First, the mechanism of structural changes in China's economy in the new era. As a direct reflection of the profound structural changes in China's economy, the digital economy has maintained rapid growth over the past decade. The industrial scale grew from 11 trillion yuan in 2012 to 45.5 trillion yuan in 2021, with a nominal year-on-year increase of 16.2%, surpassing the nominal GDP growth rate by 3.4 percentage points during the same period. The share of the digital economy in GDP rose from 21.6% in 2012 to 39.8% in 2021, making China the second-largest digital economy in the world, after the United States. Whether in terms of industrial digitalization development or the scale of digital industries, China ranks among the global leaders. At the same time, the computing power economy, as the "foundation" of the digital economy, has seen an average annual growth rate exceeding 30% over the past five years. In 2021, the core computing power industry reached a scale of 1.5 trillion yuan, with the cloud computing industry exceeding 300 billion yuan, the Internet Data Center (IDC) market surpassing 150 billion yuan, and the core artificial intelligence industry exceeding 400 billion yuan. The computing power industry has made continuous breakthroughs in infrastructure construction, industry ecosystems, standardization, technological research and development, applications, and security systems. China has become the largest and most technologically advanced country in global network infrastructure, playing a pivotal role in the global digital economy.

From a technological perspective, the reason why computing power can drive the development of the digital economy and accelerate the profound structural changes in China's economy is that the foundation for the creation and development of the digital economy is big data. In fact, big data existed objectively before the emergence of the digital economy, but its value was not as highly recognized as it is today. On the other hand, due to technological limitations and the lack of application scenarios, the vast amounts of big data accumulated by countries in fields such as economics, society, and technology were mostly static materials for a long period of time, and they were not regarded as core assets or crucial information playing an irreplaceable role in production and life as they are today. Therefore, the key drivers for promoting the application of big data, apart from the government's demand for application services in the modernization of national systems and governance capabilities, and the market-savvy entrepreneurs, are the rapid development of technologies such as computers, 5G, big data, cloud computing, the Internet of Things (IoT), artificial intelligence, and blockchain, which have made application scenarios a reality. Of course, the widespread use of intelligent algorithms as mathematical tools for big data analysis and the continuous construction and systematization of computing power platforms are the most solid foundation for the digital economy to become a critical pillar of the national economy.

Second, the manifestations of how computing power drives profound structural changes in China's economy. The structural transformation of China's economy driven by computing power is primarily reflected in two key aspects: developmental drivers and industrial forms. In terms of developmental drivers, computing power serves as the endogenous force behind both industrial digitalization and the digital industrialization process. The massive demand for data processing and digital applications continuously places new requirements on the development of computing power from the demand side. Meanwhile, improvements in computing capabilities and the increasing complexity of algorithms provide a continuous source of innovation and momentum for the digital economy from the supply side. In fact, it is the rapid advancement in foundational computing, intelligent computing, and supercomputing that has enabled China to gain a leading edge in areas such as mobile payment, social media, online retail, mobile communications, streaming media, digital finance, smart healthcare, intelligent transportation, and national governance. Existing studies have shown a positive correlation between the level of computing power and economic growth. The higher the "computing power index"—which comprises computing, storage, data transmission capabilities, and the development environment—the greater its contribution to the added value of the digital economy and even to the country's GDP growth. In terms of industrial forms, the accelerated construction of ultra-large-scale data centers by national and local governments, along with capable enterprises, has fostered the emergence of leading consumer and industrial application scenarios. This is closely linked with digital transformation initiatives, especially through the collaborative innovation of 5G, artificial intelligence, and the industrial internet, which together enable the dual integration of the consumer internet and the industrial internet. These developments have given rise to a group of digital enterprises with distinctive business models and strong competitive vitality. On the other hand, with the widespread application of computing tools such as cloud computing, edge computing, intelligent computing, and heterogeneous computing in the manufacturing sector, new possibilities are emerging. By combining scenario presentation, dynamic perception, and interactive experience, these technologies are not only reconstructing and empowering the manufacturing industry, but also promoting the formation and development of an intelligent industrial ecosystem.

Computing Power Economy Plays a Crucial Role in Enhancing the Core Competitiveness of China's Economy

Against the backdrop of increasingly intense global competition over leadership in the digital economy and frontier industries, key technological fields such as artificial intelligence, 5G, quantum information science, biotechnology, biomanufacturing, green energy, materials science, digital finance, and deep space and deep-sea exploration have become strategic focal points for major economies and enterprises, which are ramping up their investments in research and development. As the world's second-largest economy and the second-largest R&D investor, China is transitioning its economic growth model from one primarily driven by capital and labor inputs to one increasingly powered by endogenous technological progress and human capital development. This shift is especially evident since the Fourth Plenary Session of the 19th CPC Central Committee identified data as a production factor on par with labor, capital, land, knowledge, technology, and management. Data has rapidly become a critical resource and core asset. The digital economy—underpinned by computing power—has thus risen to a position of strategic significance in China's national economic agenda. The central government and relevant authorities have issued the *Outline of the Digital Economy Development Strategy* and the *14th Five-Year Plan for Digital Economy Development*, while also setting a long-term development vision through 2035. China has also introduced global initiatives such as the *Global Data Security Initiative* and the *Initiative on Jointly Building a Community with a Shared Future in Cyberspace*, and has applied to join the *Digital Economy Partnership Agreement* (DEPA). In parallel, it has enacted legal and regulatory frameworks to support the healthy development of the digital economy. These efforts aim to foster high-quality digital economic growth, build a modern digital market system with strong international competitiveness, and enhance China's core economic competitiveness during its transformation and upgrading process.

First, computing power has become a key productive force in the digital economy era. As a critical driving factor behind the development of information and communication technology (ICT) industries, computing power—alongside thermal and electrical power in the industrial economy—has emerged as one of the three essential productive forces for human production, daily life, governance, and development in the twenty-first century. It also serves as an indicator of core momentum in the processes of industrial digitization and digital industrialization. In terms of digital industrialization, ultra-large-scale data centers are not only essential to the survival and growth of internet tech firms and data-driven digital enterprises, but also provide the foundational support for extending and expanding the service boundaries of these companies. On the industrial digitization side, once traditional manufacturing, commerce, and financial services sectors adopt digital and intelligent technologies powered by computing capabilities, they can achieve innovations in production efficiency and business models, enhance user experience, and restructure upstream and downstream segments of the value chain. This, in turn, reduces transaction costs and boosts overall enterprise competitiveness.

In the digital economy era, the level and scale of computing power are not only closely tied to a country's level of economic development, but have also become a key strategic focus for enhancing national competitiveness. Countries such as the United States, China, the European Union, and Japan have placed significant emphasis on investments in supercomputing and quantum computing, recognizing computing power as a critical productive force for strengthening national core competitiveness in the digital age. As global competition over computing power intensifies, these regions currently rank among the top four worldwide in terms of total computing capacity. The United States leads in foundational computing power, while China maintains a global leadership position in intelligent computing. In February 2022, China officially launched the "Eastern Data, Western Computing" project. This initiative leverages the resource endowments of the western regions—such as favorable environmental conditions, climate, and energy supply—and connects them with the computing demand and market-driven applications of the eastern regions. Through east-west coordination and complementary advantages, the project aims to build an integrated computing infrastructure system. Its ultimate goal is to optimize the allocation of computing resources nationwide and support China's pursuit of high-quality economic development.

Second, the computing power economy is poised to drive China in establishing a new era of competitive advantage. The role of computing power in the development of the digital economy—and indeed, in the broader national economic system—is not only reflected in its function as a new productive force, but also in its wide range of application scenarios and the vast potential of the "computing power +" model to empower various industries, thus shaping the future of the computing power economy. From a medium- to long-term perspective, China is well-positioned to lead in this domain due to its possession of the world's largest information infrastructure, a highly developed information and communication technology (ICT) industry, advanced application scenarios, a vast consumer market, and existing competitive strengths in several cutting-edge technological and industrial fields. Combined with its tradition of coordinated efforts and investment in overcoming critical technological bottlenecks, a continuously improving innovation and entrepreneurship ecosystem, and a growing pool of market-sensitive entrepreneurs, China has the capacity to scale up and strengthen its computing power economy. With support from capital markets and investment forces, China may continue to enhance its computing power capabilities, fostering the emergence of a new form of productivity suited to the digital economy era. This, in turn, could enable a wave of innovative enterprises with unique technological advantages to closely align with evolving consumer demands, spurring the development of new industries, new business models, and novel service formats. In due course, this environment is likely to incubate a number of "unicorn" companies, and—leveraging the value discovery function of capital markets—forge China's core economic competitiveness in the first half of the twenty-first century.

Opportunities and Constraints Facing the Development of Computing Power Economy

Over the past four decades since the launch of reform and opening-up, China's economy has undergone a sustained transformation in its growth model and development approach through structural reforms and comprehensive strategic planning. The country has shifted from a growth pattern driven primarily by government-led investment and labor-intensive industries to one led by improvements in total factor productivity, marking a fundamental departure from the previous unsustainable mode of extensive development characterized by high input, high energy consumption, high pollution, low output, low quality, and low efficiency.

First, the transformation of China's economy requires the computing power economy to play a strategically leading role. Guided by the new development philosophy of "innovation, coordination, green development, openness, and shared growth," and aligned with China's green and sustainable development transition in achieving its "dual carbon" goals, the country is set to advance economic transformation and systemic reform throughout the 14th Five-Year Plan period and up to 2060. In this process, a new wave of technological revolution—driven by digital technology and computing power—will comprehensively accelerate the digital transformation of China's production models, lifestyles, and governance systems, fostering profound economic change and unleashing vast growth potential.

It is precisely China's sustained investment in foundational and cross-cutting technologies for the digital industry, along with its efforts to build a computing power industry system centered on large-scale data centers, that has enabled the country to largely "run alongside" developed nations—particularly the United States—in the current wave of technological revolution and industrial transformation, and even "lead" in certain areas. From the perspective of global industrial trends, the digital industry is not only a leading sector in its own right but also serves as a powerful enabler of other industries through advances in computing technologies. As such, it plays an increasingly strategic role in guiding China's economic transformation and upgrading its position in the global value chain. For example, China's rapidly growing intelligent vehicle industry places high demands on computing power, algorithms, and related data processing capabilities. Whether this industry can scale from its current market size of hundreds of billions of yuan to a trillion-yuan level will depend to a large extent on whether computing power can develop ahead of demand.

Second, the computing power economy will play an empowering role and provide new growth drivers. The digital transformation of China's economy inherently involves the empowerment of the real economy by digital technologies, and in the process of advancing the upgrading of the service sector, it continuously nurtures new technologies and industries. This, in turn, blurs the traditional boundaries of industrial sectors, forming an economic structure where the real economy is digitized, and the digital economy is materialized.

On one hand, as market demand integrates with rapidly evolving computing technologies and computing power levels, it not only drives new development opportunities for the upstream, midstream, and downstream industries within the computing power industry chain, but also empowers traditional and modern sectors such as manufacturing, transportation, financial services, shopping, healthcare, media and entertainment, social networks, and education. By upgrading and transforming underlying technologies, it enhances the competitiveness of traditional industries and accelerates the quality improvement and efficiency enhancement of emerging industries. On the other hand, the modernization of national governance systems and governance capabilities, as well as the digital transformation of the economy and society, provide unprecedented market opportunities and application spaces for the high-quality development of high-performance computing and its supporting industries from the demand side. Especially with the development of computing power systems toward trends such as high-speed ubiquity, cloud-network integration, and intelligent agility, disruptive changes are expected in certain consumer sectors, giving rise to new business models and consumption trends, and creating new growth drivers.

Third, the "East Data West Computing" project will profoundly impact the development of China's digital economy. From the perspective of the system support required for the development of the computing power economy, the "East Data West Computing Project" (referred to as East Data West Computing), launched in February 2022, is a strategic arrangement for China to build its competitive advantage in the digital economy era. Whether from the development layout, practical needs, industrial collaboration, or the promotion of common prosperity, it is a strategically significant initiative. China possesses almost all the necessary elements for developing a digital economy, and provinces such as Guizhou and Ningxia in the western regions have long been deepening the construction of big data centers, thus pioneering exploration for underdeveloped regions to "overtake" through the development of the digital economy. Combined with the growing computing power demand in the eastern regions, the "East Data West Computing" project has become a key support for driving China's digital economy toward rapid and healthy development during the 14th Five-Year Plan period. It is foreseeable that as the national computing hubs and data center clusters, primarily located in the western regions, are fully completed, they will, together with major projects like "West-to-East Power Transmission" and "West-to-East Gas Transmission," become the cornerstone for the high-quality development and stable growth of China's economy.

Although China's computing power scale ranks among the top in the world, with continuous improvements in computing infrastructure construction and innovation capabilities, as well as increasing levels of computing power application and industrialization, there are still gaps in many areas when it comes to meeting the requirements for high-quality development of the computing power economy. These gaps involve key areas such as the autonomy and controllability of critical technologies, the development environment and industrial ecosystem for computing power, and the cultivation of international competitiveness in the computing power industry. These issues need to be gradually addressed and improved as China continues to develop its computing power economy.

Fourth, the high-quality development of China's computing power economy requires a supporting factor system. Just as the high-quality development of the Chinese economy requires a high level of institutional supply and market-based allocation of factors, high levels of innovation-driven and green sustainable development, and high levels of openness and regional balanced coordination, the growing computing power economy, in order to achieve high-quality development during the 14th Five-Year Plan period and over the medium- to long-term development goals, also cannot do without the mechanism design and innovation under the overall national digital economy development plan and layout. This includes the construction of supporting laws and regulations to protect the healthy development of the computing power industry; it also requires the full development and continuous improvement of the computing power factor market, as well as high-level research and development investment and cost savings to maintain green sustainable development. Furthermore, high-level openness and international cooperation are fundamental to the high-quality development of the computing power economy. Only under high-level international cooperation can China enhance its voice in the global digital economy development process and in the formulation of rules and standards.

Fifth, the high-quality development of the computing power economy faces key technological bottlenecks. The rapid development of China's computing power economy in recent years has largely been driven by the growing consumer demand during the digital transformation process, with endogenous growth based on independent innovation being relatively weak. Although the number of supercomputers, which reflects the development level of computing platforms, ranks first in the world, and total computing power is second only to the United States and Japan, China still faces constraints in key areas required for platform construction, such as chips, algorithm software, and particularly operating systems, where it remains heavily dependent on the United States. For example, the recently enacted *2022 U.S. Chips and Science Act* directly targets the weaknesses in China's semiconductor industry. This law stipulates that U.S. chip companies receiving government subsidies cannot increase production of advanced process chips smaller than 28 nanometers in mainland China for the next 10 years. This move will significantly impact industries in mainland China, such as smartphones and autonomous driving. The tightening of export controls on high-performance computers, their chips, artificial intelligence, and other related technologies will further expose the risk exposure of China's computing power industry, while also pushing China to leverage the advantages of its national system, integrate cutting-edge scientific and technological forces, increase research and development investment, and break through the key technological bottlenecks that constrain the high-quality development of the computing power economy.

Sixth, the high-quality development of the computing power economy faces industrial ecosystem bottlenecks. Although China's computing power economy has not started late and has strong application capabilities, and its industrial development environment and financial support are continuously improving, there are still several development bottlenecks. In addition to the focus on application and the neglect of research and development, issues such as the coordination and integration of software development and full-system clusters required for high-quality development of the computing power economy, the optimization of the business environment, commercial model innovation, and how government-led computing power investments can be organically integrated with market forces, still face many challenges that need to be overcome. From a global perspective on the development trends of the computing power industry, while government support for the industry and investment in public computing platforms are important, the power of the market, especially private high-tech enterprises with strong research foundations and high sensitivity to market and technological trends, is more likely to leverage their inherent advantages, becoming key players in cultivating new business models for the computing power economy, innovating new commercial models, and transforming them into platform productivity.

Seventh, the high-quality development of the computing power economy faces global competitive pressure. As computing power becomes the focal point of strategic competition among countries, accelerating the layout of computing power, increasing technological research and development efforts, and enhancing industrial application levels, especially ensuring the autonomy and comprehensive competitive advantages of the computing power industry chain, are key national strategies for powerful players such as the United States, the European Union, Japan, and the United Kingdom. For example, in the highly competitive global cloud computing LaaS market, the United States leads the ecosystem evolution. Although Alibaba Cloud ranked third globally in market share in 2021, behind Amazon and Microsoft, and ranked first in the Asia-Pacific region, most of its business is concentrated in the domestic market. Similarly, Huawei Cloud and Tencent Cloud, ranked fifth and sixth globally, also primarily focus on the domestic market. This indicates that Chinese computing power companies urgently need to enhance their international competitiveness. On the other hand, although Chinese companies have made significant progress in data center hardware manufacturing in recent years, the "choke point" issue remains severe. The United States is leading the establishment of a closed chip alliance, "CHIP4," with Japan, South Korea, and Taiwan, aiming to strategically block China's access to advanced chip manufacturing technology, equipment, and talent, with the ultimate goal of excluding China from the global chip supply chain. While China holds key components and raw material supplies for the semiconductor industry and countries like Japan and South Korea are cautious about this alliance, the possibility of this goal being realized is not high. However, China must pay close attention to the international pressure faced by the high-quality development of its computing power industry and prepare in advance to achieve autonomous control of the industry's supply chain as soon as possible.

Strategic Thinking and Policy Recommendations for the High-Quality Development of Computing Power Economy

General Secretary Jinping Xi emphasized in the 34th collective study session of the Political Bureau of the Central Committee in October 2021 that China must continuously strengthen, optimize, and expand its digital economy. In the previous sessions of the 20th Chinese Academy of Sciences, the 15th Chinese Academy of Engineering, and the tenth National Congress of the China Association for Science and Technology, he made a series of important instructions on accelerating the construction of a technologically strong country and achieving high-level technological self-reliance and strength. General Secretary Jinping Xi's important discourse on the digital economy has provided strategic guidance for the high-quality development of China's computing power economy. Based on the constraints and strategic bottlenecks encountered in the development of computing power economy, the following thoughts and suggestions are proposed for the high-quality development of China's computing power economy.

First, it is crucial to deeply understand the strategic competitive landscape of global computing power economy development. Currently, the global computing power industry follows general trends in the computer industry, such as the continued relevance of Moore's Law in the field of computing chips. However, innovations in computing power theory and practice are undergoing transformative changes, with the exploration and development of quantum computing, photonic computing, and brain-inspired computing potentially leading a new revolution in the computing power industry. China's deep technological accumulation and research progress in these areas will help drive leapfrog development of the computing power industry during the "14th Five-Year Plan" period. Therefore, China urgently needs to grasp the pulse of global changes in computing power technology and industry, actively create an innovation ecosystem that promotes the high-quality development of the computing power economy, fully leverage the value discovery function of the capital market, provide precise financing services to maximize the innovative potential of market players in the computing power industry, deepen independent R&D, empower the real economy, and break through the key technological bottlenecks limiting the high-quality development of the computing power economy, thereby strengthening China's competitive advantage in the computing power industry.

Second, it is essential to quickly master the key technologies required for the high-quality development of the computing power economy. From the perspective of global trends in computing power technology and industry development, both developed countries and emerging or developing countries with related development foundations do not want to miss the opportunity to lead the new round of industrial development driven by big data, computing power, algorithms, and other technologies. Mastering core technologies is the prerequisite for seeking leadership in industrial competition. Currently, China's computing power industry still relies to some extent on external supply for foundational technologies and key manufacturing. If there is extreme pressure or a sudden disruption in supply, it will severely impact the normal operation and development of the industry, exposing the vulnerabilities and risks of the industrial system, which are increasingly apparent in an uncertain world. Therefore, it is essential to approach this issue with a sense of urgency, fully leverage the advantages of the new national system, focus on overcoming the key core technologies and frontier technologies that restrict the high-quality development of the computing power economy, and also respect scientific principles and industrial development laws. Strategic leadership from top talent should guide the high-quality development of the computing power economy, fostering a broad and continuous exploration of foundational technologies and key manufacturing capabilities among powerful market players.

Third, it is crucial to foster the industrial competitive ecosystem required for the high-quality development of the computing power economy. In the context of digital transformation being a significant feature of human society and economic development in the twenty-first century, the innovation ecosystem and corresponding industrial competitive ecosystem that support the development of the digital economy, including the computing power economy, must be continuously optimized. This requires the government to not only focus on advancing major technological and platform developments but also align with the trend of computing power-driven industrial innovation and technological transformation. The government should guide the computing power economy to develop along a path that respects human rationality and serves the creation of a better life for humanity. Additionally, it must strengthen legislative protection and compliance in areas such as data development and utilization, data asset pricing, privacy protection, and public safety. It is also essential to correctly manage the relationship between the government and private enterprises that hold massive amounts of data in terms of data ownership and usage. Based on the goal of expanding, strengthening, and optimizing the computing power industry, the government should lead the establishment of a sound open-source operational mechanism, with particular emphasis on supporting financial services, transportation, healthcare, and other sectors that significantly contribute to enhancing economic development. This will help collectively improve the core competitiveness of platform enterprises and foster the industrial competitive ecosystem necessary for the high-quality development of the computing power economy.

Fourth, combining high-level openness and international cooperation with self-reliance and control. The computing power economy, due to its inherent technological foresight and strategic leadership, has already become and will continue to be a key area of strategic competition among major global economies. While the U.S., EU, and Japan are highly vigilant of each other, they have also been cautious about the technological progress and industrial development of emerging economies. In particular, the United States has introduced a series of measures in recent years aimed at suppressing China's computing power industry, including sanctions and attempts to create exclusive "small circles" and "high walls." These actions have severely deviated from the principles of technological and global industrial development, disrupting the exchange and cooperation between governments and enterprises worldwide. This poses a significant challenge to China's efforts in conducting international cooperation in the computing power field.

However, the trend of global economic integration is irreversible. China must not only pay close attention to and take effective measures to overcome the many constraints that limit international cooperation in the computing power industry, but also seize the opportunity to actively participate in international digital economy organizations and steadily advance the construction of the "Digital Silk Road." By adhering to high-level openness, China can strengthen international cooperation between governments, enterprises, and civil society to jointly promote the development of the computing power economy. On the other hand, achieving self-reliance and control over key core technologies in computing power is always the foundational logic for high-quality development in the computing power economy. Key core technologies cannot be bought; China must firmly grasp the initiative in the development of computing power.

Chapter 14
Shared Prosperity under the Logic of Global Cooperation

China Firmly Holds the Initiative in Opening-Up, Unleashing Long-Term Development Dividends

On July 6, 2018, the United States, which had long dominated the global economic, trade, and financial division of labor since 1944, undermined the cornerstone of Sino-US relations and launched a trade friction. In recent years, the United States has employed various tactics to dismantle the global political, economic, and security framework, with only one goal: to reshape its superpower role in this changing world.

Undeniably, the United States is the most powerful country in the world today. However, when focusing on China's substantial trade surplus in the economic and trade relations between the two countries, it overlooks deliberately several critical points: the US's longstanding service trade surplus with China, as well as the huge annual returns of American enterprises operating in China. It also ignores the importance of the trillions of dollars of U.S. treasury bonds held by China which supports the economic growth and government spending of the United States.

The United States is determined to break the "American consume—Chinese produce" division of labor pattern, with the intention of undermining China's core interests within the global value chain, eroding China's wealth accumulated since the reform and opening up to bottom, and preventing China from catching up with the United States in real economy.

However, America cannot short the trade system of China, the second largest economy in the world, in today's highly integrated global economic and trade system, even if it is the only superpower in the world. Moreover, after over 40 years of reform and opening up, China has already formed a highly open and conscious society. It not only keeps on devoting itself to significantly relaxing market access and continuously improving the investment environment, but also to opening up import channels and actively expanding imports of high-quality products. It is also committed to building bilateral and multilateral free trade systems, releasing the

Y. Zhang, *Addressing Uncertainty*, Understanding China,
https://doi.org/10.1007/978-981-92-2692-4_14

dividends of China's reform and development to both domestic and foreign participants through vast market space and growing demand for products and services.

British people with deep financial intuition believed that RMB internationalization would release the largest financial dividend in the evolution of international monetary system in the first half of the twenty-first century as early to a few years ago. Therefore, the UK has made great efforts to build London into an offshore center for the Chinese yuan and a gateway for the Chinese capital market to connect with international investors in recent years, in order to share the dividends of RMB internationalization and consolidate London's position as an international financial center.

China has grown from a backward economy almost isolated from the global production and trade chain 40 or so years ago to one of the only two super economies in the world today, with a GDP exceeding 10 trillion US dollars. The underlying reason for this achievement is that China seeks stable development and international cooperation through a gradual opening-up logic. In fact, thanks to over 40 years of opening up to the outside world and deepening reforms, China has become one of the countries with the strongest supply capacity for industrial manufactured goods in the world, as well as a trading power deeply embedded in the global value chain.

China is widely recognized as one of the foremost beneficiaries of economic globalization, therefore, China will never be that foolish to lock itself in solitary room. With China's initial completion of industrialization and commitment to further opening up, the dividends released by China to international markets, including the US market, are no longer limited to general market opportunity sharing, but rather systematic products and services of high-quality and affordable prices. This process brought long-term and stable benefits to consumers from worldwide, including the US. Obviously, rational market entities will not easily give up this welfare. It should be a rational arrangement between governments and enterprises of all countries to promote further opening up of the economic and financial system and to facilitate trade.

The first wave of dividends released to the international market by China's reform and opening up spanned from 1978, when it started, to 2000, when China joined the WTO. During this era, China has mainly provided business opportunities based on joint ventures and sole proprietorships, market supply that had long been in short, primary products and high-quality products with affordable price to international investors and consumers. The second wave of is between 2001 to 2016, when China kept on providing international investors with investment opportunities for real industry along the extension of the trade value chain, and various benefits brought by the continuous opening up of the financial market.

Since the 19th National Congress of the Communist Party of China in 2017, China has implemented a wide array of major opening-up measures, including significantly relaxing market access, publishing the implementation schedule of opening measures of the financial industry beyond expectation, building free trade ports, further optimizing the business environment, continuously shortening the negative list for foreign investment access, especially focusing on strengthening intellectual property protection, explicitly opposing forced technology transfer, and actively expanding imports, etc. These actions demonstrated China's open mindedness of comprehensively expanding opening-up to the outside world as an important lever to promote economic development and economic globalization.

The expanding Chinese market will not shut its door to the United States. The strategic value of the economic relationship between China and the United States should extend far beyond their annual bilateral trade volume of about $700 billion or concerns over the US government, but far more from just data concentrating at the $383 billion trade deficit. This relationship is not merely a matter about how the two super economies, ranked first and second of world's economic scale, face a series of tricky problems in today's world. In fact, global economic development, trade growth, and financial stability all call on Chinese and American decision-makers to eliminate disagreements, promote the free flow of goods and capital, find the greatest common denominator in the development of economic and trade relations between the two countries, and gain benefits from sharing and win-win situations.

The global economic development history of the past 300 years has proven that free trade is the optimal path for countries to achieve complementary advantages in their factor endowments in increasingly globalized production and trade. American leaders may want to review the core ideas presented by Friedman in *Capitalism and Freedom*, which had a significant impact on President Reagan's economic policies. This representative figure of the Chicago School advocated for active non-intervention by the government throughout his life, as well as free trade and reduced tariffs. No unilateral or multilateral force in the world today can easily divide China's core value chain. The US's attempts to replicate its strategy against China is counterproductive. Cooperative game theory is the appropriate strategy choice.

China's Deepened Openness Injects New Momentum into Globalization

The Special Management Measures for Foreign Investment Access (Negative List) released in 2018 further narrowed the scope of foreign investment approval, marking the substantive stage of China's comprehensive opening up of market access across the primary, secondary, and tertiary industries. This negative list involves the opening up of 22 sectors including finance, transportation, commercial circulation, professional services, manufacturing, infrastructure, energy, resources, agriculture, etc., which have long been targeted by foreign investment. Multinational companies with greatly sensitive senses have already launched relevant layouts in indicator open cities like Shanghai. The most representative example would be Tesla, the first wholly foreign-owned automobile manufacturing enterprise post-Negative list, signed an agreement with Shanghai Municipal Government to build a Tesla super factory in Shanghai that integrates research, manufacturing, sales and other functions. As one of the world's most attractive markets, China has done solid work in matching international business logic, and relevant financial institutions in Shanghai will provide syndicated loan services for Tesla to build the factory in China.

On the other hand, according to the *European Business in China Business Confidence Survey 2018*,[1] more than half of its member companies plan to expand their operations in China. Earlier that year, the world's second and fourth largest economies, China and Germany not only signed over 20 cooperation agreements in areas such as economy and trade, new energy vehicles, technology, and agriculture, with a total amount of nearly 30 billion US dollars, but also jointly appealed opposition to the trade war and advocated for practical cooperation to uphold multilateralism.

China especially needs to maintain the determination of national development and the foresight of foreign policy, to grasp the trend of global economic development precisely, to defend globalization and free trade resolutely at this key period when anti-globalization (in a sense) and obvious trade protectionism tendencies may become sever constraints on global economic growth and trade development, and the driving force preference for promoting globalization in major developed countries has significantly declined. The more uncertain the global economy is, the more it is necessary to further integrate and even lead economic globalization through deep opening up, and enhance China's economic competitiveness and resilience to external shocks in participating in the process of global economic integration.

It is generally believed that globalization has been hindered by protectionism in recent years, largely due to the lack of momentum for US to continue promoting globalization, or because of the absence of effective alternatives to allow other engines to enter the existing power system when US refused to step on the accelerator. In other words, when the United States, as the biggest promoter and beneficiary of globalization, discovered that the trend of globalization and the explicit and implicit benefits it brings are increasingly beyond control, and its willingness and ability to pay for globalization are inevitably decreasing, the rise of "anti-globalization" isolationism becomes a phased expression of state behavior. And the UK, which already has a certain sense of community of shared destiny with the United States, chose Brexit. It is also an expression of the exquisite and rational nationalism that the UK, which still has ambitions but has significantly declined in strength, has always adopted.

If viewed from the perspective of global economic competition and pattern changes, the decline of globalization is due to the fact that developed countries, which used to play the most important driving force of economic globalization, have shown a certain degree of uneasy as emerging countries grow stronger and more willing and capable of participating in global economic governance reforms. Since the Industrial Revolution, Europeans and Americans have long dominated

[1] Published in June 20th, 2018 by European Chamber.

global industries and financial capital. However, they now face discomfort with cross-border capital from emerging countries becoming important participants in global resource allocation. Although mainstream Western financial media believe that American companies remain at the helm of globalization, with the best of them already adept at cross-border management and allocating resources to regions yielding the highest returns. They also acknowledge that even if Apple were to build factories in the United States and pay American workers American level wages, it would take considerable time to match the manufacturing speed, precision, and flexibility it achieved with its partners in China. And this is under the assumption that the Chinese partners no longer improve ever after.

In fact, if we view from another perspective, the formation of the industrial division of labor between China and the United States since China's accession to the WTO has a quite reasonable side, and it is essentially a benefit-sharing mechanism. In this benefit sharing mechanism, China is clearly not the dominant party. Even within the global industrial chain division of labor represented by Apple, where China has benefited a lot, it remains totally a downstream worker. If, according to the logic of some Americans, even the products assembly part of the value chain for Apple products is to remain in the United States, it would likely prove neither practical nor economical for American industrial capital.

All rational market entities should understand that with the ongoing technological advancements, global market expansion and wealth reallocation are inevitable. The intrinsic momentum of globalization driven by free flow of factors and cost savings in transactions is also hard to contain. In today's world, no country or enterprise can ignore the interconnectedness of industrial chains, supply chains, service chains, and even value chains. No capital or national power can block the rational flow of global factors by building various barriers. In other words, politicians can satisfy the behavioral preferences of certain interest groups, and even the interest preference at the national level, through short-term policies, but it is almost impossible for them to single reverse globalization or completely withdraw from the existing track of globalization on their own.

As a responsible emerging power, China should unite and lead the participants of globalization to the greatest possible extent, promote the flow of capital, technology, and other related factors, while establishing a mechanism for sharing interests, continuously releasing the dividends of globalization, and lead globalization away from the "tragedy of the commons" dilemma inherent in its dynamic structure.

In today's world where guarantors of the global economy are facing structural deficiencies, self-interest at the national level is clearly on the rise, and free trade occasionally struggle to advance, China's concrete and deep opening-up actions are promoting further internationalization and facilitation of global resource allocation. This is not only a national behavior of providing new market opportunities to global market entities and releasing relevant opening-up dividends, but also reflects a firm will to inject fresh impetus into globalization constrained by uncertain factors interaction. History has proven and will continue to prove that globalization, though not Pareto optimal nor perfect, is an irreplaceable path for promoting effective global economic growth.

Why the "Pandemic Accelerates China–West Decoupling" Narrative Is Fallacious

In 2020, during the outbreak and duration of the COVID-19, Western media have successively commented on the impact of the epidemic, believing that it will accelerate the process of industrial chain decoupling between China and some developed countries, and may urge more multinational enterprises to rethink the vulnerability of relying on China's supply chain. Predictions were made that COVID-19 may lead to a great reshuffle of the industrial chain in Asia and even the whole world. However, even they acknowledged that no economy can easily replace China's pivotal role in the global supply chain at least for now.

Objectively speaking, it is understandable that Western media pay attention to the impact of the COVID-19 on China and the global economy and industry, and specially to the temporary difficulties faced by Western multinational enterprises in China. But as mainstream media, they should conduct professional analysis on the impact of the epidemic at that time based on comprehensive information and precise data, and release objective and thorough reports. Today, global economy and society heavily depend on information production and transmission; thus the media plays an increasingly important role in national and even global governance systems, which requires the media to always maintain rationality and a sense of responsibility.

This COVID-19 epidemic is an emergency, but such incidents are not new in human history. In fact, no country, society, or individual can remain isolated from various uncertainties. There is no doubt that the COVID-19 has had a certain impact on China's economy, but since China's reform and opening-up, especially since its accession to the WTO, the "most complete industrial chain in the world" has become better and better. It is impossible that because of this epidemic, there will be such a so-called "break" as portrayed by Western media, or the decoupling of the industrial chain between the world's two largest economies that some international trade skeptics have "expected".

Firstly, both the division and cooperation of labor in the industrial chain between China and the United States, as well as the formation and development of China as a global supply chain pivot, are grounded in inherent economic logic. They possess both cyclical and phased characteristics of global industrial production and industrial pattern changes, as well as stable characteristics within the cycle.

From the perspective of global industrial development history, from the second half of the eighteenth century to the 1980s, a global industrial division of labor pattern emerged, with Britain, the United States, and Japan serving sequentially as the "world factory" and "world manufacturing center", which lasted for about 200 years. Since China began deepening its reform and expanding opening-up since 1990s, it has swiftly grown into the world's largest exporter and manufacturer and has achieved relatively stable benefits in the division of labor in the global value chain, marked by its accession to the WTO in 2001. China has achieved so with improved foreign trade conditions, global industrial transfer, and relying on comparative

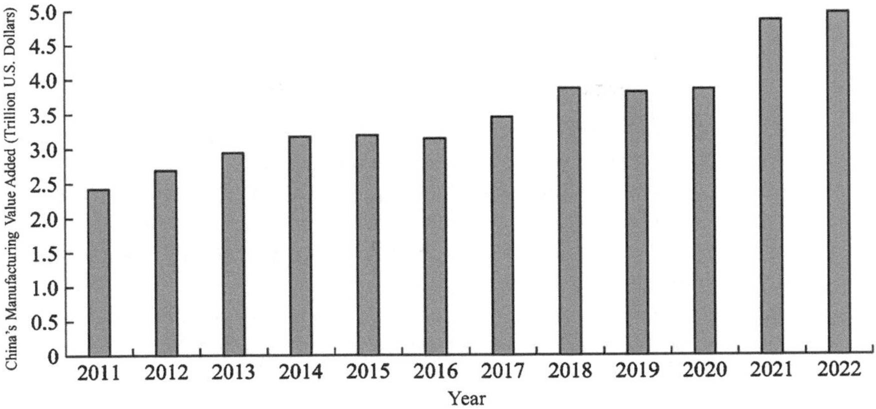

Fig. 14.1 China's manufacturing value added, 2011–2022. Data Source: National Bureau of Statistics of China

advantages like labor costs, at the same time. The added value of China's manufacturing industry has ranked first in the world for 13 consecutive years. From 2011 to 2022, this trend is illustrated in Fig. 14.1. China was also able to become an emerging economy with relatively complete high, medium, and low industrial chains in the global manufacturing industry around 2010.

Although major developed countries have implemented measures such as "re-industrialization" and "manufacturing return" around 2009, the results have been minimal so far. This underscores the difficulty even the most resource-integrated developed country governments face to shift the global industrial chain division of labor pattern by human will. Meanwhile, emerging countries such as India and Vietnam are not available with the basic conditions to replace China in the short term, due to constraints in infrastructure, economic development level, and related endowments. The author estimates that by around 2030, the division of labor in the global industrial chain will remain relatively stable.

Secondly, the enormous development dividends released by China to regions and the world based on the development of manufacturing, trade value chain upgrades, and deep and high-level financial opening will constitute the core link of the globalization dividend in the first half of the twenty-first century. These dividends also serve as an unstoppable force for global economic integration, transcending individuals' will.

China is progressively evolving from a manufacturing and trading power to an industrial and capital power by continuously expanding opening to the outside world and embedding itself into the global trade value chain. By leveraging sound institutional design, China is pioneering a new phase of economic opening-up, providing replicable business model design and regional and global financial services through the global allocation of high-quality production capacity. In addition, by enhancing relevant international coordination and mobilization capabilities, combined with the internationalization of the RMB and continuously released dividends of economic openness and foreign trade development, China has built a more dynamic internal and external economic linkage system.

Thirdly, in today's world of global economic integration, zero sum games cause no benefit but harm. For visionary politicians, business leaders, and other stakeholders, whether it is global economic growth, financial stability, trade rules improvement, industrial chains upgrading and changing, or effective resolution of complex issues such as trade disputes among countries, it cannot be achieved without respect for market regulations and international rules, as well as division of labor and cooperation based on consensus and coordination.

After years of debate and reflection, the irreversibility of globalization has once again become an international consensus. Given this reality, the whole world should work together to drive irrational impulses away.

"1+6" Round Table Dialogue: Prospects for China and the World Economy in the Post-Pandemic Era

From November 21 to 22, 2020, as the world was still grappling with the sever challenges posed by COVID-19, it was a crucial moment for testing global collective wisdom and national capacities for economic and social governance. During this time, the 15th G20 Leaders' Summit held in video format approved the G20 Actions to Support World Trade and Investment in Response to COVID-19, and achieved positive consensus on major issues such as developing the digital economy, maintaining multilateral trade, and achieving global economic and financial stability. These all demonstrated the determination of major economies in the world to work together to address common challenges.

Following the G20 summit, former Chinese Premier Li Keqiang held the fifth "1+6" Round table dialogue, along with heads of major international economic organizations, including David Malpass (World Band President),[2] Kristalina Georgieva (IMF Managing Director), Alan Wolff (former Deputy Director General of the WTO), Guy Ryder (ILO Director-General), Ángel Gurría (former OECD Secretary-General), and Randal Quarles (Financial Stability Board President), via video conference. They managed to discuss and exchange ideas on the world economic situation and global economic governance in the post pandemic era, China's development during the 14th Five Year Plan period, especially deepening reform and opening up. This was not only a simple continuation of the previous four successfully held round table dialogues, but also an international action by China and major international economic organizations to jointly solve major global economic

[2] David R. Malpass was the 13th President of the World Bank Group (WBG), April 9, 2019-June 1, 2023.

issues in the context of the lingering shadow of the pandemic and the serious interference of protectionism and unilateralism in the global trading system.

The "1+6" Round table, initiated in July 2016, represents a "new phenomenon" in the field of global economic governance in recent years, and there are not many related mechanism arrangements. From 2009 to 2016, China's economy experienced a leapfrog development with an annual growth of $1 trillion, jumping from $4 trillion to $11 trillion, contributing an average of over 30% to global economic growth. As a result, China turned to be the "anchor of stability" for the global economy. As the largest emerging economy, China has kept opening up and released development dividends to the world, providing new public goods like the Asian Infrastructure Investment Bank during this period.

In this context, regular round table dialogues between Chinese leaders and heads of the six major international economic organizations serve not only as a window for the international community to understand China's major economic policy trends and development plans, but also an important platform for China to exchange views and jointly seek solutions to major global issues with major international economic organizations. The round table dialogues indicate that major international economic organizations valued China's expanding marginal role and influence in global economic governance more, which is closely related to China's responsible image as a major power in responding to the 2008 international financial crisis.

In response to the 2008 international financial crisis, China not only stabilized its economic fundamentals through effective macro policies, but also stabilized the global financial market through practical actions. China plays a crucial role in driving global economy recovery and demonstrates international responsibility as an emerging power within the G20 framework. As is known to all, since the G20 came into being as a global economic governance platform jointly run by developed and developing countries, it has played a stabilizing role in dealing with the critical moments of major crisis tests, including the financial crisis, COVID-19 and so on. The G20 has actually replaced the G7 as the main force in global economic governance. This significant shift mostly indicates that developed countries have accepted the necessity and importance of developing countries' participation in global governance at the technological level, and also shows that the era of superpowers solely responsible for the stability of the global economic and financial system since the establishment of the Bretton Woods system has come to an end.

In practice, multilateral financial institutions such as the IMF and the World Bank are witnessing strengthened cooperation among the United States, as the actual leading country, and developing countries such as China. For example, China's voting rights in the World Bank and IMF have risen to third place, inferior only to the United States and Japan. Among the top 10 members with the largest IMF shares, 4 are developing countries (China, Brazil, India, and Russia). China's position in the governance structures of the two major organizations mentioned above has also been improved.

The G20 Hangzhou Summit especially marked China's active leading role in global economic governance as an important milestone. At the summit, China convinced the theme of "building an innovative, dynamic, interconnected, and inclusive world economy." It also comprehensively explained its global economic governance concept to the world for the first time during the summit, through President Xi Jinping's keynote speech and a series of bilateral or multilateral action initiatives. It also first placed development issues in a prominent position in global macro policy coordination, and formed a global multilateral investment rule framework. What's more, it first released a presidential statement on climate change and included "green finance" to the G20 agenda. These firsts indicated that China not only has the capability to design important issues in global economic governance, but also has the ability to coordinate and take action, thus establishing China's position as an active leader in global economic governance. Since then, countries have increasingly prioritized aligning their economic policies with China.

The "1+6" Round table not only helps China to further understand the policy direction of major international economic organizations, enhancing its subject consciousness and cooperation capacity in international economic governance, but also significantly facilitates the construction of bilateral and multilateral communication and coordination mechanisms for major international economic organizations on the basis of further understanding China's economic policy direction and development strategies.

As a major external variable, the huge impact of COVID-19 on the global economy has led to a large-scale resurgence of "depression economics", which once cornered the wisdom supply of global macroeconomists. The crisis can be regarded as an important benchmark for testing the resilience of economies in extraordinary times, as well as the stability and resilience of global industrial and supply chains. As the world's second largest economy and the first to be impacted by the epidemic, China's ability to stabilize its economic fundamentals in a relatively short time and become the only major economy in the world to achieve positive growth in 2020, as well as its comprehensive response capabilities and relevant experience summary response to major crises and risk tests, are clearly of great concern to the heads of major international economic organizations.

With the formulation of the 14th Five Year Plan and the proposal of long-term goals for 2035 at the Fifth Plenary Session of the 19th Central Committee of the Communist Party of China, China will accelerate the construction of a "dual circulation" development pattern, promote high-quality economic development with a more open mindset and courage, and release the dividends of reform and development to domestic and foreign market entities with vast market space and continuously expanding service demands. It is expected that the release of this dividend will be based on the upgrading and development of the manufacturing industry, the continuous improvement and industrial application of digital technology, high standards of opening-up, and the construction of the "the Belt and Road" and financial internationalization, which will constitute a new impetus for economic globalization and trade and investment facilitation in the first half of the twenty-first century.

Promoting economic growth, facilitating trade, maintaining financial stability, and leading the world towards a more balanced, open, inclusive, and mutually beneficial governance era are the historical missions that responsible global participants face together. At this critical moment, Chinese leaders and heads of the six major international economic organizations are jointly assessing China's and the world's economic outlook in the post-pandemic era, which is a key move to reignite global economic recovery.

China and the CPTPP: High-Standard Openness to Foster Regional Shared Prosperity

After China sent an important signal of its active consideration to join the CPTPP, the prospects of economic cooperation in the Asia-Pacific region and even across the Pacific have attracted worldwide attention, sparking optimistic expectations.

As the leading country of the CPTPP, Japan has reached a bilateral tariff reduction policy with China for the first time under the RCEP framework, signed in November 2020. The mutual benefits on imports and exports between China and Japan will significantly enhance the sense of gain for consumers in both countries. On the other hand, during the visit of then Chinese State Councilor Wang Yi, Japan also reached a consensus with China on jointly promoting the early implementation of RCEP, actively advancing negotiations on a free trade negotiation agreement among China, Japan, S. Korea, and regional cooperation processes.

Meanwhile, The Prime Minister of Australia, another crucial member of the CPTPP, highly affirmed China's economic development achievements and their spillover effects on the Australian and even global economy. The Australian Trade Minister also warmly welcomed China's intention to join the CPTPP. It is evident that regional entities with robust capabilities harbor high expectations of China. As the paramount driving force for global economic growth and the hub of global value and supply chains, China's deep integration into regional economic and trade integration will definitely bring incremental dividends.

Regarding the CPTPP and its predecessor, *the Trans Pacific Partnership* (TPP), it is indisputable that these regional trade groups with certain political senses, have always been characterized by high standards and strict requirements throughout the negotiation and signing process. To this day, The CPTPP has been considered the highest standard free trade agreement in the world. It should be mentioned that as the leading country of the CPTPP, Japan pragmatically suspended some provisions that posed uniform implementation after the United States withdrew from the TPP, but still preserved 95% of them, achieving a good balance.

What else shall be mentioned is that China's previously targeted standards for state-owned enterprises, designated monopolies, labor standards, competition policies, environmental protection, and other aspects have actually become strict standards that are no longer difficult to connect and implement with China's deepening reforms and high-level opening up in related fields in recent years. Even the sensitive issue of intellectual property protection is anticipated to be smoothly resolved with China's significant progress in this field.

The target set for relevant key reform areas in *the CPC Central Committee's proposals for formulating the 14th Five-Year Plan (2021–2025) for National Economic and Social Development and the Long-Range Objectives Through the Year 2035* adopted at the Fifth Plenary Session of the 19th Central Committee, underscore China's unwavering commitment. Whether it is the construction of a high-standard market system, property rights system reform and market-oriented factor allocation reform, or the establishment and improvement of a fair competition system and the construction of a new system of higher-level open economy, or even the settlement of the high-standard design and implementation timetable for ecological civilization construction, all reflect China's determination to devote itself to the standard and timetable with a spirit of "time waits for no one", and further promote deep level reform and high-level opening up to achieve high-quality development.

Therefore, after concluding RCEP with its largest trading partner ASEAN, as well as important trading partners such as Japan, South Korea, Australia, and New Zealand, China has taken the initiative to align with the CPTPP, distinguished by stringent rule-based access. This is not merely a full confidence in China's economic reform and opening-up achievements based on a careful evaluation of the agreement, but also an optimistic expectation for the reform progress in the medium and long-term development period from the 14th Five Year Plan to 2035, based on the high overlap of zero tariff coverage in the field of goods trade between RCEP and CPTPP.

As for the current situation of regional economic and trade cooperation and bilateral or multilateral economic and trade relations, the expectations of CPTPP members (including the potential member United States) for China to join the agreement may be no less intense than China's own. Take the economic and trade relations between the core members of CPTPP, Japan and South Korea, and China for instance. In 2012, during the golden age of Sino-Japanese trade, bilateral trade volume between the two countries reached 329.45 billion US dollars, yet it fell below this level in 2020. As for the trade between China and South Korea, the bilateral trade volume between the two countries in 2012 was 215.1 billion US dollars, and the trade with China accounting for 20% of South Korea's total foreign trade. In 2013, the bilateral trade volume between China and South Korea approached 300 billion US dollars. However, 7 years later, in 2020, the bilateral trade volume between China and South Korea was only 285.58 billion US dollars. (See Fig. 14.2 for details).

Financial leaders and market professionals in Japan and South Korea are well aware that as the world's most promising large market, China's cumulative commodity imports are expected to exceed 22 trillion US dollar in the next 10 years. Such colossal purchasing power of the market is undoubtedly an easy development dividend for Japan and South Korea, which are struggling with weak external demand. Therefore, although Japan still occasionally yearns for the flying geese paradigm of East Asian economic development proposed in the past, facing the fact that China's economic scale has completely surpassed Japan's, and facing China's

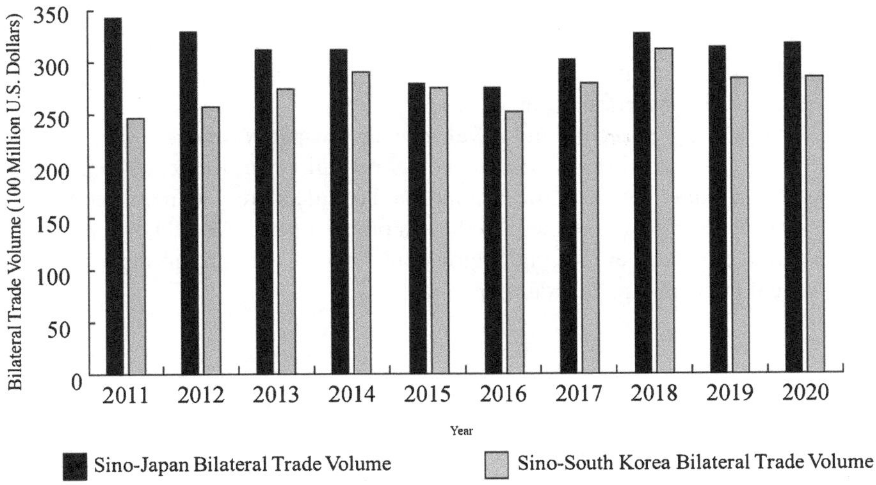

Fig. 14.2 Bilateral trade volume between China-Japan, and China-South Korea, 2011–2020. Data Source: National Bureau of Statistics of China

growing trade power and strong "purchasing power", it naturally hopes that China can join the CPTPP at the right time.

From the perspective changes of global industrial development and in patterns of division of labor, as well as changes in the export of industrial capital from leading industrialized countries, the pattern of "China produce and US consume" formed by China and the United States around 2007 will face certain degree of rupture after 10 years due to the economic and trade friction between the two country. However, the trend of China's economic development and the improvement of its trade value chain will not be interrupted. As long as the Chinese economy can maintain an average annual effective growth rate of around 5%, the size of the Chinese economy will surpass that of the United States by 2035, and China will also become the world's largest capital exporting country and the largest consumer market by then.

For over a decade, China has been playing a crucial core role in the global value chain. Recent studies have shown that global value chains account for nearly three-quarters of the growth share in global trade, with China being the most important source of this growth, commanding nearly one-third of the global supply of intermediate goods. As China has been committed to moving towards the mid-to-high end of the global value chain, it has begun to play a pivotal role in the global industrial chain. China has not only ascended to the high end of the global value chain in fields such as information and high-end equipment manufacturing, but also formed an international division of labor pattern with China as the upstream country and regional manufacturing centers such as Vietnam as the downstream country in the mid-to-low end of the global industrial chain division of labor.

From historical experience, it is difficult for the world's largest economy to maintain its status as both the largest producer and consumer in the long run. This indicates that China is likely to exist as the world's largest importer in the global trade pattern in the first half of the twenty-first century and continue to release import dividends. This is undoubtedly a huge opportunity for CPTPP members to promote their economic development.

Regional and global economic development, prosperity, and stability call for internationally responsible decision-makers from all countries to transcend disagreements, promote the free flow of goods and capital, and benefits of facilitation and sharing. If China can join the CPTPP in a proper time, it would unleash a positive external effect of enhancing regional prosperity and promoting symbiotic development through high-standard open docking.

China Removes Barriers to CPTPP Accession through Openness

Relevant reports indicate that China has engaged in technical negotiations with many members of the CPTPP, and analyzed that the attitude of the United States and its allies may be a key influencing factor in China's application for approval. From a technical perspective, there are no fundamental obstacles preventing China to join the CPTPP. The attitude of Japan, as the leading country of the CPTPP, and of the more influential stance of the United States hod significance, but China's own will and open mindedness are paramount.

The CPTPP and its predecessor TPP are essentially mega-regional trade blocs based on the characteristics of the US-Japan paradigm. This model shares some commonalities with the past when economic globalization mainly served the global allocation of capital, technology, and resources for developed countries or regions such as Europe, America, and Japan. But in today's world the economic, technological, and trade landscape have undergone fundamental changes, with emerging countries and developing nations now jointly drive global economic growth and facilitate trade and investment. These countries are deeply involved in the process of economic globalization and have formed a systematic and orderly division of labor system with developed countries.

Although China has become a major economy with relatively complete high, medium, and low industrial chains in the global manufacturing industry around 2010, and has occupied nearly one-third of the global intermediate goods supply as well as has confirmed its core hub position in the global industrial and supply chains with massive export data, the highly complementary industrial and trade division of labor between China and developed countries such as the United States and Japan will remain relatively stable in the foreseeable future.

The industrial division of labor has been deeply integrated into the international economic system, especially in Chinese economy, the global value chain system. To achieve the upgrading and optimization of the industrial structure, it is inseparable from the improvement of the supply capacity of local enterprises based on independent technological innovation, as well as the deep participation of foreign investment, particularly the early establishment of a high-standard market system. In recent years, China has implemented the Pre-establishment National Treatment and Negative List model, promoted the all-round opening up of modern service industries, manufacturing industries, and agriculture to the outside world, and allowed foreign investment to hold or operate in more sectors like financial services and high-end manufacturing. The formal implementation of the "Foreign Investment Law" and "Regulations on Optimizing the Business Environment", along with the abolition of the case-by-case approval system for foreign investments exemplifies this open approach in policy.

The widened market access, continuous optimization of the business environment, and the enhancing intellectual property rights protection indicate that, in the context of the overall irreversible trend of global economic and trade integration and deep association of the global value chain, China continues to release dividends to the international market with more active and open institutional arrangements, and that China is also taking practical actions to eliminate the so-called "Samuelson's worries" raised by trade protectionists.

To sum up, although economic and trade globalization is not perfect, it remains an irreplaceable path to foster effective global economic growth and maintain the integrity of industrial and supply chains. China, committed to improve its market system standards, will not avoid any high-standard free trade agreements, including the CPTPP, and will work together with major economies to build a better new world by deeply participating in and even leading the process of globalization.

The "Golden Age" of Emerging Markets Is Far from over

In July 2021, *The Economist*, a British weekly magazine, published an article on its official website to downplaying the economic growth prospects of emerging markets. It argued that due to the impacts of COVID-19, global economic turbulence, protectionism, insufficient financial resources and other factors, emerging markets may bid farewell to the "golden age" in advance and lose the time window to catch up with and surpass wealthy countries again.

Viewing these analyses as kind of cautionary insights, they retain certain reference value. Objectively speaking, countries such as Brazil, Russia, and South Africa in emerging markets have indeed encountered sever economic challenges in recent years. In particular, under the impact of the COVID-19 from 2020 to 2021, Brazil's national governance was on the verge of bankruptcy, leading to serious economic contraction, substantial currency devaluation, sharp increase in deficits, public debt and a growing impoverished population. Consequently, Brazil's GDP fell out of the top ten in the world. In the first half of 2019, just before the outbreak of the epidemic, Brazil announced in the WTO that it upgraded its status as a developing country to a developed country. It can be seen that under the impact of the major external variable, the COVID-19, the resilience or systemic loss-absorbing capacity of Brazil's overall economic system is far from reaching the level of a standard power.

In addition, the Russian economy is facing serious challenges due to the dual impact of COVID-19 and the US sanctions. However, Russia, which is rich in oil and gas resources and holds an important position in regional and global oil and gas supply, has overall better economic fundamentals compared to Brazil.

As for India, which brimming with confidence, it has also lost its former luster under the impact of the pandemic. In 2020, its per capital GDP fell below $2000, and the momentum of catching up with developed countries has weakened. Therefore, at the key moment when global economy is facing uncertainty, Western public opinions pointing out the problems existing in emerging markets is conducive to helping relevant countries rationally position their own development coordinates.

But what they fail to point out is that many of the economic challenges confronting emerging markets are not unique to themselves, but rather universal international issues. In fact, the overall economic performance of G7 members such as the United States and the United Kingdom have also been lackluster under the impact of the pandemic. Their national governance has faced difficulties even verging on failure: the economy has shrunk significantly, the currency has been severely over issued, the government has been borrowing to survive, large-scale bankruptcies of enterprises, soaring unemployment rates among the ordinary people, and so on. If we apply the title of *The Economist*'s commentary on emerging markets, it can totally be described that "Unrest and economic under performance haunt the emerging world." Moreover, if analyzed from a historical and reality perspective, the economic difficulties faced by many emerging economies are to some extent caused by the former suzerain countries and today's "preacher". They are the bitter fruit of these emerging economies disregarding their own national conditions, blindly copying the economic models of developed countries, or blindly following the economic policies of the United States.

In addition, similar pessimistic rhetoric in the West intentionally overlooks China's current development status and growth potential as the world's largest emerging economy. China is not only an important member of the BRICS, but also the member with the strongest economic strength. In 2020, China's GDP exceeded 14.7 trillion US dollars, accounting for over 70% of the total GDP of BRICS. It can be said that China is the most qualified country to represent emerging markets. This can also be seen from the 2021 *Fortune* "Global 500 list", where China has a total of 143 companies on the list, ranking first in the world in terms of the number of companies on the list. What's more, countries with more than 10 companies on the list, except for China, are all developed countries. It is worth noting that emerging economies such as India, Brazil, and Russia, despite facing certain economic difficulties in recent years, still have 7, 6, and 4 companies respectively selected on the list, indicating that these countries' companies still maintain considerable international competitiveness.

It should also be mentioned that today's emerging markets are no longer limited to BRICS, but encompass other emerging economies among G20 members, as well as developing countries with large population bases and good economic development momentum such as Vietnam, the Philippines, Bangladesh, Nigeria, etc.

Statistics show that in 2020, Indonesia was among the 16 countries with a GDP exceeding 1 trillion US dollars worldwide. As the fourth most populous country in the world, Indonesia's medium to long-term economic development prospects may surpass Brazil's. As for Vietnam, with a population of nearly 100 million and rapidly developing foreign trade, it is widely regarded as an emerging economy with significant value in the global supply and industrial chains. In 2020, Vietnam's total import and export volume reached 545 billion US dollars, which is equivalent to one seventh of the United States'. Relying on its abundant population dividend, advantageous geographical location, and industrial docking capabilities, Vietnam is expected to further elevate its economic development level in the future.

From the perspective of global trends in industry, technology transfer, and capital allocation, emerging markets will continue to maintain a relatively optimistic growth trend in the first half of the twenty-first century, thanks to opening-up to the outside world, demographic dividends, and continuously emerging market space and consumption potential, although fluctuations and even setbacks for a certain time are inevitable.

Under the wave of digitization, the medium to long-term growth of emerging markets will increasingly depend on core endogenous variables such as increasing returns to scale, technological progress, and human capital growth brought about by knowledge, information, research and development, or innovation. Especially emerging economies represented by China will continue to lead a new round of economic globalization through high-level reform and opening up, global allocation of high-quality production capacity, and sustained release of market and consumption dividends, and further drive the overall development of emerging market economies in this process.

China Aligns with the CPTPP through Building a High-Standard Market System

China's bit to join CPTPP has risen a wide attention, which is universally recognized by the public opinion as the mark of the determination and action for the world's second largest economy to continuously drive a higher standard opening up.

The Global Trade and Investment System Is Undergoing Restructuring

2021 marked the 20th anniversary of China's accession to the WTO. China has roughly gone through three stages of learning to adapt, understanding to apply and deeply involving to international trade and investment rules during its 20 years in WTO.

The progress China has made is remarkable to the world both in the negotiation of global trading rules and the practice of global trade. It has become an integral part of global economic system, not only as the biggest goods trading country of the world but also with a long run progress in the service trade field.

According to the statistical data, during the 13th Five Year Plan period (2016–2020), China's cumulative import and export of service trade reached 3.6 trillion US dollars, achieving an increase of 29.7% compared to the previous Five Year Plan period (2011–2015). It is now, the second largest service trade country in the world after the United States, which has earned a huge surplus in service trade with China for a long time.

Moreover, China also serves as a linchpin in three major chains in the world today, namely the industrial chain, supply chain, and value chain.

Of course, there are some sorts of scattered, blocked, or national egoism trend in global trade, which further hindered the integration of the global economy. Frictions appeared frequently among major economies, and it harmed welfare of the broad consumers while increasing the trade cost. Even the WTO, as the most important benchmark of global commercial liberalism, once faced existential threats due to such pressures.

These all make it particularly necessary to reshape the global trading system and promote the development of global economic governance towards openness, inclusiveness, orderliness, and nondiscrimination. In recent years, international trade and investment rules have increasingly focused on regional trade agreements (RTAs) concluded between countries, like USMCA and RCEP. On the other hand, as the cornerstone of global free trade, the WTO is also facing enormous pressure for reform.

The CPTPP not only needs to find an effective mechanism for resolving endless trade disputes among its members, but also needs to adapt to new changes in global trade. Especially, the digital economy and digital trade of various countries have made rapid progress in recent years while many countries and regions have comprehensively promoted digital transformation, giving rise to new formats, models, and application scenarios of digital trade, greatly accelerating the digitalization process of global trade, and even establishing digital trade as a dominant force in the global market to a certain extent. It is urgent for all countries to work together to establish international standards for digital trade. It is also the driving force and urgency for the WTO to undergo self-reform to adapt to technological progress and trade development.

Not Merely a Second "WTO Accession"

I do not quite agree with the notion that China's accession to the CPTPP is akin to a second "accession to the WTO". Although in terms of time, this is a major international economic and trade action taken by China 20 years after its accession to the WTO, it represents a natural progress in China's economic development, a logical expression of its promotion of high-level opening up and the construction of a high-standard market system; Furthermore, it is an endogenous need for China to build a modern economic system, improve the socialist market economy system, and deeply integrate into global trade and investment as well as the new round of industrial division of labor.

According to *China's WTO Accession Protocol*, China should have been recognized as a "market economy country" on December 11, 2016, 15 years after its accession. In legal terms, these clauses made at China's accession were called the "sunset clauses", which means that according to the protocol, no matter what happens, the clauses would automatically terminate on December 11, 2016, and transform China into a market economy country. However, developed economies such as Europe, America, and Japan have been reluctant to recognize China's status as market economy. The reason is simple. In their view, once China is regarded as a market economy country, it would be much more difficult to throw anti-dumping lawsuits against China, and grants China's exports to major trading partners greater advantages. Just as the saying goes that any major economic issue is a political issue, and that's the truth.

However, China's process of expanding its opening up to the world and accelerating the construction of a high-standard market system remains unwavering. China has not only prioritized the construction of a high-standard market system, the establishment and improvement of a fair competition system, the construction of a new system for higher-level open economy, the reform of the property rights system and the reform of market-oriented factors allocation in economic reform in the 14th Five Year Plan and 2035 long-term goals. It also released *China unveils action plan on building high-standard market system*, aiming for basic completion of a unified, open, competitive, well regulated, and well governed high-standard market system by around 2035.

In fact, China, with sharpening market intuition and growing international competitiveness, emphasizes more applying the five fundamental elements for an effectively operating market as important reference frames for building it, and also building a competent government, namely information symmetry, integrity, perfect competition, effective and appropriate protection of property rights, and minimizing the negative utility of third parties.

Stepping for a Mature Market Economy

Aspects like China's previous targeted state-owned enterprises and designated monopolies, labor protection, competition policy, financial regulation, and environmental protection, etc., have actually become no longer a strict standard that is difficult to attach to and to implement compared to the recognized highest standard free trade agreement in the world today, CPTPP, after the deepening reforms and high-level opening up in related fields in recent years, especially the introduction of measures such as negative lists, foreign investment access, and market oriented processes.

Even the sensitive protection of intellectual property rights is expected to be easily resolved with China's significant progress in this field in recent years.

The Opinions on Ideological and Political Work in the New Era released in July 2021 showed that almost every policy of reform and opening up signifies an orderly alignment between China and the world's highest standards of openness.

According to the relevant plans, Shanghai Pudong would achieve two-way docking between onshore and offshore RMB assets, creating a highly coordinated market. That is to say, it would incorporate standardized financial products such as stocks, bond, foreign exchange, futures, insurance, bills and non-standard financial products like trust assets, asset management, and debt financing, into the category of tradable international financial assets, and conduct transactions on platforms with international access or that currently without but can find international interfaces. It would also require to combine Shanghai's positioning as a bridgehead for the construction of the "the Belt and Road" and a forefront for high-level reform and opening up, based on appropriately referring the trading and development path of the global dollar asset system.

To successfully achieve the goals above, it is necessary to prepare a check list for Shanghai Pudong in areas such as market access, market pricing, international integration of trading systems and legal arrangements, with the support of the state.

Therefore, China's bid to join the CPTPP not only marks the determination of the world's most dynamic emerging economy to deeply integrate into the world's highest standard free trade agreement, but also reflects China's logical arrangement of accelerating market access reform, industrial regulation, and economic upgrading in promoting the construction of a high-standard market system.

Twenty Years after WTO Accession: Exploring the Economic Logic of Global Shared Prosperity

It is without question that if we were to select the best practices of emerging economies in the first half of the twenty-first century, particularly those driving economic growth and national modernization through opening up to the outside world, China would definitely be the most representative sample of major countries.

Former German Chancellor Merkel stated in a 2021 interview with domestic media about China's economic achievements that when she first took office in 2005, China's GDP was 2.2 trillion US dollars, slightly below Germany's 2.8 trillion US dollars. By 2020, China's GDP had reached 14.7 trillion US dollars, while Germany's GDP is 3.8 trillion US dollars (Fig. 14.3). In Merkel's view, although Germany remains a relatively prosperous country, its economic scale clearly pales in comparison to China's, which is also an important reason why Germany must maintain close economic ties with China.

Merkel has been known for her rationality and prudence, as one of the most international respected politicians of the twenty-first century. She guided Germany

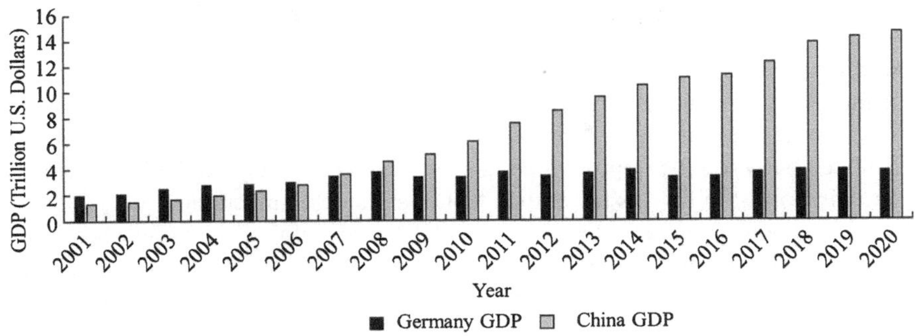

Fig. 14.3 Comparison of GDP between China and Germany, 2011–2020. Data Source: National Bureau of Statistics of China; German Federal Statistical Office

to remarkable economic achievement during her past 16 years leadership. To Germany, China's economic and trade achievements since joining the WTO in 2001, and its increasing needs for goods and consumption have provided huge export market for German products and also become a significant resource for Germany to import high quality products and services.

The rationale behind I viewing Germany and Sino-German trade as critical observation points for analyzing the national effects and global value of China's accession to the WTO is that Germany is one of the major developed countries in the world, with a relatively balanced economic structure and a stable system for a long time.

It is also one of China's major trading partners with the closest bilateral economic and trade ties, the most stable relationships, and the highest respective benefits. It can be said that although Germany is thousands of miles away from China, it is an economic neighbor that transcends geography and institutions, and is also a typical representative of promoting economic prosperity through trade and investment between countries.

As is well known, China's opening-up started without a pre-existing blueprint. China's accession to the WTO went through 15 years of arduous negotiations, during which negotiators aged from "black hair" to "white hair". Finally, on December 11, 2001, China officially joined the WTO as its 143rd member. From the perspective of national economic practice, China found the interface to participate in global production and trade division of labor through reform and opening up in 1978, and found the rule foundation to accelerate integration into the global economic and trade system through its accession to the WTO in 2001, greatly promoting institutional opening and the construction of its own market system. For example, since China's accession to the WTO, based on the need to modify relevant laws, regulations, and policies to comply with WTO rules, the Chinese central government has cleared over 2000 regulations and departmental rules, and local governments have cleared over 190,000 local policies and regulations, covering various aspects such as trade, investment, and intellectual property protection.

Since joining the WTO, China has also become a model for developing countries in terms of intellectual property protection and handling of WTO dispute settlement mechanisms. China has fully fulfilled its accession, especially concerning market opening. China had already fulfilled all tariff reduction commitments by the end of 2010, and the current average tariff level is 7.4%. If the weighted average tariff is calculated based on the import value, the average tariff level is only 3.4%. China's overall import tariff level is lower than that of all developing country members, and is close to the average tariff level of around 3% in developed countries such as the United States and Japan. The slight higher tariff reflects China's ongoing industrialization, and it is impossible to lower the tax rate to a level that is detached from its own development level and affordability.

In fact, the Office of the United States Trade Representative has acknowledged in its 2017 and 2018 annual reports that China has fulfilled its tariff commitments and removed publicly available non-tariff barriers such as import quotas. As for China's attitude towards international fair trade rules, former WTO Director General Pascal Lamy once made a fair assessment, stating that China has not abused international trade rules or evaded them through deception. The fact has approved that since China's accession to the WTO, all previous rulings on specific cases regarding the WTO dispute settlement mechanism have been strictly enforced, and there has not been a single case where the sued party has applied for retaliation for not accepting the ruling.

With the development of China's economy and the improvement of its competitiveness, China will have the conditions to proactively reduce tariffs in a timely manner in the future. On top of overall tariff reductions, structural tariff cuts will be carried out in the consumer sector to achieve mutual benefits and win-win results between China and its trading partners. On the other hand, driven by China's accession to the WTO, it has continuously expanded its opening-up to the outside world and embedded itself deeper into the global trade value chain. This evolution propels China from a manufacturing and trading powerhouse to an industrial and trading powerhouse.

After 2013, China began to explore deep-level reform and high-level opening up, providing replicable business model design and regional and global construction of financial services through the global allocation of high-quality production capacity. In addition, with the improvement of relevant international coordination and mobilization capabilities, combined with the internationalization of RMB, China has continuously released dividends of economic opening up and foreign trade development, and built a more dynamic internal and external economic linkage system. Previous studies show that China's practice of opening up based on free trade and comparative advantage is somewhat consistent with a series of classic trade theories by Western economists such as Smith, Ricardo, Heckscher, and Orin. This indicates that China's opening-up not only follows the general laws of economic development, but also exhibits increasingly significant international universality.

Taking the 20th anniversary of its accession to the WTO as an opportunity, China aims to enhance its ability to align with the highest international standards in areas including market access, goods trade, service trade, intellectual property, labor protection, state-owned enterprises and designated monopolies, competition policy, financial regulation, environmental protection, and climate response through sustained high-level opening up. China is actively promoting bilateral and multilateral investment and trade agreements with key regional and global economies to establish a long-term and stable market access mechanism. As an important beneficiary of globalization, multilateral trade, and opening up, China also shoulders the historical mission and role of a dividend releaser, constantly exploring the economic logic of global prosperity and coexistence.

What Are the Barriers to China's Accession to the CPTPP?

The attitudes of existing CPTPP members towards China's formal application to join vary. Among them, Japan, the current leading country of the agreement, is clearly not as actively cooperating and supporting China's accession as it was during the RCEP negotiation process. Some Japanese politicians questioned whether China is prepared to comply with the highest standards or rules of the CPTPP.

Although Singapore, Vietnam, Malaysia, and other countries have expressed support for China's accession to the CPTPP, other members of the CPTPP have veto power over the applicants. Therefore, whether China can ultimately join depends not only on the results of bilateral negotiations between China and the existing 11 members, but also on whether all members can adopt a consensus attitude in the end. Focusing on Japan in detail, the reason for temporarily refusing is twofold: firstly, given the dominant force behind the CPTPP, the United States, has yet to declare its intentions regarding joining, Japan fears that expressing support for China's accession too early may irritate the United States; Secondly, Japan, which has long passed the peak of its trade influence, is indeed unwilling to let China, a "giant", join, due to the "head goose mentality", fearing that Japan's authority in the organization will be greatly diluted, and China is likely to replace Japan as the rule leader and biggest beneficiary country. Japan's plan is to reject or delay China's accession as long as possible, while observing changes in the attitude of the United States. If the US rejects China's accession or uses it as a bargaining chip, Japan will work with the US to gain some incremental bargaining chips on trade issues with China.

The author believes that the United States may join the CPTPP during the Biden administration, which is a basic logical extension of the Biden administration's global economic strategy and policies. From the perspective of expected economic benefits, American think tanks have already set a record. Once the United States joins, it will boost its GDP by 130 billion US dollars annually in the next decade. Moreover, the United States is constantly monitoring China's growing power and expanding trade influence. If Japan fails to stop China from joining the CPTPP in the end, and the United States is unwilling to join, it would mean a loss of global trade leadership in the eyes of the US, which is absolutely unacceptable. Therefore, from the perspectives of cooperative and non-cooperative game dynamics, the three major economies of China, the United States, and Japan will engage in multiple rounds of games on the CPTPP issue until they reach a game equilibrium and come up with a mutually acceptable solution.

Let's analyze the rules again. The 30 chapters of CPTPP can be categorized into six major areas: trade in goods, trade in services, investment, rules, cooperation and facilitation, and general legal provisions. From its evolutionary history, the most important market access negotiations and new rule making were mainly led and driven by the United States. Despite withdrawing from the TPP negotiations during the Trump administration, Japan pragmatically froze 22 difficult to implement clauses and retained over 95% of them in the process of taking over the scaled down version of the agreement, making the CPTPP still the highest standard trade agreement in the world today.

If we carefully analyze the comparable larger differences between China's current institutional design and rule implement in these six major areas like environmental protection. China has already committed the "dual carbon" goal to the world. Even in the intellectual property protection, data policy, state-owned enterprises (SOEs) and designated monopolies, labor rights protection, and combating corruption and commercial bribery, which have been worrisome in the United States and Japan, China also has the confidence to achieve orderly integration with the highest international standards, with it actively promoting the implementation of WTO agreements on intellectual property rights, regulatory reforms on data openness, and international integration and adaptability reforms in state-owned enterprise reform and labor policy.

Of course, as the CPTPP is widely recognized as the least flexible and the most standardized free trade agreements in the world today, China needs to reform its current domestic system based on a thorough understanding of its rules and standards, while also avoiding cutting corners to fit in. In other words, China certainly needs to promote domestic market-oriented reforms and global trade integration by joining high-level trade agreements, but it also needs to avoid being led by rigid rules. Moreover, the issue of rules is clearly not the real obstacle for China to join the CPTPP, but rather the politicization of some members.

RCEP Comes into Effect: Injecting Expectation of Stability into the Uncertain World Economy

On January 1st, 2022, The RCEP officially came into effect, marking the world's largest free trade zone. This monumental initiative is promoting regional and global economic integration with a pragmatic attitude and solid actions, which is composed of 15 members representing nearly 30% of the world's population and economy.

RCEP has established an unprecedented paradigm for regional economic cooperation and prosperous coexistence. It was originally conceived and proposed by

ASEAN, inviting China, Japan, South Korea, Australia, New Zealand, and India to participate together ("10+6"), aiming to establish a unified market of 16 countries by reducing tariff and non-tariff barriers. Given the agreement covers the largest population and has the most diverse composition of members, it is usually difficult to unify the demands of all parties, resulting in hinders on negotiations and even some midway drops. But with the joint efforts of ASEAN, China, Japan, South Korea, Australia, New Zealand, and others, the relevant contracting parties finally signed the world's largest free trade agreement on November 15, 2020, through 31 rounds of formal negotiations and over 400 rounds of repeated consultations.

RCEP will bring tangible benefits to its members. It reflects the current international economic and trade rules and the direction of high-level open development. It is also a cooperative game between Asia-Pacific countries with significant differences in economic development levels and institutional systems, overcoming the "synthesis fallacy" and committed to promoting trade and investment facilitation, promoting the free flow of goods and capital, and consolidating and developing the high-level institutional arrangements established by the multilateral trading system. From the text of the agreement, it includes 20 chapters including trade in goods, rules of origin, trade in services, investment, intellectual property, electronic commerce, competition, small and medium enterprises, economic and technical cooperation, government procurement, dispute settlement.

Its core principle is highly cooperative to the purpose and aims of the WTO. For example, with the effect of RCEP, the rules of origin, so called "paper gold", would immediately becomes a significant certification for the participants to enjoy preferential treatment like cut down of tariffs. It fully reflects the world's most major export powers has undertaken the responsibility of promoting global economic development also trade and investment facilitation, as the new supporters of public products in free trade.

The implementation of RCEP has enhanced the stability and resilience of global industrial and supply chains. In the era of highly integrated global economy and trade, maintaining the stability of industrial and supply chains is an important prerequisite for ensuring the normal production, trade, and livelihood of all countries. Before the outbreak of COVID-19, the division and cooperation of the global industrial chain and the formation of the supply chain center followed their own inherent economic logic, which not only has the cyclical and phased characteristics of the changes in global industrial production and industrial pattern, but also has the stability characteristics under the expected determination. However, the epidemic has had a huge impact on the global industrial and supply chains, coupled with some countries focusing on the security and stability of their own industrial and supply chains through self-serving national policies, causing local ruptures in the global industrial chain and making the supply chain more fragile, exacerbating global economic turbulence and affecting the process of economic recovery.

Post-COVID-19 outbreak, China, as the hub of the global industrial chain and supply chain, not only ensured that the global anti-epidemic material supply chain remained intact, but also, together with Japan, South Korea, ASEAN and other countries, endeavored to restore economic normalcy and promote the convergence of industrial chains and supply chains in East Asia, Southeast Asia and even the world. China has collaborated with relevant parties to promote substantial progress in RCEP negotiations on important issues such as trade in goods, trade in services, investment, and ultimately signed agreements, reflecting the responsibility of RCEP members.

With the enforcement of RCEP, China and Japan, as the world's second and third largest economies, will forge closer industrial divisions of labor and cooperation with other regional members based on investment and trade agreements, and gain collective behavioral space in the new round of global industrial chain reconstruction.

According to the accumulation rules in the RCEP rules of origin, when determining the origin qualification of products, members consider the origin materials of other contracting parties in the free trade agreement used in product production as the origin materials of the contracting party where the product is produced. In fact, this reduces the threshold for products to obtain origin qualifications, greatly mobilizes the enthusiasm and initiative of small and medium-sized enterprises in RCEP members to use the rules of origin accumulation, significantly promotes the optimization of regional production resources and the division of labor and cooperation within products, especially the production and trade development of intermediate goods. These improvements are conducive to enhancing the stability and resilience of industrial and supply chains.

The implementation of RCEP provides a guarantee for saving transaction costs for regional market entities. Like other high-level investment and trade agreements, RCEP is an international agreement based on and aimed at zero tariffs. The tariff reductions among RCEP members are mainly based on the commitment to "immediately reduce tariffs to zero and phase tariffs down to zero within 10 years", and more than 90% of goods trade between members will ultimately achieve zero tariffs. At present, ASEAN has surpassed the European Union to become China's largest trading partner, with a bilateral trade volume reached 6.52 trillion yuan in 2022, accounting for 15.5% of China's total foreign trade. While Japan, as China's fifth largest trading partner, saw a bilateral trade volume of 2.38 trillion yuan in 2022, accounting for 5.67% of China's total foreign trade. According to the China Japan tariff reduction arrangement, with the implementation of RCEP, China's average tariff on Japanese goods will ultimately decrease from the current 9.76% to 0.04%, and Japan's average tariff on Chinese goods will ultimately decrease from the current 7.47% to near zero. China will gradually exempt about 86% of Japanese products from import tariffs under the RCEP agreement framework, and Japan will exempt 85.6% of Chinese products from import tariffs. Obviously, the effectiveness of the agreement will provide a solid guarantee for saving transaction costs between market entities within the region. In 2021, China's contribution to global import growth soared to an impressive 13.4%.

As for the facilitation arrangement of goods trade, the RCEP contracting parties have made high-level commitments on customs procedures, inspection and quarantine, technical standards, etc., especially the commitment to release goods within 48 hours after arrival as far as possible, and strive to release express and perishable goods within 6 hours after arrival. From the perspective of saving transaction costs and promoting trade development, the institutional arrangement of unified trade terms mentioned above will greatly improve the efficiency of logistics clearance, making regional trade more convenient and transparent, fair and predictable, and then significantly boost mutual exports among members in the region. As for the opening up and facilitation of trade in services, the contracting parties have also made firm commitments to implement negative list management for trade in services in the fifth year after the agreement comes into effect (January 1, 2027).

The implementation of RCEP not only helps Chinese export enterprises explore the export markets of members in the region and drill out their export potential, but also greatly benefits China's major trading partners in undertaking the dividends of China's economic development based on high-level trade agreements and open commitments. The release of these dividends will be accompanied by significant relaxation of market access in China, continuous improvement of investment environment, and high-level opening up of the financial services industry to the world, forming more opportunities from China based on vast market space and continuously expanding service demand, driven by high-level institutional opening, and guaranteed by the stability and resilience of industrial and supply chains.

The Dilemma of a "Two-Track" Global Economic Recovery Is Not Insoluble

The emergence of a "dual track" recovery in the global economy has raised increasing concerns among international organizations and analysts. In its *Global Economic Prospects*, January 2022, the World Bank warned that slow progress in vaccination, limited policy responses, and the traumatic effects of the pandemic have led to significantly weaker recoveries in emerging and developing countries compared to the developed countries, leading to further inequality. The head of the World Bank also highlighted a "huge gap" between the growth rates of rich and poor countries, with the per capital income of developed countries will increase by 5% in 2021, but that of low-income countries will only increase by 0.5%. The IMF also echoed these warnings of the "dual track" recovery from six months ago in *World Economic Prospects*, Jan 2022, predicting that developed countries would return to pre-pandemic trends in 2022, but some emerging and developing countries would experience significant economic losses in the medium term. Some worried Western media have proposed a prescription to avoid a "dual track" recovery: ensuring equal access to vaccines and strengthening global cooperation to achieve a more equitable recovery.

Adequate information, accurate data and scientific analysis are prerequisites for rational decision-making and judgment. Since the outbreak of the COVID-19 epidemic, its unprecedented, multi-round impacts have tested the systemic flexibility and absorption capacity of countries and regions. During this process, developed countries, emerging economies, and developing countries, due to their respective economic fundamentals, policy tool availability, and especially differences in national governance systems and capabilities, have faced problems like asynchronous economic recovery, structural differentiation, and even widening North South divide after rounds of impacts of the pandemic. These are all unavoidable objective realities in the real world.

While countries around the world generally struggle with inadequate capacity to cope with the impact of the epidemic, extensive vaccination, testing and treatment, as well as the development of new antiviral drugs, remain optimal strategies. All of this depends on sufficient financial and technological support, reliable health infrastructure, and equitable global vaccine distribution. However, as of early 2022, only about 4% of the population in low-income countries have been fully vaccinated, starkly contrasting with approximately 70% in high-income countries.

Another fact is that the number of people living in extreme poverty in 2021 surged by 70 million compared to pre-pandemic levels, reversing years of global progress. The fundamental reason for the above phenomenon is that the existing global division of labor pattern has been further exacerbated by the impact of the epidemic, leading to a widening gap between the North and the South. For example, after the outbreak of the epidemic, millions filed for unemployment benefits in the United States, while according to the $1.9 trillion "US Relief Program" signed by the Biden administration in March 2021, every adult with an annual income below $75,000 can receive a subsidy of $1400, and each child can receive an additional subsidy of $1400; If field as a family with an annual income under $150,000 can receive $2800, and a family of four can receive $5600. In other words, the "disadvantaged groups" assisted by the US government are the "American style poor" with an annual income of less than $75,000. Although they have encountered temporary difficulties under the impact of the epidemic, including losing their jobs, these "disadvantaged groups" in the United States, compared to the situation of people in some developing countries in Asia, Africa, and Latin America under the epidemic, the former are crying out for pain, while the latter are truly suffering.

In terms of the economic performance of emerging economies after the impact of the pandemic, issues such as weak recovery, hard landings, high macro leverage, and uncertain expectations are due to both internal reasons, like weak economic fundamentals, unreasonable economic structure, excessive reliance on foreign investment, high risk exposure, and mistakes in responding to the pandemic, as well as the impact of unlimited quantitative easing policies launched by the United States during the pandemic. Sorting out the monetary and fiscal response measures taken by the United States since the global spread of the epidemic, including injecting liquidity to stabilize market sentiment, providing direct assistance and even taking over companies facing bankruptcy due to the impact of the epidemic, and directly rescuing the lower-class people, the total expenditure is no less than 5 trillion US dollars. Subsequently, the Federal Reserve ended its asset purchase program in March 2022 and initiated a rate hike cycle in response to inflation caused by severe monetary overabundance. This large-scale water release and pumping behavior based on the interests of the US economy has already and will continue to have serious negative spillover effects, making it difficult for emerging economies to emerge from an independent recovery market, in the context where the US dollar remains the world's most important pricing, trading, and reserve currency.

However, despite the severe economic recovery challenges of emerging economies, there have been some encouraging changes in the global economy, including the stability and resilience of global industrial and supply chains being repaired and strengthened to some extent after repeated impacts and even partial ruptures caused by the pandemic. The global supply-demand dual center pattern has undergone changes that are conducive to boosting the exports of emerging economies as China accelerates the integration of domestic and foreign trade and facilitates the domestic and international dual circulation.

Moreover, the implementation of RCEP has laid the foundation for emerging economies to benefit from the dividends of China's growth. In fact, ASEAN, which is home to many emerging economies, has replaced the European Union and the United States as China's largest trading partner, and will form closer industrial division of labor and cooperation with China as RCEP is implemented. Major emerging economies such as Russia, Brazil, India, and South Africa, under the framework of the BRICS countries, will continue to receive numerous dividends from China's high-level economic opening, combined with the substantial market access liberalization, continuous improvements of investment environment, and expanding consumer demand. It is expected that the above-mentioned countries will be able to repair their economic fundamentals affected by the epidemic in short time, and are expected to usher in a new growth cycle thereafter.

Postscript

If one were to encapsulate the operational characteristics of the world economy since the twenty-first century in a single word, "uncertainty" would probably be the best footnote. Over the past decade, in the hundreds of economic and financial forums or closed-door seminars I have attended, "uncertainty" has either served as the theme or emerged as a recurring keyword in the discourse of speakers. In short, this is one of the core topics that neither conference organizers nor attendees can avoid. Indeed, a consensus has gradually taken shape: the greatest certainty in today's world is its uncertainty.

Why has the world become increasingly uncertain since the beginning of the twenty-first century—especially in the aftermath of the once-in-a-century global financial crisis in 2008? This is probably an economic and social problem that all market participants, including economic researchers, are very interested in but also difficult to solve independently. In particular, in today's world where big data is rapidly getting ubiquitous, driving artificial intelligence towards large-scale and even ultra-large-scale models, the static assumptions about economic and social development that humans used to make are becoming increasingly difficult to achieve in the real world. Researchers engaged in macroeconomic analysis and forecasting, even authoritative economists from the International Monetary Fund or the World Bank, are increasingly aware that they are engaged in one of the most complex and challenging jobs in the world. As a result, they often find themselves compelled to revise their analytical conclusions and forecast data on a quarterly, or even monthly, basis.

Economic research has long favored the use of assumptions, and economists thrive on using theorems and models to validate their economic intuitions about the real world. However, 15 years after the outbreak of the global financial crisis, if one were to challenge mainstream economists to reflect on whether they have failed in their responsibilities and what work they have done in the past few years for global economic recovery and the prevention of another crisis, perhaps no economist can provide a convincing answer. In fact, the self-reflection of mainstream economics regarding the financial crisis remains insufficient to this day. The policy

Y. Zhang, *Addressing Uncertainty*, Understanding China,
https://doi.org/10.1007/978-981-92-2692-4

prescriptions for economic recovery and so-called stronger economic growth issued by major international economic organizations, including the World Bank and IMF, have largely failed to diagnose the root causes accurately, let alone administer remedies of adequate strength. No one dares to say that the "virus" of this financial crisis has been cleared, nor can anyone rule out the possibility of an even more severe financial crisis in the future.

15 years ago, I wrote an article predicting that the global economy would confront a daunting decade or even an economic winter, which met with considerable skepticism at that time. However, after retrospections of the false recovery and series of uncertainties of the global economy in recent years, readers should keep their own rational judgment. I have also noticed that nowadays, various "chief economists" at home and abroad are rampant, churning out countless research reports day and night. Some even indulged in crafting alarmist. And some economists engage in rounds of debates around a certain topic, red-faced and sweat-drenched, all for the sake of attention. These are actually alternative expressions of the flux economy. Economists should not think that they are definitely smarter than the market, nor should they take the pride that they understand the internal logic of government, market, and rule of law better than ordinary micro market entities.

I also noticed that over the past decade, international financial capital has eagerly anticipated China becoming a super target captured by the "Minsky moment" and lock onto the dominant position of China's economic development. However, China has been fortified its defenses against such risks with extreme vigilance, keen intuition, and sophisticated governance to prevent this "beggar thy neighbor" strategic thinking from being implemented in China in recent years.

This world has always been fraught with uncertain, teeming with risk factors lurking in every corner. No one can accurately pinpoint future development expectations, and no nation can ensure that its development is not affected by external interference. Just as a single individual will always encounter various challenges and accidents throughout their limited life, short to decades and up to hundred years. It is in the alternative sense of the "Minsky moment", that even the strongest individuals have their own helplessness and weakness. However, on the other hand, the world advances every day, and behind each step forward steeped in human ingenuity and toil. Of course, despite the escalating complexity of this process, fundamentally, it is the extraction of various forms of learning aggregates.

This manuscript is based on nearly a hundred essays, commentaries, and interviews I have published in recent years (mainly in the past three years), each meticulously revised. Most of the relevant discussions, commentaries and interviews were written by invitation, and many articles and analytical views were reprinted or adopted by major platforms such as *People's Daily Online, CPC News Network, Qiu Shi Network, the State Council of the People's Republic of China Website, Xinhua Net, Guangming Online, CCTV.com, the CCDI and NCS Website,*[1] *China.*

[1] CCDI: the Central Commission for Discipline Inspection of the Communist Party of China; NCS: the National Commission of Supervision of the People's Republic of China

com.cn, China Daily Website, China Economic Net, as well as overseas English-language media outlets, resulting in extensive social impact.

This book aims to present readers the concerns of a Chinese economist and senior financial columnist about the resurgence of "Depression Economics". It encapsulates my strategic thinking on solving the series of uncertainties confronting China and the world's economic development.

This book follows the same style as my best-selling books *Dollar Logic: Behind the Currency of the Kidnapping and Murder and War* and *China's Economy Breakou*t published a few years ago, but emphasizes the depth and foresight of problem analysis. It takes the rigor and readability of economic words of expression into account at the same time, which not only serves for readers' fast reading, but also inspires them to think deeply through forward-looking predictions and analysis of major practical issues.

During the editing and publishing process of this book, I received invaluable assistance from my graduate students Fan Shumei and Zhang Ruoya, who did a lot of constructive work in updating data, figure production, and text organization. I would like to express my special thanks to them! The two students have agile thinking, strong comprehension ability, and the potential to become outstanding researchers.

Lastly, I would like to express my special thanks to Ms. Yang Liming , the dedicated editor of this book, for her meticulous organization and high-level editing. During the publication process of this book, Ms. Yang engaged in numerous detailed discussions with me, striving to ensure that every word is accurately expressed without falling into clichés. It can be said that without her wholehearted dedication and hands-on creation, this book would not have been published as scheduled.

Kolibri 360 GmbH
Ferdinand-Jühlke-Straße 7
99095 Erfurt, Deutschland
produktsicherheit@kolibri360.de